W9-APR-202

BUILDING
FINE FURNITURE

BUILDING FINE FURNITURE

A Simple, Uncomplicated Method

G. William Scherer

Sterling Publishing Co., Inc. New York

Library of Congress Cataloging-in-Publication Data

Scherer, G. William.
  Building fine furniture : a simple, uncomplicated method / G.
William Scherer.
        p.   cm.
  Includes index.
  ISBN 0-8069-8712-X
  1. Furniture making — Amateurs' manuals.   2. Cabinetwork — Amateurs'
manuals.   I. Title.
TT195.S33   1992
684.1'04 — dc20   92-21741
                                                                        CIP

1   3   5   7   9   10   8   6   4   2

Published in 1992 by Sterling Publishing Company, Inc.
387 Park Avenue South, New York, NY 10016
© 1992 by William Scherer
℅ Canadian Manda Group, P.O. Box 920, Station U
Toronto, Ontario, Canada M8Z 5P9
Distributed in Great Britain and Europe by Cassell PLC
Villiers House, 41/47 Strand, London WC2N 5JE, England
Distributed in Australia by Capricorn Link Ltd.
P.O. Box 665, Lane Cove, NSW 2066
Manufactured in the United States of America
All rights reserved

Sterling ISBN 0-8069-8712-X

CONTENTS

Introduction

Many an amateur woodworker has looked at a beautiful piece of furniture and enviously wished he could build such a difficult project. Though he has access to plans in woodworking books and project magazines, he considers these drawings too complicated to be of practical use.

It may surprise such woodworkers to learn that these "difficult" projects can indeed be built in a series of simple, sequential steps without the need for expensive machinery or joints such as mortise-and-tenon or dowelled joints. And, furthermore, this furniture can be built without having to glue up solid lumber panels that seem to always twist and warp and require endless hours of planing, scraping, and sanding.

The following pages contain information about a system of woodworking that is geared specifically for the wood hobbyist with limited machinery, space, and skills. This system has been developed by a woodworking teacher and professional cabinetmaker with almost 50 years of experience. Once this system has been mastered, it can be used to build furniture and cabinets of one's own design or to reproduce more expensive pieces that are seen in furniture catalogues and showrooms. Step-by-step instructions and hundreds of drawings and photos describe and illustrate how to build fine traditional or contemporary desks, chests of drawers, bookshelves, and cabinets, as well as many other furniture pieces. All facets of furniture building are covered, from purchasing and handling the building material to acquiring the proper machinery and tools and to applying a beautiful hand-rubbed finish to the project.

This book was written for amateurs who want to sharpen their woodworking skills and build professional-looking furniture. Reading and studying the sequentialized lessons in this volume is the first step towards accomplishing this goal, but studying is not enough. Learning by actually building some of the projects is still the best way to become thoroughly familiar with the author's system and to become a skilled amateur woodworker. Such an opportunity is presented in the following pages.

William Scherer

CHAPTER ONE

The Casework System of Woodworking

Many beginning woodworkers have taken up furniture-building with energy and enthusiasm, in the hope that they will be able to create sophisticated and professional-looking pieces of furniture. Armed only with the limited woodworking knowledge gained in "shop" classes, a few hand tools and, perhaps, a table saw and some other portable electric tools, these woodworkers soon sadly discover that it is extremely difficult to build anything of consequence.

The greatest reason for the hobbyist's difficulties is the system of woodworking he or she is using to build the furniture. This system, taught in most woodworking classes, calls for furniture projects to be built from glued-up panels of solid lumber that are laboriously hand-planed, -scraped and -sanded. Wood joints are always made with carefully machined mortise-and-tenon or dowel joints (Illus. 1-1 and 1-2). With the proper machinery, these joinery methods can be accomplished quite readily. The hobbyist, however, discovers that these methods are beyond the capabilities of his limited home shop.

The system of woodworking described in this chapter and used for the projects in this book requires only a minimum of machinery and hand tools, very seldom uses mortise-and-tenon or dowel joints, and never requires the builder to glue-up large panels from solid lum-

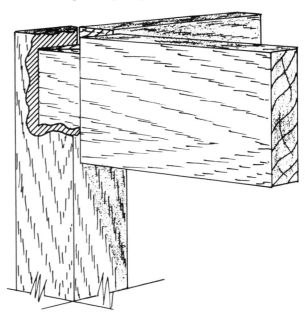

Illus. 1-1. In the traditional method of making furniture, table legs are mortised and tenoned from two directions.

9

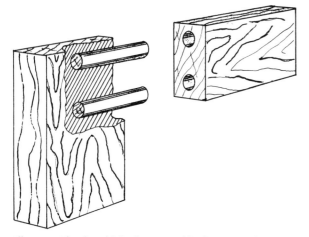
Illus. 1-2. The dowel joint is not used in the casework system.

ber! This casework method of constructing furniture and cabinets is adapted from industrial methods used by today's television cabinet manufacturers and makers of fine mass-produced kitchen cabinets. These manufacturers have developed a woodworking technology that makes use of modern materials and methods. These techniques can be adapted to build professional-looking, strong, yet inexpensive furniture and cabinets. In this system, furniture and cabinets are built using a screwed face frame and ¼-inch plywood for the sides, backs, and top.

There are several main differences between the casework method and traditional furniture-making. They are listed below.

1. In the Casework Method, Plywood Is Substituted for Lumber. Much time and money is saved when reinforced ¼-inch plywood panels are used instead of solid-lumber panels. In the traditional method of furniture-making, expensive grades of kiln-dried, hardwood lumber must be purchased to glue into knot-free, matched-grain panels. These better grades are usually the highest priced grades that the lumber dealer stocks. Often, too, a milling charge must be paid to have this lumber planed to the thickness desired.

As an example, ¼-inch-thick black walnut plywood, grade A-3, is listed in the most

recent catalogue of a wholesale hardwood lumber supplier for $1.82 per square foot. One-inch-thick walnut lumber, on the other hand, wholesales for a base cost of $2.92 a board foot, kiln-dried and rough (unplaned), and comes in random widths and lengths. To this base price must be added nine cents per foot for planing to the desired thickness, nine to 23 cents per foot for selecting boards of a specified width, and ten to 22 cents per foot for picking lengths to the customer's order!

Even using the lowest charges for selecting and planing the wood, the base price for walnut lumber quickly reaches $3.21 per board foot. If ¾-inch plywood is to be used, the price per square foot in grade A-2 wholesales for $3.42. It is easy to calculate that a considerable savings results from using ¼-inch plywood panels in place of solid lumber or ¾-inch plywood.

It should also be noted that good-quality hardwood plywood with its matched-grain veneers is much more attractive than solid lumber.

2. Casework Furniture Is Designed with a Face Frame. Furniture being built with ¼-inch plywood must be designed with a face frame. A face frame is defined as "a furniture- or cabinet-facing structure, usually of lumber, composed of horizontal and vertical pieces that frame the openings for the drawers and doors." The vertical pieces of the face frame are called stiles, and the horizontal pieces are called rails (Illus. 1-3).

Certainly no cabinet or furniture project can be built without using some solid lumber pieces. The goal, naturally, is to attempt to minimize the amount of this more expensive lumber being used and to emphasize the less-expensive and lower grades when lumber is required.

Although the face frame is built of solid-lumber pieces, these pieces are, for the most part, narrow rippings that can economically

Illus. 1-3. A face frame is required on casework projects.

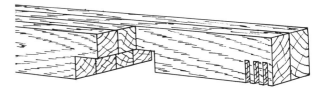

Illus. 1-4. Face-frame rails are bundled together and notched on the table saw.

be ripped from the No. 1 common grade rather than the select grade. The knots and blemishes can easily be avoided in the lower grade with careful planning and cutting.

In addition, the casework face frame does not have to be face-nailed. Most mortised or dowelled face frames are nailed through their bodies when they are fastened to the main body of the furniture piece or cabinet being built. These nails must be "set" below the surface of the wood, and the resulting holes filled with matching wood filler. The filler must then be scraped and sanded very clean. This is not a problem with the casework method, because the ¼-inch plywood sides are fastened to the face frame by gluing and nailing the panels to the *sides* with small brads; this eliminates any unsightly filled nail holes on the front, where they are much more noticeable. If the color of the wood and the filler are well matched, these small brad heads become virtually invisible.

3. A Unique Machining Method Is Used. A unique and timesaving method of cutting the notches in the rails of the face frame that will later receive the stiles is called the "bundling" method. In this technique, all the horizontal pieces are stacked or "bundled" together, nailed, and then the notches are sawed simultaneously on the table saw (Illus. 1-4). This method is fully described and illustrated in Chapter Six.

4. Screw Joints Are Used Instead of Mortise-and-Tenon or Dowel Joints. In the casework system, a screw joint is used instead of a mortise-and-tenon or dowel joint to assemble the stiles and rails of the face frame (Illus. 1-5). These screw joints can be fabricated quickly and easily with only a portable electric drill, selected bits, a countersink, and a screwdriver. No special or expensive machinery such as a mortiser, a dowelling machine, or even a dowelling jig is needed. The screw joint can be quickly learned and is very strong, and the face frame that is joined by this means requires no clamping time while the glue is setting, and can be put to use immediately after assembly.

5. A Small Selection of Power and Hand Tools Are Needed for Casework Furniture Building. The table saw and jointer are essential to any means of furniture-making. The table saw can be

Illus. 1-5. Rails are attached to stiles with screws.

used to rip, crosscut, mitre, cut dadoes (when used with the dado head accessory), and cut moulding on a fancy edge (when used with the moulding head accessory). The jointer performs such functions as straightening, smoothing, tapering, rabbeting, squaring edges, and even some surfacing.

Some portable electric tools will also prove valuable when the casework method of furniture-building is being used. A router can be used to machine decorative edges on wood and plastic laminate, which is often used on modern furniture. The sabre saw does a respectable job of cutting curves. Although slower than a band saw, it is less expensive and can cut into a panel without the lead-in cuts that the band saw would require. With its many accessories, the 1/4-inch or 3/8-inch electric drill is a tool that can perform a myriad of chores ranging from drilling, driving screws, sanding, countersinking, etc. A finish sander and a good oscillating sander will also prove valuable. Consideration should also be given to acquiring a belt sander, which can effectively remove knife marks left by the jointer.

A basic set of hand tools will also prove helpful. Included in this set should be a hammer, saws, assorted screwdrivers, a measuring tape, various pliers, and a square or two. A more complete set is described in Chapter Two.

As described in this chapter, there are several differences between the casework method of building furniture and traditional methods. In the following chapters you will learn how to use the casework method to efficiently build desks, chests of drawers, cabinets, and entertainment centers.

The Basic Woodworking Shop

This chapter focuses on the tools and equipment needed to create a "working" shop—one in which most woodworking operations and techniques can be accomplished with a minimum amount of cash and space. After you have learned additional woodworking skills and gained more experience, you will find yourself investing in additional tools that will prove helpful in the workshop.

It would be folly to recommend that a beginner should rush out and purchase a complete line of woodworking machines and set up a shop that costs several thousand dollars. Better advice would be to purchase the items recommended in this chapter over a period of time and *after* a few projects have been successfully completed, for it is not outside the realm of possibility that you may discover you are not as enthralled with woodworking as you originally thought.

POWER TOOLS

As cited in Chapter One, the table saw and jointer are two power tools that are essential in the home workshop. There are other tools that will prove extremely helpful. All these tools and ways to determine the specific type best suited for you are described below.

TABLE SAW

Purchasing a Table Saw

Almost without exception, woodworking experts recommend that the table saw be the first machine purchased when setting up a shop. But the purchaser can become truly befuddled when looking over the market, for table saws come in many sizes, horsepowers, specifications, and brands. When determining which type of table saw to select, remember that the machinery being sought for the hobbyist's shop is considerably different in specifications and price from that used in a professional cabinet shop.

There are several guidelines you should follow when investigating the table-saw market. First, buy a table saw from a manufacturer whose products have been on the market for years and which have a good reputation. Nothing is more discouraging than to own a machine for a few years and discover, when a repair part is needed, that the company is no longer in business and parts are not available.

Second, look for a table-saw top that is made from cast iron rather than sheet metal, and make sure that the finish on the metal is smooth and polished. Third, look for a table saw that meets the following specifications:

1. It should be able to accommodate a saw blade no smaller than 8 inches in diameter or larger than 10 inches in diameter.

2. The horsepower rating of the motor should not be less than ¾ horsepower or more than 1½ horsepower. A home workshop table saw with a horsepower rating of ¾ to 1 horsepower will work efficiently.

3. The ripping capacity of the table saw should be no less than 25 inches, as this will allow the operator to rip down the middle of a 4 × 8-foot sheet of plywood or a sheet of particle board that may be 49 inches wide.

4. The saw blade and blade-raising mechanism should enable the operator to saw through at the minimum a 2-inch-thick board with an 8-inch blade, and through a 3-inch piece with a 10-inch blade.

5. A tilting arbor saw (one on which the blade tilts) is preferable over a tilting table saw.

6. The rip fence should be easily and quickly adjusted, yet very accurate and positive when locked in position. It should be constructed of quality materials, for it will be used frequently.

7. The other setting controls should be easily visible, accurate, and handily located. The on-off switch in particular should be located in an easily accessible spot on the machine.

8. Make sure that the voltage requirement of the table saw—110V or 220V—is the same used in the workshop. If

not, you may have to do rewiring in the shop.

9. Find out what accessories come with the machine, such as a blade guard, mitre gauge, and stand. If the motor is separate, is it included or an extra? What about the switch mechanism? That, too, could be an additional charge!

Table-Saw Recommendations

There are several types and brands of table saws available that will prove valuable to an amateur woodworker. Delta, Powermatic and Sears manufacture quality table saws that compare quite favorably pricewise with any on the market. Delta's 10-inch contractor's table saw is as fine a product as is available (Illus. 2-1). Not only will it provide a lifetime of service, but parts always seem to be available for Delta products no matter how old the machine is.

Definitely worthy of consideration is Delta's 9-inch table saw and 4-inch jointer combination (Illus. 2-2). Although the 4-inch jointer may be a bit small by professional stan-

Illus. 2-1. The 10-inch table saw is ideal for the home shop. (Photo courtesy of Delta International Machinery Corp.)

Illus. 2-2. The table saw and jointer are essential woodshop tools.

made, less expensive copies of this machine manufactured by Grizzly and Jet also perform adequately.

Table-Saw Accessories

The table saw can be made to perform a number of auxiliary functions with the addition of a few accessories. If you do not have a spindle shaper in your workshop, a moulding head may be purchased that will do a respectable job of machining edges on tabletops, cabinet-door edges, etc. (Illus. 2-4 and 2-5). Although the moulding head does not cut as quickly as a spindle shaper, it can still do an adequate job if several light cuts are made instead of just one heavy cut. Many patterned knives are available for the moulding head that will make a wide variety of cuts.

A dado-head set should also be purchased (Illus. 2-6). With this set of blades and interior chippers, you can plow grooves and dadoes either with or across the grain of lumber pieces. Usually, a dado-head set will allow the operator to make grooves from $1/8$ to $13/16$ inch wide.

Also available for grooving is a single dado blade that can be adjusted to various

dards, it does an adequate job in the home workshop, especially when used with a work-supporting outfeed roller.

If a cabinet-shop type of table saw is preferred and the cost is not a factor, the 10-inch Delta Unisaw is the standard of that market (Illus. 2–3). However, it retails for well over $1000 when completely equipped. Foreign-

Illus. 2-3. The Unisaw is widely used in cabinet shops. (Photo courtesy of Delta International Machinery Corp.)

15

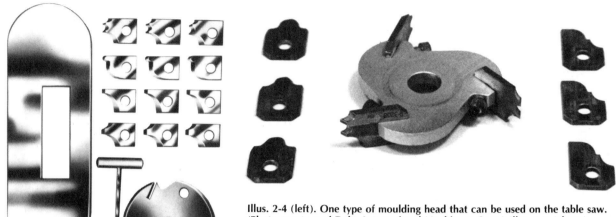

Illus. 2-4 (left). One type of moulding head that can be used on the table saw. (Photo courtesy of Delta International Machinery Corp.) Illus. 2-5 (above). Another type of moulding head that can be used on the table saw.

Illus. 2-6. A dado-head set requires a table insert.

widths by just turning a dial. These blades usually come equipped with carbide-tipped teeth for long wear, and will also make grooves from ¼ to ¹³⁄₁₆ inch wide. Both of these accessories require a dado-head table insert to use with the moulding head or the dado head (Illus. 2-7).

If a mitre gauge is not standard equipment with the saw being purchased, definitely purchase one. This accessory is used to make all angle cuts and crosscuts. The mitre gauge should have adjustable stops at the 45- and 90-degree positions for ease of setting.

Some consideration should also be given to adding side extension wings to the tabletop to increase the load-bearing area of the top.

JOINTER

The jointer complements the table saw nicely in the woodshop. No shop should be without one. It is used to straighten a piece of lumber before the lumber is ripped by the table saw, and again to remove the rough marks made by the table saw on the ripped board and to bring the board to its final width. Other chores performed by the jointer include rabbeting, tapering, bevelling, chamfering, and even some surfacing.

Illus. 2-7. An adjustable, carbide- tipped dado blade. (Photo courtesy of Delta International Machinery Corp.)

Illus. 2-8. The 6-inch jointer enjoys wide popularity. (Photo courtesy of Delta International Machinery Corp.)

The 6-inch jointer shown in Illus. 2-8 enjoys the widest use in cabinet shops and, possibly, home workshops. It is more popular than the 4-inch jointer because its tables are longer than those on the 4-inch models. These longer tables make it easier to straighten and smooth long boards when no helper is present to support the board as it comes off the machine.

However, the 4-inch jointer may prove to be more appealing to some woodworkers. This smaller machine costs considerably less than the 6-inch jointer. Also, when an out-feed support roller is used, the 4-inch jointer will do everything its larger companion will do except plane a 6-inch-wide board.

Following are additional factors to consider when shopping for a jointer:

1. The machine should be made of cast iron, and have well-polished tables and smooth, working table adjustments.
2. Both the front and rear tables should be adjustable. The in-feed table adjusts for depth of cut, and the out-feed table should be adjustable to the cutterhead. It is much more difficult to adjust the cutterhead knives to the out-feed table when the knives have become worn.
3. The guard should move freely as work is pushed through the machine. It should also spring back quickly over the cutterhead after the work has cleared the knives.
4. The jointer fence should be able to be adjusted easily and accurately, in both width and angle of cut, and have stops at 45 and 90 degrees. The fence should be able to be tilted both to the right and the left.

5. The cutterhead should have a minimum of three knives positively held in the head. Three knives result in a much smoother finish, with fewer "knife marks per inch" than would result with a cutterhead with only two knives.

6. Finally, determine if the price includes the stand, motor, pulleys, and belts.

After the jointer knives have been resharpened a number of times after becoming dull, the out-feed table often becomes slightly higher than the cutters. If the out-feed table is adjustable, it is a simple matter to correct this. However, if the out-feed table is not adjustable, then all of the knives in the cutterhead must be reset to conform to the position of the out-feed table. This is a timeconsuming job, and can be easily forestalled by purchasing a jointer with both tables adjustable.

COMBINATION MACHINES

No doubt, the budding woodworker will want to consider the combination machines that are available for hobbyists. Shopsmith sells one such very popular machine (Illus. 2-9). There are advantages and disadvantages to buying a combination machine. The first advantage is that a *total* combination machine is comparable in price to a good table saw and jointer, yet it includes a table saw, jointer, drill press, disc sander, lathe, and even a band saw. Be aware, however, that the basic combination machine consists of a drill press and lathe, and all the other tools mentioned are additional purchased accessories that must be placed in position as their use is required.

The second advantage is that a combination machine requires little shop space. This could be very useful for the hobbyist whose space is quite limited. Third, a unit such as the Shopsmith is a well-built and finely engineered piece of equipment that has been on the market for many years and has proved itself to be a quality machine.

There are also disadvantages to using a combination machine. First, the individual machine units have very small tables and machining surfaces. It becomes laborious when handling large pieces of plywood and lumber. Second, it is difficult to use the table saw and jointer in the manner most beneficial to the

Illus. 2-9. Shopsmith manufactures an excellent combination machine. (Photo courtesy of Shopsmith, Inc.)

woodworker when using a combination machine such as the Shopsmith. This is because the relationship that is so important to a serious woodworker is difficult to maintain on a unit such as the Shopsmith as the jointer on a Shopsmith machine is an accessory that must be mounted onto the basic unit when its use is desired. Third, the operator is constantly changing from one woodworking operation to another by mounting the various machine accessories as their use is dictated.

Also worthy of serious investigation is a French-manufactured combination machine called the Katy K-5 Wood Machining Center (Illus. 2-10). This ruggedly engineered unit possesses five basic woodworking machines: the table saw, spindle shaper, mortiser, surfacer, and the jointer, which also operates as a surface planer. This is a unique operation because the work is run *over* the top of the cutterhead to perform the jointer chores and *under* the cutterhead when thickness planing is desired. All of the individual machines are full-

Illus. 2-10. The Kity machine combines five basic woodworking machines: the table saw, the spindle shaper, the mortiser, the surfacer, and the jointer. (Photo courtesy of Ferris Machinery, Blue Springs, MO)

size and can be operated by simply changing the drive belt from one to another. The table saw/jointer relationship is basically maintained, but the operator must move the belt from one to the other as required.

PORTABLE ELECTRIC TOOLS

Once the table saw and jointer are purchased, it is entirely possible to build furniture the casework way using these two machines and a variety of much less expensive portable electric machines. The table saw and jointer are used for ripping, crosscutting, smoothing, grooving, dadoing, straightening, rabbeting, and making moulding. However, many operations remain that often need to be performed in building a quality wood project. These operations include drilling, sanding, cutting curves in wood, and efficiently shaping edges. Although there are expensive full-size machines that perform these functions, portable electric tools will, in most cases, accomplish the same operations at a fraction of the cost. These tools are described below.

Electric Drill

The electric drill should be the first portable tool purchased for a homeowner's tool kit. Electric drills come in what may seem to be a bewildering range of sizes, prices, and specifications that range from the discount-store "do-it-yourself" model to the higher-quality industrial-grade model. The electric drill is categorized first by the capacity of the chuck. For example, a ¼-inch drill can handle a drill bit no larger in diameter than ¼ inch. Electric drills are also categorized as either single- or variable-speed drills. Many of the variable-speed units have a reversing feature.

The power of the electric drill is designated by the amperage of the motor, and the speed may vary from machine to machine. Some variable-speed drills range in speed from 0 to 2500 rpm. Some of the more powerful drills have amperages that can range from 2 to 3.2 amperes. Also available is a rechargeable, cordless drill that can be taken from job to job.

The home workshop owner should be perfectly satisfied with a modestly priced ⅜-inch, single-speed drill, although a variable-speed drill with a reversing feature will also prove useful. This latter tool, slightly more expensive, can be used to drill holes, drive and extract screws, and for a number of other chores when used with the proper accessories. These accessories are described below.

Electric-Drill Accessories   When used with the many accessories available, the electric drill can be a very versatile tool. The following accessories should be used in the home workshop (Illus. 2-11):

A. One countersink with a ¼-inch shank and an 82-degree angle
B. One set of countersink bits (available in various sizes to accommodate different-size wood screws)
C. One set of high-speed drills, ¹⁄₁₆ through ¼ inch, in increments of ¹⁄₆₄ inch
D. One set of spade-bits, ⅜ through 1 inch, in increments of ¹⁄₁₆ inch
E. One or 2 small sanding drums in different sizes
F. One set of assorted hole saws
G. Two screw-driving bits—a slotted and a Phillips head bit

Other accessories that may prove useful are a dowelling jig and an electric drill guide. An electric drill guide is a unique accessory that ensures accurate 90-degree holes.

Portable Jigsaw (Sabre or Bayonet Saw)

One of the basic operations in the woodshop is the cutting of curves in wood. The full-size machine that usually accomplishes this is the band saw. Many woodworkers use the less-expensive sabre saw. Not only will the sabre saw cut curves in wood, it will also perform some jobs that are not possible with the band saw. For example, the sabre saw can be used to make cutouts in large plywood panels, to make sink cutouts in countertops, and to cut holes in panels where a lead-in cut (such as the band saw must make) is not desirable. Because this tool is used so much and on a variety of wood thicknesses, it might be well

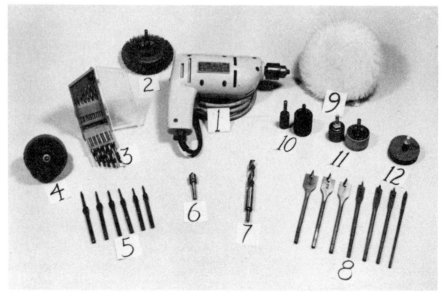

Illus. 2-11. An electric drill and its accessories: 1, ¼-inch electric drill; 2, wire brush; 3, assorted bits ¹⁄₁₆ to ¼ inch in diameter; 4, hole saw; 5, assorted countersink bits; 6, ½-inch rose-type countersink; 7, ½-inch drill bit with ¼-inch shank; 8, power bit set, bits ¼ to 1 inch in diameter; 9, lamb's wool polisher; 10, assorted wood rasps; 11, assorted sanders; and 12, grinding wheel with ¼-inch shank.

to spend a bit more money and purchase one of the higher-quality machines. The higher-quality machine will cut much faster through thicker material than will its less expensive counterpart (Illus. 2-12).

Finishing Sander

The well-equipped workshop will have both a finishing sander and portable belt sander (Illus. 2-13). These two sanders help woodworkers to avoid laborious hand sanding that is often part of woodworking. However, purchasing both sanders can be expensive, so the home woodworker usually decides to purchase only one. The finishing sander will probably prove to be the better selection, for two reasons. First, much more finish-sanding than belt-sanding is done on a furniture project, so the finishing sander will be more useful. Second, the belt sander is used primarily to give furniture face frames their initial sanding. This is a job that *can* be done with the finishing sander, although much more slowly, and if the joints are poorly made, a hand plane might be required to do some cleanup work.

Discount stores carry inexpensive finishing sanders that will serve the home woodworker quite well. Most finishing sanders operate with an orbital (circular) sanding action of the pad, although at least one sander

Illus. 2-12. Portable electric tools. Left: portable circle saw. Center: router. Right: portable jigsaw (sabre saw).

Illus. 2-13. Left: finish sander. Right: portable belt sander.

on the market can be switched from orbital to straight-line action. The larger models take $4\frac{1}{2} \times 11$-inch sandpaper (one-half of a standard sheet), but the less-expensive sanders have a smaller sanding surface and take one-third of a standard sheet, or $3\frac{5}{8} \times 9$-inch sandpaper. There is also a smaller sander on the market that takes only $4\frac{1}{2} \times 5\frac{1}{2}$-inch sandpaper.

Portable Belt Sander

The serious woodworker will soon decide to invest in a portable belt sander, as it is the only machine that will efficiently remove machining marks or "planer waves" left by the jointer and surfacer (Illus. 2-13). Available in a wide variety of sizes, this sander does a rapid job of surface- and edge-sanding.

The belt sander's size is determined by the width and length of the sanding belt that it will accommodate. The more common belt sanders range in size from 3×21 inches to 4×24 inches. One of the more popular and commonly used belt sanders is the 3×24-inch size. A good, heavy-duty portable belt sander is expensive, so shop carefully for one.

Many of the sanders on the market come equipped with a dust-catching bag. Although this feature is desirable insofar as partial dust control is concerned, the bag often seems to get in the way during the sanding.

Router

The router is put to extensive use in the home woodshop (Illus. 2-12). It can do the job of the very expensive spindle shaper and also cut grooves, dadoes, and edge moulding. Although some of these operations can be accomplished on the table saw with the moulding head and the dado-head set, the router is often handier and makes a smoother cut. The router can also be used for lipping drawer fronts in various shapes, as well as to trim plastic laminate with carbide trimmer bits.

There is a seemingly unlimited variety of both high-speed tool steel and carbide-tipped router cutters or "bits" available. Mail-order firms, discount stores, and building-supply dealers all usually carry a good supply of router cutters.

Routers are designated by the horsepower the machine generates. The horsepower rating of a router can range from $\frac{1}{2}$ to $3\frac{1}{2}$ hp. A router with a rating of 1 hp would make a very satisfactory machine for the home woodworker. A router listed as a "hobby"-type router has a horsepower rating of $\frac{1}{2}$ hp.

The speed of a router is also an important factor. Most routers generate speeds of over 20,000 rpm when operating under no load. This ensures a smooth cut.

Many accessories are available that increase the versatility of the router. Often, a table is purchased (or built) that will convert the router into a small spindle shaper. The router is mounted upside down under the table, and the work is moved rather than the router (Illus. 2-14). Dovetail fixtures are commonly used with the router to produce the fine-looking drawer joints that appear on high-quality furniture. Although many other operations are advertised in craft magazines by router cutter merchants, be aware that

Illus. 2-14. The router can be mounted under a router table for a stationary operation.

these almost always involve cutters with a shank diameter of ½ inch, rather than the ¼-inch shanks used in the smaller machines.

Portable Circular Saw

This is another portable tool that isn't essential in the home workshop, but can prove helpful (Illus. 2-12). If the table saw must be used for cutoff work, the portable circular saw can be used to rough-cut the stock to length, and the table saw to finish-cut the stock. It is quite awkward to handle boards 10 to 12 feet long and to cut them to specific lengths on the table saw, even when using out-feed supports. The circular saw can be used to rough-cut plastic laminate and plywood sheets to specified sizes.

Circular saws are classified by the size of the saw blade they will accommodate—usually 5½ to 7¼ inches—as well as their horsepower. They range in horsepower from ¾ to over 2 hp. The hobbyist can get good use out of one of the less-expensive models on the market such as those on sale at discount stores.

Bench Grinder

Although not classified as a portable machine, the bench grinder is quite small and is a necessity in the shop (Illus. 2-15). It is needed to sharpen plane irons, chisels, drill bits, hook scrapers, and for many other jobs. An inexpensive bench grinder can be purchased at the leading mail-order firms or discount stores. Accessories are available for buffing and polishing, and special wheels are also available for sharpening carbide-tipped tools.

POWER TOOL ADDITIONS

As you become a more proficient woodworker and the projects more sophisticated, you may decide to add several machines to the home workshop.

Illus. 2-15. Bench grinder. (Photo courtesy of Delta International Machinery Corp.)

DRILL PRESS

The drill press is basically used to drill perfectly perpendicular as well as slanted holes of

Illus. 2-16. This drill press has a foot lever. (Photo courtesy of Delta International Machinery Corp.)

various sizes (Illus. 2-16). With the proper accessories, it can also be used as a drum sander and as a mortiser. The mortising attachment is especially useful when you are building projects that have legs, such as tables and chairs (Illus. 2-17).

There are many inexpensive foreign-made, bench drill presses on the market. Most of these have a table that does not tilt for angle drilling, but you can compensate for this disadvantage with shop-built jigs.

Illus. 2-18. A lathe is used to shape wood in-the-round.

Illus. 2-17. A mortising attachment for the drill press.

WOOD LATHE

The only machine that can be used to shape wood in-the-round is the wood lathe. Most ornamental furniture has turnings that are shaped with a wood lathe (Illus. 2-18). Sizes of lathes are designated by the turning capability, or "swing," of the machine, that is, the largest diameter of material that can be mounted in the lathe.

The size of a lathe is also designated by the length of material that can be mounted between the centers of the lathe. For example, if a lathe is designated as one with a 12-inch swing and a 30-inch capacity, the operator can turn a bowl blank that is 12 inches in diameter, or mount a piece of wood for turning between centers that is 30 inches long.

All lathes have a mechanism for changing the speed of the material being turned. This mechanism can be a highly sophisticated variable-speed device or simply a belt that is changed on step pulleys.

There is a vast array of lathes available on the market which come in a wide range of prices. Discount building centers sell foreign-manufactured bench lathes with a 12-inch swing and a 29-inch capacity for a price suitable for most hobbyists. Other manufacturers market heavy-duty lathes designed for use by the wood turner who does a lot of lathe work and bowl turning.

Along with the lathe, the purchaser must also acquire a good set of turning chisels and faceplates in various sizes. If a bench lathe is purchased, some thought must be given to where the lathe will be installed—either on a bench or on a shop-built table designed by the owner.

BAND SAW

Although the sabre saw does an adequate job of cutting curves in wood, it has definite limitations when cutting hardwood and wood thicker than ¾ inch (Illus. 2-19). A band saw is a continuous cutting blade mounted on two, sometimes three, wheels. The blades are available in various widths. The thinner the blade, the smaller the diameter of a curve the blade can cut.

Illus. 2-19. The 14-inch band saw is widely used in both home and professional shops. (Photo courtesy of Delta International Machinery Corp.)

Band saws are designated by the diameter of the wheels that carry the blade. Smaller two-wheel 10- and 12-inch machines will do an adequate job in the home workshop. There are even 6-inch three-wheel band saws on the market that perform adequately.

The Delta 14-inch band saw has been the standard of the school woodshop, home workshop, and the smaller cabinet shop for many years. Foreign manufacturers have been quick to copy this band saw and other Delta machines.

HAND TOOLS

There are many jobs in the home workshop that can only be accomplished with a particular hand tool. When purchasing these tools, make quality your first priority. You will be using these tools in the workshop for many years. Take excellent care of these tools.

The tools that are described in this section will comprise a solid basic kit on which to build.

SMOOTHING AND SCRAPING TOOLS

Planes

Although the jointer is considered to be the basic wood-smoothing machine, there are many times that the only tool that will do the job is the hand plane. The following planes should be available in a home workshop:
  A. One 9-inch smoothing plane (either smooth or one with a corrugated bottom) or one 14-inch jack plane (either smooth or one with a corrugated bottom).
  B. One 6-inch block plane with an adjustable blade.

Files and Rasps

Several wood files and rasps should be in the

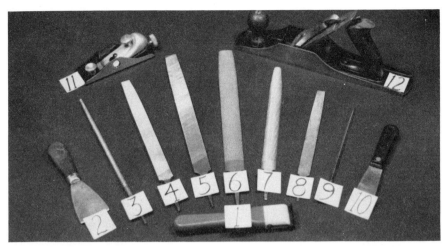

Illus. 2-20. Smoothing and scraping tools: 1, hook scraper; 2, two-inch blade scraper; 3, rat-tail or round file; 4, wood file; 5, ten-inch mill file; 6, half-round wood rasp; 7, half-round wood file; 8, eight-inch bastard mill file; 9, seven-inch slim-taper file; 10, one-and-one-quarter-inch putty knife; 11, six-inch block plane; and 12, fourteen-inch jack plane.

woodworker's tool collection. There should also be several metal files, for they will be used to sharpen saw and scraper blades, etc. Also available is a Surform smoothing tool, which can prove useful. Following is a list of files and rasps that should be a part of the basic hand-tool kit:

1. Wood files:
   A. One each flat and half-round
   B. One round (or rat-tail) wood file
   Note: Some manufacturers have discontinued making "wood" files because they are too closely related to the regular half-round, round, and flat metal files. They recommend using the metal files for use on wood as well as metal.
2. Wood rasps used for more rapid removal of material, because they have a coarser cutting action.
   A. One 10-inch-long half-round, flat, and round cabinet rasp.
3. Metal files: mill and taper (triangular). The mill file is used for sharpening circular-saw blades, draw-filing, and finishing metal. Taper files are used to sharpen all types of saws with 60-degree-angle teeth.
   A. One 8-inch bastard mill file.
   B. One 7-inch, extra-slim-taper saw file.

C. One 5-inch extra-slim-taper saw file.

Wood Scrapers

Wood scrapers are used to scrape off dried glue or wood filler and to remove minor blemishes and scratches on the wood surface. They are easily sharpened with a file (or on the disc sander), and replacement blades may be purchased for most wood scrapers. The Red Devil flip-over wood scraper works well for either coarse or fine work.

   A. One wood scraper, with a 1½-inch blade.

Putty Knives

Putty knives are versatile tools used to apply wood fillers, glaze a window, and for other chores.

   A. One 1⅛-inch common putty knife
   B. One 2-inch stiff-blade putty knife

DRILLING TOOLS AND ACCESSORIES

Although the portable electric drill with its wide array of accessories has practically replaced hand-drilling tools, the furniture builder might still want to consider purchasing some of the tools listed in this section. The possibility still exists that work might have to

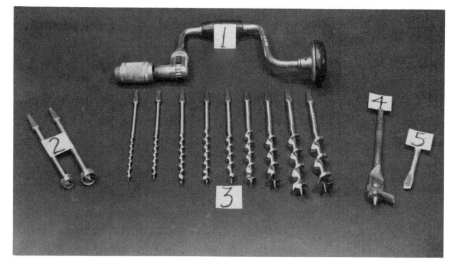

Illus. 2-21. Drilling tools and accessories: 1, ten-inch ratchet brace; 2, Forstner bits; 3, auger bits, ¼ to 1 inch; 4, expansive bit, ⅞ to 3 inches; and 5, screwdriver bit.

be done in an area that doesn't have electricity. A brace and a set of bits could be indispensable in such a situation. However, the brace and bits often languish on the tool rack for months and months without even being put to use. For this reason, the purchase of the following items might well be postponed for some time.

A. One ratchet brace with a 10-inch sweep
B. One set of auger bits, ¼ through 1 inch (in ¹⁄₁₆-inch increments)
C. One expansive bit, ⅞ to 3 inches
D. One screwdriver bit, size No. 5 (⁵⁄₁₆-inch tip)

CLAMPING AND HOLDING TOOLS

Purchase the following clamps initially, and then add clamps as the occasion demands.

A. Six 4-inch C-clamps
B. Six 6-inch C-clamps
C. Two 2-foot-long bar clamps
D. Two 4-foot-long bar clamps
E. Two pairs of Pony® pipe clamp fixtures. (These fixtures are used with ordinary ¾-inch pipe as the bar. Sections of pipe may be screwed together to provide clamps of almost unlimited length.)

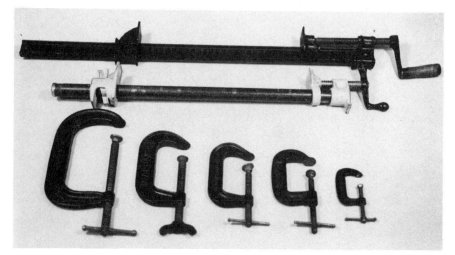

Illus. 2-22. Clamping and holding tools. At top is a 24-inch bar clamp. In the center is a pipe clamp. On the bottom are assorted C-clamps.

27

MEASURING, SQUARING, AND LEVELLING TOOLS

The following are among the most used in the woodshop:

A. One 10- or 12-foot-long power-return measuring tape, with a ¾-inch-wide blade
B. One steel square, with a 24-inch body and 16-inch tongue. (Purchase the less expensive type that does not have the carpenter's rafter scales.)
C. One combination square with a 12-inch removable blade
D. One try square with an 8-inch blade
E. One sliding T-bevel with an 8-inch blade
F. One 24- or 48-inch level with two levels and two plumbs
G. One 9-inch torpedo level
H. One 8-inch wing divider
I. One pencil compass

HAMMERS AND SCREWDRIVERS

As with most tools on the market today, there are high-quality hammers and screwdrivers available and ones of lesser quality. Keep a minimum of two hammers in the toolbox, as well as a wide assortment of screwdrivers. Buy higher-quality tools and use them correctly, and you will get many years of use out of them. Following is a list of hammers and

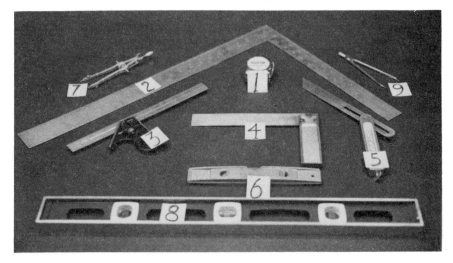

Illus. 2-23. Measuring, squaring, and levelling tools: 1, ten- or twelve-foot retractable steel tape; 2, twenty-four × sixteen-inch square; 3, combination square; 4, try square; 5, sliding T-bevel; 6, torpedo level; 7, pencil compass; 8, twenty-four-inch level; 9, dividers.

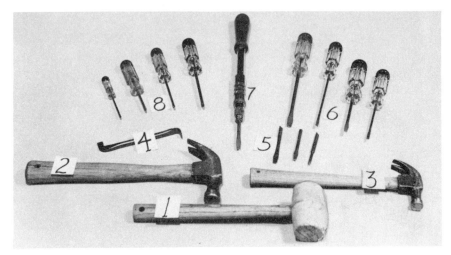

Illus. 2-24. Hammers and screwdrivers: 1, rubber mallet; 2, thirteen-ounce claw hammer; 3, seven-ounce claw hammer; 4 offset screwdriver; 5, ratchet screwdriver bits; 6, assorted regular screwdrivers; 7, automatic-return ratchet screwdriver; 8, assorted Phillips head screwdrivers.

screwdrivers that should be included in the workshop:

A. One 13- or 16-ounce claw hammer
B. One 7- or 8-ounce claw hammer. (The 7- or 8-ounce claw hammer is especially handy for pounding finish nails, brads, etc., in furniture work where your hands can get in the way.)
C. One 13-ounce rubber mallet
D. One spiral spring-return ratchet screwdriver that extends out to about 25 inches. (Purchase this screwdriver with assorted driver bits that can be used for both slotted and Phillips screw heads. Yankee makes one about this size.)
E. Assorted hand screwdrivers for both slotted and Phillips screw heads ranging in size from 2 inches to 10 inches long
F. Offset screwdriver for both slotted and Phillips screw heads

SAWING, CUTTING, AND RIPPING TOOLS

The list of tools in this category is quite lengthy and covers several types of hand tools. They are as follows:

Saws

The handsaw is still used considerably in the day-to-day work of the furniture and cabinet-maker. The purchase of one good wood-cutting handsaw is usually sufficient. This should be the crosscut saw, because a hand ripsaw is very seldom used.

A. One 10-point (10 points to the inch) crosscut saw
B. One hacksaw (adjustable for 8- to 12-inch blades)
C. One coping saw with about a 6-inch throat
D. One mitre box. (This can range in complexity from a simple hardwood box to the more expensive automatic metal mitre box.)

Cutting Tools

A. One set of wood chisels ($\frac{1}{4}$, $\frac{1}{2}$, $\frac{3}{4}$, 1, and $1\frac{1}{4}$ inches)
B. One utility knife
C. One $\frac{1}{2}$-inch cold chisel
D. One 10-inch tin snips
E. One pair of 8-inch straight shears
F. One glass cutter

RIPPING TOOLS

A. One $\frac{1}{2} \times 12$-inch ripping bar
B. One pry bar (Wonder bar)

SAFETY EQUIPMENT

Perhaps nothing is more important but more overlooked than some of the more common safety items for the woodshop. These items

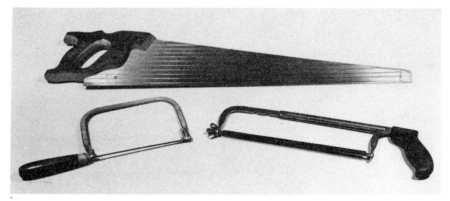

Illus. 2-25. Handsaws. At top is a 10-point crosscut saw. At left is a coping saw. At right is a hacksaw.

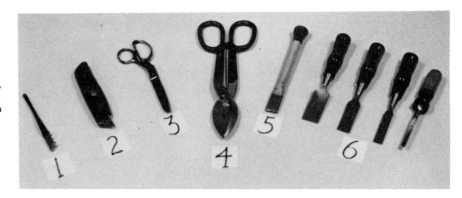

Illus. 2-26. Cutting tools: 1, glass cutter; 2, utility knife; 3, scissors; 4, tin snips; 5, cold chisel; 6, assorted wood chisels ranging in size from ¼ to 1 inch.

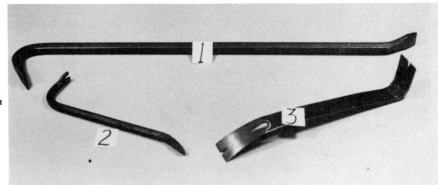

Illus. 2-27. Ripping tools: 1, three-quarter × twenty-four-inch ripping bar; 2, one-half × twelve-inch ripping bar; 3, pry bar (Wonder bar).

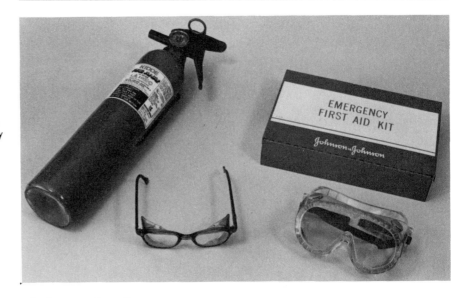

Illus. 2-28. Safety equipment. From left to right: fire extinguisher; safety glasses; first-aid kit; and safety goggles.

should be on hand in the workshop and *used* as safe practise demands. They are as follows:

A. One first-aid kit
B. One pair of safety glasses and/or goggles
C. One 8-inch, clear face shield
D. One fire extinguisher (foam and/or CO_2 type)

Pliers, Nippers, and Wrenches

A. Two slip-joint combination pliers (6 and 8 inches)
B. One pair of side-cutting long-nose pliers (6 inches)
C. One 7-inch cutting nipper
D. One 8-inch adjustable wrench

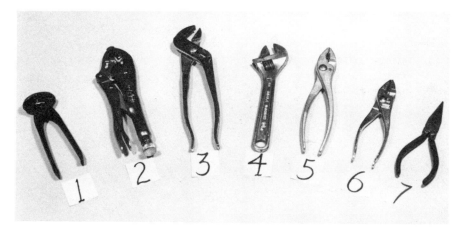

Illus. 2-29. Pliers, nippers, and wrenches: 1, end-cutting nippers; 2, Vice-Grip wrench; 3, slip-joint pliers; 4, eight-inch adjustable wrench; 5, eight-inch combination pliers; 6, six-inch combination pliers; 7, long-nose, side-cutting pliers.

Illus. 2-30. Miscellaneous tools: 1, a set of Allen wrenches; 2, two-thirty-second- and three-thirty-second-inch nail sets; 3, wire brush; 4, combination bench sharpening stone; and 5, oil can.

E. One 7-inch Vise-Grip wrench
F. One pair of 10-inch utility pliers (Rib Joint)

Other Tools

A. One combination sharpening stone with oil and oil can
B. One set of Allen wrenches ($5/64$ to $1/4$ inch)
C. Two nail sets ($2/32$ and $3/32$ inch)
D. One nail puller
E. One wire brush

SHOP ACCESSORIES

There are certain additions to the woodshop that are needed to build woodworking projects with a certain degree of efficiency. Fortunately, many of these can be built by the craftsperson, and are generally inexpensive.

WORKBENCH

Certainly the first accessory in a woodshop should be a sturdy workbench to which a woodworking vise can be attached. The vise should be one that possesses 4×7-inch jaws. It should also have the sliding, rapid-action feature that allows it to be opened or closed quickly. The jaws should be cushioned with pieces of hardwood so that wood, when placed in the vise, will not come in contact with metal surfaces (Illus. 2-31).

There are many different plans for workbenches to be found in craft magazines, but most of these do not provide for drawer or shelf storage. You can easily fabricate a workbench with storage space by purchasing inexpensive base units from a discount building-supply dealer and fastening them together into one continuous cabinet to the length desired.

Illus. 2-31. A good woodworking vise is indispensable.

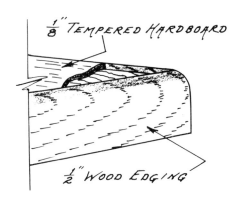

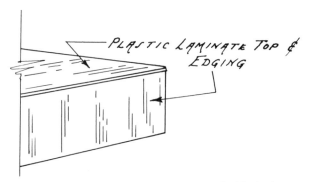

Illus. 2-32. The workbench top can be covered with plastic laminate or tempered hardboard.

The height of these units is about 35¼ inches, which, when the top is added, provides an excellent working height of 36 inches.

The workbench is an excellent shop project that will acquaint the builder with basic kitchen cabinet construction as well as drawer building and installation. (Note: Although drawer building is thoroughly covered in this book, kitchen cabinet building is not. For a complete volume on kitchen cabinet construction, refer to *Designing, Building, and Installing Custom Cabinets for the Home,* by Scherer, available from Prentice-Hall, Inc., Englewood Cliffs, N.J. 07632.) The workbench top can be made from ¾-inch particle board or plywood or from standard 2-inch planks. The top must extend past the end of the bench to accommodate the width of the vise being used. This extension must also be built up to a thickness of about 2 inches or whatever are the mounting requirements of the vise.

After firmly securing the vise to the bench top, cover the top with plastic laminate or, as an inexpensive alternative, ⅛-inch tempered hardboard. If laminate is used to cover the bench top, build up the front edge to a thickness of about 1½ inches and apply laminate to this edge as well (Illus. 2-32). If hardboard is used on the top, apply an edging of wood. Give the hardboard covering a couple of coats of satin varnish to add an attractive finish to the workbench.

SAWHORSES

Among the handiest accessories in the shop are pairs of sawhorses. At least one, preferably two, pair 30 inches high should be available. Another pair about 23½ inches high will also prove helpful during certain stages of furniture construction. These shorter horses are especially good for supporting furniture pieces at a convenient height when you are sanding with the belt and finish sanders.

Not only do these horses provide auxiliary working surfaces of the correct height, but they are invaluable for supporting lumber and plywood while you are cutting to length and even ripping with the portable circle saw. Cushion the 23½-inch-high horses with scraps of soft carpeting so that furniture pieces can be supported without being scratched or marring in any way.

Illus. 2-33 shows a sturdy sawhorse that is fairly easy to build and should give many years of service. Any sawhorse you work with should be sturdy. Many of the commercial, metal sawhorse devices on the market are not sturdy enough to adequately support a chest or desk project. Build several sawhorses of the design illustrated for inexpensive work support in the shop.

The sawhorses can serve other functions in the home workshop. With the addition of a height-extension device, as shown in Illus. 2-33, the sawhorses can be used to support large sheets of plywood or particle board while being ripped on the table saw. This is especially important to the person who is working alone in the shop and must handle these heavy, awkward pieces.

These height-extension devices can be further improved when old-fashioned, metal roller skate wheels are added to them to further ease the handling of large pieces. (See Illus. 5-17 and 5-18 on page 76.) These old-fashioned roller skates can often be bought at garage sales for very little money. Note in Illus. 5-17 and 5-18 that one height-extension device has its wheels the long way of the device, and the other has its wheels set across the support piece. One horse is used to support the work as it comes off the saw table, and the other is used to support the piece at the side of the saw table. When using these work-support rollers make sure that they are lined up *parallel* to the saw table or they will fail to guide the plywood sheet straight and true.

WALL CABINET STORAGE

Another early project for the woodshop might well be the addition of some wall cabinets for the storage of such things as paints and stains, sandpaper, assorted screws, brads, and small nails, etc. (Illus. 2-34). The craftsperson will soon accumulate a myriad of such items that need to be stored neatly and out of sight. Of course, open shelves can be built for this storage, but they collect an enormous amount of dust when the sanders are used. (*Designing, Building, and Installing Custom Cabinets for the Home*, by Scherer, also contains plans and directions for building wall cabinets.)

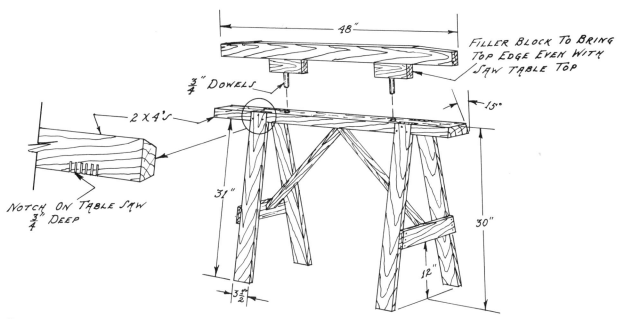

Illus. 2-33. A sawhorse with a table-saw work support.

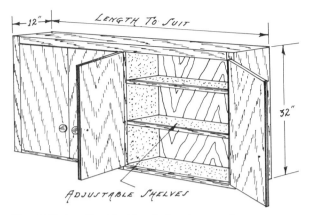

Illus. 2-34. A wall cabinet for storing shop supplies.

WALL SHELVING

Some sturdy shelving or wall brackets will no doubt be needed for the storage of lumber pieces. Either buy adjustable supports that fit into metal shelf track or make supports in the shop. In either case, be certain to line up the brackets carefully so they support the lumber pieces absolutely straight. Nothing is more discouraging than to discover that a piece of lumber is warped and wavy after being stored on uneven shelf brackets.

WORKSHOP AIDS FOR THE MORE EXPERIENCED WOODWORKER

So far in this chapter only the basic needs of a woodshop have been addressed. The items described in this section will make woodworking more enjoyable, efficient, and make possible for woodworkers with more experience the accomplishment of furniture projects of greater scope and sophistication.

WOOD SHAPER

A wood shaper should be one of the first machines added to the workshop by more experienced woodworkers. It is with the wood shaper that fancy moulded edges, flutings, cathedral-type raised panels, and many other furniture decorations can be made quickly and smoothly on either straight or curved edges. Shaper cutter sets are available with which the woodworker can make window sash and machine the intricate coped joints on the stiles and rails of furniture doors. Although the router will accomplish some of the above operations, the shaper will do these jobs far faster and with much greater ease for the operator.

However, even a small, light-duty wood shaper, complete with motor and stand, a good assortment of cutters, and the necessary accessories to do efficient work, can cost a considerable amount of money (Illus. 2-35).

Interchangeable spindles are available for some shaper models which allow the owner to

Illus. 2-35. A small wood shaper. (Photo courtesy of Delta International Machinery Corp.)

perform even more intricate machining. Accessories often purchased with the shaper include spring hold-downs, a ring guard, table extensions, sliding shaper jig, and a starting pin.

One word of caution: The shaper is not a machine for woodworking beginners. This machine requires a knowledgeable and skilled operator who is well versed in the safe operation of the machine and knows exactly what job the shaper is suited for.

DOWELLING JIG

Although dowel joints are seldom, if ever, required when building furniture the casework way, occasionally a situation arises in which a joint is required that cannot be assembled by screws. When faced with this problem, the woodworker has mainly two choices: Use either the mortise-and-tenon joint or the simpler dowel joint. There are many dowelling jigs on the market that make the fabrication of this joint quite easy (Illus. 2-36). To correctly and quickly align the matching holes to receive the dowel pegs, simply position the jig correctly and use a drill bit of the proper size.

Illus. 2-36. Use of a dowelling jig results in accurate dowel joints.

Some woodworkers prefer to save even the minor expense of a dowelling jig and use metal dowel centers to correctly line up the holes for a dowel joint (Illus. 2-37). After the first holes are drilled for the dowel pegs, metal centers are inserted into these holes and the two pieces to be joined are simply pressed together to transfer the centers to the corresponding piece. Drill the holes straight and true to ensure a well-fit joint.

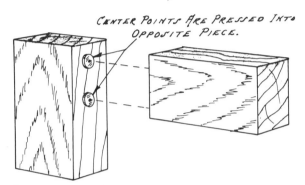

Illus. 2-37. Inexpensive metal dowel centers are used to match dowel hole centers.

DOVETAILING JIG

Furniture drawers manufactured with the very highest quality construction techniques have a dovetail joint that fastens the drawer sides to the drawer front (Illus. 2-38). Fortunately, there are metal jigs available that, when used with the router and the correct cutter, make this complicated joint reasonably easy to build (Illus. 2-39). Although these jigs are expensive, they work very well and can be used to make a strong and good-looking

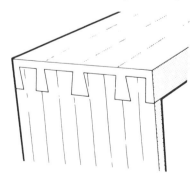

Illus. 2-38. The dovetail joint is used to attach drawer sides to the drawer front.

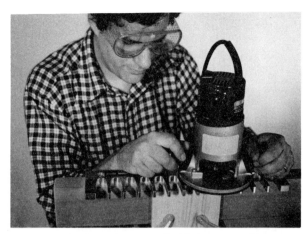
Illus. 2-39. The dovetail jig is used with the router. (Photo courtesy of Keller and Company)

drawer. Most home woodworkers, however, rely mainly upon the simple glued-and-nailed butt joint to fasten their drawer sides to the drawer fronts.

PURCHASING TOOLS AND MACHINERY

Shop carefully when buying tools and machinery. The leading machinery makers have placed ads in the most popular craft magazines, so the prices of equipment can easily be determined and compared. Many offer to ship their products with no freight cost to the customer. If the purchase of a brand-name woodworking machine is being contemplated, don't hesitate if you are thinking about buying a machine through magazine advertising. Be somewhat wary, however, of foreign, cut-rate manufacturers, because it could be difficult to have parts replaced or complain about the product. If you will need help setting up the machine and will need operating instructions, it may be wise to purchase the machine from a local woodworking machinery distributor.

USED EQUIPMENT

Most major city newspapers have a "Tools and Machinery" section or something similar in their classified ads. Here tools and ma-chines of all descriptions are advertised for sale almost daily, and to the *knowledgeable* purchaser this can be a terrific opportunity. Note the emphasis on the word knowledgeable. The purchaser has to be able to determine if the bearings of the machine are worn to the point of replacement, if the control and adjustment features all work properly, and if the motor and its bearings are in good shape. It is also important to ascertain what accessories are included with the purchase and the shape they are in, and if replacement parts can be easily obtained. Nothing is more discouraging than to purchase a piece of equipment at what would seem to be a real bargain, only to discover that the company has gone out of business and parts are scarce or no longer available.

Garage sales can also be an amazing source of used hand tools, portable electric tools, and even machinery items. Tools at these sales are usually very inexpensive and, if not, haggling is often the standard strategy for obtaining what may be considered the correct cost. For example, at a garage sale the author obtained a Delta 10-inch table saw, complete with stand, ¾ hp motor, and accessories, for $85, and a Delta 4-inch jointer for $15! Of course, these types of bargains are somewhat unusual, but it is always possible to find a bargain at any garage sale.

SHOP LAYOUT AND MACHINE LOCATION

The area where the shop is located is another concern that must soon be faced. Adequate space is important, not only for machine location, but for storage of lumber and supplies and for an assembly area as well. However, "adequate" is a relative term and what one craftsperson considers adequate might well be thought to be completely inadequate by another. The space requirements for a woodworker's shop are completely dependent upon the ambitions the hobbyist has, the amount and type of machinery that is to be housed, and, most important of all, the kind of woodworking projects that generally will be undertaken. After all, a shop designed to produce only small items such as toys, turnings, or "one-night" projects would require much less in square feet than a shop in which chests, desks, and even kitchen cabinet units are to be constructed.

BASEMENT SHOP

Many woodworkers initially locate their shop in a portion of the basement. If the basement is unfinished—that is, not partitioned off—there is usually enough space, and heat, light, and power will most likely be available and adequate. However, the dust clouds that are generated by the machines and especially the sanders in a finished or unfinished basement can rise from the basement and cover everything throughout the entire house.

Another problem with a basement shop is that everything has to be carried up or down the basement stairs. This includes the machinery when it is initially installed, plywood, lumber, and supplies, and, finally, completed projects that are removed.

For the above-described reasons, it is recommended that a workshop be located in the basement only if other space is absolutely not available.

SINGLE-CAR-GARAGE SHOP

Many hobby shops are successfully carried on in a single-car garage, even though space is at a premium. It is not unusual to find even a professional cabinetmaker operating out of this limited space. This type of operation requires keeping machine needs to a minimum and using a very small assembly area. Imagine attempting to fabricate a full set of cabinets for a good-sized kitchen in a 12 × 22-foot ga-

rage. This can be done more successfully in the South (or in the summer in the North) where winter heating is not so much of a problem and much of the assembly work can be done out of doors.

Be aware, too, that using a single-car garage for the shop practically forestalls the use of this space for housing the car. The machines alone will take up the space needed for the car.

TWO-CAR-GARAGE SHOP

A 24 × 24-foot double garage makes an adequate woodworking shop for either the hobbyist or the one-man professional. The 576 square feet allows adequate space for machinery, assembly, and storage. The owner of two cars, however, will find at least one and sometimes both sitting in the driveway when ambitious projects are underway. Illus. 2-40 shows a floor plan for a 24 × 24-foot double-garage shop that is well equipped with many tools, machinery, and accessories.

MACHINE LOCATION

The table saw and the jointer, being the most used machines, are usually located near the center of the work area and close to the assembly area. This keeps walking distance to a minimum. Try to locate these machines so there is a minimum distance of 8 to 10 feet both in front of and in back of the saw and jointer. This will facilitate the handling and sawing of plywood sheets. For ripping longer material it might be necessary to open the garage door for a few minutes. For this reason, it is often advisable to cut long material to rough length with the portable circle saw prior to ripping it on the table saw.

Other machines can be located along available wall space. This way, they can be easily moved towards the shop's open space if lengthy material runs are required. Many

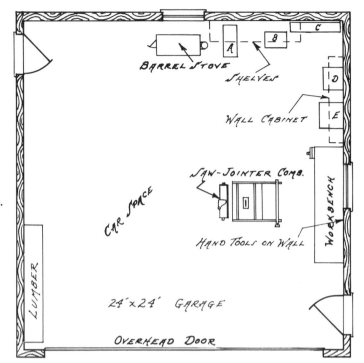

Illus. 2-40. A double garage provides adequate space for a home workshop.

BARREL STOVE

SHELVES

A

B

C

D

E

WALL CABINET

A. JIG SAW
B. GRINDER
C. LATHE
D. BAND SAW
E. SHAPER

SAW-JOINTER COMB.

CAR SPACE

WORKBENCH

HAND TOOLS ON WALL

LUMBER

24' x 24' GARAGE

OVERHEAD DOOR

woodworkers install locking-type casters on the stands of their machinery. This makes it much easier to move them around the shop as required.

LIGHTING THE WORKSHOP

With the number of inexpensive fluorescent shop lights available at any discount store, there is no excuse for having a poorly lighted shop. Four or five of these fixtures strategically mounted onto the ceiling of the shop and above the workbench will provide proper lighting and ensure safety.

PROVIDING POWER FOR THE WORKSHOP

Several 110-volt outlets should be located throughout the shop. These outlets should be equipped with adequate fuse or circuit-breaker strength to carry the load of horsepower needed for the table saw and jointer. If the circuit will handle those machines, it will usually be able to handle the other machines, as it is rare that more than one machine is running at a time. If the shop circuit breakers are constantly tripping, it would be wise to seek the advice of a competent electrician to assist in providing adequate electricity to the shop area.

Several good extension cords are a must in the shop because portable power tools are in almost constant use and these cords should be of adequate size to carry the amperage needed.

HAND-TOOL STORAGE

Hobbyists are very clever when it comes to designing storage for hand tools. Many hang peg boards to the walls with the wire hangers sold for various purposes, while others design their own fixtures for hanging these tools. Whatever system is used, the tools should be handily located near or above the workbench and kept in such a way that the tools are not dulled or harmed by the type of storage rack used.

HEATING THE WORKSHOP

Adequate heat must be provided for the shop area in the northern regions if any work is to be accomplished in the winter months. This is one advantage the basement shop has over the detached garage shop. Many northern shop owners heat with a small wood stove, figuring to burn the scrap generated by the shop projects that are underway. This is rarely adequate and soon wood must be purchased, especially when the stove is burned steadily throughout the working day.

In most communities, a wood stove must be installed according to the existing code. The correct type of chimney must also be provided. Check this with the local building inspector, and follow his recommendations exactly. Before installing a workshop in your home, contact the insurance agent who handles your homeowner's insurance to determine whether any regulations must be followed to satisfy the insurance company's requirements.

If heating with wood is not a viable option, use either fuel oil or gas (natural or propane). A circulating fuel oil stove will adequately heat a small shop, especially if the ceiling and walls are insulated. A 200-gallon fuel oil tank will ensure a good supply of oil, and fuel will not have to be constantly reordered for it. Gas wall heaters or units suspended from the ceiling are other alternatives that bear investigation. These are very efficient but rather costly and might be beyond the needs of a hobby shop owner

For *occasional* heat, kerosene heaters may be considered. Be very careful, however, that there is plenty of adequate ventilation when using these heaters! The same may also be said for Knipco heaters. These heaters generate a lot of BTUs, but always make sure that there is adequate ventilation if using them.

Finally, always have a good fire extinguisher on hand, mounted within easy reach. Make sure that it is charged, ready for use!

CHAPTER THREE

Purchasing Wood Material

The cost of any furniture project is determined by the labor put into making the project and the materials used. Since the home craftsman provides his own labor, this is not really a factor, unless the furniture piece is being built in the hope of realizing a profit. The cost of materials is, however. Although the hobbyist will want to purchase materials as inexpensively as possible, the quality of those materials must also be taken into consideration. A project that has been built from shoddy material can be immediately detected, even to the most indiscriminate observer.

In the casework method of building furniture, less expensive material is used, but this material should never be of a low grade. Also, some of this less expensive material requires more labor than the more expensive material. For example, it may take a bit more labor to apply reinforcing strips to plywood.

This chapter contains information on purchasing material and on the types and costs of softwood and hardwood lumber, plywood, particle board, plastic laminate, and shop supplies.

HARDWOOD LUMBER AND PLYWOOD

The home craftsperson should have a working knowledge of the more common species of lumber and plywood used in furniture construction. This knowledge will not only help in the purchase of lumber and plywood, but also in determining which species is most appropriate for the project under consideration. There are many factors that determine which species to use. These factors are described below.

KINDS OF HARDWOOD LUMBER USED IN FURNITURE

Generally speaking, hardwood lumber is far more preferred for furniture construction than is softwood lumber. All species usually are *first* classified as either hard or soft. The trees from which the lumber comes is a determining factor in this classification. Hardwood comes from deciduous (leafed) trees, and softwood from coniferous (needle-bearing) trees. This can be confusing, because a wood designated as hard may not actually be hard. For example, fir, a conifer, produces wood that is harder than basswood, which is a deciduous tree! The following list will probably prove helpful because it classifies wood according to its *actual* hardness or softness, rather than the type of tree from which it comes:

SOFT	MEDIUM	HARD
Balsa	Butternut	Ash
Basswood	Fir	Birch
Pine (all)	Elm	Cherry
Redwood	Mahogany (all)	Maple
Cedar, Western	Cedar, Eastern	Oak, red
Willow	Gum	Oak, white
		Walnut, black

Although the above list is by no means complete, it does cover the most commonly used varieties for making furniture.

A second means of classifying wood is to designate it either as *open-grained* or *closed-grained*. An open-grained wood is one whose pores are quite obvious, such as oak. If you tried to paint an oak board, you would observe that even several coats of paint will not cover up the tiny pinholes that keep reappearing in the surface of the wood. These are the pores of the wood. The pores of open-grained wood need special treatment prior to finishing. This is important to the furniture builder because a paste wood filler usually has to be brushed and rubbed into the pores of open-grained woods in order to secure a satisfactory finish. Closed-grained woods, on the other hand, require no such treatment. Here is a listing of the above species classified as closed- or open-grained:

CLOSED-GRAINED	OPEN-GRAINED
Basswood	Ash
Birch	Butternut
Cedar	Oak
Cherry	Mahogany (all)
Elm	Walnut, black
Fir	Teak
Gum	
Maple	
Redwood	

PROPERTIES OF COMMON FURNITURE WOODS

In this chapter, only the more popular furniture woods that have matching plywood available are identified and described. These are the woods that can be used to build furniture the casework way, because this system is built upon the availability and use of lumber and its matching plywood in both ¼- and ¾-inch thicknesses. This makes it much easier for the woodworker, as there are over 100,000 different varieties of woods from several hundred species that are used in the woodworking industry.

A recent catalogue from a wholesale lumber and plywood dealer had these following species of hardwood plywood listed: ash, birch, cherry, maple, mahogany, red oak, teak, red cedar, walnut, and white oak.

Ash (White) This wood is widely used for baseball bats and other sports equipment. Ash is strong, stiff, and somewhat heavy, and it works fairly easily with well-sharpened hand and machine tools. It has a grain pattern similar to that on white oak, but has a more tannish color. Native ash in the northern regions of the United States tends to be considerably darker, and is often called black ash. Early furniture builders used the darker variety to build their kitchen sets with bent-wood chair backs because ash bends easily with proper steaming and forming. Ash is not used extensively today in furniture-building, but white ash is used for tool handles for shovels, rakes, hoes, etc.

Birch Birch is one of the most popular cabinet and furniture woods used by kitchen and furniture manufacturers. It can range in color from very white to reddish brown, and many cabinet builders order it in either color. Dark birch is often difficult to distinguish from cherry and maple. Birch tends to have a curly grain; this makes it difficult to work with hand tools, because the grain will "tear out," sometimes even when being machined. It is often used interchangeably with maple. Birch finishes nicely and can be stained to match other darker woods. Work it very carefully by scraping and sanding it; this will prevent a "cloudy" appearance when stained.

Black Walnut Black walnut has been the favorite species of wood of furniture builders and buyers, since colonial days. It possesses a beauty of color and grain pattern that surpasses almost all other furniture woods, and yet is easy to work and finish. Walnut is an open-grained wood, so it requires the use of a paste wood filler prior to finishing. It will range in color from almost a purplish brown to light brown, and has white streaks of sapwood. Walnut accepts nearly every modern finish and, when finished, turns a rich, dark brown color that most woodworkers prize very highly. Walnut, however, is becoming rarer and thus more expensive, with many of the best logs being made into veneer for plywood.

Cherry This wood is a favorite of fine period-styled furniture builders because it possesses a beautiful color and grain pattern and can be worked more easily than many other species. Cherry works easily with either hand tools or machines and sands to a smooth finish. Cherry ranges from light to dark reddish brown heartwood color, is closed-grain, and takes stain nicely.

Mahogany (African, Honduran, Philippine) Fine furniture builders often use the African and Honduran mahoganies. These woods are reddish brown, open-grained, and have a nice grain pattern. Both are easy to work, and after their grains are filled, a fine finish can be easily produced. Philippine mahogany, on the other hand, is softer, lighter (although it darkens as it is exposed to light), and less expensive than the other varieties. Lauan is a species of mahogany that is made into inexpensive plywood and can be substituted for the more costly type. Most retail lumber dealers stock this plywood. It is used for cabinet backs, drawer, bottoms, and for flooring underlayment. They also will stock the Philippine mahogany or Lauan lumber. Handled correctly, Lauan plywood can be used in furniture building, but it has a coarse, open grain that might require two applications of paste wood filler. Because it is relatively inexpensive, the home woodworker should investigate the availability and workability of Lauan and Philippine mahogany for building nice-looking furniture projects.

Maple This is another quality hardwood often used in the manufacturing of fine furniture. It is hard and strong, but fairly easy to work with good-quality, sharp hand tools and machine blades. Occasionally, a highly prized, unusual grain is found in this species. This grain is called "birds-eye" because of its peculiar, eye-like grain formation. Maple turns well on the lathe, and is used for flooring, bowling alleys, and other wooden specialities. It is usually light tan with darker shades and streaks. Maple will finish to a highly polished surface, because it is very closed-grained.

Red Cedar Typically the aromatic wood that is used for cedar chests and closet lining, cedar is a soft, closed-grained wood that is red with white sapwood streaks. Cedar is used primarily for special applications such as chests and other unusual items, and has little application in the furniture or cabinet field.

Red Oak Red oak is still used a great deal on kitchen cabinets. Much furniture is also constructed of this fine hardwood. Oak is easily identified; it is very hard and heavy, open-grained, and fairly difficult to work with hand tools. Oak is usually a light brownish tan and has a very prominent grain pattern that shows up when stained with the darker stains. Most lumber dealers stock a good supply of red oak in both lumber and plywood, so it is easily available to the home woodworker.

Teak This is one of the more exotic woods that has a limited use in the furniture industry. Teak is a very hard, dense wood (so dense, it will not float) that ranges in color from light brown to a honey tone. Because the wood feels oily it needs special handling when it is being glued and finished. Carbide tools are usually needed when working teak.

White Oak Other than for specialty furniture, store fixtures, and cabinetry items, white oak does not have a large use in the furniture field. It is very hard, strong, and durable, and has an open grain and a very light tan color. It has long been used as a favorite wood for building barrels, and enjoys a popularity among shipbuilders as well.

FURNITURE APPLICATION FOR HARDWOOD LUMBER AND PLYWOOD

Today, less expensive lines of furniture are constructed with a mixture of plywood and solid lumber. Indeed, it is rare to find a piece that is entirely solid lumber except in the very expensive lines. A dining-room table may well have its legs made from lumber, and the skirt

and top made from veneered stock or plywood. Chests of drawers will often have this same mixture, with the interior portions of the chests, such as drawer sides, backs, bracing, etc., made from softwood, softwood plywood, or even particle board. The general rule is that if it can be readily seen in the finished piece of furniture, the material must be either solid lumber or matching hardwood plywood. Drawer fronts, for example, are often made from either lumber or plywood, depending upon the style and the cost of the finished item. Face frames, door frames, trim, mouldings, and leg stock are usually made of hardwood lumber, but side panels and drawer fronts and tops may often be made of hardwood plywood.

PURCHASING LUMBER AND PLYWOOD

The home woodworker faces a real problem in attempting to purchase lumber and plywood from the local lumber dealer when something besides red oak, birch or, perhaps, mahogany is desired. In some of the larger cities, there are a few lumber dealers who are beginning to cater to the hobby market and claim to stock nearly any species of lumber or plywood. However, for the most part, the hobbyist must rely on either the local dealer or a local cabinetmaker who is nice enough to order for him from a wholesaler.

How Lumber and Plywood Are Sold

Generally speaking, hardwood lumber is sold by the species, grade, and thickness, with the basic unit of measure being the board foot. The cost is based on the number of board feet multiplied by the price per board foot. Plywood, on the other hand, is sold by the square foot, with these factors affecting the price: species, thickness, and core material. Thus, plywood is purchased by calculating the number of square feet of a selected variety and multiplying it by the cost per square foot.

Calculating Board Feet

To intelligently purchase lumber you should have working knowledge of how board feet are computed. Board feet is usually abbreviated as bd. ft. A board foot is a piece of lumber that is 1 inch thick by 12 inches wide and 12 inches long, or 1 inch × 12 inches × 1 foot (or other combinations of dimensions that total 144 cubic inches). Lumber thinner than 1 inch is still calculated at the 1-inch thickness, and lumber over 1 inch thick is figured in multiples of ¼ inch up to 2 inches thick (Illus. 3-1).

Another common abbreviation used in the lumber business is RW & L (or simply RWL), meaning "random width and length." This abbreviation applies to the selection of pieces in a lumber order. Ordering specific widths and lengths will mean a slight additional charge, and a full foot of length must always be paid for.

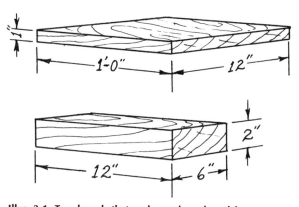

Illus. 3-1. Two boards that each equal one board foot.

Calculating a problem in board feet is a rather simple arithmetic process that can be mastered with some practice. The basic formula for calculating the number of board feet in a given board is:

$$\frac{\text{no. pieces} \times \text{width (in.)} \times \text{thickness (in.)} \times \text{length (ft.)}}{12}$$

Example A: $\dfrac{10 \text{ pieces } 2 \times 4 \text{ and } 10 \text{ feet long}}{12}$

Calculation: $10 \times 2 \times 4 \times 10 = 800$
800 divided by 12 = 66⅔ bd. ft.
Cost = 66⅔ × price per board foot

Example B: Three pieces of oak are ordered 1 × 8 and 12 feet long

Calculation: $\dfrac{3 \times 1 \times 8 \times 12}{12}$
$3 \times 8 = 24$ bd. ft.
(Note: Where 12 appears both above and below the formula line, the two numbers can be cancelled out and the remaining numbers multiplied.)

In practical retail use the fractional portion of a board foot is rounded off to the nearest whole foot using the standard round-off rule: If the fraction is less than half a foot, drop it; if it is half or over, move up to the next foot.

Lumber thicker than 1 inch (four-quarter) is designated by adding quarters to the standard ¼ designation. Therefore, lumber measuring 1¼ inches thick is called 5/4 (five-quarter), lumber 1½ inches thick is known as 6/4 (six-quarter), lumber 1¾ inches thick is 7/4 (seven-quarter), and lumber 2 inches thick is 8/4 (eight-quarter). To calculate the cost of lumber in the 5/4 thickness, simply calculate the number of board feet for the 1-inch thickness and then add ¼ more. Thus, 6 pieces 5/4 × 8 and 12 feet long are calculated as follows:

6 pieces 1 × 8 × 12 feet
12

6 × 8 = 48
48 × ¼ = 12
48 + 12 = 60 bd. ft.

Once you have reached this figure, multiply it by its cost per board foot. For example, if the lumber costs $2.50 per board foot, multiply 60 × $2.50.

If using an electronic calculator, enter the problem thus: 6 × 1.25 × 8 = 60 bd. ft. To determine the cost of the lumber, next multiply the amount of board feet by the cost per board foot. For example, if you have calculated that you will use 60 board feet, and the lumber costs $2.50 per board foot, multiply 60 × $2.50. In each case of extra thickness, substitute the decimal equivalent in the formula. For example, 5/4 = 1.25, 6/4 = 1.50, and 7/4 = 1.75. Of course, 2 inches is entered directly as 2.

Lumber Thickness Measurements

The *actual* measurements of a board are not the same as its described, or *nominal*, size. When a standard 2 × 4 is purchased, for example, what is actually received is a piece of lumber 1½ × 3½ inches. This is because lumber is sized at the sawmill, where it is first sawed to rough size from the still-green log. Because of shrinkage in the drying process and the amount removed in the planing mill, the finished piece is considerably smaller than it was before it was sized (Table 3-1).

It is important for the woodworker to be aware of the S2S (surfaced two sides) dimensions of the hardwoods that are commonly used in furniture building. If an order specifies 1-inch oak S2S, the lumber received will measure 13/16 inch thick. If the order specifies oak ¾ inch thick, a milling charge will probably have to be paid to plane the boards to the ¾-inch thickness. When ordering or purchasing hardwood lumber, make sure you distinguish between the thickness of lumber you are ordering and that which you will actually receive.

Nominal (rough)	*Surfaced 2 sides (S2S)*
1"	13/16"
1¼"	1 1/16"
1½"	1 5/16"
2"	1 ¾"
3"	2 ¾"
4"	3 ¾"

Table 3-1. Standard hardwood lumber dimensions. (Table courtesy of National Hardwood Lumber Association)

Softwood lumber has a different set of milling rules. When sold at retail in the finished state or S4S, it has the measurements shown in Table 3-2.

Nominal		*Actual*	*Nominal*		*Actual*
1 × 2	=	¾" × 1½"	2 × 10	=	1½" × 9¼"
1 × 3	=	¾" × 2½"	2 × 12	=	1½" × 11¼"
1 × 4	=	¾" × 3½"	3 × 3	=	2½" × 2½"
1 × 5	=	¾" × 4½"	3 × 4	=	2½" × 3½"
1 × 6	=	¾" × 5½"	3 × 6	=	2½" × 5½"
1 × 8	=	¾" × 7¼"	3 × 8	=	2½" × 7¼"
1 × 10	=	¾" × 9¼"	3 × 10	=	2½" × 9¼"
1 × 12	=	¾" × 11¼"	3 × 12	=	2½" × 11¼"
2 × 2	=	1½" × 1½"	4 × 4	=	3½" × 3½"
2 × 3	=	1½" × 2½"	4 × 6	=	3½" × 5½"
2 × 4	=	1½" × 3½"	4 × 8	=	3½" × 7¼"
2 × 6	=	1½" × 5½"	4 × 10	=	3½" × 9¼"
2 × 8	=	1½" × 7¼"	4 × 12	=	3½" × 11¼"

Table 3-2. The actual dimensions of softwood lumber after it has been surfaced four sides (S4S).

Grading of Hardwood Lumber

The National Hardwood Lumber Association has had grading rules for hardwood lumber for many years. They are the result of a need expressed by the furniture industry to obtain some uniformity as to the grading of its product. Grading is done according to the number of defects present in any given board, or, of special interest to the woodworker, the amount of defect-free lumber that can be obtained from a board. Grading is a complicated subject, and it is not necessary for the hobbyist to understand it fully. However, it is a good idea to have a basic knowledge of lumber grades, so that you can purchase lumber intelligently.

FAS (first and seconds)

This is the top grade of lumber found in the hardwoods. FAS hardwood lumber has clear rippings on the poorer face of a board that is at least 4 inches wide × 5 feet long or 3 inches wide × 5 feet long. FAS is graded from the poorer face, so the opposite side is of even better quality. Walnut, cherry, red gum, and poplar must have at least two-thirds heartwood on one face. Clear rippings must be ten-twelfths of the surface, with a minimum board width of 6 inches and a minimum length of 8 feet.

Selects

A select board is FAS on its better face. Where only one side is commonly seen, this grade is good enough for cabinet and furniture work. There must be no holes or decay in the board, and the opposite side must be grade No. 1 Common. The minimum width of selects is 4 inches and the minimum length is 6 feet.

No. 1 Common

This is a grade used on the poorer-quality face of a board. No. 1 common hardwood lumber is considered the most practical to purchase for home furniture and cabinet building, because it produces clear rippings on 66% of a board that must be 4 inches wide and 2 feet long or 3 inches wide and 3 feet long. In practical use, No. 1 Common can produce clear rippings 1½ to 2 inches wide by 8 to 10 feet long. This makes it ideal for face frames such as are used in the casework method of building furniture.

No. 2 Common

Again this is a grade used on the poorer side, and a board with such a grade must produce clear rippings 3 inches wide by 2 feet long over six-twelfths of its surface. This grade of lumber may be useful in the production of frames for raised panel doors, where shorter, clear rippings can be used.

There are lower grades, but unless one is building a project that requires only very short, clear pieces, these lower grades are not a practical purchase for the furniture builder.

SOFTWOODS

SOFTWOOD APPLICATIONS IN FURNITURE BUILDING

Whereas hardwoods are used where they can be seen in furniture construction, softwoods are used where they are not ordinarily visible. Not to be overlooked is the vast use made of softwoods such as the various pine varieties in building Shaker and some colonial furniture. Knotty pine is also used extensively by builders of Early American-styled pieces. Softwoods are used in fine furniture built of hardwood for many interior bracing and support pieces, drawer sides and backs, drawer runners, and for plywood reinforcing strips.

The varieties of softwood available to the craftsperson will vary from region to region. The hobbyist should attempt to make use of the species that are the least expensive. Softwoods available in most northern regions of the country include various species of pine, fir, basswood, native poplar, and even aspen.

GRADING OF SOFTWOOD LUMBER

The Department of Commerce's National Bureau of Standards has supplied the industry with grading rules for softwood lumber under the title "American Lumber Standards." The softwood grading system is even more bewildering than the grading system for hardwoods. Familiarity with the following grades of softwood lumber should be adequate for most home woodworkers:

No. 1 Common Seldom will one find lumber of this grade in the local lumberyard. It is practically clear, defect-free lumber.

No. 2 Common Excellent for painted surfaces, shelves, and panelling.

No. 3 Common Much the same as No. 2 Common, with a few more allowable defects. It should be used where strength and an attractive appearance are required.

No. 4 Common This grade is commonly used in the construction of cement forms, sub-floors, and other uses where it will not ordinarily be seen.

Shop-grade Factory Select The two top shop grades are of the most interest to the furniture builder, because these grades yield the most in long, clear rippings that can be used as reinforcing pieces and bracing on the interior of furniture. Factory-select softwood lumber must produce clear cuttings of 70% in these boards: boards 9½ inches wide or wider by 18 inches long or longer; boards 5 inches wide or wider by 36 inches long or longer; boards 9½ inches wide or wider and less than 36 inches long if good on both sides; or boards 4 inches wide or wider by 36 inches long or longer if they are C select grade or better.

No. 1 Shop Much the same as factory select, except the yield percent drops to 50 to 70%.

No. 2 Shop Is graded in relationship to No. 1 shop grade in that this grade need yield only 33 to 50% of the No. 1 size in clear rippings.

PURCHASING HARDWOOD PLYWOOD

Because the furniture builder will be buying a considerable amount of hardwood plywood for use in the casework system, he should have a basic knowledge of the thicknesses, grades, and core materials available.

GRADES OF HARDWOOD PLYWOOD

Furniture-grade plywood in the ¾-inch thickness (and to some extent in the ¼-inch thickness) is graded based on several factors: species, quality of veneer surfaces, type of grain, the color of the veneer on some species, and the type of core to which the veneered surface is applied.

Veneer
The home furniture builder will be most often interested in *veneer* of three grades: A-2, A-3, and shop. These grades are described below:

A-2 (good two sides) Both veneered sides of the 4 × 8-foot sheet are of the species ordered, as, for example, oak. The faces must be of smoothly cut, high-quality veneers which are carefully matched as to color and grain. No defects should appear on either side. This grade is used extensively for drawer fronts and furniture doors where both sides of the piece will be seen.

A-3 (good one side) Only one side of the panel fits the description of the A-2 grade. The opposite or back side will contain a variety of types of defects. Hardwood plywood of this grade is used for end panels and tops of furniture where only one side is visible.

Shop (shop-grade) Slight defects are allowed in this grade. It is ordinarily used where the sheet will be cut into smaller pieces and the defects can be eliminated. It's also used for backs of furniture and cabinets with glass doors such as china cabinets, gun cabinets, etc.

Red oak (Rotary cut) — Veneer core

⅛" 4 × 8 A-3
¼" 4 × 8 A-3
    4 × 8 A-2
⅜" 4 × 8 A-2
½" 4 × 8 A-2
¾" 4 × 6 A-2
    4 × 7 A-2
    4 × 8 A-2
    4 × 8 Shop grade

Red oak (Plain sliced) — Veneer core

¾" 4 × 8 A-2

Red oak (Rotary cut) — Solid lbr. core

¾" 4 × 6 A-2 (Aspen core)
    4 × 8 A-2 (Aspen core)
    72 × 24" A-2 Door stock (Bass. core).
    72 × 30"
    72 × 36"
    72 × 42"
    72 × 48"

Red oak (Rotary cut) — Fiber core

½" 4 × 8 A-2
¾" 4 × 8 A-2
    60 × 24" A-2 Door stock
    60 × 30"
    60 × 36"
    60 × 42"
    60 × 48"

Table 3-3. Typical catalogue listing of hardwood plywood.

CORE MATERIAL

The *core material* of plywood ranges in quality. Three distinct types are used for ¾-inch-thick plywood:

Lumber Core
The interior material is solid lumber strips. This plywood is often used in high-quality furniture drawer fronts and doors. Aspen and basswood are often used for the core material. This is usually the highest-priced grade of plywood.

Veneer Core
The panel is made of "sandwiches" of three, five, seven, or nine plies. The five- and seven-ply types are most often used in furniture building. The inner plies are placed at right angles to each other as the panel is built.

Particle Core
This type of plywood is being used more and more often in the less expensive varieties of furniture construction because it is the least costly of the three types. It is a very stable panel that is seldom subject to warping, although its weight is sometimes a problem and it has less screw-holding power than the others.

OTHER FACTORS

Finally, the thickness of the plywood, the type of grain specified, and the species determine the cost of hardwood plywood. Sometimes a customer can save money if he orders plywood from the dealer in large quantities. Typical catalogue descriptions are given in Table 3-3.

Note that when the material is described, the width is always listed first and the length second. For plywood this is extremely important, as the dimension description determines the direction of the grain. Thus a 4 × 8-foot piece of plywood will have the grain running the 8-foot length. However, if the dimension of the panel is given as 72 × 24 inches, the grain will run the 24-inch length.

SOFTWOOD PLYWOOD

FURNITURE APPLICATIONS

Softwood plywood in the ¼-inch thickness is widely used for such applications as furniture backs and drawer bottoms. Douglas fir plywood has over the years been the standard species used for these applications, although some 70 species of wood are used in the manufacture of softwood plywood. In recent years, more and more use has been made of some of the less expensive hardwood plywoods and particle board. Lauan plywood in the ¼-inch thickness is one such plywood. The appearance of Lauan is excellent, and it costs only a few cents more per square foot than fir. Particle board in various thicknesses is being used for interior partitions, drawer sides, and backs, bottoms, shelves, and furniture backs. Typically, ½-inch-thick particle board is used for drawer sides and backs.

GRADES OF SOFTWOOD PLYWOOD

Softwood plywood is divided into two basic types: interior and exterior. Exterior softwood plywood is bonded with waterproof glue, but the interior is bonded with just water-resistant glue. For practical furniture purposes, the grade designations range from A to D, with A being the best quality. Only the interior grade is ordinarily used for furniture use, but many lumber dealers stock only the exterior glued panels.

Grade A
Smooth and paintable. Patches are permitted in this grade, usually in the form of round "plugs" or small, football-shaped repairs. Grades A-D are widely used for furniture backs. Years ago, fir plywood was used widely for cabinet and some furniture panels. Today it is almost impossible to obtain fir plywood, even in grade A, without these unsightly patches, which make it impractical to use for furniture and cabinet building where the finished plywood will be seen.

Grade B
Solid surface veneer. Plugs and tight knots are permitted in this grade of softwood plywood. It is a good grade to use for partitions and drawer sides in grade B-B, where both sides can be seen.

Grade C and C Plugged
Knotholes up to 1½ inches and splits up to ½ inch are permitted in these grades under certain conditions. No use is made of this or lower grades in furniture building. Grades C and C plugged softwood plywood are used primarily as a backing for the A grade such as A-C.

Grade D
Used for interior plies and backs for Grade A-D, for example.

SIZES OF SOFTWOOD PLYWOOD

Although softwood panels are more commonly sold in 4 × 8-foot sheets, they are also obtainable in widths of 36, 48, and 60 inches. Softwood plywood is available on the market in thicknesses that range from ¼ to 1¼ inches, lengths from 60 to 144 inches, in 1-foot increments. A typical catalogue listing of a wholesaler's stock is illustrated in Table 3-4.

Fir				
¼	4 × 8	AA		Int
¼	4 × 8	AD		Int
¼	4 × 8	AC		Ext
¼	4 × 8	Sanded Shop		
⅜	4 × 8	AD		Int
⅜	4 × 8	AC		Ext
⅜	4 × 8	Sanded shop		
⅜	4 × 8	CDX sheathing		Ext
½	4 × 8	BB		Int
½	4 × 8	AD		Int
½	4 × 8	AC		Ext
½	4 × 8	Sanded shop		
½	4 × 8	CDX sheathing		Ext
⅝	4 × 8	BB		Int
⅝	4 × 8	AD		Int
⅝	4 × 8	AC		Ext
⅝	4 × 8	Sanded shop		
⅝	4 × 8	CDX sheathing		Ext
¾	4 × 8	AA		Int
¾	4 × 8	BB		Int
¾	4 × 8	AD		Int
¾	4 × 8	AC		Ext
¾	4 × 8	Sanded shop		
¾	4 × 8	CDX sheathing		Ext

Table 3-4. A catalogue listing of softwood plywood.

PARTICLE BOARD

Particle board, both veneered and plain, is one of the newer human-made materials being widely used in the furniture industry. Made of sawdust, shavings, etc., particle board, especially in the heavier densities, has many practical applications and has largely replaced softwood plywood for many things in furniture building. When this product was first marketed, only the underlayment grade was available. Furniture and cabinet builders used it for shelving and were very disappointed when the shelves sagged under even an average load. Despite the cost savings, particle board received notoriety and was no longer used in the furniture industry. Later it was manufactured in the 45-pound density with a nice, smooth surface. From this point on, it has been used by furniture and cabinet builders.

TYPICAL USES OF PARTICLE BOARD

Particle board is most widely used in thicknesses of ½ and ¾ inch. One-half-inch-thick particle board is used for drawer sides and backs, and ¾-inch-thick particle board is used for bottoms in the casework furniture methods. Where plastic laminate is to be applied, ¾-inch particle board is commonly used. For shelving, such as used on an armoire, ¾-inch-thick particle board is used with a shelf edging of wood to match the furniture wood being used.

Also available for drawer bottoms, sides, and furniture backs is a direct-print oak grain imposed on the ¼- and ½-inch-thick particle board. The drawer side stock is sold in strips 4⅝, 7½, 9½, and 24 inches wide by 97 inches long and is sold by the lineal foot. The ¾-inch-thick oak-grained particle board used for shelving is sold in pieces 11½ inches wide by 97 inches long, and is also sold by the lineal foot.

Where ½- and ¾-inch-thick particle board is used for shelves and drawer sides, the unsightly inner material of the panel has to be covered with a facing strip. Typically, this strip matches the other hardwood of the furniture piece, and on the drawer sides a cap strip is applied, which makes a neat and more expensive-looking drawer.

AVAILABLE SIZES OF PARTICLE BOARD

Standard sheets of particle board are an inch wider and longer than sheets of plywood. They are 49 inches by 97 inches. This extra inch is an advantage because two full 24-inch or four full 12-inch pieces can be ripped from this standard 49-inch sheet. These oversize pieces are still sold at the 48 × 96-inch price with no extra charge. Particle board is available in thicknesses that range from ⅜ to 1⅛ inches. A catalogue listing of available sizes from a wholesale outlet is shown in Table 3-5.

VENEERED FIBRE-CORE HARDWOOD PANELS

This seems to be the least expensive veneered panel available today, and many lumber dealers stock this item in 4 × 8-foot sheets. The inner core is a very fine sawdust-like material that shapes easily and holds up reasonably well in use. It is hard on standard tools, so carbide-tipped blades and cutters are almost a necessity when machining this material for any length of time. The glue used in bonding the core material has a rapid dulling effect on tool-steel blades. Of course, a wood banding must be applied to those exposed edges that will be seen in the finished product.

There are two main disadvantages to using this product. First, it is heavy. Second, when it is knocked around, the veneer can be chipped. This exposes the rather unsightly interior. Many builders still prefer to use lumber- or veneer-core plywood for their high-quality projects.

Particleboard	Fiberboard

Particleboard

Duraflake & Korpine (45 lb. density)

⅜	49 × 97 ......(4 × 8 billing)
⅜	49 × 121 ....(4 × 10 billing)
⅜	49 × 145 ....(4 × 12 billing)
½	49 × 97 ......(4 × 8 billing)
½	49 × 121 ....(4 × 10 Billing)
⅝	49 × 97 ......(4 × 8 billing)
¹¹⁄₁₆	49 × 97 ......(4 × 8 billing)
¾	23¼ × 145 .(24 × 144 billing)
	25 × 97 ....
	25 × 121 ....
	25 × 145 ....
	30 × 97 ....
	30 × 121 ....
	30 × 145 ....
	36 × 97 ....
	36 × 121 ....
	36 × 145 ....
	49 × 97 ......(4 × 8 billing)
	49 × 121 ....(4 × 10 billing)
	49 × 145 ....(4 × 12 billing)
	49 × 193 ....(4 × 16 billing)
	60½ × 97 .....(5 × 8 billing)
	60½ × 121 ...(5 × 10 billing)
	60½ × 145 ...(5 × 12 billing)
1″	49 × 97 ......(4 × 8 billing)
	49 × 121 ....(4 × 10 billing)
1⅛″	49 × 97 ......(4 × 8 billing)
	49 × 121 ....(4 × 10 billing)

Fiberboard

Glacier edge—Medium density Fiberboard (MDF)

³⁄₁₆	61 × 97 ......(5 × 8 billing)
¼	49 × 97 ......(4 × 8 billing)
⅜	49 × 97 ......(4 × 8 billing)
⁷⁄₁₆	49 × 97 ......(4 × 8 billing)
½	49 × 97 ......(4 × 8 billing)
⅝	49 × 97 ......(4 × 8 billing)
¾	49 × 97 ......(4 × 8 billing)
1	49 × 97 ......(4 × 8 billing)

Drawer sides & bottoms—(MDF) Direct print—Oak woodgrain

½	4⅝ × 97 ....
½	7½ × 97 ....
½	9½ × 97 ....
¼	24 × 97 ....

Shelving—(MDF) Direct print—Oak woodgrain

34	11½ × 97 ....
¾	11½ × 121 ....

Korpine—Shelving (Bull-nosed)

¾	11½ × 97 ....
	11½ × 121 ....
	11½ × 145 ....

Table 3-5. A catalogue listing of particle board and fibreboard.

ORDERING LUMBER, PLYWOOD, PARTICLE BOARD, AND PLASTIC LAMINATE

The home woodworker should have a fair working knowledge of how to order lumber and plywood, so it will be easier to do business with lumber and plywood suppliers.

ORDERING HARDWOOD LUMBER

When the furniture builder's needs are best met by ordering specific widths and lengths and the stock needs to be surfaced, an order will look like this: *6 pcs.-4/4 × 6 × 10 ft. No. 1 Comm. Red Oak-KD-S2S ¾ in.* The dealer is being told in logical sequence the following: (1) the number of pieces and the thickness, width, and length of those pieces desired; (2)

the grade of hardwood acceptable; (3) the species of hardwood being ordered; (4) that the lumber should be kiln dried (never use green lumber for fine furniture and use air-dried lumber very rarely); and (5) that the lumber should be surfaced to a thickness of ¾ inch. Remember, if the above order had just stated S2S, the lumber received would be ¹³⁄₁₆ inch thick.

If the job requires no particular widths and lengths, the order would look like this: *30 bd. ft. 4/4 No. 1 Comm. Red Oak-RWL-S2S ¾ in.*

The dealer is now being told the following: (1) that the woodworker wants to purchase a number of red oak boards in various widths and lengths that total 30 bd. ft.; (2) that the woodworker wants the grade to be No. 1 Common; and (3) that the boards should be planed to a thickness of ¾ inch.

ORDERING SOFTWOOD LUMBER

The specifications for ordering softwood lumber are not quite as demanding as for hardwood lumber. Usually, a visit to the local lumber dealer is all that is needed to determine the requirements for ordering softwood. The lumberyard has softwood such as pine stacked in piles according to length, width, and grade. Let's assume that the hobbyist needs eight pieces of 1 × 8 pine 12 feet long of No. 2 grade. The clerk at the yard is given this order, and the customer accompanies him or her to that part of the yard where this material is stored. Usually (at least in smaller towns), the clerk will assist in picking the boards, so the better ones are used to fill the order. These boards are already S4S and cut to accurate length and width.

If ordering must be done to a supplier out of town, the same type of information must be given the dealer as was done for the hardwood varieties. A typical order might look like this: *100 bd. ft. 4/4 No. 2 Shop, Ponderosa Pine RWL-KD-S2S.* If exact-sized softwood boards

are needed, the order may look like this: *8 pcs. 1 × 8-12 No. 2 Shop, Ponderosa Pine.* This order will be filled with eight pices of Ponderosa pine in the No. 2 shop grade that measure ¾ inch thick × 7¼ inches wide × 12 feet long and are surfaced on all four sides.

ORDERING PLYWOOD AND PARTICLE BOARD

When ordering plywood, give a complete, accurate description. A typical order for Douglas fir plywood might look like this: *12 pcs. ¼ in. 4 × 8 AD Doug. Fir. Ply.* This sequence of descriptive items is standard and should be followed closely. In this order, the customer is doing the following: (1) ordering 12 pieces, (2) specifying that they be ¼ inch thick; (3) that they be in 4 × 8-foot sheets; (4) that they be grade AD; (5) that they be of interior-type glue; and (6) that they come from Douglas fir species.

An order for hardwood plywood might look like this: *4 pcs. ¾ in. 4 × 8 A-2 Red Oak Ply (Rotary Cut).* Now the customer has told the dealer that what is needed are: (1) four pieces; (2) that the pieces be ¾ inch thick; (3) that the pieces be 4 × 8; (4) that the pieces be grade A2; (5) that the pieces be cut from red oak species; and (6) that the veneer should be rotary cut. Rotary cut specifies a grain that has a wavy, beautiful pattern, as opposed to "plain-sliced," which has the grain running in almost straight lines.

An order for particle board would be of the same sequence, for example, as follows: *8 pcs. ½ in. × 49 in. × 121 in. Duraflake 45 lb.*

How Plywood and Particle Board Are Priced

Rather than pricing plywood per board foot, as is done in the lumber industry, plywood makers simply charge by the *square foot.* Each species in its various thicknesses will have a different per-square-foot price. As an example, ¾-inch red oak plywood that is ¾ inch thick and grade A2 might be priced at $1.50 per square foot. A 4×8-foot sheet would cost $48.00 (32 sq. ft.×$1.50=$48.00, plus tax and delivery if required).

How Plastic Laminate Is Priced and Sold

Decorative plastic laminate is used for countertops and for the tops of tables as well as other pieces of furniture. It is a very durable material and is available in hundreds of wood grains and colored finishes. Some common trade names are Formica, Wilson Art, Nevemar, and Consoweld.

Standard Sizes Available

Because plastic laminate is rather expensive, it is well to know the standard sheet sizes available so that the furniture maker can plan carefully to obtain the most economical cutting from a standard size. Table 3-6 shows a listing of one manufacturer's standard available sizes. Many discount lumber dealers carry some of the more popular patterns in just one standard size, but the local lumber dealer is usually happy to special order any pattern in the size that is selected.

Grade 10—Standard material (includes -949 white and -909 black)				
24 × 48	30 × 48	36 × 48	48 × 48	
24 × 60	30 × 60	36 × 60	48 × 60	60 × 60
24 × 72	30 × 72	36 × 72	48 × 72	60 × 72
24 × 96	30 × 96	36 × 96	48 × 96	60 × 96
24 × 120	30 × 120	36 × 120	48 × 120	60 × 120
24 × 144	30 × 144	36 × 144	48 × 144	60 × 144

Table 3-6. The range of available sizes of plastic-laminate sheets.

SUPPLIES FOR THE HOME WOODSHOP

Certain supplies should be kept on hand most of the time so that constant trips to the hardware store and lumberyard are not necessary. Large amounts of these materials are not needed, but an adequate supply should be available and stored in an organized manner for quick and easy access.

GLUE

Most woodworkers use one of two familiar types of glue on the market for gluing wood: white or yellow wood glue. Both are excellent products, but yellow glue is more effective for gluing wood. Franklin's Titebond and Elmer's Professional Carpenter's Wood Glue are examples of the yellow aliphatic resin glue and are available in quantities that range from small squeeze bottles up to 5-gallon pails. These glues "grab" fast, yet allow sufficient open time for positioning material. If the temperature in the woodshop is 60 degrees or greater, usually one half-hour to an hour of clamping time is all that is required if no strain is to be placed on the glue joint for a time.

Yellow glues provide excellent joint strength, are non-staining, and clean up with water. Every effort should be made to clean up the glue that is squeezed out of a clamped joint. Even a thin film of glue allowed to remain and dry will present problems. If the dried glue is not completely removed, the stain or finish, when applied later, will not be able to penetrate the wood and will show up as a light, unattractive blotch. Either white or yellow glue should be kept from freezing during the winter months.

There are several other types of glue that may have a use in the woodshop at times. Some furniture builders still prefer to use plastic resin glue. This is a urea resin that is available in powder form and is mixed with water just prior to its use. This glue is considered highly water-resistant, but is not considered waterproof. The inconvenience of having to mix it, the rather long setting time, and the short pot life are reasons why this glue is not as popular as it once was.

If a waterproof glue is required, use the phenol-resorcinol type. This comes in two parts—a liquid and a powder—that must be mixed together before the glue can be used. This glue is widely used in boat building and for making outdoor furniture, but does not have much application in everyday furniture work.

Some purists in the furniture-making profession still use the old "hot" glue in which hide glue is heated in an electric glue pot. Another similar product is liquid hide glue that comes ready to use in liquid form. Most home woodworkers do not use these glues to any extent.

Contact Cement

This is a special adhesive that is used primarily for adhering plastic laminate to its underlayment, which is usually particle board or plywood. To use this latex-type glue, brush, roll, or spray it onto both surfaces to be joined, allow it to dry, and then press the surfaces together using a small roller. Once the surfaces meet, no adjustment is possible.

Contact cement is highly volatile and must be used with adequate ventilation. There is a water-based variation of contact cement on the market that is not dangerous to use, but it is quite slow to dry in comparison with the volatile type. Contact cement is available in small tubes, pints, quarts, gallons, and even drums for the industrial user. Most hardware and building supply dealers carry contact cement up to the gallon size.

Epoxy Glue

This adhesive is used in special situations such as gluing teak or where a good gap-filling glue is needed. It is waterproof and comes in two parts that must be mixed before using. Epoxy glue sets for use in about 5 to 10 minutes, although there is a slower-setting glue available that allows more open time. It is very strong and is often used by furniture repairers for regluing parts that are worn and fit poorly. Most hardware stores carry this adhesive, which is available in small two-tube containers and is rather expensive.

WOOD FILLERS

Plastic Wood

There are various products on the market that are used for filling dents, defects, and set nails. One of the most common is Plastic Wood, which is available in colors to match the most common furniture woods. Other well-known fillers are Famowood and Durotite. Keep small cans of this wood filler on hand for filling various wood colors. Use natural filler on pine, birch, beech, and other near-white woods, oak filler on fir, cherry, and oak, and walnut and mahogany fillers on those two woods. Lacquer thinner is used as a thinner and solvent for this material, which can become quite dry in the can after a period of time. Techniques of applying and working with these fillers are described in detail in Chapter Six. Note that plastic wood is applied *before* the finish is applied, and is scraped and sanded to blend with the raw wood.

Putty Sticks

This is a semi-solid, crayon-like filler that is available in many colors and is usually applied *after* the stain and a sealer coat are applied to the wood. It is widely used for covering the nail-head holes made in installing finished wall panelling.

Shellac Patch Sticks

These solid shellac pieces come in many colors to match various stained and natural finishes. They must be applied with a small heated knife similar to a palette knife, although an electric knife is available for this purpose. A shellac patch stick quickly hardens and then must be rubbed with very light rubbing paper and naphtha to the level of the surrounding surface. It is a professional product used by restorers and furniture repair people and takes quite a bit of experience to use successfully.

Unlike the other products described in

this section, shellac sticks cannot be bought at hardware or paint stores. A complete set of these sticks is available from the Woodworker's Store, Box 44, Rogers, MN 55374-9514, and is listed in the company's catalogue, which is available on request for $1.00.

SANDPAPER AND SANDER BELTS

Sandpaper and sander belts have become increasingly expensive over the past several years and should be purchased carefully. If at all possible, purchase both from a wholesaler or mail-order firm in standard packaged amounts to obtain the best buy. This will be less expensive than buying the products from a hardware store or through a woodworking catalogue.

Be aware that both "open coat" and "closed coat" sander belts and sandpaper sheets are available. This coating designation refers to the spread of abrasive particles on the paper or belt. The abrasive particles on open-coat sander belts and sandpaper sheets are spread rather thinly, so the belts and sandpaper are less inclined to fill up with resins from the wood being sanded. Open-coat sander belts and sandpaper do, however, sand a bit slower than those with closed coats.

Open-coat aluminum-oxide sandpaper in the 9×11-inch size works very well for general hand-sanding and when using the finishing sander. This type of sandpaper can be cut quickly to the size required for the finished sander, which is usually one-third of a sheet. Table 3-7 illustrates the grits usually available. A supply of 80A-, 120A-, 220A-, and 320A-grit sandpaper will accomplish nearly all sanding jobs. Note: using grits coarser than 120A in the finishing sander may result in "swirl" marks on the surface of the wood. Much laborious scraping and resanding are required to remove them.

Garnet and silicon-carbide sandpaper are also available. Garnet is a reddish-brown min-

Production paper "C and D" wt. All prices per sheet			Production paper "A" wt. All prices per sheet		
	Minimum package	Unit		Minimum Package	Unit
9 × 11	100	1000	9 × 11	100	1000
150C			320 A		
120C			280A		
100C			240A		
			220A		
9 × 11	50	500	180A		
			150A		
80D			120A		
60D			100A		
50D					
40D			9 × 11	50	500
			80A		

Table 3-7. Available grits for production sandpaper.

eral of medium hardness and is widely used for reconditioning surfaces before finishing. It is recommended for the removal of varnish, paint, or lacquer. Silicon carbide is a black, shiny mineral and is widely used on rubbing paper for producing fine finishes. Silicon carbide is bonded to its backing with waterproof adhesive and can be used with water as a lubricant for rubbing out a finish. Table 3-8 lists grits available for silicon-carbide rubbing paper.

	Minimum Package	Unit
9 × 11	50	500
600A		
500A		
400A		
320A		
280A		
220A		

Table 3-8. Standard grits of silicon-carbide sandpaper.

Production cloth belts (sander belts) are available in sizes and grits to fit all standard portable belt sanders as well as stationary and stroke-sanding machines. Try to purchase the open-coat belts. Table 3-10 lists the grits, belt sizes, and standard packaging that a leading wholesaler stocks.

While the tough Aluminum Oxide mineral can penetrate metals, these belts are primarily intended for wood-working operations.

Production cloth belts, closed coat All prices per belt					
	Minimum package	Unit		Minimum package	Unit
3 × 21	10	50	**4 × 27**	10	50
120×			120×		
100×			100×		
80×			80×		
60×			60×		
50×					
40×					
3 × 24	10	50	**4 × 37¹³⁄₁₆**	10	50
120×			120×		
100×			100×		
80×			80×		
60×			60×		
50×					
40×					
4 × 21¾	10	50	**6 × 48**	10	20
120×			120×		
100×			100×		
80×			80×		
60×			60×		
4 × 24	10	50			
120×					
100×					
80×					
60×					
50×					

Table 3-9. Available belt sizes and grits for sander belts.

Because sanding materials are becoming increasingly expensive, many woodworkers make use of abrasive cleaner sticks to remove the resins and gums that clog the abrasive and slow the sanding action. These are sold by woodworking supply houses and are usually advertised in the craft magazines. Note, however, that an old rubber sole from a sneaker or other sport shoe works just as well to clean sander belts, and does not cost anything.

NAILS AND BRADS

Finish Nails A good supply of various sizes of nails and brads should be kept on hand. Finish nails in sizes 4d and 6d will satisfy most requirements, although they are available in sizes from 3d to 9d (Illus. 3-2).

Wire Brads A box or two of 16-gauge (diameter) wire brads ¾ and 1 inch long should be stocked. The brads are small, flat-headed, mild-steel nails with sharp points that look like miniature finish nails. They are available in lenghts of ½ to 1½ inches, and in gauge sizes from 20 to 14. Sixteen- or 18-gauge wire brads are good to work with.

3d 4d 5d 6d 7d 8d 9d
FINISHING NAILS

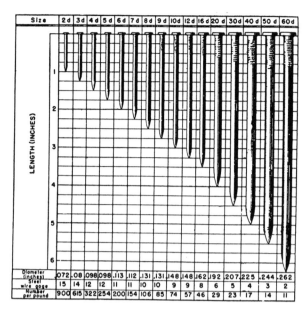

Illus. 3-2 (far left). Comparative sizes of finishing nails. Table 3-10 (left). The table depicts the sizes, gauges, and lengths of box nails.

Box Nails

Box nails should be purchased with a resin coating (simply called "coated") in sizes 4d, 6d, and 8d. The resin coating on this nail gives it excellent holding power in comparison to the regular box nail. Table 3-10 illustrates the comparative sizes of box nails. Table 3-11 shows the size, length, and gauge of all wire nails.

A 1-inch nail is used considerably in the casework system, but it is quite difficult to locate in quantity. Most 1-inch nails come in small boxes. They are bright steel with little holding power. The best 1-inch nails to purchase for nailing plywood to its reinforcing strip, as is done often in the casework system, are the small, colored, ring-shanked nails used for nailing wall panelling. These nails come in 1-inch lengths and have excellent holding power. The 1-inch length is just right for nailing ¼-inch plywood to ¾-inch reinforcing strips. A nail that is any longer will pop through on the inside of the furniture back and snag things with its sharp point. Any

WIRE NAILS

Size	Length (In.)	Common		Finishing		Casing and Box		Spikes	
		Gauge	No. per lb.	Gauge	No. per lb.	Gauge	No. per lb.	Gauge	p
2d	1	15	876	16½	1,351	15½	1,010		
3d	1¼	14	568	15½	807	14½	635		
4d	1½	12½	316	15	584	14	473		
5d	1¾	12½	271	15	500	14	406		
6d	2	11½	174	13	309	12½	236		
7d	2¼	11½	161	13	238	12½	210		
8d	2½	10¼	106	12½	189	11½	108		
10d	3	9	69	11½	121	10½	94	6	
12d	3¼	9	63	11½	113	10½	87	6	
16d	3½	8	49	11	90	10	71	5	
20d	4	6	31	10	62	9	52	4	
30d	4½	5	24			9	46	3	
40d	5	4	18			8	35	2	
50d	5½	3	14					1	
60d	6	2	11					1	
	7							5/16	
	8							3/8	
	9							3/8	
	10							3/8	
	12							3/8	

Table 3-11. The comparative data on all wire nails.

building supply dealer who retails wall panelling will stock these 1-inch nails in various colors.

Screws

In the casework method of furniture building, screws are used extensively. Screws 1¼, 1½, and 2½ inches long, all in the No. 8 size, should be on hand. For greatest economy, these screws should be purchased in boxes of 100 rather than in the small packets available in most stores. The chart in Table 3-12 illustrates the correct drill sizes to use for both the pilot and the shank holes for various screw diameters. For example, a No. 8 wood screw calls for a ³⁄₃₂-inch pilot hole in hardwood and a shank hole of ¹¹⁄₆₄ inch.

It is important that the correct shank and pilot holes be drilled so that boards can be fastened together properly with screws (Illus. 3-2). The available gauges and lengths of flathead wood screws are shown in Table 3-13.

	0	1	2	3	4	5	6	7	8	9	10	11	12	14	16	18	20
DIAMETER DIMENSIONS IN INCHES AT BODY	.060	.073	.086	.099	.112	.125	.138	.151	.164	.177	.190	.203	.216	.242	.268	.294	.320
TWIST BIT SIZES For Round, Flat and Oval Head Screws in Drilling Shank and Pilot Holes.																	
SHANK HOLE HARD & SOFT WOOD	¹⁄₁₆	⁵⁄₆₄	³⁄₃₂	⁷⁄₆₄	⁷⁄₆₄	⅛	⁹⁄₆₄	⁵⁄₃₂	¹¹⁄₆₄	³⁄₁₆	³⁄₁₆	¹³⁄₆₄	⁷⁄₃₂	¼	¹⁷⁄₆₄	¹⁹⁄₆₄	²¹⁄₆₄
PILOT HOLE SOFT WOOD	¹⁄₆₄	¹⁄₃₂	¹⁄₃₂	³⁄₆₄	³⁄₆₄	¹⁄₁₆	¹⁄₁₆	¹⁄₁₆	⁵⁄₆₄	⁵⁄₆₄	³⁄₃₂	³⁄₃₂	⁷⁄₆₄	⁷⁄₆₄	⁹⁄₆₄	⁹⁄₆₄	¹¹⁄₆₄
PILOT HOLE HARD WOOD	¹⁄₃₂	¹⁄₃₂	³⁄₆₄	¹⁄₁₆	¹⁄₁₆	⁵⁄₆₄	⁵⁄₆₄	³⁄₃₂	³⁄₃₂	⁷⁄₆₄	⁷⁄₆₄	⅛	⅛	⁹⁄₆₄	⁵⁄₃₂	³⁄₁₆	¹³⁄₆₄
AUGER BIT SIZES FOR COUNTERSUNK HEADS			3	4	4	4	5	5	6	6	6	7	7	8	9	10	11

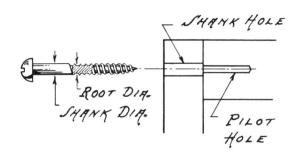

Table 3-12 (above left). The proper drill sizes for shank and pilot holes. Illus. 3-2 (above right). The proper drilling technique for fastening boards with screws.

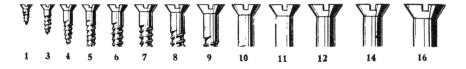

1   3   4   5   6   7   8   9   10   11   12   14   16

Table 3-13. The comparative lengths and gauges of flathead wood screws.

LENGTH	GAUGE NUMBERS																	
	0	1	2	3	4	5	6	7	8	9	10	11	12	14	16	18	20	24
¼ INCH	0	1	2	3														
⅜ INCH			2	3	4	5	6	7										
½ INCH			2	3	4	5	6	7	8									
⅝ INCH				3	4	5	6	7	8	9	10							
¾ INCH					4	5	6	7	8	9	10	11						
⅞ INCH							6	7	8	9	10	11	12					
1 INCH							6	7	8	9	10	11	12	14				
1¼ INCH								7	8	9	10	11	12	14	16			
1½ INCH							6	7	8	9	10	11	12	14	16	18		
1¾ INCH									8	9	10	11	12	14	16	18	20	
2 INCH									8	9	10	11	12	14	16	18	20	
2¼ INCH										9	10	11	12	14	16	18	20	
2½ INCH													12	14	16	18	20	
2¾ INCH														14	16	18	20	
3 INCH															16	18	20	
3½ INCH																18	20	24
4 INCH																18	20	24

CHAPTER FOUR

Planning the Furniture Project

Once the shop is located and equipped with the proper machines, hand tools, and accessories, the actual work can begin! For your first project, do not start with something that exceeds your woodworking knowledge and experience. It is better to continue to study magazine articles and books on techniques and undertake some rather simple projects that will provide valuable experiences with tools and machinery. However, when you are ready for a major project, you'll discover that many good design ideas can be found in the available woodworking literature.

WOODWORKING LITERATURE

CRAFT MAGAZINES

A visit to almost any magazine rack in a bookstore or supermarket will reveal a number of excellent woodworking magazines. Some of these cater to the novice, and some to the more advanced woodworker and others to woodworkers of all skill levels. All contain articles on techniques and are filled with projects ranging from simple wooden toys to measured drawings of famous furniture reproductions.

WOODWORKING BOOKS

Most public libraries will usually have an entire section of books that deal with the practical arts. Chief among these will be books on cabinetmaking, furniture building, toy making, carpentry, and home remodelling. Many are of recent publication and are well worth reading and studying. Libraries provide an excellent and inexpensive means of learning about woodworking, as well as finding plans for furniture.

FURNITURE CATALOGUES

Another excellent source of ideas for the home shop are furniture catalogues and advertisements in the newspapers by furniture retailers. Many of the leading home magazines such as *Better Homes and Gardens, House Beautiful,* and *Home and Garden* contain a section listing catalogues available from leading furniture manufacturers. These include such companies as Ethan Allen, Pennsylvania House, Baker, Lane, Drexel, and Harden. The catalogues contain beautiful furniture pieces that may well inspire you to duplicate them in the home shop. These catalogues are particularly useful because the overall dimensions are given for each individual piece of furniture illustrated. This makes it easy for the home craftsperson to prepare a simple working drawing of the item to be reproduced.

PREPARING A DRAWING

No woodworker, no matter how experienced, starts cutting lumber for a project without making some preliminary drawings and calculating the sizes, quantity, and cost of the lumber. Whether the drawings are just simple sketches or fairly accurate scale drawings, they allow the builder to determine the sizes of the various pieces and their relationship to each other. If the drawings are drawn to scale, the builder will be able to better visualize the finished product. In any event, before the actual building starts, sit down with paper and pencil and prepare dimensioned sketches of the project from which a materials list may be made. If a drawing board, T-square, and other drawing instruments are available, make a scaled drawing.

Note: The material on planning and estimating that follows contains instructions for the traditional-styled chest of drawers featured in Chapter Six. Before continuing, refer to this project to become acquainted with it and some of the construction techniques that will be used.

PREPARING A SIMPLE SKETCH

An elaborate drawing is not always necessary. A reasonably accurate pencil sketch will often suffice. The chest of drawers used for the project in Chapter Six could be built from the sketches shown in Illus. 4-1 and 4-2. The per-

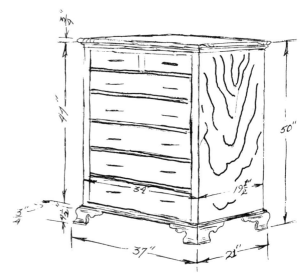

Illus. 4-1. A simple freehand sketch often makes an adequate plan.

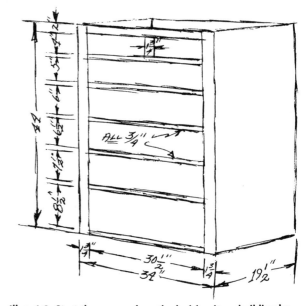

Illus. 4-2. Start the casework method of furniture building by computing the face-frame dimensions.

spective sketch in Illus. 4-1 gives the overall dimensions for the chest of drawers' length, depth, and height. The front-view sketch shown in Illus. 4-2 gives the exact dimensions of the face frame, which is the starting point for any furniture built the casework way. Besides the face-frame details, preparing the sketch will help determine the following: (1) the height of the legs; (2) the thickness of the top; (3) the amount to allow for the moulding between the legs and the "basic box," which is the main part of the chest; (4) the actual dimensions of the face frame members; and (5) the dimensions of the side panels.

After completing the sketches and adding the dimensions, calculate the amount of material to be purchased. Also prepare an exact cutting list of pieces that will be taken to the shop and followed carefully when the actual machining of the various pieces begins. Be very careful when calculating the amount of material and preparing a cutting list. Mistakes made on paper can lead to costly miscalculations when cutting hardwood or plywood!

DETERMINING MATERIAL AMOUNTS AND COSTS

Unless money is of no concern, make a close estimate of the required amounts of the various materials used in building the selected project. First determine exactly what will be used in building the project, which in our example is a chest of drawers. Basically, the chest will be built with the materials shown in Table 3-1.

DETERMINING AMOUNTS OF MATERIALS

Hardwood Lumber   The amount of hardwood lumber to purchase is usually the first problem faced when attempting to determine the cost of a project. Looking at the sketch, list the various parts of the chest that will be made from hardwood. These are the face frame, legs, bottom moulding, top edging, and cove moulding.

Next, take each item separately and determine the sizes of the hardwood pieces used to make it. For example:

Face frame
Stiles: Two pieces ¾ × 1¾ × 44 inches
Top rail: One piece ¾ × 2 × 30½ inches
Drawer rails: Five pieces ¾ × 1¾ × 32 inches
Top drawer divider piece: One piece ¾ × 1¾ × 4¾ inches

Legs
Leg blanks: Six pieces ¾ × 4½ × 8 inches

Bottom Moulding
Front: One piece ¾ × 2½ × 37 inches
Sides: Two pieces ¾ × 2½ × 22 inches

MATERIAL	USE
Hardwood lumber	Face frame, legs, mouldings, and top edgings
¾-inch hardwood plywood	Drawer fronts
¼-inch hardwood plywood	End panels and top (perhaps drawer fronts)
1-inch softwood lumber	Plywood reinforcement, drawer runners, cross-braces
¼-inch softwood plywood	Drawer bottoms and cabinet backs
½-inch particle board (or plywood)	Drawer sides and backs
¾-inch particle board (or plywood)	Chest bottom
Hardware	Drawer pulls and thumbtacks
Miscellaneous supplies	Glue, sandpaper and belts, nails, screws, brads, and finishing materials

Table 4-1. Material used to build a chest of drawers.

Top Edging

Front: One piece ¾ × 2½ × 39 inches
Sides: Two pieces ¾ × 2½ × 23 inches

Cove Moulding

Front and two sides: One piece ¾ × ¾ × 6
  feet

Some of the dimensions will be approximate for those pieces that will have mitred ends, because these pieces have to be at least 2 inches longer than the basic chest to allow enough length for the mitres.

The next step is to convert the above dimensioned pieces into standard boards of hardwood lumber from which the pieces can be machined. These pieces of lumber can then be ordered or purchased from the local lumber dealer. It will take some calculations to arrive at a fairly accurate estimate of the quantities needed. Four factors must be considered when making such calculations. First, some waste and leftover scrap must be allowed for. Second, when estimating quantities it is best to think in terms of what rippings can be garnered from a certain width board. Illus. 4-3 depicts the pieces that can be ripped from an

8 × 10 hardwood board which really is only 7½ inches wide but is 120 inches long. Third, the width of the saw blade, about ⅛ inch, must be factored into the calculation. Finally, remember that the dimensions of the material calculated in Step 1 are the *dressed*, or final, size desired, which means the pieces should be ripped a bit oversize to allow for smoothing on the jointer. Actually, many of these width dimensions are approximations. The drawer rails, for example, could just as well be ¹⁄₁₆ inch or so narrower to make economical use of a standard board width.

LAYOUT AND CUTTING PLAN

Start with the five drawer rails, which are each 1¾ inches wide. Four of these rails, ripped at exactly 1¾ inches, may be obtained from a 7½-inch board with very little material left over. These four pieces will use slightly more than 32 inches of the length of the 10-foot board. The next 44 inches of the board will yield the two stiles and the 2-inch top rail, and the last 44 inches will yield the two long pieces for the bottom moulding, the top edging, and two of the shorter side pieces. It is

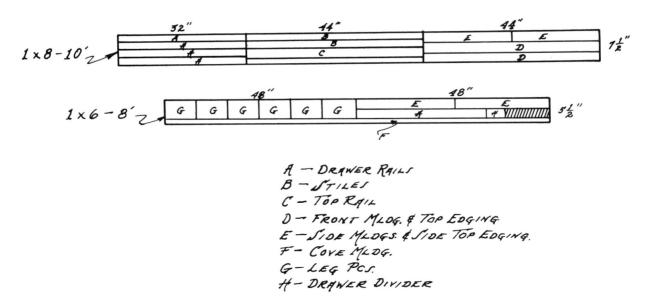

A — DRAWER RAILS
B — STILES
C — TOP RAIL
D — FRONT MLDG. & TOP EDGING
E — SIDE MLDGS. & SIDE TOP EDGING.
F — COVE MLDG.
G — LEG PCS.
H — DRAWER DIVIDER

Illus. 4-3. Lumber-cutting plan for the hardwood pieces needed for the sketched chest of drawers.

good practice to first add ½ inch to the 32-inch section before cutting it off the board. Next, cut the 44-inch section off—again allowing about ½ inch. Then rip the pieces required. Finally, cut the pieces to exact length using a stop jig so that all the furniture components, such as the drawer rails, are exactly the same.

The second board, a 1 × 6 that is 8 feet long, will yield the remaining pieces (Illus. 4-3). Run the cove edging on this board before ripping the ¾-inch strip, as it is much easier to handle. Shape the edge with the cove cutter, and then rip the strip off the board. Next, cut 48 inches off for use as the six required leg pieces. Finally, rip about 2½ inches from the remaining piece. This leaves a strip for the fifth drawer rail and the very short drawer divider piece.

One reason very little material is wasted in this example is because select lumber with no flaws is being used. If No. 1 Common were to be used, extra lumber would have to be purchased and careful calculations made to secure the required rippings. Below are ways to lay out and plan the material in the most economic way when using different types of material.

If the drawer fronts are to be fabricated from hardwood lumber, additional footage will have to be calculated. In this example, however, ¾-inch hardwood plywood is going to be used for the drawer fronts.

¾-Inch-Thick Hardwood Plywood

The builder can use three different types of material for drawer fronts: solid lumber, ¼-inch plywood that may be glued to ½-inch plywood or particle board, or ¾-inch plywood. He also has to decide whether to use veneer- or fibre-core-grade plywood. For this example, ¾-inch hardwood plywood is going to be used for the drawer fronts.

Determine the opening dimensions of the chest front, disregarding the drawer rails. This opening measures about 30½ × 41½ inches. This will be a piece of ¾-inch material that measures 48 × 36 inches. Note that the dimensions have been enlarged to the nearest foot, which is the way the material will probably have to be purchased. Also, be certain that the 48-inch dimension is listed first, as this determines that the grain will run in the 36-inch direction. This is important if horizontal grain is desired for the drawer fronts, which most often is used for traditional chests. All seven drawer fronts can be cut from this panel.

If the lumber dealer will not cut a 4 × 8-foot sheet, try one of the cabinet shops in the area. They may even have smaller pieces they want to get rid of that can be used for the drawer fronts. Hopefully, it will not be necessary to purchase an entire sheet of plywood to secure just the 12 square feet needed.

¼-Inch-Thick Hardwood Plywood

One-quarter-inch-thick plywood is going to be used for the two side panels and the top. No matter how this footage is calculated, it will not cut economically from a 4 × 8-foot sheet. However, if Lauan and Philippine mahogany are being used, the chest back and drawer bottoms can also be made from ¼-inch-thick plywood. The two side panels will require a piece of ¼-inch plywood that is 4 × 3 feet. The top will take a piece about 2 × 3 feet. Again, a cabinet shop might be the best bet for purchasing these three pieces. Otherwise, it will probably be necessary to buy a whole 4 × 8-foot sheet from the lumberyard.

1-Inch Softwood Lumber

This is not an expensive item, so just purchase a couple of No. 3 pine boards that are 1 × 8 and 10 feet long and plan on cutting the knots out when machining the pieces needed.

¼-Inch Softwood Plywood

This probably will be ¼-inch fir plywood or similar inexpensive plywood. It will be used for the back of the chest and the drawer bottoms. These are the pieces that will be needed:

Drawer bottom: Five pieces ¼ × 19 × 30 inches
Drawer bottom: Two pieces ¼ × 14 × 19 inches (sizes are approximate)

One 4 × 8-foot piece of plywood will furnish all the drawer bottoms (Illus 4-4). The chest back will require a piece of plywood 4 × 3 feet. Most lumber dealers will cut a sheet of softwood plywood to the size ordered, but, if your dealer won't, a full sheet will have to be purchased.

½-Inch Particle Board

One-half-inch particle board will be used for the drawer sides and backs. One-half-inch fir plywood can also be used if it can be purchased in the B–B grade. This type of plywood in the A–D grade, the most commonly stocked grade in lumberyards, will have many knots on the D side. Choose the heavy-density particle board ordinarily used for cabinet work. Do *not* use the underlayment grade. Many lumber dealers are now stocking this in both the ¾- and ½-inch thicknesses.

Estimate the amount required by simply using the approximate dimensions of the inside of the chest. This results in the following calculation:

Drawer sides: Two pieces ½ × 19 × (approximately) 42 inches
Drawer backs: One piece ½ × (approximately) 30 × (approximately) 42 inches

These three pieces will yield the sides and backs, with some material to spare. Unless these pieces can be purchased in approximate size from a cabinet shop, a full 4 × 8-foot sheet will have to be bought at the lumberyard. Illus. 4-5 shows the cutting pattern.

¾-Inch Particle Board

Three-quarter-inch plywood in the A–D grade can be used on the chest bottom because only the one surface will be seen, and this surface is on the inside of the chest. Do not use a thinner plywood or particle board because this could result in a weak chest. Only one piece, ¾ × 19 × 34 inches, is required.

If buying the particle board from a lumber dealer, you may have to purchase a 2 × 4-foot piece. A cabinet shop may either have a "leftover" piece equal to that size or be willing to cut the piece to the needed dimensions. In either case, the piece will have to be recut to

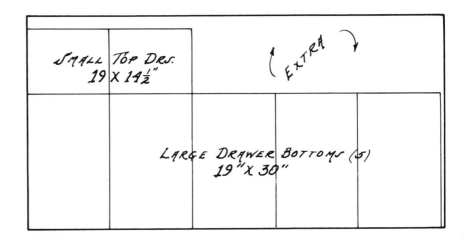

Illus. 4-4. Cutting plan for ¼-inch plywood drawer bottoms.

the exact dimensions when installed in the chest.

Hardware

Twelve period-styled pulls will be needed. These can be purchased at discount, hardware, and building supply stores. Discount stores usually have a good stock of furniture and cabinet hardware at reasonable prices. Traditional-styled drawer pulls are usually available at most of the above-mentioned retailers. Furniture hardware can also be bought through mail-order firms that cater to woodworkers.

After all of the above quantities are determined, it is a simple matter to calculate the cost of the materials by calling or visiting various dealers and asking for their price per foot or board foot. Some real savings can be garnered by shopping around.

PREPARING A MATERIAL CUTTING LIST

Ordinarily, this is accomplished at the same time the quantity estimate is being made, as was demonstrated earlier in this chapter. The face-frame cutting list, for example, should be exactly dimensioned. You can take it to the table saw and refer to it frequently while machining the parts. Most of the dimensions of the other components of the project should be taken from the project itself as it progresses. The dimensions for the plywood back, for example, should be determined by measuring the rear of the assembled face frame. Chapter Six covers this subject thoroughly. By following this method, accuracy is ensured and mistakes are held to an absolute minimum.

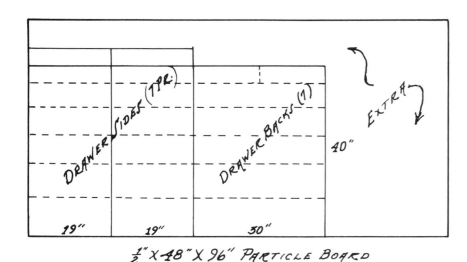

Illus. 4-5. Cutting plan for drawer sides and backs of ½-inch particle board.

CHAPTER FIVE

Working with Lumber and Plywood

A skilled woodworker can perform even the most difficult operations with smoothness and ease. He has attained this skill level for the following reasons: (1) He can make exact measurements and can cut accurately to those measurements. (2) He knows what the machines can accomplish and keeps those machines sharp and accurately adjusted. (3) He works safely, using all the guards intended for a particular machine. (4) He knows the capacity and rate of feed for these machines and does not exceed that rate or force the material beyond the machines' capabilities. (5) He uses jigs and fixtures, often shop-made, for ease of cutting and handling materials. (6) He plans carefully, thus holding errors and miscuts to an absolute minimum. (7) He is always willing to observe, listen, and learn about new techniques, materials, and machinery. (8) He is willing to share his knowledge, techniques, and experiences with other devoted woodworkers.

The information contained in this chapter focuses on how to measure and cut accurately, how to adjust the machines for accuracy, and which jigs will prove particularly helpful in the workshop.

MEASURING

The number of amateur woodworkers who have not mastered the very basic technique of accurately measuring and cutting is amazing. This is an essential part of woodworking. More errors and miscuts can probably be attributed to poor measuring than any other factor.

Three things are required to accurately measure and cut: (1) an accurate measuring device (2) a sharp pencil and (3) a good "eye." They are described below.

MEASURING DEVICES

There are several tapes, rules, and squares available that can be used for measuring in woodworking. Some are of better quality than others. These measuring devices are often used for special purposes.

Retractable Metal Tape All woodworkers should have a good power-return metal tape from a name-brand manufacturer such as Stanley. This tape should be at least ten feet long or even longer if kitchen cabinets as well as furniture projects will be built. The tape should also have a movable, hooked end so it will be accurate for either inside or outside measuring. The markings should be clear, dark, and finely defined, with both feet and inches clearly printed on a white or yellow background. The first few inches should be divided into 32nds and 16ths. The balance of the tape should be divided into feet and inches, and the inches divided into 16ths. Many tapes will also have 16-inch wall stud spacing marked as well. A quality tape, kept lightly oiled, should last for years.

Six-foot Folding Rule
Some hobbyists still use a wooden, six-foot folding rule. Although it is an accurate measuring tool, it has some serious shortcomings. First, it breaks easily. Second, it does not have a hooked end, which means that you have to maneuver it carefully with your fingers to determine that it is flush with the end of the board being measured. Third, its six-foot length is a handicap when materials longer than six feet are being used.

Framing Square
This convenient tool can be used as both a measuring device and a square. It is excellent for drawing square lines and for testing the squareness of large openings that are found on furniture and cabinetry. The inch marks on the edges of some squares are divided into different divisions — into 10ths and 12ths, for example. These divisions are sometimes needed when inches are being divided into odd fractions.

One blade of a framing square is exactly 24 inches long. It can be used to quickly locate the center of a 48-inch panel and also as a 24-inch marking gauge. The markings used for measuring are very accurate and, if the square is kept polished, easy to read. A quick 45-degree angle can be drawn by using the same numbers on the blade (body) and tongue placed along the edge of a board (Illus. 5-1).

Using the tip of the blade and the tip of the tongue will give 30- and 60-degree angles on a board (Illus. 5-2).

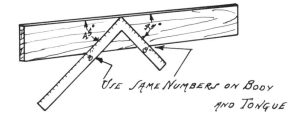

Illus. 5-1. Using the framing square to lay out a 45-degree angle.

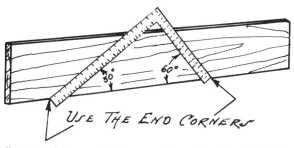

Illus. 5-2. Thirty- and 60-degree angles can be determined with the framing square.

Combination Square
This versatile tool is one of the most used in the workshop for several reasons. First, it is used as a try square to draw square lines and to test the squareness of edges and ends of boards. Second, the blade can be removed from the handle and used as an accurate bench rule. It has inch divisions of 32nds, 16ths, and 8ths. Third, because the square possesses a sliding handle, it can be used as a marking gauge, a depth gauge, and a locating jig. Fourth, there is a small level built into the handle that is useful at times. Finally, there is a small awl recessed into the handle that can be removed and used for pinpricking locations of centers for drilling, and other tasks.

A Sharp Pencil
Because cutting pieces accurately to length on the table saw requires sawing to the line or mark, the finer that mark

or line is made the more accurate the cut can be. Though some old-time woodworkers do their marking with a sharp knife, most craftspersons will be satisfied with a sharp pencil that they sharpen frequently while measuring.

CUTTING TECHNIQUES

The real test of accuracy when making a cut is to *cut as close to the line as is possible and still allow the line to remain on the wood*. So in learning to cut to length, the woodworker must develop the technique of using the mitre gauge to move the wood into the saw blade so that the blade is cutting as close to the mark as possible. Here are two techniques to help develop this skill:

1. Make the mark or line on the edge of the piece of wood that will first come in contact with the saw blade.
2. Move the wood slowly towards the saw blade and allow the blade to just nick the board a bit wide of the mark. Now it is an easy matter to adjust the work slightly to have the blade cut just to the mark.

Remember, a board that is cut too short is useless, but one cut a bit too long can always be trimmed.

ADJUSTING THE MACHINES

TABLE SAW

Adjusting the Mitre Gauge

If the mitre gauge on a table saw is not set absolutely square, you will not be able to cut square cutoffs. The easiest way to set the mitre gauge is to set it square in relationship to the saw blade itself. This is done with the try, or triangle, square, as shown in Illus. 5-3. Make an end cut on a 3- or 4-inch board and

Illus. 5-3. A triangle or try square can be used to set the mitre gauge square with the saw blade.

check it with the square to ensure that the setting is correct. Check the mitre gauge often, because it is used frequently and can quickly become misaligned.

Adjusting the Rip Fence

The table saw will only rip material accurately if it is equipped with a sharp blade with adequate "set" and if the rip fence is adjusted properly in relationship to the blade. One of the first table-saw adjustments that must be made is the proper adjustment of the rip fence in relationship to the saw blade. A binding saw is partially caused by the fence being out of parallel to the blade.

To set the fence correctly, first loosen the adjusting bolt heads at the rear of the fence. Cut two blocks of wood to the exact width of the table slot and insert these at the front and rear of the slot. Now, bring the fence into position so it just touches both blocks; then tighten the adjustment bolts. Some woodworkers prefer to have the fence slightly wider at the rear and will place a piece of note paper between the block and the fence (Illus. 5-4).

Setting the Ripping Gauge

Almost all rip fences have an adjustable pointer that indicates the ripping width. This

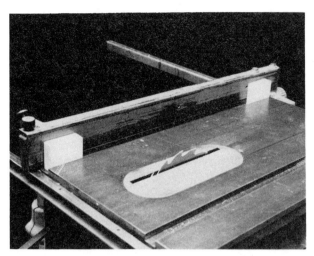
Illus. 5-4. Setting the saw fence parallel with the blade.

scale is imprinted on the fence guide rail. To maintain the accuracy of the pointer it is necessary to adjust it each time a different blade is used, because each blade will have a different set.

To set the pointer, use the tape measure to set the fence a certain distance from the saw blade, for example, 4 inches. Be sure the measurement is made from a saw tooth that is set *to the right.* Now, run a scrap piece of wood into the blade and measure the piece to ensure that the saw is cutting exactly 4 inches. If it is not, adjust the fence until the cut is exactly 4 inches.

Next, set the rip pointer exactly on the 4-inch line on the scale on the guide rail. Double-check the pointer setting by moving the fence to the 8-inch mark and again run a test cut. Then move the fence to the 20-inch mark and make another test cut. Each setting should produce the correct ripping width indicated by the pointer setting.

Many saw operators use the pointer only for rough cutting or when a "jointer cut" allowance must be made. For very accurate cuts, use a tape measure to set the fence.

Accurate "Leftover" Ripping   The previous section describes only the accurate rip-

ping of material that will be pushed between the saw blade and the rip fence. Very often, it is necessary to rip material where the portion between the fence and blade is the discard and does not have to be accurately cut, as, for example, when ripping 80 inches from a 96-inch piece of plywood. The rip fence will have to be set at 16 inches, *including the saw blade.* This means that the measurement must be made from the rip fence to a saw tooth set *to the left.* It is always an excellent idea to bring the sheet of plywood to the saw, just allow the saw blade to touch the material, and then measure the piece to see that 80 inches is actually remaining before making the completed cut.

JOINTER

The jointer is another machine that can accomplish accurate work only if the fence and tables are set perfectly. The fence must be set absolutely square in order to produce truly square edges on the lumber being dressed. Both the in-feed and out-feed tables must be set correctly in order to joint lumber straight and true.

Setting the Fence   Almost every jointer possesses a tilt scale and stops for adjusting and tilting the fence. These stops are adjustable, and the fence can rapidly be tilted to 45 degrees and then back to 90 degrees. It is important that these settings are accurate and kept properly adjusted. Set the fence first in the 90-degree position by checking it with a try square or other perfect 90-degree measuring device. With the fence set at 90 degrees, set the adjustable stop so this exact setting can be returned to. Now, do the same for the 45-degree position. Use only the handle of the combination square for an accurate 45-degree setting device.

Finally, adjust the pointer so that it accurately points to the 90-degree markings on the scale.

Adjusting the Tables A jointer has an in-feed and an out-feed table. The out-feed table is the one that requires accurate adjustment. If this table is too low, a "clip" is made on the end of the board as it leaves the cutterhead. If this table is too high, the board being jointed will be slightly tapered—that is, less wood will be removed by the knives as the edge of the board is moved over the cutterhead. An easy means of setting the out-feed table correctly is as follows:

1. Set the in-feed table for about a 1/16-inch-deep cut.
2. Set the out-feed table slightly lower.
3. Run the edge of a board over the cutterhead until it moves onto the out-feed table about 1 inch.
4. Adjust the out-feed table upwards until it exactly reaches the edge of the board at the 1/16-inch depth of cut made by the cutterhead (Illus. 5-5).
5. Complete a cut to determine that no "clip" is made at the end of the board.

TABLE-SAW JIGS

There are several jigs that the hobbyist can build in the shop that will make the table saw more efficient and useful. These are not difficult to build, but will make some tasks, such as mitring, easier and more accurate. Two shop-built jigs that will prove indispensable are the mitring jig and the cutoff jig. Both jigs replace the mitre gauge. They have fairly large surfaces and edges that hold the work firmly and it slides with the jig in the grooves of the table-saw top. The other jigs described in this section either aid in ripping or provide assistance when the moulding head is being used on the table saw.

MITRING JIG

This is a relatively easy jig to build, as Illus. 5-6 reveals. The base piece of ¾-inch plywood or particle board should be about as large as the table-saw top. The two hardwood runners should be attached to the bottom carefully so that the jig slides easily but no play is evident in the runners. Rubbing the runners with paraffin will help the jig slide easily.

Lay out the mitring guides accurately in relationship to the saw blade. Do this with the framing square so that each guide makes an exact 45-degree angle with the blade. Glue a strip of coarse sandpaper along the edge of each guide to help prevent the work from drifting as it is being cut. The small piece across the two guides acts as a guard as the blade completes the mitre. If laid out and assembled accurately, this jig does an excellent job of mitring.

SLIDING CUTOFF JIG

This jig is especially convenient when cutting off wide pieces of lumber or plywood. The mitre gauge does not provide much guiding

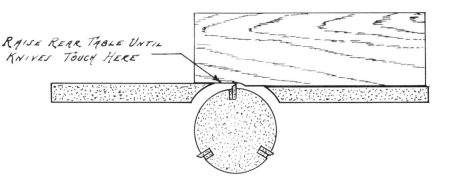

Illus. 5-5. Setting the jointer out-feed table.

RAISE REAR TABLE UNTIL KNIVES TOUCH HERE

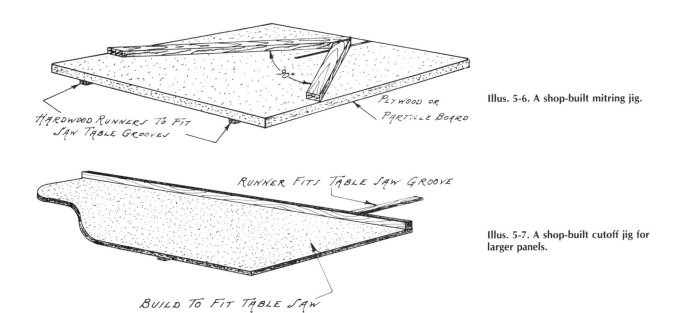

Illus. 5-6. A shop-built mitring jig.

HARDWOOD RUNNERS TO FIT
SAW TABLE GROOVES

PLYWOOD OR
PARTICLE BOARD

RUNNER FITS TABLE SAW GROOVE

Illus. 5-7. A shop-built cutoff jig for
larger panels.

BUILD TO FIT TABLE SAW

surface for large pieces and cannot be used to obtain perfectly square cuts. Illus. 5-7 shows a sliding jig that holds wider pieces firmly and uses the groove in the table-saw top for guidance. Build the jig to fit the table saw. Then install the guide runner and saw the right-hand edge on the table saw. Attach the holding fence at a perfect right angle to the right-hand edge. When using this jig, simply align the mark on the board to be cut with the right-hand edge of the jig for accurate sawing.

LENGTH CUTOFF JIGS

One problem beginners face is cutting several pieces to exactly the same length. For example, four legs for a table must be exactly the same length, as do stiles and rails on a piece of furniture. There are several means of accomplishing exact multiple cuts on the table saw, depending upon the length of the pieces being cut. They are described below.

Stop Rods in the Mitre Gauge   For cutting short pieces to length, use the stop rods that fit into the mitre gauge. Illus. 5-8 depicts their use. For most applications, install the

hooked stop to the left of the mitre gauge so there is no danger of the saw blade hitting the stop rod or the cutoff piece wedging between the blade and the stop.

Rip Fence   The rip fence is probably the most convenient cutoff jig for pieces up to 24 inches because it can simply be set at the length desired. The only danger is that the piece being cut off might wedge between the saw blade and the fence and come flying out of the saw. This can easily be prevented by always using the mitre gauge to control the piece being cut off. This means that the mitre gauge must be *between the saw blade and the fence* for all multiple-cut operations where the pieces are longer than the mitre gauge is wide (Illus. 5-9).

To cut off pieces shorter than the width of the mitre gauge, simply clamp a piece of wood to the fence. The pieces that will be cut off will be butted against this piece of wood, rather than against the fence itself (Illus. 5-10). This way, when the pieces are cut there is room between the saw blade and the fence and there is little danger of the loose pieces wedging.

Illus. 5-8. Stop rods are used for making multiple length cuts.

Illus. 5-9. The saw fence can be used as a cutoff jig.

Illus. 5-10. For short cutoffs, clamp a piece of wood to the fence.

A Cutoff Jig for Longer Pieces

Pieces longer than 24 inches are usually cut with a radial arm saw or power mitre box. If these tools are not available, the table saw will work well if used with a fairly simple cutoff jig with an adjustable stop piece, as shown in Illus. 5-11 and 5-12. The jig is clamped to the rails of the table saw, and is used with the mitre gauge to control the pieces being cut. The arm with the stop block can be made of varying lengths, so almost any length of cutoff can be accommodated. Use supporting sawhorses to hold and catch the boards as they are being sawed.

ATTACHMENTS FOR THE RIP FENCE

Occasionally, the rip fence requires some attachments for special operations. These are simple to make and can be easily attached to the fence when needed.

Moulding-Head Fence

When using the moulding head in the table saw, you must attach a ¾-inch wood or plywood auxiliary fence to the rip fence to prevent the knives hitting the metal fence (Illus. 5-13). Most rip fences have screw holes for just this purpose, so it is easy to install the auxiliary fence. The first time the auxiliary fence is used, raise the moulding head gradually to cut the relief area into the wood.

Attachments for Cutting Thin Material

Very thin material such as plastic laminate or veneer will slip under the rip fence when being sawed. To prevent this, two attachments should be made. The first is used when the rip fence is in position on the saw table. It is simply a piece of wood that is attached to the rip fence. This piece of wood fits snugly against the table and closes the gap between the fence and the table (Illus. 5-14). The second is an aid to be used when the rip fence is to the right of the table and clamped to the guide rails. When the rip fence is used in such a position, thin material will move around and slip under the rip fence and cannot be properly guided into the saw blade. It is easy to build an attachment from wood that has a supporting lip on the bottom that will hold the thin material as it is being ripped (Illus. 5-15).

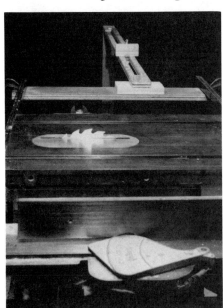

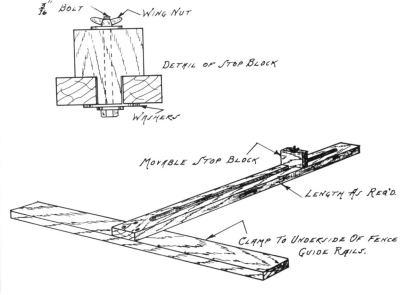

Illus. 5-11. (above left). An adjustable shop-built cutoff jig for longer pieces. Illus. 5-12. (above right). Details of the cutoff jig.

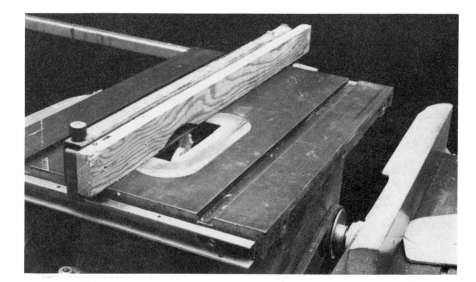

Illus. 5-13. An auxiliary fence is needed when the moulding head is used.

Illus. 5-14. An auxiliary fence is also needed for very thin stock.

Illus. 5-15. A lipped auxiliary fence is used to support thin stock.

TABLE SAW AND JOINTER TECHNIQUES

Before engaging in the actual furniture-building procedures, it is important that you learn how to properly handle plywood and lumber when using a table saw or jointer. The information that is presented in this section describes how to handle lumber and plywood skillfully and safely.

RIPPING ON THE TABLE SAW

Straightening the Lumber Edge
One problem the woodworker constantly faces is cutting straight lumber rippings with the table saw. To obtain straight rippings, the edge of the board placed against the rip fence must be straight! To straighten the edge of the board do the following: Sight along the edge of that piece. Determine whether that edge should be straightened on the jointer before sawing. If the edge has to be straightened, use the jointer to remove both concave and convex edges by repeatedly passing the board over the cutter-head in just those areas where the material should be removed. Make these jointer cuts until the entire length of the board makes contact with the cutters, and the edge is finally straightened. Sometimes the curvature of the edge is so great that it is faster and easier to remove the curvature by using the portable circle saw. In such a situation, snap a chalk line on the board and straighten the edge with the circle saw (Illus. 5-16).

Jointing Allowance
Always remove saw marks from lumber. This is called "dressing the lumber." When ripping lumber, allow extra material for dressing the pieces on the jointer. If both edges of a board require dressing, allow about $1/16$ inch. If only one edge will need jointing, allow slightly over $1/32$ inch. For example, if the net width of a board should be exactly 2 inches, the ripping will be $2\frac{1}{16}$ inches. Set the jointer to make a cut slightly less than $1/32$ inch and run the edge into the cutter about an inch. Flip the board over and do the same with the other edge.

Next, measure the net result. If the 2-inch measurement has not been reached, lower the in-feed table slightly and try again until an exact net measurement of 2 inches is reached. If a scrap piece of the ripping is available, do the setting with it—just be sure that the scrap is the same as the original ripping, which was $2\frac{1}{16}$ inches. Some craftspersons feel more comfortable allowing more than $1/16$ inch for the jointing allowance. This is a decision that the individual operator should make.

HANDLING PLYWOOD SHEETS ON THE TABLE SAW

A 4×8-foot piece of $3/4$-inch plywood or particle board is difficult to handle for a person working alone in the workshop, even if he has a large table saw. If a smaller saw is being used, some ingenuity is required.

In Chapter Two it was recommended that you build several sawhorses and equip at least two of them with height extensions that make use of roller skate wheels. Illus. 5-17 and 5-18 present the details for making these roller supports. These supports can be used to

SNAP A CHALK LINE

Illus. 5-16. Snap a chalk line and use the circle saw to straighten badly curved lumber.

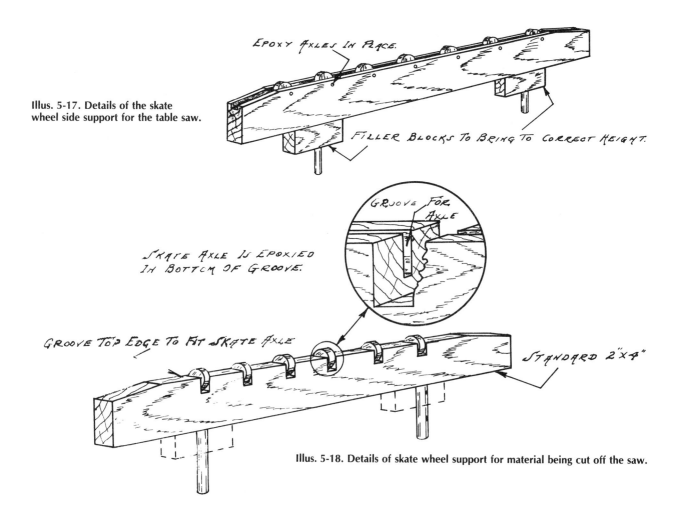

EPOXY AXLES IN PLACE.

Illus. 5-17. Details of the skate wheel side support for the table saw.

FILLER BLOCKS TO BRING TO CORRECT HEIGHT.

GROOVE FOR AXLE

SKATE AXLE IS EPOXIED IN BOTTOM OF GROOVE.

GROOVE TOP EDGE TO FIT SKATE AXLE

STANDARD 2"x4"

Illus. 5-18. Details of skate wheel support for material being cut off the saw.

handle sheets of plywood as long as they are lined up parallel to the table saw. The top of the rollers should be the same height as the table saw.

To use these supports to cut the plywood, simply lift the front edge of the plywood sheet onto the saw, walk to the back, and then lift the piece to feed it into the saw. The two rollers will support the piece from the side and as it comes off the saw (Illus. 5-19). After the cut has been completed, the pieces just remain in place until the operator removes them. The rollers work equally well for supporting long pieces of plywood and lumber when cutting to length.

HANDLING LONG LUMBER PIECES ON THE TABLE SAW

The roller skate support is also helpful when long pieces of lumber must be ripped. The wheels are placed close enough together so that at least two wheels are touching the board at all times.

For a narrow board that might not hit the wheels, rip the board to about half its length, remove it from the saw, reverse it (keeping the same edge against the rip fence), and complete the cut.

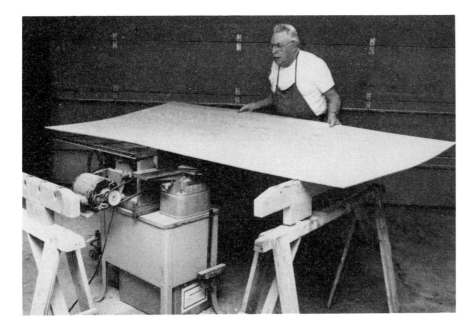

HANDLING LONG PIECES ON THE JOINTER

Another type of roller support can be built to support long pieces coming off the jointer. This should be constructed so that it is adjustable in height for use at the shaper, table saw, or other machines. Illus. 5-20 gives the build-

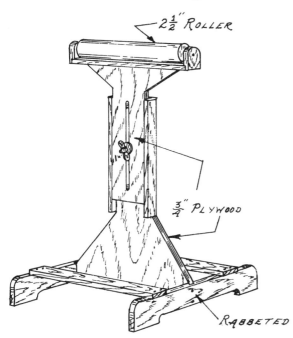

Illus. 5-20. A shop-built adjustable roller support for the jointer.

ing details for making such a support. The roller can be turned on the lathe, and the end holes drilled on the drill press, to get them as straight as possible. The axles are simply 3/8-inch lag screws that have had their heads removed with the hacksaw after they have been driven into the ends of the roller. For ease of operation, rub the axles with paraffin prior to installation.

When this support is used at the jointer, it must be set at the exact height of the out-feed table. To set the roller, position a straight piece of wood on the out-feed table and raise the roller just high enough to meet the bottom edge of this piece (Illus. 5-21).

SPECIAL TECHNIQUES FOR WORKING WITH PLYWOOD

Plywood or veneered particle board is especially easy to use to build furniture. No gluing of panels is required, and the beauty of a panel covered with rotary-cut veneer is hard to surpass. The main difficulty encountered when working with these panels is covering the unsightly inner core. This section of the chapter

Illus. 5-21. Setting the roller support even with the jointer out-feed table.

will concern itself with techniques to band the edges of plywood and to join the corners.

BANDING THE EDGES OF PLYWOOD PANELS

There are several methods commonly used to cover the inner plies of panels. Some require sophisticated machinery, and others can be done quite successfully in the home shop.

Edge-banding with Veneer   Industrial woodworking plants use machines called edge banders to mechanically apply veneer to the edge of plywood panels. These machines automatically apply hot glue, feed the veneer into position, apply pressure, and trim the veneer. Small cabinet shops have less-sophisticated edge banders that are also less costly. Both types, however, would be beyond the means of the home woodworker.

Rolls of veneer for edge banding are available to the hobbyist that simply require a hot iron to apply. These veneers come in a variety of species which include the common cabinet woods. After application, trim the veneer with a sharp hand plane to meet the dimensions of the panel.

Banding with Solid Lumber   Perhaps the most common method of hiding the plywood core used by the home woodworker is to cover it with a thin strip of solid lumber. When using this method, first joint a ¾-inch board and then rip a thin strip ³⁄₁₆ or ¼ inch wide (or wider, if desired) off the board. Next, glue this strip and nail it with ¾-inch brads to the edge of the panel with the jointed or smooth side against the panel's edge; this makes for a tight fit. The only precaution that must be taken is to predrill holes for the brads so that the strip does not split. After applying the strip to the panel, deeply set the brads and fill the holes with matching plastic wood. Then run this rough edge lightly over the jointer. Next, sand the edging with the belt and finish sander to complete the process. Lumber edging has one advantage over veneer edging: it can be hit occasionally without chipping away and revealing the core of the panel.

Some craftspersons use other techniques for banding ¾-inch panels by attaching wider pieces of solid lumber to the edges. Most of these techniques require the use of a spindle shaper to do an efficient job of installation because a tongue-and-groove joint is often used (Illus. 5-22).

Plastic Edge-banding   Many furniture and cabinet builders use a plastic moulding to finish the edges of shelving. This is a T-shaped moulding that is pressed into a routed groove in the edge of the shelving. The edging is available in tan, brown, black, or white, and in 12-foot lengths or 500-foot coils. A ¹⁄₁₆-inch slot cutter for the router is needed to make the installation. This is a fast and easy means of edging interior shelves (Illus. 5-23). This edging is available from the Woodworker's Store, Rogers, MN, 55374. This company also has an oak T-moulding that requires a ¼ × ¼-inch groove to install it on ¾-inch panels. This moulding comes in 3- or 4-foot pieces (Illus. 5-24).

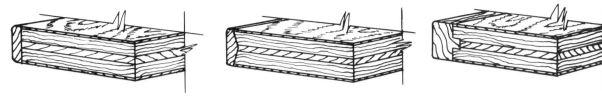

Illus. 5-22. Three different nosings used to cover plywood edges.

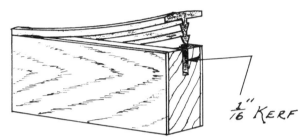

$\frac{1}{16}''$ KERF

Illus. 5-23. Plastic nosing is available to use on plywood edges.

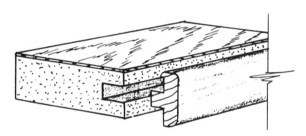

Illus. 5-24. A commercial wooden nosing is available for edging plywood.

CORNERING PLYWOOD PANELS

Another technique that must be mastered is the joining of plywood at a corner. Three common methods for both ¼- and ¾-inch panels are described in this section.

The Mitred Corner
The most common means of joining ¾-inch plywood panels at the corner is to use the mitre joint. Mitring requires an accurate table-saw setting of 45 degrees and a sharp, smooth-cutting saw blade. Set the blade by using the handle of the combination square or other 45-degree instrument. Always make test cuts, and then check the assembly with the square to see that the corner is exactly 90 degrees.

Before assembling the two pieces, drill holes for the brads. When assembling them, apply a liberal coating of glue to the joint. Then match the points of the mitres carefully and hold the two pieces firmly as you drive in the first nails. Nails should be driven from both sides of the assembly, and the pieces should be held in the 90-degree position until the glue has set. Set the nails and, using matching plastic wood, fill the holes and any slight gaps in the mitred joint. Sand and scrape the excess filler from the two sides; be careful not to damage the thin veneer.

The mitre joint can also be used for joining ¼-inch panels, but the sides must be reinforced with a ¾ × ¾-inch backing strip (Illus. 5-25). Do not attempt to drive the brads into the end grain of the plywood; instead, drive them into the reinforcing strip. Strips of masking tape placed along the edge of the joint will keep the veneers tightly together until the glue dries.

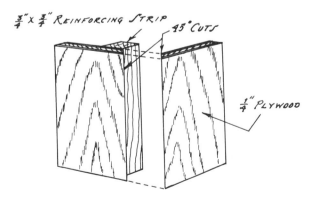

Illus. 5-25. Mitring ¼-inch plywood using a backup piece.

The Lumber "Filler" Corner This is probably the easiest method of making a satisfactory corner for ¼-inch plywood. Glue and clamp a ¾ × 1-inch reinforcing strip to one of the sides, and hold the opposite side back ⅜ inch to ½ inch. Then fill this space with a lumber strip that is slightly thicker and wider than the space between the panels (Illus. 5-26). Glue and nail the strip in place using fine ¾-inch brads after predrilling holes for them. After setting the brads, fill the holes and any slight gaps along the cornering strip with plastic wood. With a very sharp block plane, hook scraper, and sandpaper, work the filler strip down to just meet the side panels.

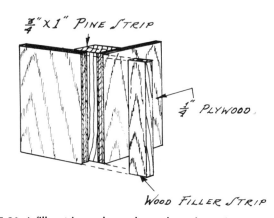

Illus. 5-26. A filler strip can be used to make a plywood corner.

The Veneered Corner Although the veneered corner is the most difficult to make, it is the most attractive when used with ¼-inch panelling because no interruption in the grain pattern is noticeable (Illus. 5-27). This is the one disadvantage to the filler corner, because the solid lumber strip sometimes is quite evident and does not match the adjoining panels. This, too, requires a reinforcing strip and the careful sawing of the plywood so only the veneer remains on one of the pieces. Detailed instructions are given for making this joint in Chapter Six, so they will not be duplicated here.

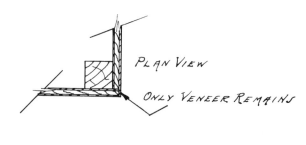

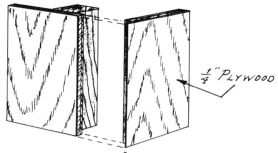

Illus. 5-27. The "veneered corner" method of cornering ¼-inch plywood.

PREVENTING VENEER FROM SPLINTERING

Veneer can splinter on the underside of the plywood panel when it is being sawed on the table saw, or when it is being rabbeted or grooved with the dado set. This makes a very unsightly joint. Although matching plastic wood can be used to fill the splintered areas, this is time-consuming and a close inspection reveals the filler. A fine-toothed, sharp saw blade will minimize this problem, but some splintering still occurs. It is better to prevent splintering completely by using one of the techniques described below.

Scoring One of the easiest methods of preventing splintering is to use a sharp knife to score the plywood right next to the path of the saw blade. Use a straight edge and be certain to cut through the veneer with the knife even if a couple of knife strokes must be made. Use this technique any time splintering is a concern.

Using Masking Tape Another way to prevent veneer from splintering is to apply a strip of masking tape directly over and along the path of the saw blade. This technique is not quite as successful as the scoring technique, but it is slightly faster and will usually do a satisfactory job. If it is critical that splintering be prevented, use the scoring technique.

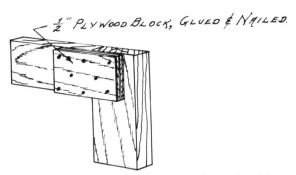

Illus. 5-28. A block of wood is used to reinforce a butt joint.

MAKING THE SIMPLE WOODWORKING JOINTS

The strength and appearance of any wood joint depends upon the accuracy of its layout and fabrication as well as the method used in assembling that joint. The following joints are ones that the woodworker will have to use occasionally.

BUTT JOINT

This joint is simply two pieces of wood butted together at right angles and assembled with screws or "butt blocks." To create a good butt joint, make sure that the mitre gauge is set absolutely square when cutting the adjoining pieces, and that the pieces are held in that position until they are assembled. The casework system of furniture building makes extensive use of the screwed butt joint. The details for making this joint and hiding the screw heads are presented in Chapter Six.

This joint is often assembled and held together with butt blocks of ½ inch plywood or even pine (Illus. 5-28). The face frame on inexpensive cabinetry is often assembled with butt blocks. Glue is placed in the joint, and the butt block is then glued and nailed in position on the back side of the joint.

MITRE JOINTS

Illus. 5-29 depicts several different mitre joints. All must be cut exactly at 45 degrees and assembled with care. The mitre joint is

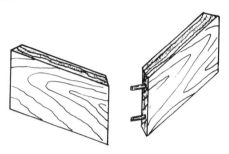

DOWELED EDGE MITRE

SPLINED FLAT MITRE

PLAIN FLAT MITRE

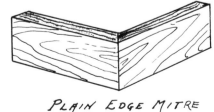

PLAIN EDGE MITRE

Illus. 5-29. Various types of mitre joints.

weak unless reinforced with a spline or with dowels. Assembly is often a problem, too, as the pieces have a tendency to slip out of position while being nailed or clamped.

There are on the market various clamping devices for holding the pieces while assembling them. One device is the picture frame clamp, but this is limited as to the width of pieces it will accommodate (Illus. 5-30). A "wedge" board is an effective means of assembling a shallow box or framework made of wider pieces. It exerts enough pressure to make attractive mitres (Illus. 5-31). Wax paper placed under each corner will prevent the frame from sticking to the board upon which

the frame is assembled. Always check the corners with the framing square while assembling, to ensure that the framework is square and that the mitres match exactly.

Another device available is the web or strap clamp with metal corners that will pull the framework together. Often the pieces can simply be placed in the vise and held there while being nailed together.

LAP JOINTS

The joints shown in Illus. 5-32 are all variations of the lap joint. The success of these joints depends upon the accuracy of the layout

Illus. 5-30. A commercial picture-frame, or mitring, clamp.

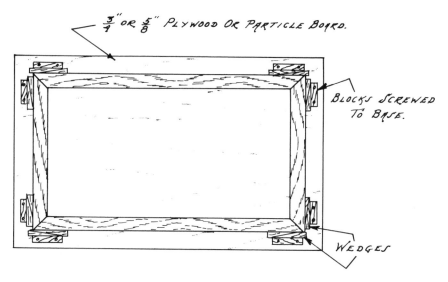

Illus. 5-31. A wedge board can be made for clamping large mitred frames.

82

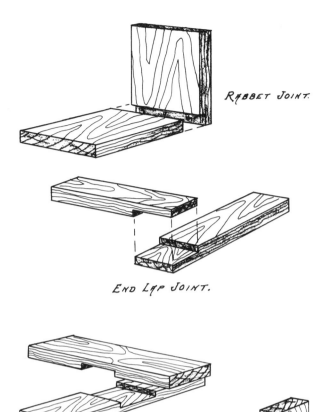

Illus. 5-32. Common lap joints and the rabbet joint.

DADO JOINTS

Illus. 5-33 depicts the two most frequently used dado joints. These are made by using the dado head (or other dadoing device) in the table saw. The assembled dado head should be the same width as the wood being used. The dado head is equipped with 1/16- and 1/8-inch "chippers" that fit between the two outside saw blades. Cut some thin "doughnut" shims from thin cardboard. Place these shims between chippers if a minor adjustment in width is needed to match the exact thickness of the wood.

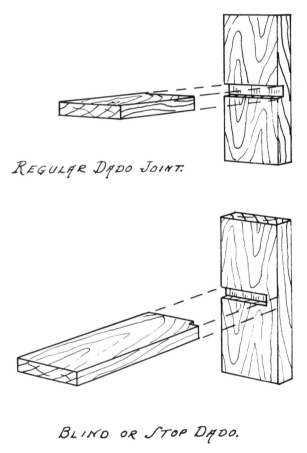

Illus. 5-33. Commonly used dado joints.

and how accurately the craftsperson saws "to the lines" with the dado head mounted in the table saw. Test the cutting action of the dado head on scrap lumber until the cut it makes is exactly halfway through each piece. Once this is correct, very carefully saw to the lines marking the joint. The rip fence can often be used as a "stop" so that each piece is dadoed exactly in the same place. Assemble the lap joints either with glue and clamps or, in the case of the rabbet joint, with nails. If a bookcase is being built with rabbet and dado joints, it is often assembled with glue and bar clamps.

The blind, or stop, dado is run only partway across the board and then stopped, so the dado groove will not be visible in the finished project. It is a good idea to devise a "stop" for this operation so each dado is sawed to a predetermined place. Finish the joint by using a chisel to square off the end of the groove to accommodate the board that will fit in the dado. Notch the end of the board carefully to fit around the end of the dado where it was stopped.

MORTISE-AND-TENON JOINT

Although the mortise-and-tenon joint is not used in the casework system, it may prove handy. The mortise is the squared hole drilled into one of the pieces to be assembled. The tenon is the tongue that fits into this hole (Illus. 5-34). To bore the mortise with any degree of efficiency, you will need a special piece of equipment that is attached to the drill press. (See Chapter Two, Illus. 2-17.) Lacking this attachment, use the drill press and a drill bit of the correct size to drill a series of holes to the proper depth and as close together as possible to form a rough mortise. Then use a sharp chisel to clean and square-up the opening to accommodate the tenon.

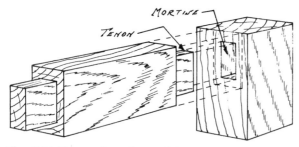

Illus. 5-34. The mortise-and-tenon joint.

The tenon is not difficult to make. Only the dado head mounted in the table saw is needed. The rip fence is used as a stop to determine the correct length of the tenon. Using a scrap piece to set the dado head at the correct height, make a cut on each side of the board and test-fit it into the mortise. Raise or lower the dado head and continue to make test cuts until the tenon fits snugly into the mortise (Illus. 5-35).

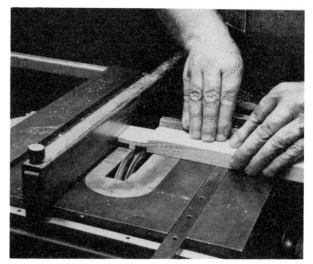

Illus. 5-35. Using the dado head on the table saw to cut a tenon.

The shoulder cut can also be made on the table saw. Make the first cut by raising the saw blade to its correct height and butting the tenon against the rip fence, which has been set at the correct distance from the blade (Illus. 5-36). Make the second cut by running the tenon into or over the saw blade, which has been raised high enough to free the shoulder piece (Illus. 5-37).

Illus. 5-36. Cutting the shoulder of the tenon.

Illus. 5-37. Cutting the shoulder of the tenon free.

DOWEL JOINT

In the home woodworker's shop the dowel joint is preferred over the mortise-and-tenon joint because virtually no special equipment is required. The single most important factor in fabricating an acceptable dowel joint is correctly aligning the centers of the matching holes that will receive the dowel pins. A second important factor is drilling the holes for the dowel pins straight and true. There are on the market dowelling jigs that correctly line up the matching centers and guide the drill bit straight and true. (See Chapter Two, Illus. 2-36). They can be purchased for a nominal amount and should be part of a shop's equipment if considerable dowelling is to be done.

For an occasional dowel joint, dowel centers are also available that work nicely. These are merely metal centers that are placed into the first holes drilled. The piece with those holes is then pushed firmly against the second board, transferring the centers to the opposite piece. (See Chapter Two, Illus. 2-37.) Dowel centers come in sets containing several commonly used diameters such as ¼, 5/16, ⅜, and ½ inch. Use the drill press to drill perfectly

true holes. If this is not possible, use the portable electric drill.

You can make the dowel pins in the shop by cutting the proper lengths from a standard dowel rod purchased at a builder's supply firm. Scratch grooves along the side of these pins to allow the air to escape from the holes and to spread the glue evenly throughout the hole. A simple fixture for accomplishing this is shown in Illus. 5-38. If there is no objection to the extra expense, dowel pins can be purchased that already have a spiral groove cut around them (Illus. 5-39).

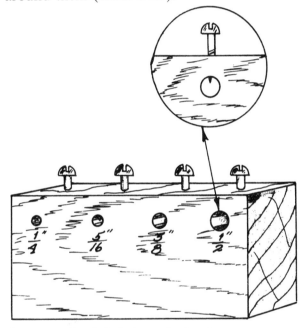

Illus. 5-38. A shop-built jig for scoring dowels.

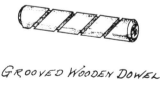

GROOVED WOODEN DOWEL

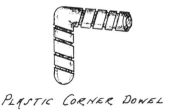

PLASTIC CORNER DOWEL

Illus. 5-39. Commercial spiral dowels.

CHAPTER SIX

Chest of Drawers

A chest of drawers is a good project on which to learn the casework system of woodworking. It requires a face frame, its sides, back, and top can be built with ¼-inch plywood, and it contains a number of drawers, so the hobbyist can become thoroughly acquainted with the techniques of drawer building. This project adapts well to the various furniture styles, too, so the builder can decide whether a traditional-styled chest or contemporary styling is preferred.

In this chapter, the craftsperson will be taken through all the steps required to build a traditional chest of drawers. By studying and mastering all of these steps, one should be able to design and build a chest of drawers in the size and style desired.

BASIC CHEST DESIGNS

There are just three basic designs of chests of drawers: the single-row chest, his-and-hers chests (or the double dresser), and the chest-on-chest. Of course, infinite combinations of these are possible and are often seen in high-quality furniture catalogues and showrooms.

THE SINGLE DRESSER

Usually taller than it is wide, the single dresser is so named because it contains just one vertical row of drawers. The top row, however, is often divided into two or even three smaller drawers (Illus. 6-1). Although the design standards will vary somewhat, the dressers will usually be built from 19 to 21 inches deep (front to back). The width of a single dresser across the front can vary widely, but is usually

Illus. 6-1. The traditional-styled, single-row chest of drawers. (Drawing courtesy of Ethan Allen, Inc.)

in the 36- to 45-inch range. If the chest is designed much wider than that, the drawers become quite bulky and unwieldy.

One variation from these standards is the tall, narrow lingerie chest, which is often designed just 22 inches wide and as high as 52 inches. This chest varies in depth and is customarily built just 17 to 18 inches deep (Illus. 6-2).

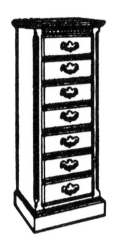

Illus. 6-2. The lingerie chest. (Drawing courtesy of Ethan Allen, Inc.)

DOUBLE DRESSER

Often termed a "his-and-hers" dresser, this chest of drawers is much longer than it is high. It contains eight or nine drawers and its top row is divided into several smaller units (Illus.

Illus. 6-3. The "his-and-hers" chest of drawers. (Drawing courtesy of Ethan Allen, Inc.)

6-3). Clothing that is usually stored in two single dressers is instead stored in this unit. An interesting variation of this design is the "triple dresser," which is simply a double dresser with a face frame divided into three drawer or door areas (instead of the usual two) and which is perhaps a few inches longer (Illus. 6-4).

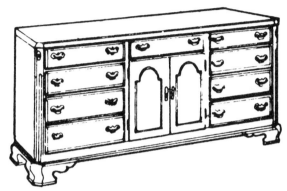

Illus. 6-4. The triple dresser. (Drawing courtesy of Ethan Allen, Inc.)

The double dresser is often 54 to 58 inches long, and triple units 64 to 68 inches long. They are 19 to 21 inches deep and vary in height from 32 to 34 inches. It is up to the builder to determine which dimensions will best suit the available space and to determine which size will make the most practical use of standard materials such as 4 × 8-foot pieces of plywood.

CHEST-ON-CHEST

Just as its name implies, the chest-on-chest is in reality one chest built on top of another. This, naturally, becomes a dresser that is quite tall and usually has just a single row of drawers (Illus. 6-5). The chest-on-chest varies in height from 51 to 55 inches, and in width from 37 to 42 inches. The depth, however, remains at approximately 20 inches. Because the upper section of the chest-on-chest is smaller in height, depth, and width than the lower section, these width and depth standards apply to

Illus. 6-5. Two variations of the chest-on-chest. (Drawing courtesy of Ethan Allen, Inc.)

the lower section and the height standards are for the combined height of the two sections.

An interesting variation of the chest-on-chest is the use of cabinet doors on the upper portion of the piece (Illus. 6-6). These are

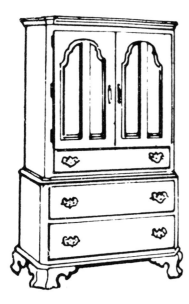

Illus. 6-6. Another variation of the chest-on-chest. (Drawing courtesy of Ethan Allen, Inc.)

often called "armoires." The upper section of an armoire is equipped with either adjustable shelves or pull-out shelves with sides, back, and front.

Note from Illus. 6-5 that sometimes the upper portion of a chest-on-chest is designed higher than the lower section, and vice versa.

STYLES OF DRESSERS

There are many different furniture styles. Roughly, however, furniture can be divided into two large categories—traditional and contemporary. Traditional styles would include such familiar styles as Colonial, French Provincial, Queen Anne, and Georgian. These separate styles are defined by things such as type of furniture base, top treatment, legs, edge shaping, hardware, the species of wood used in the construction, and even the styling of the drawer fronts and the doors.

Contemporary furniture, on the other hand, has a more severe or straight-lined design that puts to use a wide variety of modern materials.

TRADITIONAL-STYLE FURNITURE

Nearly all of the furniture shown in Illus. 6-1–6-6 is of the traditional style. Even a cursory examination of these simple sketches reveals some basic differences in period styles. Most notable is the motif of the base construction, which can vary from a plain-scrolled, solid base to the more ornate "rolled and coved" base. Illus. 6-7 shows several of these base-construction variations.

The tops on almost all traditional-styled furniture have a rounded edge which overhangs the basic structure. A cove moulding is used to fill the corner where the top and the side meet (Illus. 6-8). This top design is a basic one, and tops are often designed more ornately.

The edge treatment of drawer fronts on traditional-styled pieces will range from a sim-

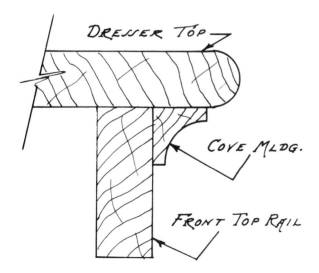

Illus. 6-7. Different base treatments are used on traditional furniture. (Drawing courtesy of Ethan Allen, Inc.)

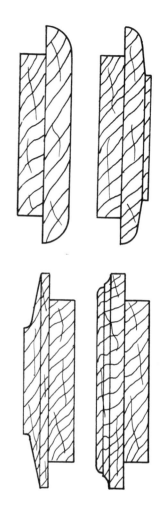

Illus. 6-9. Cross sections of typical traditional-styled drawer fronts.

Illus. 6-8. A common top design on traditional furniture.

ple rounding on the lipped drawer to a fancy edging machined with a panel-raising shaper cutter (Illus. 6-9). The main surface of the drawer front, however, is seldom adorned with overlaid mouldings, because the designer or builder wants the beautiful wood grain to highlight the piece.

Traditional pieces which have doors as part of their construction have several design variations. One design feature most often noted is the raised panel door. The raised panel itself can vary considerably, as shown in Illus. 6-10. Another variation is the louvered door. Also glass doors are frequently used on Colonial hutches. Several methods of dividing the glass into panes are employed (Illus. 6-11).

Illus. 6-10. Different styles of raised-panelled doors are used on traditional furniture. (Drawing courtesy of Ethan Allen, Inc.)

Illus. 6-11. Glass-paned and louvred doors are common on period furniture. (Drawing courtesy of Ethan Allen, Inc.)

CONTEMPORARY-STYLED FURNITURE

As described previously, modern or contemporary styling is more severe and straight-lined than its traditional counterparts. The edges of tops and drawers are most often left square, and the furniture bases or legs are simple yet functional (Illus. 6-12).

Plastic laminate is used to a great extent in contemporary furniture. So are other types of plastic, and even metals.

Illus. 6-12. A contemporary chest of drawers.

BUILDING A TRADITIONAL-STYLED CHEST OF DRAWERS

For the purpose of instruction, a straight-forward traditional-styled chest of drawers has been selected (Illus. 6-13). This dresser contains rows of single drawers, with the exception of the top row, which is divided into two smaller drawers. The base has separate corner legs that will be "rolled and coved." These legs are probably the most difficult to build but, once mastered, these techniques can be applied to other less difficult base features. Following are step-by-step instructions and accompanying illustrations for building this chest of drawers.

Illus. 6-13. A chest of drawers on which to apply the casework system of furniture-building.

BUILDING THE DRESSER'S "BASIC BOX"

Study the chest of drawers depicted in Illus. 6-13. This is the chest of drawers on which you will apply the instructions. If you were to strip away the overhanging top, cove moulding, base structure, and drawers, the "basic box" would remain. The basic box is the fundamental structure of the chest (Illus. 6-14). It is this structure that will be built first. This basic box will be reduced to its several fundamental components, each to be built separately. These separate fundamental components are the face frame, bottom, back, and the two sides.

Illus. 6-15 contains most of the dimensions for fabricating these components. Special detailed illustrations will supply the remaining required dimensions as the building of the dresser progresses.

Selecting the Species of Wood The first decision that must be made is determining what species of wood to use for the chest of drawers. Hardwood such as walnut, cherry, oak, or mahogany is recommended. These four cabinet woods have beautiful grain, are durable, and are easy to work. Walnut and cherry have more beautiful grains than oak or mahogany. Oak is more durable.

Because ¼- and ¾-inch plywood must be used with the species selected, the availability of the matching plywood might also be a factor that enters into the decision. The local lumber dealer usually has both lumber and plywood in oak and mahogany. The other species usually can be special-ordered. A good source also might be a local cabinet shop. They have lumber and plywood sources for

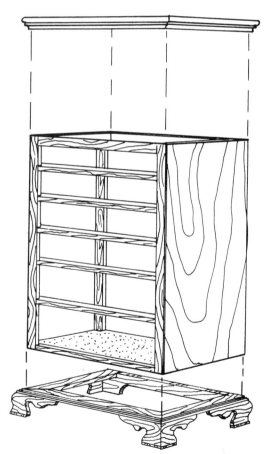

Illus. 6-14. The basic box.

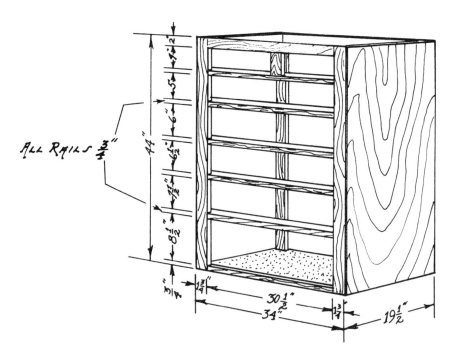

Illus. 6-15. Dimensions of the basic box.

ALL RAILS ¾"

practically all species, and they might be willing to order what is needed when they order their own material. Remember, for the face frame and most of the other lumber requirements for this project, No. 1 common grade is the most economical material to order.

Building the Face Frame

The face frame is always the first component to be built, because it contains all of the width and height dimensions as well as the arrangement and location of the drawers and/or doors (Illus. 6-16). It is from the face frame that the width dimensions of the back and bottom are calculated. Note that the overall dimensions of the basic box are smaller than the overall dimensions of the completed dresser. This is due to the overhang of the top and the extension of the rolled-and-coved legs beyond the basic box itself.

Bill of Materials

Stiles: Two pieces ¾ × 1¾ × 44 inches. Note that the stiles are 1¾ inches wide. They can vary in width from 1½ to 1¾

inches, but for best appearances should be somewhat less than 2 inches.

Top rail: One piece ¾ × 2 × 30½ inches. The top rail is 2 inches wide because a cove moulding will later cover a portion of this piece. If it is made narrower, the top rail would look quite skimpy in the finished chest. Also note that the top rail is exactly 3½ inches less than the overall width of the basic box. This 3½ inches represents the width of the two stiles.

Drawer rails: Five pieces ¾ × 1¾ × 32 inches. The drawer rails are 1½ inches longer than the top rail because each drawer rail is notched at the ends to fit behind the stiles a distance of ¾ inch (Illus. 6-16).

Top drawer divider piece: One piece ¾ × 1¾ × 4¾ inches. This piece divides the top drawer space into two equal spaces.

Run out each of the above pieces to the exact dimensions given, selecting knot-free lumber that is devoid of warp or twist.

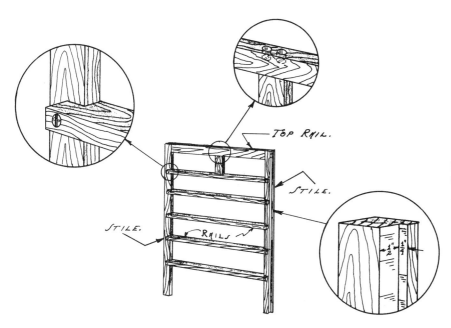

TOP RAIL.

STILE.

STILE.

RAILS

Illus. 6-16. Rear view of the face frame and its details.

Machining the Face-Frame Members After the individual pieces for the face frame have been carefully ripped, jointed, and cut to exact length, there is still some machining to be done on individual pieces prior to assembling the face frame.

First the stiles must be rabbeted to receive the ¼-inch plywood sides. The plywood when installed will also cover the heads of the screws that are used to assemble the top rail to the stiles. Also the unsightly edge of the plywood side panel will be hidden when the panel is installed in the rabbet. This rabbet is very important and must be done accurately. Measure the exact thickness of the plywood first, because ¼-inch plywood will vary in thickness as much as ¹⁄₃₂ inch. Study Illus. 6-16 to determine the exact dimensions of the rabbet. The dimensions given in Illus. 6-16 for the rabbet are ¼ × ½ inch (but the ¼-inch depth of the rabbet will vary to meet the exact thickness of the panel.)

Use the table saw to machine the rabbets in the stiles. This can be done on the jointer or the shaper, but a certain amount of "tear out" always seems to occur when these other machines are used. Set the saw fence for a ¼-

inch cut; *this should include the thickness of the saw blade*. The blade should be ½ inch high. Using a piece of scrap lumber, make a test cut to check the accuracy of the saw settings and to be certain that the resulting rabbet *is slightly deeper than the thickness of the plywood side panels*. Remember, the exposed portion of the stile can easily and quickly be planed, scraped, or sanded down to meet the plywood. However, if the plywood should be a bit above the lip of the stile, the extreme thinness of the plywood veneer makes it impossible to plane the plywood down to meet the stile without exposing the inner core and ruining the side panel. This is extremely important, so practise with a piece of scrap lumber first before making the actual cuts in the stiles.

Complete the rabbets by making two passes or cuts on the table saw. Make the first pass as described in the preceding paragraph. For the second saw cut, set the saw fence at ½ inch, *including the thickness of the blade*. The blade itself should be just a hair over ¼ inch high. Be certain the resulting rabbet has a clean, square corner, so there is nothing remaining to obstruct the plywood side panel when it is fastened in position later.

Notching the Rails The simplest and most accurate means of notching the ends of the drawer rails (five pieces) is to assemble these pieces together in a bundle and notch them all at the same time. This is accomplished by nailing the rails together using 1¼-inch nails or brads, while keeping the edges flush and the ends even (Illus. 6-17). Always select the best-looking edge of each rail and place it to the front of the bundle, as this is the edge of the rail that will be visible in the finished face frame.

Illus. 6-17. These rails are bundled together, for notching.

Remember, the rails were cut 1½ inches longer than the top rail because the rails were to have a ¾-inch notch cut at each end. Carefully mark with a pencil and a square on the bundled rails where the notches are to be cut, and carry these marks onto three sides of the bundle. This way, the marks can be seen when the bundle is turned end-for-end. Make absolutely certain that the distance between the notches is equal to the length of the top rail, even if you have to make the distance between the notches shorter.

Note: If working with hardwood such as oak or walnut, rubbing the nails with paraffin will make nailing a lot easier.

Sawing the Notches After completing the layout at the end of the rails, you are now ready to cut the notches on the table saw. *The saw blade must be exactly as high as the thickness of the lumber used for the stiles.* Normally, this would be ¾ inches, but occasionally the thickness will vary slightly, so check this saw setting very carefully.

Use the mitre gauge to support the bundle while notching. For this operation, set the mitre gauge absolutely square with the saw blade. Start the notch by sawing inside of and as close to the marking as possible. Then make a series of closely spaced saw cuts about ¹⁄₁₆ to ⅛ inch apart through the remaining distance. Illus. 6-18 and 6-19 show this operation.

After both ends of the bundle have been sawed, use a hammer to break away the material that remains between the cuts. Now, return the bundle to the saw and clean up the notch by moving the notched area slowly forward and, at the same time, back and forth across the saw blade.

After completing the notches on both ends of the bundles, double-check the distance between the notches to confirm that this is exactly equal to the length of the top rail. If the distance is slightly long, cut a bit off one notch by passing it carefully over the saw

Illus. 6-18. The saw blade must be exactly as high as the stile is thick.

94

Illus. 6-19. Make a series of cuts and break away the pieces with a hammer.

blade. If the distance between notches is short, you will have to trim the top rail to match its length with the distance between notches.

Disassemble the bundle with a screwdriver or prybar. Do not mar the edges that will be exposed on the front.

Notching the First Drawer Rail The top space in the chest will contain two drawers, so a short, vertical divider must be placed in the exact center of this space.

Select one of the rails and mark the exact location of the vertical short stile. This short stile was machined to a width of 1¾ inches, so

locate the center of the first drawer rail and then measure ⅞ inch on either side of the center mark. Draw lines at these two points; the notch will be cut between these points (Illus. 6-20).

Assembling the Face Frame After the face frame pieces have been completely machined, the face frame is ready to be assembled. Begin by fastening the two stiles to the top rail. To accomplish this, you must master the techniques for making a screw joint.

Clamp the top rail and one of the stiles in the vise (Illus. 6-21). Butt the pieces together firmly and squarely, and place glue in the joint. Use a C-clamp to align the surfaces on the front side by clamping the two pieces to a small block of wood. The following are the steps for making a screw joint. Practice on two scrap pieces before making the actual dresser joint.

1. Drill ³⁄₁₆-inch shank holes through the stile. Do not drill deeply, if at all, into the end of the top rail.
2. Countersink each hole with a ½-inch countersink, taking care not to mar the lip of the rabbet.
3. Drill ³⁄₃₂-inch pilot holes, going through the ³⁄₁₆-inch holes previously drilled and into the end of the top rail as far as the drill bit will go.

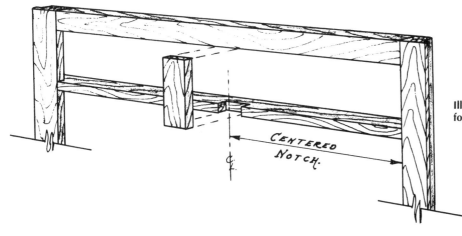

Illus. 6-20. Notch the first drawer rail for the drawer divider.

CENTERED NOTCH.

₵

Illus. 6-21. Clamp the top rail and the stile in the vise to assemble the face frame.

Illus. 6-22. A ratchet screwdriver is used to drive the 2½-inch screws.

4. Finally, drive a 2½-inch #8 flathead wood screw tightly into each hole.

Driving Screws Lubricate the threads of the screws with beeswax or mild soap to make it easier to drive the screws into the hardwood. Paraffin does not work well for driving screws. Beeswax is best because it does not contain acid. Acid and soap can corrode the screws.

A large auto-return ratchet screwdriver works well for driving screws. It is fast, and you can lock the screwdriver at full extension to obtain good leverage for the final turns. Do not attempt to drive the screws completely in with the ratchet action, because the screwdriver blade has a tendency to slip out of the screw slot under heavy pressure and damage the work. Instead, open the screwdriver to full length, lock it in this position, and turn the final few turns with your hands (Illus. 6-22).

An alternative to using the ratchet screwdriver is to use a screw-driving bit in the hand brace. This is not quite as fast nor as handy as the ratchet screwdriver, but it does generate a lot of power. The electric drill can also be used, especially if it is a variable-speed drill.

Simply mount the proper screwdriver bit in the drill chuck and carefully drive the screws home.

There are available various drill bits with countersink attachments that will drill and countersink in one operation. Most of these, however, will mar the lip of the rabbet, and thus are not usable. For production work, or to save time switching bits in the drill, use two or three drills. Used electric drills can be found at garage sales or flea markets.

Attach the second stile to the opposite end of the top rail and make sure that the lips of the rabbets are facing the same direction.

Installing the Drawer Rails Refer to the dimensions in Illus. 6-15 for the vertical spacing of the drawers in the dresser. Of course, this spacing may be changed to suit one's preference, but note in this design the drawers get progressively larger as they descend in the dresser.

To save time doing repeated measuring and to hold the rails firmly in position while screwing them in place, prepare six "gauge sticks" of scrap that measure 4, 5, 6, 6½, 7½, and 8½ inches long (or to the measurements decided upon, if different from those given).

Next, drill and countersink ³⁄₁₆-inch shank holes through the "horns" on each end of the drawer rails (Illus. 6-23).

Illus. 6-23. Drill and countersink ³⁄₁₆-inch shank holes through the horns on the drawer rails.

Lay the partially assembled face frame facedown on the floor or other large work surface and place the first drawer rail in position. Remember, the top drawer rail was notched for a center divider. Place the rail in position on the back of the face frame between the stiles and space it properly with the 4-inch gauge stick. Put a drop or two of glue under the horn and drill a ³⁄₃₂-inch pilot hole. Then fasten the horn with a 1½-inch #8 flathead wood screw, holding the rail and stile firmly together and against the gauge stick while drilling and assembling (Illus. 6-24). Move the gauge stick to the opposite end and, using the same techniques, fasten that end of the drawer rail in place.

Continue fastening each drawer rail in its proper position using the correct gauge stick until all cross rails are installed.

Installing the Short Stile Double-check the exact length of the short stile by placing it in position at the end of the drawer space. It should just reach the lower edge of the first

Illus. 6-24. Attach each drawer rail to the rear of the face frame.

drawer rail when held against the lower edge of the top rail. After checking its length, place the short rail in the notch cut for it on the front of the first drawer rail. Then glue and fasten it in position from the rear with two 1¼-inch #8 flathead wood screws. The pilot holes should be drilled beforehand.

Next, glue and clamp the upper end of the short stile in position with a C-clamp and a small block of wood (Illus. 6-26). Counter-

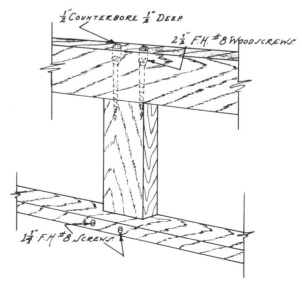

Illus. 6-25. Method of installing the center drawer divider.

Illus. 6-26. Clamp the short stile to the top rail.

bore two ½-inch holes about ½ inch deep into the top edge of the top rail. Then drill two ³⁄₁₆-inch shank holes through the remaining distance of the top rail, taking care not to drill into the upper end of the short stile.

Finally, drill ³⁄₃₂-inch pilot holes into the end of the short stile. This will require a rather long drill bit, but, if the bit is inserted in the chuck near its end, it will usually be long enough to do the job. Drive two 2½-inch #8 flathead wood screws into the joint to hold it firmly together. The face frame is now completed. Set it aside while working on the other components of the basic box.

Fabricating the Dresser Back and Bottom

The back of the dresser should be built next. This is built in ¼-inch fir or Lauan plywood, hardboard, or other inexpensive material. The ¼-inch material is then reinforced with ¾-inch pine strips (or other inexpensive lumber or even plywood rippings) that are nailed and glued to the plywood. Excellent material for the back can be purchased at discount lumber dealers' in 4 × 4-foot pieces.

Determining the Size of the Back The reason

the face frame was built first was because many of the measurements for other parts of the dresser are taken from the face frame itself. To determine the width of the back, carefully measure the distance between the rabbets on the back of the face frame. This should measure about 33½ inches, depending upon the exact depth that the rabbets were machined.

Be certain to cut the plywood back to match the exact width from the bottom of one rabbet to the bottom of the opposite rabbet (Illus. 6-27). The height of the back is the same as the height of the face frame.

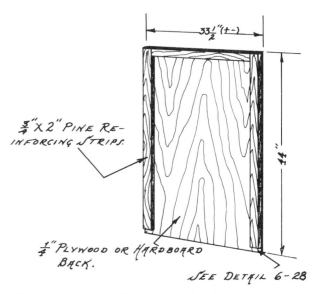
Illus. 6-27. Details for fabricating the chest back panel.

Reinforcing the Back Any ¾-inch inexpensive material—lumber or plywood—can be used to reinforce the plywood back. Three pieces will be needed. These pieces should be ripped and jointed to a width of 2 inches. Two of the pieces used to reinforce the sides of the back should be cut to a length of 43¼ inches, which is exactly ¾ inch shorter than the height of the back. This ¾-inch space is where the dresser bottom will be placed (Illus. 6-28). Use a small scrap piece of the ¾-inch bottom material and mark a line on the back at this

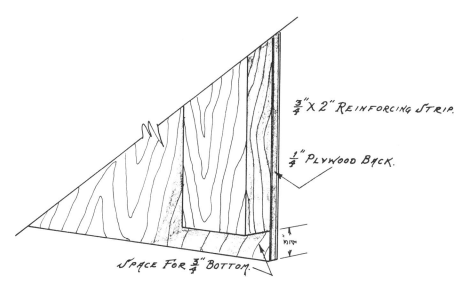

$\frac{3}{4}" \times 2"$ REINFORCING STRIP.

$\frac{1}{4}"$ PLYWOOD BACK.

SPACE FOR $\frac{3}{4}"$ BOTTOM.

Illus. 6-28. The lower corner detail of the back assembly.

exact thickness. Measure the exact length of the side reinforcers from this mark.

The top reinforcing piece will be approximately 29½ inches long. This is approximate because the exact length will be determined after the two side reinforcers are in position.

Glue and nail the side pieces into position first. Apply the strips to the good or A side of the plywood or the smooth side of the hardboard if that is what is being used for the back. Tack the strips to the plywood back, flush with the outside edges of the plywood back, with two 1-inch nails. Then flip the assembly over and nail through the plywood into the reinforcing strips as shown in Illus. 6-29. Now, cut the top strip to an exact fit between the side pieces and glue and nail it in position using the same technique. The dresser back is now completed.

Making the Dresser Bottom The material for the bottom should be at least ¾ inch thick. Fir plywood or particle board works very well for the bottom.

The bottom will be exactly as long as the back is wide and 1 inch less in width than the intended depth of the dresser. If the dresser is to be 20 inches deep, then the bottom will be ripped to a width of 19 inches. The ¼-inch

Illus. 6-29. Nail the plywood to the reinforcing strips with 1-inch nails.

back and the ¾-inch face frame make up the extra 1 inch depth. Take the measurements from the back panel itself, to be certain they match. Note that the bottom, the back, and the distance between rabbets on the face frame *must all be the same.*

Assembling the Face Frame, Back, and Bottom

Glue and nail the back to the bottom. Cut two pieces of ¼-inch plywood 2 or 3 inches wide for supports and tack-nail these pieces to the top edge of the back (Illus. 6-30). These support strips should be exactly as long as the dresser is deep. They will support the back in position as it is being nailed to the bottom.

99

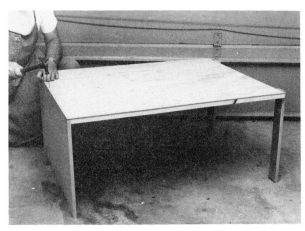

Illus. 6-30. Nail the back to the bottom. Note the use of the pieces to support the back in position.

Fastening the Face Frame to the Bottom Lay the back/bottom subassembly down on the back and place the face frame in position. Tack-nail the support strips to the top rail to hold it in position while assembling (Illus. 6-31). Glue and nail the lower end of each stile to the bottom. Drill two holes ⅜ inch from the ends of the stiles; use a 6d nail in the drill to prevent splitting the stiles. It is also a good idea to angle the nails slightly towards the inside of the dresser to prevent any splitting that might occur in the particle-board bottom. Put a drop or two of glue under the stile and, using 6d nails, fasten the stile to the bottom, keeping the bottom of the face frame rabbets exactly flush with the ends of the particle board or plywood bottom (Illus. 6-32).

Illus. 6-31. Support strips hold the face frame at the correct height.

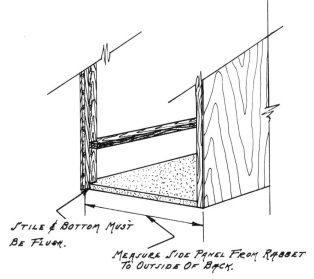

STILE & BOTTOM MUST BE FLUSH.

MEASURE SIDE PANEL FROM RABBET TO OUTSIDE OF BACK.

Illus. 6-32. Assembly detail of the face frame and bottom.

Preparing and Installing the Facing Strip Prepare a ¾ × ¾-inch facing strip for the exposed front edge of the bottom. Cut this strip to its proper length and glue and nail it in place using 4d finish nails. Set all the nails and fill the resulting holes with matching plastic wood.

Fabricating and Machining the Plywood Sides

The sides of the dresser are made from ¼-inch plywood, to match the face frame. The plywood used should have a beautiful grain pattern and no flaws. The grain should run vertically. The side panels will be exactly as high as the face frame. Determine their width by measuring from the face frame rabbet to the outside of the dresser back.

Rip the panel about ¹⁄₁₆ inch wider than needed, to allow for jointing the edge that will fit into the rabbet. Joint this edge at about a 5-degree bevel, so that it will fit tightly against the lip of the rabbet. Joint the other edge of the panel to smooth it and to trim the panel to its exact width (Illus. 6-33).

Fastening the Sides in Position Lay the

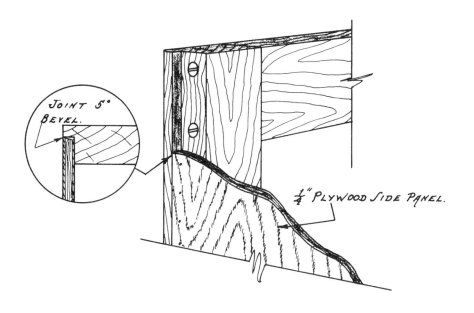

dresser on its side, place the panel in position, and check the fit all around. If it fits properly, run a bead of glue in the face-frame rabbet, and along the bottom and the edge of the back. Start fastening the sides by nailing the panel in position along the rabbet using ¾-inch brads spaced 3 to 4 inches apart. Pull the panel tightly against the lip of the rabbet while nailing. A bar clamp will help tighten this joint (Illus. 6-34).

Illus. 6-34. Nail the side panels in position with ¾-inch brads.

After nailing along the rabbet, nail along the edge of the bottom using 1-inch brads or 4d finish nails. Be sure to pull the structure into square prior to nailing along the bottom. Next, nail along the edge of the back, again using 4d finish nails. If necessary, remove the scrap support piece from the top so that the back and bottom can be pulled square and flush with the side panel.

Set all the brads and nails and fill the resulting holes with matching plastic wood. Also fill any imperfections in the face-frame joints. After the filler has dried completely, use a sharp hook scraper to remove the surplus plastic wood and sand the filled spots clean (Illus. 6-35). It is important to remove all traces of the plastic wood, because if any residue is allowed to remain a light blotch will be evident when stain is applied later. This blotch is caused by the lacquer that is a component of plastic wood. The lacquer actually seals the surrounding wood and prevents the stain from penetrating.

Sanding the Face Frame and Sides Lay the dresser on its back in preparation for sanding the face frame. Using a belt sander equipped with a 120-grit belt, carefully sand the vertical

101

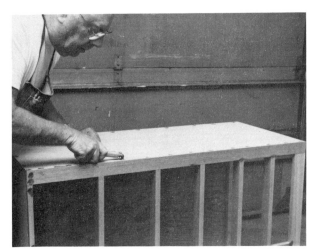

Illus. 6-35. Wipe matching plastic wood into the nail holes and, after it has dried, scrape it with the hook scraper.

members of the face frame. Hold the sander level, and do not allow it to remain stationary at any time. Guide the sander over all joints, sanding them flush and even (Illus. 6-36). Don't worry about sanding across the grain because these marks will be removed when you sand the rails. Sand the narrow drawer rails carefully. If too much sanding is done near the center of the dresser, the rails will become slightly concave. Again, it is extremely important to hold the sander level. With some practice, sanding a face frame becomes easy and perfect joints will result.

Illus. 6-36. Use a belt sander to sand the face frame and all joints flush and smooth.

Next, with the finish sander loaded with 120-grit paper, sand the entire face frame. If a few scratches remain where the belt sander has travelled across the grain, remove these with the hook scraper (Illus. 6-37).

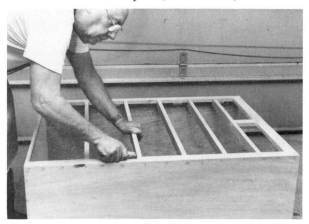

Illus. 6-37. After finish-sanding, scrape away any sander scratches.

Note: Never use the belt sander on the plywood side panels! The veneer on plywood is so thin that the belt sander can sand through it very quickly and ruin the panel. If the lip of the rabbet needs some trimming to make it flush with the surface of the side panel, use a very sharp block plane or scraper, or just hand-sand it. If a plane is used, set the blade for a very fine shaving and slightly tilt the plane, so there is no possibility that the plywood panel will be marred (Illus. 6-38).

Illus. 6-38. The block plane can be used to trim the face frame.

First sand the side panels with 120-grit paper in the finish sander, making sure that you remove all plastic-wood residue. Then sand the entire structure using 220-grit paper in the finish sander.

MAKING AND INSTALLING THE DRESSER CROSS-BRACES

To strengthen the entire structure and to also provide upper runners for the top drawers, install cross-bracing at the top of the chest. The upper runners are important, because they prevent the drawer from tipping down when it is pulled from the chest. The upper ends of the plywood side panels must also be reinforced.

Fabricating the Cross-Braces

The cross-braces are normally made of pine or other inexpensive material. Even leftover ¾-inch plywood can be used. The braces measure ¾ × 2 × 17¾ inches. The length is approximate, because this measurement must be double-checked on the dresser itself. Make this measurement at the end of the chest, not at the center, because a slight bow might exist in either the face frame or the back. Note that the 2-inch width of the cross-brace must match the width of the top rail of the face frame. If the top rail is less than 2 inches wide, then the cross-brace must be made to match it. As shown in Illus. 6-38, four cross-braces will be needed. Two will be used for top-drawer runners, and the other two will be used to reinforce the side panels.

Two small mounting blocks will also be required. These blocks measure ¾ × 2 × 4 inches and are used to install the cross-braces at the front. Rip, joint, and cut to length all of these pieces, using care to follow the dimensions exactly.

Installing the Bracing Pieces To install the top reinforcers for the side panels, glue and clamp them in position with C-clamps and scrap pieces, to prevent marring the panels (Illus. 6-40). Next, glue and clamp the small mounting blocks to the inside of the top rail. Locate these so that the top runner, when installed, will be very close to the center of the drawer opening.

After the glue has dried, square the top runners in position and hold them there by placing a bar clamp across the top of the dresser (Illus. 6-41). Using a countersink bit for #8 screws, run two holes through the cross-brace. Then glue and drive two 1½-inch #8 flathead wood screws to hold the runners to the sides of the mounting blocks. Fasten the rear of the runners with either 2-inch #8 flathead wood screws or by driving eight-penny, ring-shank box nails through the cabinet back

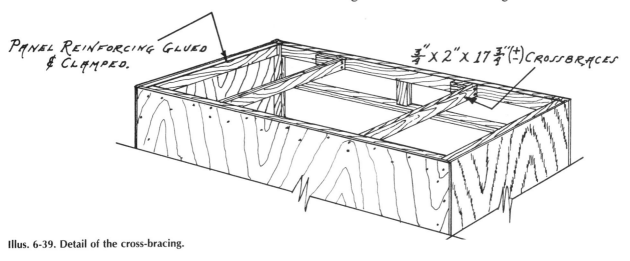

Illus. 6-39. Detail of the cross-bracing.

Illus. 6-40. Glue and clamp the panel reinforcers and mounting blocks in place.

Illus. 6-41. Use a bar clamp to hold the cross-braces in place while fastening them.

into the ends of the cross-bracing. If using box nails, lay the structure on the floor, face frame down, while nailing so that it will not be chipped or marred while being pounded.

Installing Optional Reinforcement

It is a good idea to add extra reinforcement to certain parts of the structure. This reinforcement consists of glue blocks that are "rub-glued" into place. These glue blocks are made of inexpensive scrap material. Prepare a number of them (Illus. 6-42). By installing the blocks at the recommended places, you strengthen the joint considerably.

The rub-gluing process is a very easy yet effective cabinetmaker's technique. Spread a good layer of glue on each side of the block, place it in position, and simply rub it back and

forth in place for a few seconds until resistance is felt and it is difficult to move the block anymore. When dry, the block will remain firmly glued in its position, and will reinforce and strengthen the adjoining spot. Place a few of these blocks along the rabbet joint where the plywood fits into the stile, in each upper corner where the back and sides meet, and where the face frame and the side-panel reinforcing piece meet.

CONSTRUCTING THE DRESSER BASE

The basic box has now been completed. The next step is to construct the base structure. The chest of drawers shown in Illus. 6-13 and 6-14 has "rolled and coved" legs, so the instructions that follow are for making this type of base. Although there are many other base designs that could be built, this leg design is standard on many traditional chests.

Making and Installing the Bottom Moulding

Examine Illus. 6-13–6-15 carefully, because these drawings show the relationship of the various base pieces. Note that the basic box has narrow moulded pieces attached directly to its bottom, and that the coved legs are attached to these moulded pieces.

Milling the Bottom Moulding Three pieces will be needed to make the bottom moulding. Two pieces should be approximately ¾ × 2½ × 22 inches. Another piece should be approximately ¾ × 2½ × 37 inches. The length of the pieces is approximate because each of them must have an allowance for the 45-degree mitres on its ends. Try to cut each piece very close to the dimensions given.

After cutting the material to the above dimensions, machine a bead-and-cove on one edge of each piece (Illus. 6-43). You can ac-

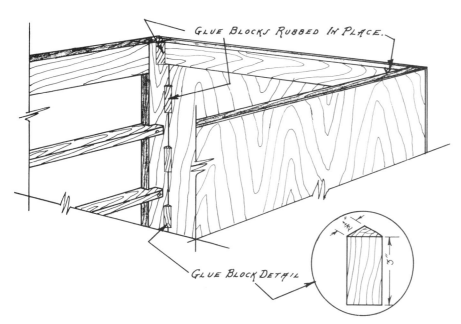

GLUE BLOCKS RUBBED IN PLACE.

GLUE BLOCK DETAIL

Illus. 6-42. Rub-glue the reinforcing blocks in place.

Illus. 6-43. The moulding head can be used in the table saw to machine the bead-and-cove edge.

complish this with the table saw by using a Delta cutter No. 35-243 in the moulding head or with a spindle shaper using a Delta three-wing cutter, No. 09-135 or 09-136. If only a router is available, use a roman ogee router bit. This will slightly change the pattern of the moulding, but this change will hardly be noticeable. If using the moulding head in the table saw, make a series of light cuts when machining this edge rather than one heavy cut.

Mitring the Bottom Moulding The mitres on the ends of these three pieces must be cut very accurately. This can be accomplished with a hand mitre box, the mitre gauge accessory for the table saw, or, best of all, by using a mitring jig built for the table saw (Illus. 6-44 and 6-45). This mitring jig is easy to build and, if laid out accurately, will produce exact mitres every time. Always use a sharp saw blade. A dull blade will "drift" slightly and throw the resulting mitre cut off a bit.

As indicated in Illus. 6-46, the bottom moulding will stick out from the basic box about ¾ inch. First, cut the mitres on the two side pieces, making sure to cut left and right sides, tack them in position on the dresser bottom after carefully lining them up, and then mark and cut the pieces to length. You can easily restore the pieces to their correct position by placing the nails back in their holes where they were tacked.

Next, mitre just one end of the longer front piece. Hold the point of this mitre against the mitred point of one of the side pieces and mark exactly where the point of the *opposite* mitred side piece hits the front piece (Illus. 6-47). At this point, make the

Illus. 6-44. The mitring jig can be used to mitre the bottom moulding.

Illus. 6-45. Bottom view of the mitring jig.

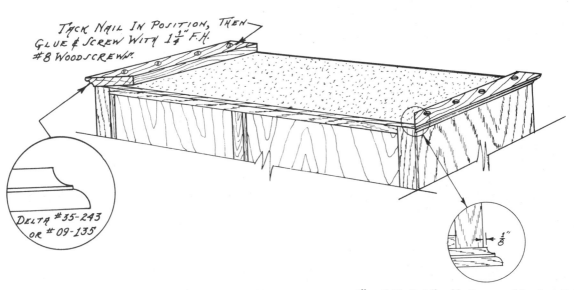

TACK NAIL IN POSITION, THEN GLUE & SCREW WITH 1¼" F.H. #8 WOODSCREWS.

DELTA #35-243 OR #09-135

⅛"

Illus. 6-46. Details of bottom moulding installation.

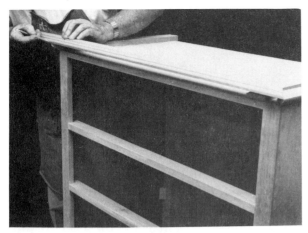

Illus. 6-47. Determining the length of the front bottom moulding piece.

second mitre cut at the *opposite angle* from the first mitre. Test-fit the front piece against the two side pieces to determine how well the mitres fit together. You can use a disc sander to make slight adjustments on the mitres of the front moulding piece in order to get the pieces to fit perfectly.

After the mitre joints have been perfected, place glue in the joints and tack the front piece in position. Then, using a countersink bit for 1¼-inch #8 flathead screws, fasten all three pieces to the bottom of the chest.

Fill any slight imperfections in the joints with matching plastic wood. After the filler has dried, sand the joints clean and smooth.

Making and Installing the "Rolled and Coved" Legs

One attractive feature on traditional-styled furniture is the use of a short leg that has a coved and curved shape. Although these legs are not difficult to build, they do present somewhat of a challenge. The following steps will make it easy to design furniture with "rolled and coved" legs.

Bill of Materials As indicated in Illus. 6-13, six pieces, each about 8 inches long, will be required to make these legs. Two pieces of stock are needed from which to cut the individual leg blanks. These pieces should be ¾ × 4½ × 25 inches. Machine the two pieces to these exact dimensions. Use defect-free lumber.

Making the Cove Cuts on the Leg Stock

Make the cove cuts on the table saw, using either the saw blade or the moulding head

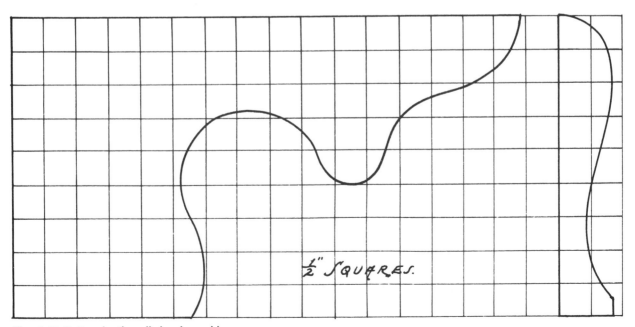

½" SQUARES.

Illus. 6-48. Pattern for the rolled-and-coved legs.

with a straight knife. The width of the cove is determined by the angle at which the piece of leg stock is run over the saw blade. Illus. 6-49 shows the auxiliary fence layout for running the cove cuts. The angle at which to place this auxiliary fence can be determined by following these steps:

1. Raise the saw blade to the desired depth of the cove, in this case ⅜ inch, or halfway through the stock piece. Make a rough pencil sketch of the desired depth and width of the cove on the end of the board.
2. Place the leg blank on the opposite side of the saw blade and experiment by moving the board at various angles to observe what effect this has on the resulting cove width. Note that as the angle increases, the cove cut gets narrower.
3. Angle the board so that the resulting cove will start about ⅜ inch from the bottom edge of the blank and will be about 2½ inches wide. Then clamp the auxiliary fence to the table saw in this position using two C-clamps.
4. Next, lower the saw blade so it will cut no deeper than ¹⁄₁₆ inch. Run the

two boards over the blade at this saw setting, holding the boards firmly against the auxiliary fence.
5. Raise the saw blade about ¹⁄₁₆ inch and again run the leg blanks over the blade. Repeat this process until the desired ⅜-inch depth of cove is reached.

Shaping the Upper Portion of the Leg Make a template from a scrap piece of ¼-inch plywood or plastic laminate in the desired finished shape of the leg (Illus. 6-50). Remove as much as possible from the upper corner by running the pieces over the jointer at 45 degrees. Then hand-plane the pieces to the correct curve, checking often with the template along the length of the pieces.

Cutting the Leg Pattern First, cut the leg blanks into six 8-inch pieces. Then, cut 45-degree paired mitres on the ends of four of the pieces that will be the front legs. Check the table saw blade to be sure the cut is exactly 45 degrees. *This is important, because you are making a left-hand and a right-hand mitre for each assembled leg.* Next, make a cardboard or plywood template for the leg pattern from the

Illus. 6-49. The table saw set up to make cove cuts.

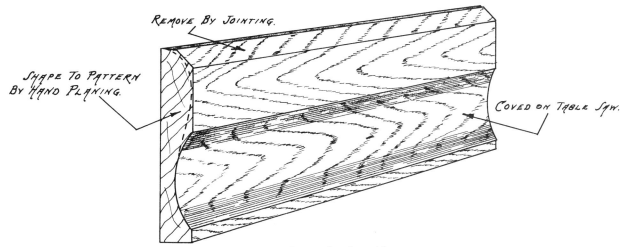

REMOVE BY JOINTING.

SHAPE TO PATTERN BY HAND PLANING.

COVED ON TABLE SAW.

Illus. 6-50. Hand-plane the blank to the proper shape using the template for guidance.

drawing shown in Illus 6-48. Transfer this pattern to each leg piece; again, be absolutely certain that a left and right side is made for each leg assembly and for the two back legs.

Cut the pattern on each leg piece using a jigsaw, sabre saw or, if neither of these is available, a coping saw. Sand the jig-sawed cuts on the area of the legs that will be seen.

Starting with 60- or 80-grit sandpaper, sand the coved area of the legs to remove the saw marks. Use progressively finer sandpaper until all blade marks are removed. Then sand the upper curved portion of the legs. This sanding was not done earlier because much labor would have been wasted in sanding those areas that were later cut away.

Assembling the Legs Arrange the legs in the vise (Illus. 6-51). Place glue in the mitre joint and then nail the two sides together. Before nailing the two sides, however, drill a nail into them to prevent splitting the pieces. Use 4d finish nails for this assembly. Set all nails and fill the holes with matching plastic wood. If you notice any slight discrepancy in the mitred joint, sand or plane the sides so that they match perfectly.

Leg Reinforcing and Mounting Pieces As shown in Illus 6-52, you must apply reinforc-

Illus. 6-51. Clamp the leg pieces in the vise for assembling.

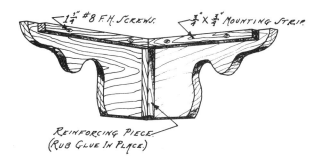

1¼" #8 F.H. SCREWS.   ¾" X ¾" MOUNTING STRIP.

REINFORCING PIECE. (RUB GLUE IN PLACE.)

Illus. 6-52. Inside view of leg assembly showing mounting strips and reinforcer in place.

ing pieces and mounting strips to the inside of each assembled front leg. Apply only mounting strips to the rear legs at this time. Cut about five feet of ¾ × ¾-inch material from pine or other inexpensive lumber. This will be used for the mounting strips. Cut this five-foot length into pieces about 7 inches long. Mitre one end of each piece at 45 degrees. (These mounting strips are cut a bit shorter than the legs so that they will not be seen.)

Next, drill and countersink four ³⁄₁₆-inch holes in each piece. Two holes will be used for fastening the strips to the leg assembly. The other two are for fastening the legs to the bottom of the chest. It is easier to drill the holes prior to assembly than afterwards.

Next, glue and tack-nail the mounting strips in position absolutely flush with the top edge of the leg assembly. Drill a ³⁄₃₂-inch pilot hole and permanently secure the strips with 1-inch #8 flathead wood screws. Then rubglue a ¾ × ¾-inch piece in the corner of each front leg to reinforce the mitre joint. Finally, sand the assembled legs. Remove all traces of plastic wood and glue.

Mounting the Legs on the Chest Mount the front legs to the bottom moulding piece with screws and glue. Position the legs so that only the leg lumber is visible and none of the pine mounting strip can be seen (Illus. 6-53). Tack-nail the legs in position. Then complete the mounting by drilling ³⁄₃₂-inch pilot holes and fastening the leg assemblies with 1¼-inch #8 flathead wood screws.

Mount the rear legs in the same manner.

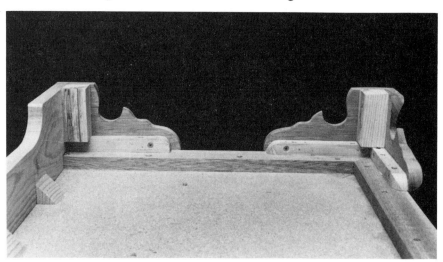

Illus. 6-53. View of legs installed on bottom moulding and back stretcher in place.

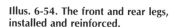

Illus. 6-54. The front and rear legs, installed and reinforced.

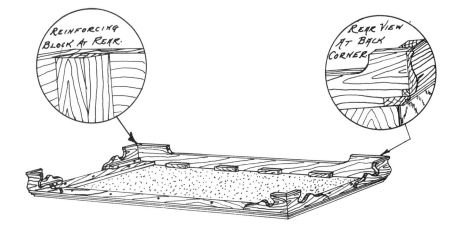

Make sure that the legs are even with the end of the bottom moulding. Make a ¾-inch plywood or pine reinforcing piece to install between the two back legs and across the back of the chest (Illus. 6-54). This piece will have to be notched accurately around the bottom mouldings and cut in the pattern shown in Illus. 6-54. Screw this back-reinforcing piece to the chest bottom by counterdrilling with a ½-inch drill bit and using 2-inch #8 flathead wood screws. Fasten the rear legs to this reinforcer by predrilling with a nail in the drill and gluing and nailing with 4d finish nails.

Rub-glue a reinforcing block in each corner of the rear legs. Use a block that's about 1½ inches square. These back legs must be reinforced well because they are only ⅜ inch thick at the bottom of the coved portion. Finally, rub-glue several ¾ × ¾ × 4-inch blocks along the joint where the chest bottom and the back leg reinforcer meet.

Alternative Traditional Base Designs

Illus. 6-7 shows several variations for traditional furniture base designs. Some are easier to build than the rolled-and-coved legs just covered, and some are slightly more difficult.

Scrolled Straight Base This traditional-styled base is constructed of flat lumber and does not require coving and shaping operations. The base pieces are 4½ to 5 inches high and must be mitred to extend outside the bottom moulding (Illus. 6-55). After the desired pattern is drawn and transferred to the pieces, use the jigsaw or sabre saw to cut the design. Shape the top edge of the pieces with a quarter-round cutter using either the spindle shaper or the router. Sand the base pieces with the belt sander, followed by the finish sander.

Fasten full-length ¾ × ¾-inch mounting strips to the back of these pieces using the same method as described for the rolled and

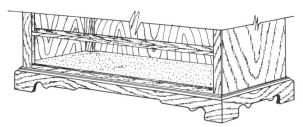

Illus. 6-55. The scrolled straight base.

coved legs. Be sure to drill the holes for fastening the base to the bottom moulding before fastening the strips to the back of the base pieces. Tack the pieces in position on the bottom moulding. Then glue and screw them in place using 1¼-inch #8 flathead wood screws. Fasten the mitred corners together by predrilling with a nail and then nailing them together with 4d finish nails. Set all nails and fill the holes with matching plastic wood. After it dries, sand the surfaces smooth and clean.

Rolled-and-Coved Full-Length Base This traditional base is a flat base with rolled-and-coved legs (Illus. 6-56). Machine full-length pieces for the front and sides. Then cove and shape these pieces as you did the shorter corner legs. After the three pieces are shaped and sanded, mitre and cut the ends to fit the bottom moulding.

Next, cut the pattern with a jigsaw. Then make the mounting strips and apply them to the rear of the pieces. Finally, install the three base pieces using the same method as used for the scrolled straight base.

Patterned Single-Piece Base This type of traditional base requires only one front piece with the desired pattern scroll-sawed along its length. Although this is, perhaps, the easiest base to build, some changes must be made in the basic box construction to accommodate this front piece. Note that Illus. 6-57 shows the face frame extended in length to cover the

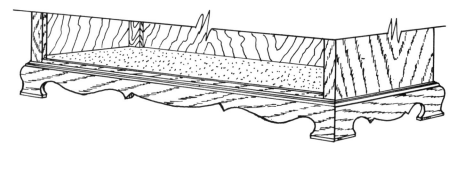

Illus. 6-56. The full-length rolled-and-coved base.

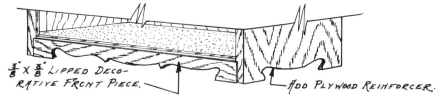

Illus. 6-57. The patterned single-piece base.

⅜" × ⅜" LIPPED DECO-RATIVE FRONT PIECE.

ADD PLYWOOD REINFORCER.

space where the base construction would be installed in the other types of bases already described. No bottom moulding is used, and the side panels and the face frame extend all the way to the floor. A matching pattern is cut along the bottom of the ¼-inch side panels (which are reinforced with ½- or ¾-inch pine or particle board pieces that are placed slightly higher than the cut pattern).

To install this front base piece, cut a ⅜-inch rabbet along the two ends and the top edge. Thus, the piece must be machined $1\frac{1}{16}$ inch longer and ⅜ inch wider than the space in which it will be installed. (The $1\frac{1}{16}$-inch measurement allows for an extra $\frac{1}{16}$ inch so the piece will slip into position easily.)

After the rabbets are cut, shape the top edge and the ends with a "rounding over" cutter that has an attractive design using either the router or the shaper. Sand the entire piece carefully and then glue it in position. Make several small ⅜ × ⅜-inch glue blocks and rub-glue these in position on the back side of the base piece.

MAKING AND INSTALLING THE DRESSER TOP

Do not fabricate the top of the chest at this time. Instead, skip ahead to Chapter Seven and build and install the drawers. It is much easier to install the drawers before the top is completed on a chest or desk. When you have built and installed the drawers, read the information presented in this section for building and installing the dresser top.

Instructions are given here for building a dresser top that has a ¼-inch plywood panel, as do the sides of the project. The plywood must be set into a frame of solid lumber. If the builder prefers, a top may be built of ¾-inch plywood and edge-banded to cover the inner core of the plywood. The ¼-inch top, however, is much less expensive and, once the fabricating techniques have been mastered, is reasonably easy to build.

Making the Top Retaining Pieces
Illus. 6-58 illustrates the relationship between the solid-lumber top retaining pieces, the ¼-inch plywood top panel, and the chest itself. These three retaining pieces must be machined carefully and accurately. Use lumber that does not have blemishes of any type.

Bill of Materials Two pieces ¾ × 2½ × 23 inches will be needed for the two side members. One piece ¾ × 2½ × 39 inches will be required for the front member. The length is approximate, but make sure that each piece is long enough to accommodate the mitres that must be cut on the ends.

Machining Required on the Top-Edging Pieces

After the three pieces are machined to the above dimensions, round one edge of each piece using either the router, the shaper, or the moulding head in the table saw. A ⅜-inch quarter-round knife or cutter will do this job in two passes.

A rabbet must be cut in each piece; the plywood top panel must fit precisely into this rabbet. The dimensions for this rabbet are given in Illus. 6-58. First, check the thickness of the plywood panel to determine if it is exactly ¼ inch thick. Then set the fence on the table saw to this exact thickness. Remember, the thickness of the blade must be included in this saw setting, and the measurement must be made to a "left side" saw tooth. Raise the blade so that it is 1¼ inches high and make a test cut on a piece of scrap. Check the ¼-inch depth of the rabbet against the plywood panel to determine that it either matches exactly or is a "hair" deeper than the plywood is thick. (A "hair" is defined by master woodworkers

as "about the thickness of a piece of typing paper.")

The depth of this rabbet should be as exact as possible. If the rabbet is not deep enough, the plywood would be above the surrounding wood frame. This would pose a problem because the plywood cannot be sanded or planed down to meet the framework. If the rabbet is too deep, you will have to do a lot of sanding or planing on the framework to match the top surface of the plywood.

After determining that the cut will be made to the proper depth, make the first cut of the rabbet on all three pieces. Then lower the blade to about ¼ inch high, move the fence to make a 1¼-inch cut (again including the saw blade), and make a test cut to determine that a clean, square rabbet will result.

Mitring and Cutting the Pieces to Length

Mitre one end of each short piece, planning for a right- and left-hand side! At this time, mitre only one end of the longer front piece. The best means of determining the correct length of these pieces while locating their proper overhang is to build a simple "overhang" jig, as shown in Illus 6-59. Simply place the jig in position at the front corner of the chest, butt the mitred end of the side piece

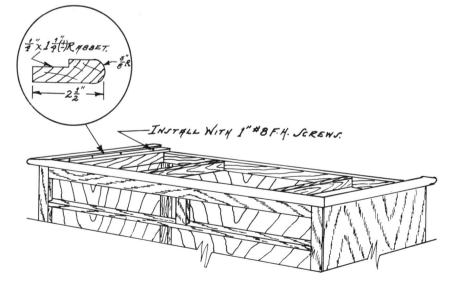

Illus. 6-58. Detail of the top edging.

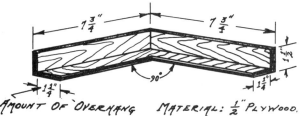

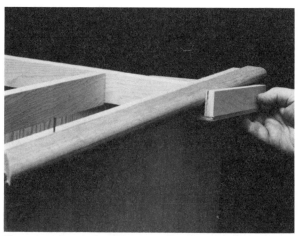

Illus. 6-59. Build an "overhang" jig to install the top edging pieces.

Illus. 6-61. The overhang jig determines the amount of overhang at the rear of the side pieces.

into the corner of the jig, and against its side and mark the end of the side piece even with the back of the dresser (Illus. 6-60 and 6-61). Both the side and the front overhang are determined by using this jig. Cut the two side pieces to length and then tack-nail them in position, again using the jig to relocate them properly. Next, cut and fit the front piece to the correct length, making opposite-direction mitre cuts on either end. Tack-nail the front piece in place after determining that the mitred joints are close to perfect and that the front and side pieces are square. Use a framing square to do this; make any slight adjustments in the location of the side pieces, if necessary, to bring the pieces into square. If making these adjustments changes the amount of overhang slightly, this will not be noticed. It is important that the pieces are installed squarely!

Glue and screw the two side pieces and the front piece permanently in position using 1-inch #8 flathead wood screws. To strengthen each mitre joint, drill a hole into the joint and then drive a 4d finish nail into the joint from each side. If there are any discrepancies in the outside edges of the mitre joints, plane and sand them flush so the points meet perfectly.

Installing the Top-Support Furring Strips

After installing the top edging pieces, you will note a gap of about ½ inch between the bottom of the rabbet and the dresser cross-braces. This space must be filled with ½ × ¾-inch strips of wood that must be flush with the bottom of the rabbet so they will solidly support the ¼-inch plywood top panel. Measure exactly how thick these support strips must be and prepare enough of this material to install on top of the two cross-braces and along the top of the dresser back. Simply nail and glue these strips in position using a 1-inch box nail (Illus. 6-62).

Fabricating and Installing the Top Panel

The ¼-inch plywood top panel is now ready to be installed in the rabbets of the top edging pieces. This must be done carefully and exactly because there is very little room for er-

Illus. 6-60. The overhang jig locates the side edging piece.

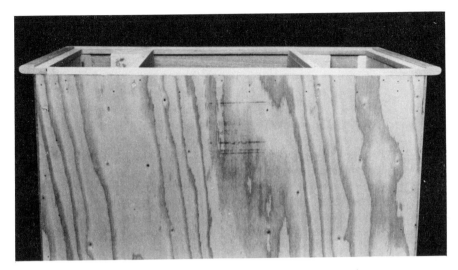

Illus. 6-62. Furring strips are installed to support the top panel.

ror. If the top edging pieces were installed exactly square, the job will be much easier. In any case, if you follow the directions precisely a nice-fitting panel will result.

Cut the Top Panel to Rough Size

Measure the opening into which the panel will be installed and cut the ¼-inch plywood piece at least ½ inch wider and 1 inch longer than this opening. The grain should run the length of the piece of plywood. Joint a 5-degree bevel along the front edge of the panel and along one end. Make a light pencil checkmark that will easily identify these two jointed edges.

Fitting the Panel into the Front and One End

Place the panel in position into the rabbets on the front edge and the first end to determine how well the two jointed edges fit (Illus. 63). The ¼-inch plywood is flexible enough so that it can easily be bent into these rabbets. With a well-sharpened block plane or by making light cuts on the jointer (still set at 5 degrees), bring the front edge and first end of the top panel to a perfect fit. Fitting this first end is usually no problem if it has been sawed perfectly square and if the top edging pieces have been installed square.

Fitting the Second End

With the panel still in its position in the rabbets, mark its exact length where it will drop into the opposite end rabbet (Illus. 6-64). Mark the panel at the rear as well and, using a straight edge, draw a line between these two marks. Check this line with the framing square to determine if it is perfectly square. If it is square, saw the panel to length to within ¹⁄₃₂–¹⁄₁₆ inch of the line. Joint this second end at 5 degrees with a very light cut on the jointer, and then test-fit the panel in the rabbets. Continue to make light jointer cuts (or hand-plane the edge) until the panel fits snugly into place.

If the line is slightly out of square, either

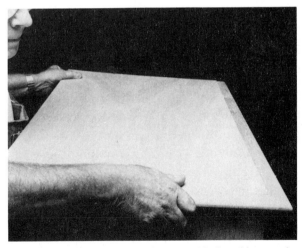

Illus. 6-63. First fit the top panel square with the rabbets on the front edge and one end.

115

Illus. 6-64. Mark the opposite end at both the front and rear.

Illus. 6-65. Glue, clamp, and weight the top panel in place.

saw to the line freehand on the table saw or, using the jointer, make light taper cuts and work gradually up to the line. Of course, a block plane can also be used to work the panel into position. Again, too much emphasis cannot be placed on having the top edging pieces installed squarely to make an easy job of fitting the top panel.

Cutting the Panel to Width Check the distance from front to back along the rabbets in each of the two side pieces. If the measurements are the same, simply rip the panel to this size, allowing slightly more width for a final jointer cut. If the measurements are not the same, rip the panel at the widest measurement and then hand-plane the back edge of the panel after it is installed.

The Final Installation of the Top Panel Run a good bead of glue along all edges that the panel will contact. Prepare a piece of ¾-inch plywood or lumber as a cushioning piece for clamping the front edge of the panel in position with several C-clamps (Illus. 6-65). Be certain that this cushioning piece contacts only the plywood panel, so the clamping pressure will push the top firmly into the front rabbet.

Make two more cushioning pieces for the panel ends and weight these down with sufficient weight to settle the panel firmly into the side rabbets. Two concrete blocks will do the job nicely.

Finally, nail the panel in place along its back edge with ¾- or 1-inch brads. Set these brads and fill the resulting holes with matching plastic wood. At this time, also fill any joint imperfections or slight gaps between the plywood edges and the rabbets. Allow the filler to dry thoroughly before scraping or sanding the excess away.

Final Sanding of the Top Panel and the Edging If the rabbet was cut to the correct depth, very little cleanup will be needed. However, it always seems that some final scraping is necessary. Using a sharp hook scraper, carefully work the excess wood down to the plywood surface; remove any dried plastic wood filler at the same time. Using only the finish sander, begin with 120-grit paper and sand the entire panel and the edging pieces. Then sand the surface with 220-grit paper. The result will be a "ready-to-finish" surface.

Installing the Cove Moulding Below the Top The final trim applied just below the top is a ¾-inch cove moulding installed along the front and two sides. Hopefully, the local lumber dealer will have this to match the lumber used to build the dresser. If not, it will have to be machined on the shaper or with the moulding head in the table saw.

Install the cove with carefully mitred joints and then glue and nail it in place using 1-inch brads (Illus. 6-66). Set the brads and fill the holes with matching wood filler. Sand the filler clean when it dries. The chest chassis is now completed.

DESIGNING AND BUILDING THE CONTEMPORARY CHEST

The contemporary chest is in many ways easier to build than the traditional chest. It does not have the coved legs or other embellishments usually placed on traditional furniture. Instead, a more straight-line motif is emphasized. The drawers in the contemporary chest are most often flush rather than the lipped drawers that are used in traditional pieces.

In this section, complete design details and building instructions are presented for a contemporary chest of drawers that is about the same overall size as the traditional chest

described earlier. Before attempting to build this piece, it would be wise to read all of the material that was presented for building the traditional chest. Many of the basic operations have been covered in detail in that section, and will be referred to often in this section.

DESIGN

Illus. 6-67 depicts the contemporary chest for which building instructions will be presented. Note the flush drawers, the contemporary-styled drawer pulls, the turned tapered legs, and the straight-lined look of this chest. Several alternative base or leg treatments are available that may be used with this style. They are shown in Illus. 6-68.

BUILDING THE FACE FRAME

As with all casework projects, construction begins with the face frame. The basic box (the frame minus the top and base) is first determined. Then the dimensions for the face frame are calculated from this structure. In this project the basic box is 42 inches wide by 19 inches deep by 27 inches high (Illus. 6-69). The major difference between a face frame designed for flush drawers and one designed for traditional cabinetry is that the drawer

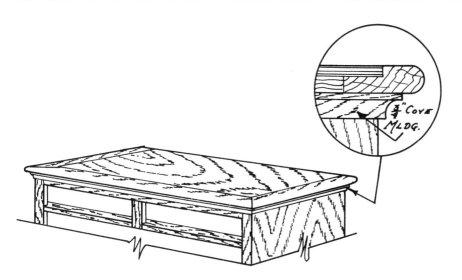

Illus. 6-66. Install cove moulding under the top.

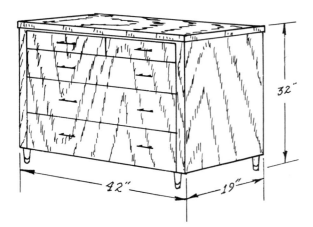

Illus. 6-67. Overall dimensions for the contemporary chest.

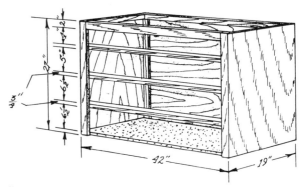

Illus. 6-69. The basic-box dimensions.

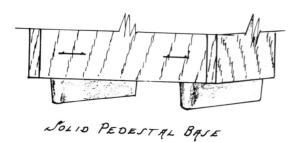

SOLID PEDESTAL BASE

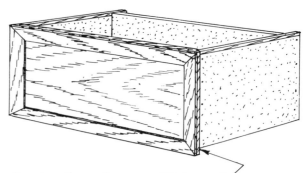

DRAWER FRONT EXTENDED TO COVER CROSS RAIL

Illus. 6-70. The lower edge of the flush drawer front is extended to cover the lower drawer rail.

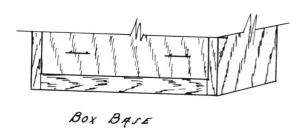

BOX BASE

Bill of Materials

The face frame is shown in Illus 6-71. Note that only three pieces of the face frame need to be the type of wood being used for the chest itself. These three pieces are the top rail and the two stiles. The other drawer rails may be fabricated from less expensive wood because

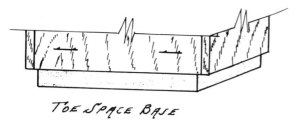

TOE SPACE BASE

Illus. 6-68. Three base treatments for a contemporary chest.

rails are fastened *behind* the stiles and are not flush with the front of the face frame. This makes it possible for the drawer fronts to be flush with the face frames (Illus. 6-70).

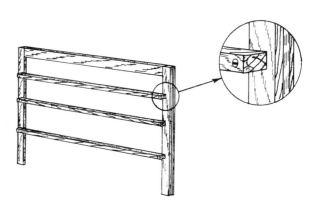

Illus. 6-71. The drawer rails are not notched, but fit behind the face-frame stiles.

they will not be seen in the finished chest. These are the dimensions of the pieces used in building the face frame:

Stiles: Two pieces ¾ × 1¾ × 27 inches.
Top rail: One piece ¾ × 2 × 38 inches.
Drawer rails: Five pieces ¾ × 1¼ × 39½ inches.

Machining the Face-Frame Pieces

After the two stiles and the top rail have been cut to the dimensions given above, rabbets will have to be cut into the stiles. Illus. 6-72 shows these rabbets, which measure ½ × ¼ inch. Use the table saw for these rabbets. Make two passes over the saw blade (Illus. 6-16). Cut the rabbet, just a "hair" deeper than the thickness of the ¼-inch plywood to be used as side panels. This is extremely important, because you cannot scrape or sand the plywood down to meet the rabbeted stiles without damaging the veneer on the plywood panel.

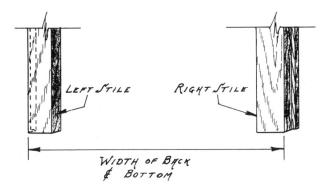

Illus. 6-72. Each stile must receive a ¼ × ½-inch rabbet.

The other five pieces may be fabricated from pine or other inexpensive wood, and require no further machining other than cutting them to their exact dimensions. Make sure that the lumber used for these rails is well seasoned, so it does not warp or twist in the finished face frame.

Assembling the Face Frame   The stiles and the top rail are joined with screw joints, described on page 96 and shown in Illus. 6-21 and 6-22.

After these pieces are assembled, screw and glue the drawer rails to the back side of the face frame (Illus. 6-71). Make the required pairs of gauge blocks to position the rails according to the depth dimensions decided upon. Illus. 6-69 has suggested dimensions for these drawers, but these may certainly be changed as desired. Note, however, that the drawers of a well-designed chest become progressively deeper as they descend in the chest from top to bottom, with the bottom drawer the deepest.

Position the first drawer rail with the gauge blocks. Glue and screw the rail in position using 1½-inch #8 flathead wood screws. Install the other four rails using the same technique and the proper gauge blocks to ensure equal spacing on both sides of the face frame.

MAKING THE BACK

The back for this contemporary chest is built exactly the same way as the back for the traditional chest. It may be built of ¼-inch fir plywood or any other inexpensive material. One-quarter-inch-thick hardboard may also be used because it is relatively inexpensive and is often available in 4 × 4-foot sheets at discount lumber dealers.

Determining the Size of the Back

The back must be cut exactly the same height and width as the face frame when measured from rabbet to rabbet (Illus. 6-72). These are very important measurements; make sure that they are correct!

Reinforcing the Chest Back   The plywood or hardboard back must be reinforced with pine strips or other inexpensive material that is ¾-inch thick. Even ¾-inch plywood scrap may be used for this reinforcement. Just as was done with the traditional chest, the side reinforcing strips must be cut exactly ¾ inch shorter than the height of the back panel, to allow room for the cabinet bottom. Illus. 6-27 and 6-28 show this clearly.

Glue and nail the strips with 1-inch nails to the back panel. Place the good, or A, side of the plywood (or the smooth side of the hardboard) to the inside of the chest.

MAKING THE BOTTOM

The bottom for the chest should be fabricated from ¾-inch fir plywood or other inexpensive ¾-inch material such as particle board. Do not attempt to save money by using thinner panelling, because you will not make as sturdy a basic box.

Dimensions of the Bottom   The length of the bottom panel must be cut exactly as long as the width of the back panel, so make sure that these two pieces match in length. The width (front to back) of the bottom will measure 1 inch less than the overall depth of the chest. This will be 18 inches if the dimensions given in Illus. 6-69 are being followed. If another depth is being used, always subtract the thickness of the face frame plus the thickness of the back panel from the desired finished depth of the chest.

ASSEMBLING THE FACE FRAME, BACK, AND BOTTOM

These assembly techniques are similar to those described for the traditional chest. Glue and nail the back to the chest bottom. Support the face frame with plywood or lumber scrap pieces, and glue and nail it to the bottom panel using six-penny finish nails. Use the "nail-in-drill" technique when nailing the face frame to

the bottom; this avoids any splitting that might occur near the ends of the rails. To avoid splitting the bottom material, slant the nails slightly in towards the center of the chest.

FABRICATING AND APPLYING THE ¼-INCH PLYWOOD SIDE PANELS

Two ¼-inch plywood panels are required for the sides. These panels should measure 18¾ × 27 inches, with the grain running the length of the panel. (Check the exact size by measuring the partially assembled chest.) Joint a five-degree bevel along the edge that fits into the rabbet on the stile. Then glue and nail the panel in place using ¾- or 1-inch brads. Pull the structure into square by lining up the face frame, bottom, and back with the side panels.

Set all the brads and fill the resulting holes with matching plastic wood, which should be scraped and sanded clean after it has dried.

COMPLETING THE BASIC BOX

Install the cross-braces and panel reinforcing pieces at the top of the chest as was done with the traditional chest. Then fill any joint imperfections and nail holes, sand the face frame carefully with both the belt sander and the finish sander, and sand the side panels with the finish sander only.

THE LEGS OR BASE

The contemporary chest will probably have either turned and tapered legs or a two-pedestal base, both of which are shown in Illus. 6-68.

Tapered Chest Legs   These legs are often available at hardware stores and building centers in sets of four in various lengths, and are ready to install on the bottom of the cabinet.

The shortest leg is 4 inches long, and they are available in longer lengths in increments of 2 inches. A set of 6-inch-long legs is needed for the contemporary chest. The set should contain four turned and tapered legs that have brass ferrules and swivel glides already attached. Clinch nut plates are also included in the set; these plates are screwed to the bottom of the chest. The legs may be attached to the nut plates on the chest bottom at an angle or straight up and down (Illus. 6-73).

Illus. 6-73. Turned and tapered legs used on a contemporary chest.

If the craftsperson has a small lathe, he can easily turn four 6-inch tapered legs from the same wood as used for the chest. It is not even necessary to purchase 2-inch stock, because the turning squares can be glued up from ¾-inch lumber into pieces about 1½ × 1½ × 7 inches. Swivel glides with brass ferrules (without the wooden tapered legs) are usually available at any hardware or home center. The ferrules on these swivel glides are available in diameters of ½, ⅝, ¾, ⅞, and 1 inch. Turn the lower end of the leg so that it will just fit inside the ferrule, and the upper end to a diameter of about 1⅜ inches.

If you are not using the swivel glides and ferrules, simply turn a 6-inch-long tapered leg with a top diameter of 1⅜ inches and a lower diameter of about ¾ inch. Use 2-inch hanger bolts (available also at most hardware stores)

to fasten the legs to the clinch nut plates. One end of these bolts has wood screws, and the other end has machine threads. To install these bolts in the legs, drill a ³⁄₁₆-inch hole into the upper end of the leg and, with good-sized pliers, turn the wood-screw end of the hanger bolt into the end of the leg. Wrap some cloth around the machine threads of the hanger bolt to prevent the pliers from damaging these threads. Use beeswax to lubricate the wood-screw threads. This makes the legs easier to install. Turn the hanger bolt into the leg so that only the machine threads are exposed.

Next, screw the leg to the clinch nut plate and determine if the plate can fit flat on the chest bottom or if the end of the hanger bolt interferes. If the end of the bolt protrudes slightly, then cut this section off with a hacksaw so the bolt is flush with the plate or drill a small hole into the chest bottom, into which you can slip the end of the bolt and prevent it from interfering when you mount the leg. Finally, install furniture glides on the bottom of all four legs.

Making a Pedestal Base

An alternative treatment for a contemporary chest is to build two tapered pedestals for the base. Two blocks of wood will have to be glued up from fir or pine. To accomplish this, machine four 1½ × 5½ × 18-inch pieces and then glue them together in pairs. Standard 2 × 6 lumber can be used effectively. Illus. 6-74 shows the taper and the curved-end pattern that must be laid out on the blocks. A band saw is used to make the cuts. Set the band-saw table to the proper tilt to cut the desired taper. Sand the bases to remove the saw marks made by the band saw, and mount the two pieces on the bottom of the chest by fastening them with 1½-inch screws driven through the bottom of the chest into the pedestals. The pedestals on contemporary furniture are usually painted a flat black.

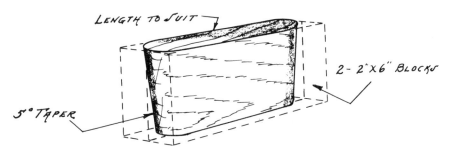

Illus. 6-74. Details of a tapered and curved pedestal base.

LENGTH TO SUIT

2-2"X6" BLOCKS

5° TAPER

FABRICATING THE TOP

The top of the contemporary chest may be made from ¾-inch plywood or from less expensive ¼-inch plywood. In either case, the unsightly edges of the top will have to be edge-banded with solid-lumber pieces or strips of matching veneer.

Fabricating a Top from ¼-Inch Plywood

The first thing that must be considered is the overall size of the top and how much overhang is desired along the front and sides. The top of a well-designed chest will overhang the basic box about ½ to ¾ inch on the three sides. So, if the basic box measures 42 inches wide and 19 inches deep, and veneer is the material to be used for edge-banding, then the basic panel for the top will have to be cut 19½ × 43 inches, with the grain running the long direction. This will result in a top overhang of just slightly more than ½ inch due to the minimal thickness of the veneer. However, if solid-lumber strips are to be used to band the edges of the top, then the top panel will have to be cut smaller, depending on the thickness of the strips to be used. Thus, if ⅜-inch strips are used for banding, and if the same ½-inch overhang is desired, cut the top panel to 19⅛ × 42¼ inches (Illus. 6-75).

Next, consideration must be given to how thick the top should be. The finished top should be a minimum of 1 inch thick, and as much as 1½ inches thick. However, if ¼-inch plywood is going to be used, it will have to be reinforced with ¾-inch lumber or plywood strips, so a 1-inch-thick top will be the result. If a thicker top is desired, either use wider lumber edge banding or, if a veneered edge is being used, build up the thickness of the top with additional reinforcing strips (Illus. 6-76).

Reinforcing the ¼-Inch Plywood Top

After cutting the top panel to the correct size, you must reinforce it with ¾ × 2-inch pine or plywood strips (Illus. 6-77). Simply glue and clamp the pieces along the edges with C-clamps, taking care to cushion the clamps so as not to mar the plywood surface. The interior crosspieces cannot be reached with clamps, but can be weighted in place with a concrete block or other weight. The reinforcing strips are mitred rather than butted at the corners. This allows the veneer to be glued to side grain rather than end grain, which is much more satisfactory.

Veneering the Top Edges

Rolls of plywood edge banding are available in most of the common hardwoods in widths of 1, 1½,

Illus. 6-75. Edge-banding details for a contemporary chest top.

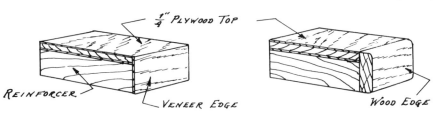

¼" PLYWOOD TOP

REINFORCER

VENEER EDGE

WOOD EDGE

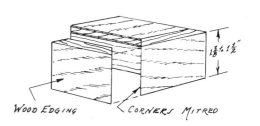

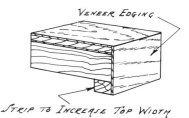

WOOD EDGING   CORNERS MITRED

VENEER EDGING

STRIP TO INCREASE TOP WIDTH

Illus. 6-76. Techniques for increasing the thickness of the top.

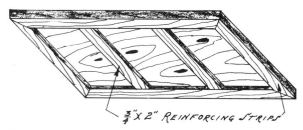

¾" X 2" REINFORCING STRIPS

Illus. 6-77. Reinforcing the ¼-inch top panel.

and 2 inches and in lengths of 6 and 8 feet. Of course, industrial users can purchase this material in coils of 250 feet and longer. Minnesota Woodworkers, Rogers, Minnesota 55374 lists this edge banding in its latest catalogue. Some of the banding can be bonded with just a warm household iron, while other veneer edge banding can only be applied properly with contact cement. In either application, allow the banding to extend slightly above the surface of the panel and then sand the veneer down so it is perfectly flush with the surface.

Edge Banding the Top with Lumber Strips

After the lumber edge-banding strips have been machined and sanded to the size desired, they must be mitred to fit on the three exposed edges of the top. Make sure that the mitring device being used makes a perfect 45-degree cut, and then mitre and fit the two end pieces first. It is good practice to cut the 45-degree mitre first, place it in position against the edge of the top, and then mark and cut the piece to the correct length at the rear of the top panel.

Either glue and clamp the strips in posi-

tion or glue and nail them to the edge of the top using 1-inch brads. If you glue and clamp the strips, there will be no nail holes to fill and sand.

After installing the two side pieces, mitre one end of the front strip, place the piece in position, and carefully mark the length at the opposite end. Mitre the other end of the piece and glue and clamp or nail it in position. Fill any small discrepancies in the joints and nail holes with matching plastic wood and, after it has dried, sand and scrape the surfaces and joints clean. Make sure that the banding strip is even with the surface of the panel; if it isn't, do whatever sanding or scraping is required to make everything flush.

FASTENING THE TOP TO THE CHEST

Perhaps the best means of fastening the top to the chest is to use cleats and screws. Prepare about ten cleats from scrap lumber that measure ¾ × ¾ × about 4 inches. Drill and countersink a ³⁄₁₆-inch hole through each cleat from one side, and two of the same-size holes from another side (Illus. 6-78). Glue and screw the cleats to the inside of the chest using the two holes and 1¼-inch #8 flathead screws. Position the countersunk single hole in the cleat on the bottom side. Space the cleats as shown in Illus. 6-79. Lay the top upside down on a padded surface to prevent any marring of the panel, and then place the chest upside down on the top. Make sure that

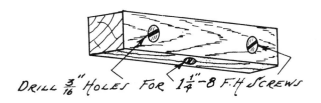

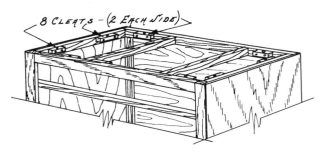

Illus. 6-78. Detail of the cleat used to fasten the top.

Illus. 6-79. Cleats installed in the chest for fastening the top.

the front of the top and two ends have the correct overhang. Then drill ³⁄₃₂-inch pilot holes and fasten the top in place using 1¼-inch #8 flathead screws (Illus. 6-80).

The chest is now complete, except for making and fitting the flush drawers. Chapter Seven contains complete instructions for the fabrication and installation of both lipped and flush drawers.

DESIGNING AND BUILDING OTHER CHESTS OF DRAWERS

After you have mastered the basic skills of the casework system by learning the material presented thus far, it is fairly easy to design and build chests of various descriptions. Just remember to isolate the basic box, build its face frame first, and then add the styling components that make the chest either traditional or contemporary.

In this section, several variations of both styles of chests will be presented.

TRADITIONAL DOUBLE DRESSER

Illus. 6-81 shows a typical traditional double dresser. Illus. 6-82 and 6-83 contain the overall dimensions, the dimensions for the basic box, and the dimensions for the face frame. If dimensions other than those presented are desired, remember that the top and legs on a traditional chest extend beyond the basic box about 1½ inches on each end and the front. So, to calculate the overall size of the basic box, subtract 3 inches from the length of the chest and 1½ inches from the depth. To calculate the height of the basic box, subtract the height of the legs (4 to 6 inches) plus the

Illus. 6-80. Place the chest on the top to fasten the top.

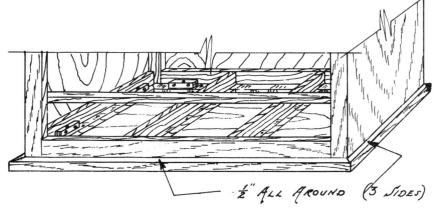

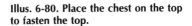

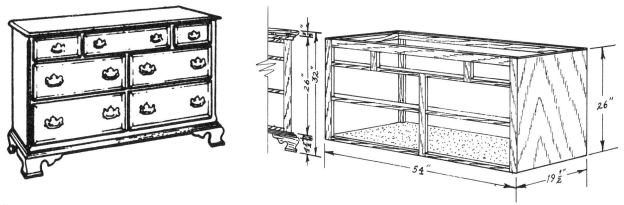

Illus. 6-81 (above left). A traditional double chest of drawers. (Drawing courtesy of Ethan Allen, Inc.) Illus. 6-82 (above right). The basic box dimensions for the double dresser.

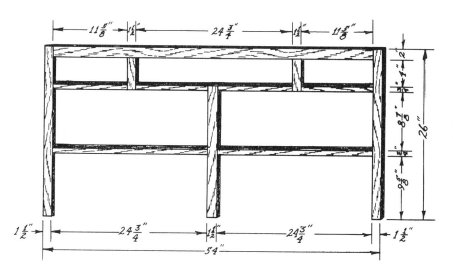

Illus. 6-83. The face-frame dimensions for the double dresser.

bottom moulding strip (¾ inch) and the dresser top (¾ inch) from the overall size of the basic box.

After determining the basic-box size, construct it as instructed previously in this chapter. Build the face frame, the cabinet back, and the bottom. Add the two side panels and their reinforcing strips and then install the cross-bracing pieces to complete the box. Make coved-and-rolled legs, apply the bottom moulding strip, complete the top panel, and install the quarter-round trim below the top. Always refer to the instructional material in the early part of this chapter if clarification is needed for building details.

TRADITIONAL CHEST-ON-CHEST

Another interesting chest of drawers that the home craftsperson might want to construct is the traditional chest-on-chest. Illus. 6-84 shows a typical chest-on-chest. Note that a chest-on-chest is really two chests—one on top of the other, with the top one slightly smaller than the lower one. Illus. 6-85 contains the overall dimensions of this dresser. Illus. 6-86 presents the face-frame dimensions for this dresser.

Follow the same procedures used for the double dresser by building the face frames first, and then the backs, bottoms, and side panels.

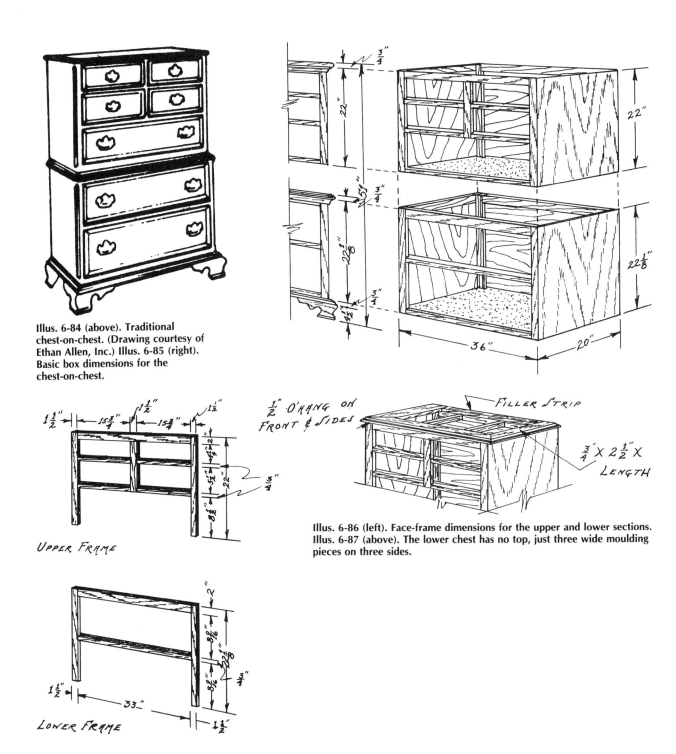

Illus. 6-84 (above). Traditional chest-on-chest. (Drawing courtesy of Ethan Allen, Inc.) Illus. 6-85 (right). Basic box dimensions for the chest-on-chest.

UPPER FRAME

LOWER FRAME

Illus. 6-86 (left). Face-frame dimensions for the upper and lower sections. Illus. 6-87 (above). The lower chest has no top, just three wide moulding pieces on three sides.

The bottom section really has no top; instead, install a wide moulding piece on the front and two ends (Illus. 6-87). Fasten the top section to the bottom section by driving screws through the particle-board bottom of the upper section. Then install small cove moulding or other attractive moulding around the base of the upper section to cover the joint where the two sections are joined.

126

Drawers

There is probably no greater challenge in furniture building than making drawers that fit and slide easily. Such drawers indicate that the chest itself is of high quality. The construction methods included in this chapter will reveal how to build smoothly running drawers that do not bind in the summer when humidity is high or rattle around in their opening in the winter. Some of the drawers featured are relatively simple to build, and others require rather complicated machinery or jigs.

TYPES OF DRAWERS

Furniture manufacturers use three different types of drawers: the lipped drawer, the flush drawer, and the overlay/box drawer. Each has a particular use, depending upon the style of furniture being built. Traditional furniture usually has the lipped or overlay drawers, and contemporary furniture most often contains drawers that are flush with the face frame.

LIPPED DRAWER

This drawer is probably the one most used in the manufacturing of furniture. It is so named because a lip or rabbet is machined on the three or four sides of the drawer front; this rabbet "laps" over the face frame and conceals the gap between the drawer and the frame. A lipped drawer, therefore, is easy to install and does not require a high level of craftsmanship (Illus. 7-1). Most kitchen cabinets contain lipped drawers, especially those made by the smaller shops.

Illus. 7-1. The lipped drawer is one of the most frequently used type of drawer.

The sides of a lipped drawer can be fastened to the drawer front with a simple butt joint, a more complicated double dado, or the sophisticated dovetail. The dovetail dado and the dado overlap are sometimes also used (Illus. 7-2). Each of these is described in detail in this chapter.

FLUSH DRAWER

The flush drawer is made so that it is even with the face frame when inserted in the chest and so the perimeter of the face frame itself remains visible around the drawers (Illus. 7-3). This type of drawer front lends itself nicely to more contemporary furniture. The drawer fronts of contemporary furniture will often be cut from the same piece of plywood and will possess beautiful matching grain from the top drawer to the bottom. Illus. 6-67 (page 118) depicts a chest with flush drawers.

These drawers are relatively easy to build, but have to be built to the exact dimensions so that the drawer does not move too loosely in or bind in its opening. The sides are joined to the drawer fronts usually with a simple rabbet joint or, on more expensive furniture, with the dovetail joint.

OVERLAY DRAWER

This type of drawer is really a variation of the lipped drawer. However, instead of machining a lip on the drawer front, the full thickness of the front of an overlay drawer spreads over the face frame. This type of drawer is quite popular with makers of high-quality contemporary kitchen cabinets as well as with build-

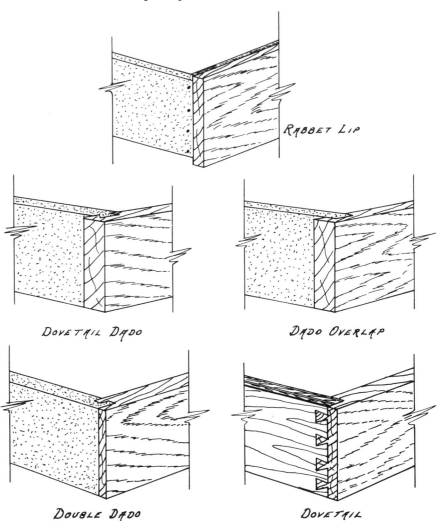

Illus. 7-2. Types of drawer joints.

RABBET LIP

DOVETAIL DADO

DADO OVERLAP

DOUBLE DADO

DOVETAIL

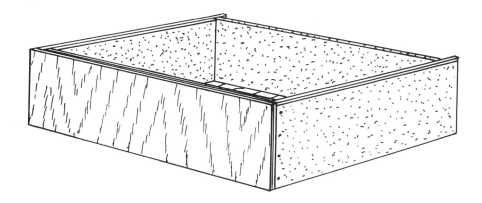

ers of both traditional and contemporary furniture.

The sides are joined to the overlay drawer front with either the dovetail dado or the "box" method (Illus. 7-4). In the box method a complete drawer of less expensive material is fabricated (boxed), and then a drawer front is attached to this box. If the fronts are out of square, they can be adjusted with commercial drawer adjusters after they are attached (Illus. 7-5).

JOINING THE DRAWER SIDES AND THE BACK

The sides of the three different types of drawers are joined to the backs in similar ways. The simplest means of accomplishing this is to use the nailed butt joint (Illus. 7-6). If the sides and front have a simple rabbet joint, then the sides do not have to be made in pairs. Most of the other methods of joining the sides to the drawer front and the back require that a left and a right drawer side be made.

The dado joint is often used to join the drawer sides and back. This is a simple joint to make that is strong when glued and nailed (Illus. 7-7). When the dado joint is used, the sides pieces should be paired. Occasionally on high-quality furniture, the drawer sides will be joined to the drawer back with dovetail joints, especially if the drawer front has been joined to the sides with this method. Although the home craftsperson will probably not be interested in this sophisticated approach to drawer building, instructions for dovetailing

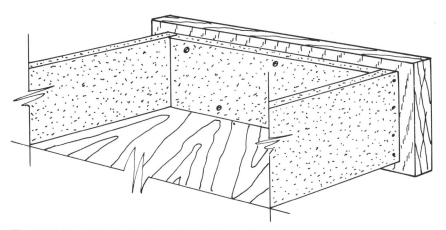

Illus. 7-4 (above left). In the box method, a drawer front is attached to the box. Illus. 7-5 (above right). The drawer adjuster is used to align the fronts on box drawers. (Photo courtesy of Julius Blum, Inc.)

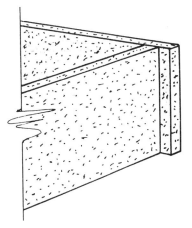

Illus. 7-6. Drawer backs are fastened to the sides with a simple butt joint.

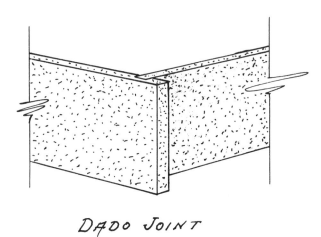

DADO JOINT

Illus. 7-7. The dado joint is also used to fasten the sides to the drawer back.

drawer sides will be presented later in this chapter.

BUILDING LIPPED DRAWERS

Because lipped drawers are the most commonly used and are relatively easy to build, instructions for fabricating this type of drawer will be presented first. To successfully build a nice-fitting and smooth-running drawer requires accurate measuring and machining. The

measurements used to machine the drawer fronts for lipped drawers must be precise, so proceed carefully and study the material thoroughly before attempting to machine a drawer front.

SELECTING THE MATERIAL FOR THE DRAWER FRONTS, SIDES, AND BACKS

The Drawer Fronts
The following are some decisions that will have to be made before the drawer fronts can be machined:

1. Will ¾-inch lumber (or thicker) or ¾-inch plywood be used for the fronts?
2. What direction will the grain run on the drawer fronts? A nice design touch on a row of vertical drawers is to have matching vertical grain. This works very well on flush drawers.
3. Will there be added mouldings, routings, etc., on the fronts that may determine the grain direction?

Drawer Sides and Back
Most drawer sides and backs are made from ½-inch material. On the finest furniture, these pieces are often machined from solid oak that has been planed to a thickness of ½ to ⅜ inch. However, most home woodworkers cannot afford such material and do not have access to a surfacer to plane the wood to the desired thickness. Do not use ¾-inch lumber for drawer sides, because this results in a very heavy and clumsy-looking drawer. Either ½-inch plywood or particle board is perhaps the best material to use, and when the raw edges of this material are capped with a hardwood strip, a nice-looking drawer side is created. (Because not much of the drawer back is seen, it is not capped with a hardwood strip.) Grade B-B fir plywood makes attractive drawer sides

because both sides are relatively free from any serious blemishes. However, this grade is difficult to purchase from the average lumber dealer, and the more commonly available A-C and A-D grades may contain too many knots or other blemishes on the C or D side.

Particle board in the ½-inch cabinet grade seems to be a successful alternative to plywood. It usually is available at most lumber dealers (or local cabinet shops). Use only the heavier-density boards. The underlayment grades are not smooth enough to make into satisfactory drawer sides. Another advantage in using particle board is that there is little waste because the sheets have no grain pattern and can be cut in any direction.

DETERMINING THE OVERALL SIZE OF A FRONT

The formula that follows results in a lipped drawer with the proper amount of "play," yet allows for thumbtack glides for the drawer. Chart 7-1 can be used to organize the measurements when several drawer fronts must be machined.

The formula for determining the overall size of a lipped drawer front is easy. Measure the face-frame opening for the drawer. Add 9/16 inch to the length of this opening. This gives you the overall length of the drawer front. Then add ⅜ inch to the height of the face-frame opening. This gives you the overall height of the drawer front.

This formula, remember, is only for a *lipped* drawer with drawer sides of ½-inch material that will be attached with butt joints to the drawer front.

MACHINING THE RABBETS

The rabbets on a lipped drawer must be machined accurately. The end rabbets are usually made on the table saw with both a horizontal and a vertical cut (Illus. 7-8 and 7-9). The rabbet along the top and bottom of the drawer front can be made with a router equipped with a ⅜-inch cutter, a spindle shaper equipped with a straight knife on the shaper, or a table saw. If using the table saw, clean up the rabbets by sanding the saw marks away. If the router is going to be used to shape

Drawer No.	Opening Width	+ 9/16"	Width of Dr. front	Opening height	+ 3/8"	Height of Dr. front

Chart 7-1. Organize the drawer-front size data by using this machining chart.

Illus. 7-8. The first rabbet cut made on the drawer-front.

Illus. 7-9. The second cut to complete the rabbet at the end of the drawer front.

the edges of the drawer fronts, do that *before* machining the rabbets!

Cut the bottom rabbet to a depth of only ⅛ inch because the crossrails used in projects built the casework way are just ¾ inch wide. If a standard ⅜-inch lip were to be machined on the bottom of the drawer front, and to the top of the drawer just below, the entire drawer rail would be covered. It is because of this ⅛-inch rabbet along the bottom of the drawer fronts that ¾-inch material can be success-

fully used for crossrails in the casework system.

Illus. 7-10 shows the dimensions for the various rabbets. The end rabbets are ⅜ x ⅞ inch. The top rabbet is ⅜ × ⅜ inch. The bottom rabbet is ⅜ × ⅛ inch.

The groove for the drawer bottom will not be cut until the drawer sides and backs are ready, so all the grooving can be done in one operation. Sand the lumber drawer fronts with the belt and finish sanders at this time.

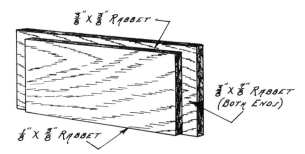

Illus. 7-10. Rabbet dimensions for the drawer front.

SHAPING THE EDGES OF THE DRAWER FRONT

The way the edges of furniture drawer fronts and doors are shaped is determined by personal preferences, the style of furniture being built, and the available shop equipment. The simplest treatment is to round the edges using a ⅜-inch-radius cutter in the router or a similar-size cutter in the spindle shaper and then sand the edges smooth. Traditional chests often have a pattern run on the edges of their drawer fronts (Illus. 7-11).

Using the Router

Shape the drawer fronts with the router *before* cutting the rabbets. If the rabbets are cut first, the guide pin on the router cutter will have nothing to rub against and the cutter can dig into and ruin the drawer front.

Shape the end grain of lumber drawer fronts first and the sides last, moving the router from left to right. By using this tech-

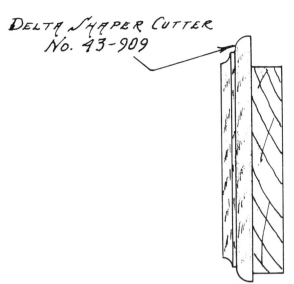

Delta Shaper Cutter
No. 43-909

Illus. 7-11. A patterned edge is often machined on the drawer front.

Illus. 7-12. The Sanding Router-Master is a foam rubber pad that firmly holds the work to be routed.

nique with either the router or the shaper, you will be able to remove any slight splits that might occur as the pass is completed on the end grain when you machine the side-grain edges. The same thing can be accomplished by routing or shaping the edges in a clockwise manner.

Some hobbyists mount their router in a router table which they have either purchased or made. This makes it much easier to shape the edges, because the drawer fronts do not have to be clamped down while they are being routed. However, there is a relatively inexpensive new product available called the Sanding Router-Master that makes routing even easier. This product is simply a rubber-like mat similar to carpet padding that holds even small pieces of wood while being shaped on the router (Illus. 7-12). It is available from the Industrial Abrasives Company, 642 North 8th Street, Box 14955, Reading, PA 19612-9954. The piece is large enough to hold a good-size cabinet door, and should last indefinitely.

MAKING THE SIDES AND BACKS

Make the sides and backs of lipped drawers exactly as high as the rabbeted inside of each drawer front. If cap strips are to be applied to the sides, rip the side pieces about ¼ inch less than the height of the rabbeted drawer front.

The length of the sides is determined by the depth of the furniture piece. A 20-inch-deep chest, for example, would have drawer sides about 18½ to 18¾ inches long. (One inch is subtracted from the overall depth of 20 inches. Also, allow slightly more to the length so the drawers do not hit the back reinforcing strips.) Make the drawer backs the same length as the rabbeted inside of the drawer front (Illus. 7-13).

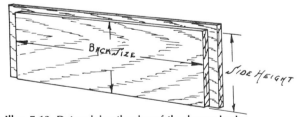

Illus. 7-13. Determining the size of the drawer back.

If the backs are to be dadoed into the drawer sides, then add an extra ½ inch to the length of the back. This measurement is for a dado that will be cut ¼ inch deep or halfway through the drawer side.

Machining and Applying Cap Strips

If the drawer sides are made from solid lumber, disregard this section on cap strips. However, if plywood or particle board is being used, cover the top edges with hardwood strips to create a professional-looking drawer (Illus. 7-15). These strips are usually made from the same species of wood from which the face frame was made. Chances are that enough leftover pieces are available from which you can rip the strips.

Each drawer will require two cap strips that measure ⅜ × ½ × 18½ inches (or the length of the drawer side). If a surfacer is available, you can quickly machine the stock to the ½-inch thickness, and then rip ⅜-inch strips from this stock. Otherwise, resaw ¾ × 2-inch or ¾ × 3-inch pieces to a ½-inch thickness, smooth them on the jointer, and then rip them into ⅜-inch strips. Joint the edge of the board prior to ripping each ⅜-inch strip. This results in a cap strip that is surfaced on three sides. Do not attempt to joint this last edge at this time, because this could be dangerous.

Applying the Strips to the Drawer Sides

1. With the smooth edge of the strip against the jointed edge of the drawer side, glue and nail the strip to the side using 1-inch brads. First, however, drill holes for the nails with a 1-inch brad in the electric drill. This will prevent the strips from splitting, especially near the end of the strip.
2. Set the 1-inch brads rather deep with the nail set, so that they do not interfere with the machining that follows.
3. Fill all holes with matching plastic wood, and let it dry.
4. Run this last rough edge over the jointer to clean up the plastic wood and the saw marks.
5. Belt-sand the drawer sides with the 120-grit belt so that the cap strips are flush with the particle board or plywood.

Easing the Edges of the Cap Strips

The drawer sides will have a professional look to them if you round or "ease" the edges of the cap strips. This can be done quickly and efficiently with a small-radius cutter in the router. Do not run the rounding the full length of the drawer side. Allow about ¾ inch of square edging to remain on each end of the side piece. This will look better where the drawer side fits into the drawer front rabbet (Illus. 7-14).

You can also use the jointer for this operation by cutting a small 45-degree chamfer on the edges of the cap strip. Lower both tables of the jointer until the desired depth of cut is reached. (Lowering both tables prevents a tapered cut.) Make a mark on the jointer fence where the piece will be dropped on the knives to start the cut, and another mark on the fence where the piece will be stopped and removed from the jointer (Illus. 7-15 and 7-16). When you use this procedure, you leave both ends square.

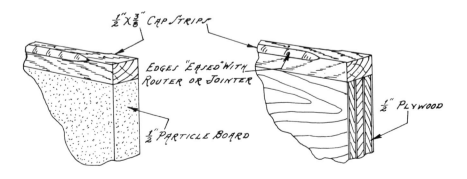

Illus. 7-14. Cap strips applied to the drawer sides hide the unsightly core of particle board or plywood.

Illus. 7-15. Mark a starting point on the jointer fence for stop-chamfering.

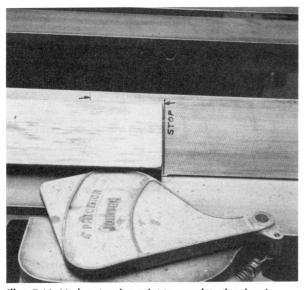

Illus. 7-16. Mark a stopping point to complete the chamfer.

SAWING AND JOINTING THE DRAWER SIDES TO THEIR CORRECT HEIGHT

With the addition of the cap strips, the side pieces can be somewhat too high. Check the exact size of the back of each drawer front where the sides will be attached and rip and joint the side pieces to those exact sizes.

GROOVING THE BOTTOMS

Machine the grooves for the plywood or hardboard drawer bottoms with a dado head in the table saw or an adjustable dado blade.

GROOVING THE SIDES AND BACKS

Using just the two outside saw blades of the dado set with, possibly, one cardboard shim between them, set the table-saw fence so that the groove is 5/16 inch above the bottom edge of the drawer side (Illus. 7-17). The groove should be wide enough so that the 1/4-inch plywood or hardboard bottom will slide easily into the groove. The groove should be 1/4 inch deep.

At this setting, run the groove for the drawer bottom on all the sides and backs. Do not do the drawer fronts at this setting!

GROOVING THE FRONTS

Because of the 1/8-inch lip on the bottom edge, you must adjust the table-saw fence to cut the groove on the back of the drawer fronts. Make a test cut on the back of one of the drawer fronts by just barely touching the wood with the dado set. Make sure that this cut matches the groove in a drawer side. When the two grooves match perfectly, cut the grooves on the back of all drawer fronts. The grooves should remain at 1/4 inch deep (Illus. 7-18).

ASSEMBLING THE DRAWERS

Although the drawer bottoms still have to be machined, it is good procedure to attach the sides to the drawer fronts prior to measuring and cutting the bottoms.

Nailing the Sides to the Fronts

1. Fasten a "stop" block to the top of the workbench, against which you can butt the drawer front while nailing the

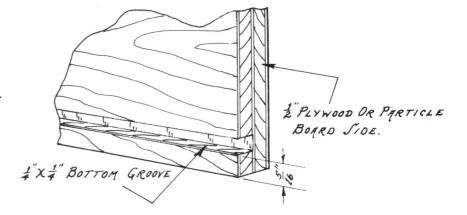

Illus. 7-17. Details for the groove for the drawer bottom.

½" PLYWOOD OR PARTICLE BOARD SIDE.

¼" X ¼" BOTTOM GROOVE

5/16"

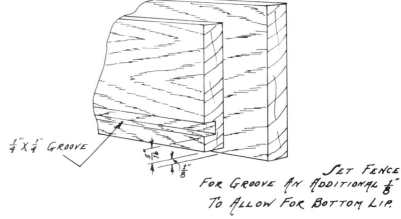

Illus. 7-18. Groove detail for the drawer front.

¼" X ¼" GROOVE

5/16" ⅛"

SET FENCE FOR GROOVE AN ADDITIONAL ⅛" TO ALLOW FOR BOTTOM LIP.

sides in position. Cover the bench with a protective cloth to prevent the drawer fronts from being scratched.

2. Using a 3d resin-coated nail or other nail with good holding power, tap the nails into the plywood sides about 1½ inches apart and about 5/16 inch from the end.

3. Run a bead of glue along the edge of the drawer front where the side will be attached.

4. Place the drawer side in position, line up the grooves exactly, and drive the nails into the drawer front. Proceed in the same manner for the opposite side. Attach all sides to their respective fronts at this time (Illus. 7-19).

Note: When tapping the nails into the

sides, slant them slightly so that the nail will be going down into the drawer front. This makes it easier to nail, and eliminates the possibility that the nail might break through the back of the drawer front. If you cannot drive the nails "home" without hitting the drawer lip, use a good-size drift punch or similar blunt device (Illus. 7-20). This will prevent you from damaging the drawer lip.

There is some debate among woodworkers as to whether the sides should be nailed to the fronts with box or finish nails. Finish nails, no doubt, have a nicer appearance, but the coated box nail has greater holding power. This decision will have to be made by the craftsperson but, in any event, the use of a good grade of glue will be of more importance than the type of nail used.

Illus. 7-19. Nail the sides to the drawer front using either finish nails or small box nails.

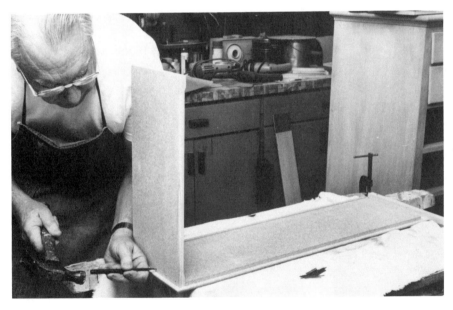

Illus. 7-20. To prevent damaging the drawer lip, drive the nails home by using a drift punch.

MEASURING AND CUTTING THE BOTTOMS

After the drawer sides are nailed to the fronts, the bottoms can be measured accurately, cut, and installed. Because the grooves in the drawer sides were cut ¼ inch deep, the bottoms will be slightly less than ½ inch wider than the length of the drawer back. About 1/16 inch less is enough clearance to slide in nicely.

Usually, many of the drawer bottoms in a chest of drawers will be the same size. They should be about ¾ inch shorter than the length of the sides. Give the A side of the plywood a good sanding with 120-grit paper in the finish sander. Slip the bottoms into their respective grooves, and then glue and nail the drawer back in position (Illus. 7-21 and 7-22). Do not glue the drawer bottoms in their grooves, because the plywood must be allowed to expand and contract.

Illus. 7-21. Slip the bottom into the grooves.

Illus. 7-22. Nail the back into place.

BUILDING FLUSH DRAWERS

There are two types of flush drawers. The first type is flush with the face frame, and has exposed drawer rails and stiles. In the second type, the stiles of the face frame are exposed, but the drawer rails are covered by the drawer fronts. Both types are addressed in this section.

TYPE ONE

Building a drawer with no lips or rabbets is relatively simple. The main problem is in determining the amount of "play" that must be built into the front so the drawer will not bind or fit too loosely. Thumbtack glides will be used when the drawer is installed, so they, too, must be taken into consideration. The rabbets in the drawer fronts will be exactly one-half the thickness of the front × the thickness of the sides. In most cases, when ¾-inch plywood is used for the fronts and ½-inch material for the sides, the rabbet will be ⅜ × ½ inch (Illus. 7-23).

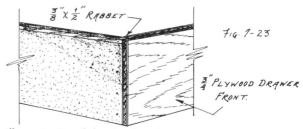

Illus. 7-23. Detail showing the side of a flush drawer attached to the front.

Tolerances Machine the front width ³⁄₁₆ inch less than the width of the opening, and ⅛ inch less than the height of the opening.

TYPE TWO

For this type of flush drawer, also subtract ³⁄₁₆ inch from the width of the drawer opening, and machine the drawer sides ⅛ inch less than the drawer opening height. However, the height of the drawer front must be extended to cover the drawer rail below the drawer—usually ¾ inch (Illus. 7-24). Usually some fitting is required when installing this type of drawer, to be certain that none of the drawer fronts clash.

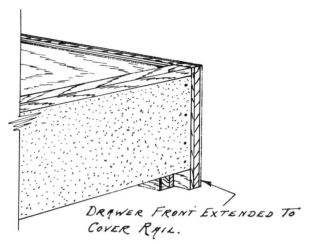

Illus. 7-24. Extend the lower edge of the front on a flush drawer to cover the drawer rail.

BUILDING OVERLAY DRAWERS

There are also two types of overlay drawers: the "boxed" overlay drawer and the dovetailed overlay drawer. Both types are described below.

"BOXED" OVERLAY DRAWER

This drawer is simply a four-sided box with a drawer front attached that overlays the face frame a desired amount. The amount of overlay is up to the individual. It can be enough to fully cover the face frame, or it can just be an overlap of ⅜ or ½ inch (Illus. 7-4).

Use the same tolerances to build the basic drawer "box" as were used for the type-one flush drawer. Then machine the drawer front to the size necessary to produce the desired overlay, and attach the drawer front to the basic drawer box with screws or "drawer adjusters."

DOVETAILED OVERLAY DRAWER

Lacking a dovetailing template fixture, the hobbyist should avoid building this style of drawer. Cut a dovetail "groove" into the back

of the drawer front that will accept the dovetail "tail" you will cut on the end of the drawer side (Illus. 7-25). Lay out the groove and tail carefully, so the completed drawer will have the same tolerances as any flush drawer. You will have to calculate the measurements carefully and use fixture setups to produce a correctly sized drawer. It is much easier to make the "boxed" overlay drawer.

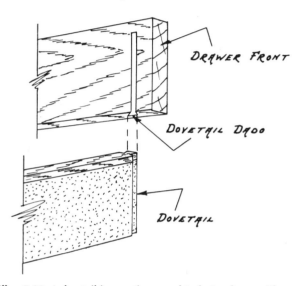

Illus. 7-25. A dovetail is sometimes used to fasten drawer sides to the front.

MAKING THE DOVETAIL JOINT

This joint is one of the classical means of joining wood pieces together. It derives its name from the shape of the joint's surfaces, which actually resemble a dove's tail. The sides of drawers in quality furniture are usually joined to the fronts with the dovetail joint. Although this book is written for the beginning woodworker, this section on dovetailing is included because it is so commonly used in the furniture industry.

DOVETAIL JIG

Dovetails can be made by using hand tools only, but this would be a laborious job indeed and would call for a degree of skill beyond most home woodworkers. Instead, make this joint by using a router in conjunction with a manufactured template device called a dovetail jig. These jigs range from a rather simple metal template to one with sophisticated adjustable "fingers" that allow the operator to make dovetails of an infinite variety and size (Illus. 7-26).

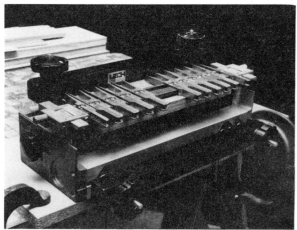

Illus. 7-26. One leading dovetail jig has adjustable fingers. (Photo courtesy of Leigh Industries Ltd.)

Almost all woodworking catalogues and supply houses carry dovetail jigs. These jigs can cost hundreds of dollars, and for this reason alone only the most serious woodworkers will use them.

Using the Dovetail Jig

Building a drawer with dovetail joints requires some careful planning. Although the drawer-front sizing formulas presented in this chapter would be applicable for dovetailed drawers, the rabbet cut measurements cannot be used because the drawer sides are "fingered" or dovetailed into the ends of the drawer fronts. To produce a perfect-fitting joint, you must locate the template accurately on both the drawer front and the ends of the drawer sides. Each manufacturer includes specific directions for the use of its template, and these

instructions should be followed explicitly. The router must be equipped with the proper template guide bushing to be able to accurately follow the outlines of the template.

The router, equipped with the proper carbide dovetail cutter, makes "tails" on the ends of the drawer sides when the sides are clamped in a vertical position in the jig. The "pins" are produced with the same router cutter, but for this cut the drawer front is clamped horizontally in the dovetail jig.

After making some practice cuts and test-fitting a joint, clamp the drawer pieces in the jig for the dovetailing. The actual operation is a simple matter of guiding the router carefully between and around the metal fingers of the template (Illus. 7-27).

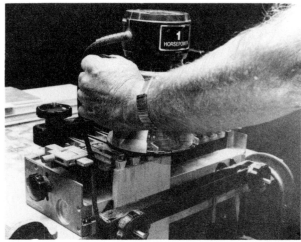

Illus. 7-27. Cut the tails by guiding the router between and around the metal fingers of a template. (Photo courtesy of Leigh Industries Ltd.)

Assembling the Dovetailed Drawer

The assembly procedure for the dovetailed drawer is the reverse of the procedure for a rabbeted drawer front with butt joints. First, fasten the sides to the drawer back, then slip the bottom into position, and, finally, glue and clamp the drawer front dovetail joints.

MACHINING THE DRAWER RUNNERS

The drawer runners in the casework system are center runners that guide the drawer through a notch cut into the bottom edge of the drawer back (Illus. 7-28). Two of these runners are often used on large drawers, such as in a chest of drawers. Pine, basswood, or a similar type of wood is used for the runners, but if a high-quality runner is desired, hardwood may be used (Illus. 7-29). Note that the center runner serves a dual purpose: (1) to guide the drawer into its opening straight and level; and (2) to act as an upper runner for the drawer just below to prevent it from tipping downwards when it is pulled from its opening.

The runner for the bottom drawer is not the same as the others. It is simply a strip of

wood ⁵⁄₁₆ × ¾ inch and as long as required that is glued and nailed to the bottom of the chest or cabinet as a guide (Illus. 7-30). Note that the ⁵⁄₁₆-inch lip on the runner is equal to the distance the bottom is inset on the drawer sides.

Note: Leave the runners slightly long, and cut them to an exact fit when installing the drawer. This way, the runners are certain to fit snugly, and the drawer will be somewhat easier to install.

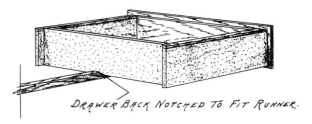

Illus. 7-28. Method of guiding a drawer with a center runner.

Illus. 7-29. To attach the runner to the drawer rail, cut a lip at the end of the runner.

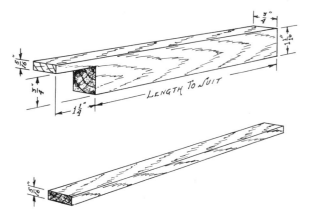

Illus. 7-30. Drawer runner detail.

MAKING SLIDE RUNNERS

Another type of center drawer guide is the slide runner. When this type of runner is used, the drawer is constructed differently. The bottom plywood is inset about ½ inch. The drawer back is not grooved for the bottom, but is machined so the bottom is nailed to it. With no notch to guide the drawer, make a separate grooved slide and fasten it to the bottom of the drawer with glue and small brads (Illus. 7-31).

The basic advantage of the slide runner is its durability. The notches cut in the bottom edge of the drawer back for the center runner can become worn, and the drawer will move around on its track. This will not happen with the slide runner, especially if the slide is made of hardwood.

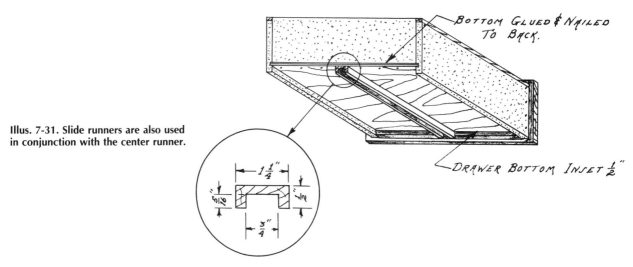

Illus. 7-31. Slide runners are also used in conjunction with the center runner.

MANUFACTURED METAL DRAWER RUNNERS

The furniture industry has been very slow to use metal drawer rollers on its products. Perhaps this has been due to the noise associated with these runners. Lately, however, the manufacturers of roller-runners have coated their runners with epoxy, and this has made a noticeable difference. Perhaps in the future, chests of drawers, desks, and other pieces of furniture will have these products.

The metal drawer runners on the market come in a wide variety of styles and designs. Be aware that the drawer formulas, measurements, and tolerances presented in this chapter for building drawers will not apply if metal runners are to be used. You will have to follow the directions and tolerances that accompany the individual manufacturer's metal runners. Once the principles of good drawer construction have been mastered, however, little difficulty should be encountered in adapting to metal drawer runners.

INSTALLING THE DRAWERS IN A CHEST OR CABINET

One of the advantages of using the center runner system is that each drawer is fit into its opening individually. This means that the lip of the drawer should fit tight and flush against the face frame of the chest. Flush drawers should be installed so that the drawer is exactly even with the face frame and no edge of the drawer is out of line with the plane of the face frame. Of course, you can simply square the center runners by using a framing square from both the side and the top of the runner, and then nail them in position. However, the drawer might not fit properly. A drawer lip could touch the face frame along the top edge, but have a slight gap along the bottom lip, or one end lip might be tight and the other end have a space between the lip and the face frame. The only sure way to have properly fitting drawers is to follow the drawer installation methods as described in this section. They only take moments to learn and, once they are mastered, you are ensured of nearly perfect-fitted and -aligned drawers. In this procedure, the bottom drawer of a row of drawers is installed first, and then you work upwards, installing each drawer atop the drawer just below.

INSTALLING DRAWERS WITH CENTER RUNNERS

If you follow these steps carefully, the result will be drawers that fit properly in a chest or cabinet. (If two runners per drawer or slide runners are to be used, follow the same procedures.)

Installing the Bottom Drawer

1. The 5/16-inch strip is the runner for the bottom drawer. Cut the strip to length by measuring from the rear of the chest to about ½ inch from the front edge of the chest.
2. Position this strip in about the middle of the drawer opening and nail it near the front end with one ¾-inch brad.
3. Place the drawer in its opening—with an equal amount of space on each side—and bump the drawer against the guide strip. Reach behind the drawer and, with a pencil, mark the back of the drawer on each side of the guide strip (Illus. 7-32).
4. Remove the drawer, turn it upside down on the workbench, and, with a handsaw, cut *on the marked lines* down to the plywood drawer bottom. Make one or two more cuts if necessary and wiggle the saw blade enough to break out the remaining material between the outside cuts. Clean up the notch down to the plywood bottom. By making the first two cuts on the marks, you are creating enough room for the drawer to slide freely on the strip guide (Illus. 7-33).
5. Replace the drawer back into its opening and slide it all the way into the chest, making certain that the drawer fits snugly against the face frame. The 5/16-inch strip will be moved to its correct position by this action.
6. Carefully pull the drawer out of the chest about 4 or 5 inches, being careful not to disturb the position of the guide.
7. Reach in behind the drawer and make a pencil mark on the chest bottom on each side of the guide (Illus. 7-34).
8. Remove the drawer from the chest and move the runner aside by pivoting it on the brad at the front of the strip. Run a bead of glue on the chest bottom where the runner will be placed, move the strip back to its marked position, and nail the runner permanently to the chest bottom using ¾-inch brads.

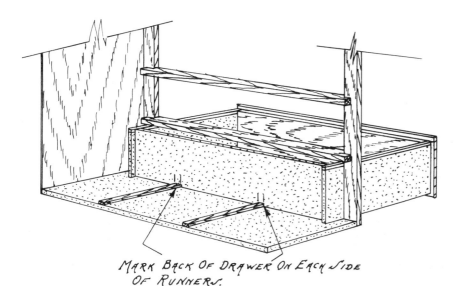

Illus. 7-32. Place the drawer in the opening and mark the back of it.

MARK BACK OF DRAWER ON EACH SIDE OF RUNNERS.

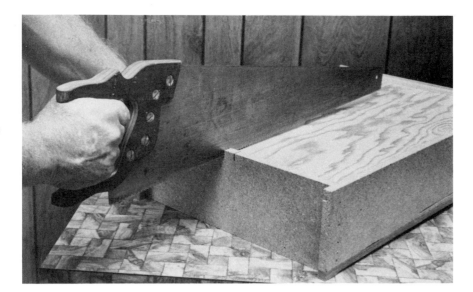

Illus. 7-34. Running the drawer into the chest will move the runners to their correct location.

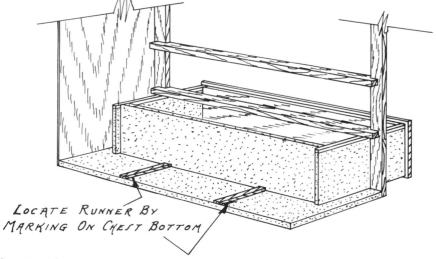

Illus. 7-33. Use a handsaw to cut the notches in the drawer back.

LOCATE RUNNER BY MARKING ON CHEST BOTTOM

Installing the Drawer That's Above the Bottom Drawer

Leave the bottom drawer in its position in the chest, while installing the drawer above it. Install this drawer as follows:

1. Saw the drawer runner (or runners) for this drawer to a length that will fit snugly in the chest and place it in position (Illus. 7-35).
2. Place a drop or two of glue under the lip of the runner and nail the runner in place with one ¾-inch brad. Apply some paraffin to the brad if nailing it into hardwood.

Note: Use a peavey under the drawer rail, so there is a surface underneath the runner when you nail it (Illus. 7-36).

The rear of the drawer runner rests on the back of the drawer below.

3. Mark and notch the back of this drawer as instructed previously.
4. Make several shims about ¾ inch wide and 3 inches long from scrap plastic laminate. These shims can also be made about the same size from ¹⁄₁₆-inch-thick strips of wood. Place one of these shims under the drawer runner

Illus. 7-35. Install the second drawer by building on the bottom drawer. (Note that shims are placed at the rear of each runner.)

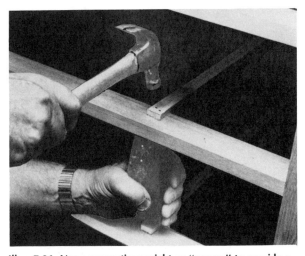

Illus. 7-36. Use a supporting weight or "peavey" to provide a solid nailing surface.

so the shim and the runner are resting on the back of the bottom drawer (Illus. 7-37).

5. Check the fit of this drawer against the face frame. If the drawer does not fit properly, do the following:

   (a) Move the drawer runner slightly either left or right to bring the end lips of the drawer front into alignment.

   (b) Place extra shims under the run-

ner if the bottom lip needs aligning.

Note: Do not place more than two or three shims under the runner. If you place too many under the runner, the drawer below will jump off its own runner when pulled from the chest.

6. After aligning the drawer, move to the rear of the chest, sight down the inside of the chest, and drive a 4d box nail through the plywood back into the rear of the runner. The first nail may miss, but the second try is usually successful. Drive two nails into the end of each runner.

7. Return to the front of the chest and drive one more ¾-inch brad through the lip of the runner.

Installing the Remaining Drawers

Install the remaining drawers by using the same method as outlined in the preceding section. Install each drawer by "building" on the drawer just below it by using the shims and adjusting the drawer runner to bring the drawer into perfect alignment.

145

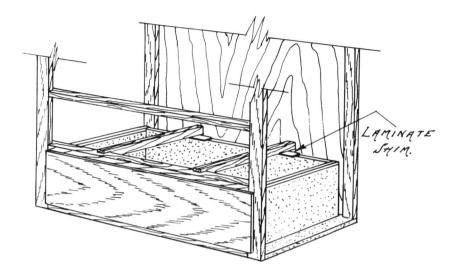

Illus. 7-37. Laminate shims are placed under the runner.

LAMINATE SHIM.

Techniques for Smoothly Running Drawers

You can ensure that the drawers run extremely smoothly by using thumbtacks and paraffin. Push two No. 4 thumbtacks into the left and right corners of each drawer opening—and one thumbtack into the notch at the back of the drawer. Place another thumbtack on top of the drawer back so that it is directly *under* the drawer runner for the drawer above (Illus. 7-38). Now each point of friction has a metal glide. Using a block of paraffin, rub all the contact surfaces: the bottom edges of the drawer sides, the drawer runner for each drawer, and the underside of each drawer runner. Also rub some paraffin on the heads of the thumbtacks. Now give the drawer a try. You'll find that it slides effortlessly!

Fabricating the Chest Top

After all of the drawers have been made and installed, go back to Chapter Six for instructions on fabricating the top of the chest. This will be the last building step in completing a fine piece of furniture. After the top is done, add a finish to the chest. (See Chapter Sixteen)

Illus. 7-38. Place thumbtacks at friction points for smooth-running drawers.

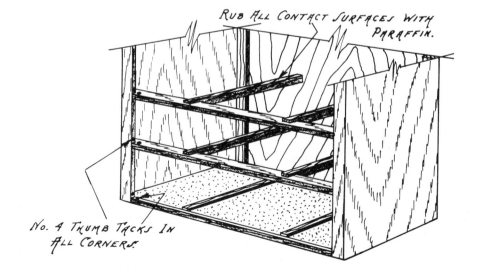

RUB ALL CONTACT SURFACES WITH PARAFFIN.

NO. 4 THUMB TACKS IN ALL CORNERS.

Desks

Desks are very popular projects for wood-workers, and this chapter contains building instructions for several styles and types. Desks are functional pieces of furniture that can be designed to blend with the motif of the home or office. The casework system lends itself nicely to the building of desks. One word of caution: Do not attempt to build a desk project from this chapter unless you have mastered the casework woodworking techniques and drawer construction procedures in Chapters Six and Seven. These techniques and procedures will be constantly referred to in this chapter.

DESIGNING DESKS

As with most furniture, desks fall into two design categories: traditional and contemporary. The traditional furniture features that were described for chests of drawers in Chapter Six are virtually the same for desks: rolled-and-coved legs (or cabriole legs as they are often called), lipped drawers with moulded edges, and an overhanging top with a rounded edge accompanied by a cove moulding below. The contemporary desk, on the other hand, is more straight-lined in appearance, presents a modern, functional look, and does not have any fancy mouldings or other period accruements.

BASIC DESIGN FEATURES

Besides being categorized as traditional or contemporary, all desks are designed with particular features and for specific uses. These design characteristics are described below:

Double- and Single-Pedestal Desks

The majority of desks are either double- or single-pedestal desks. A double-pedestal desk has a row of drawers on either side of the kneehole (Illus. 8-1). A single-pedestal desk has just a single row of drawers to the right or left of the kneehole (Illus. 8-2). Pedestals can be a design feature in traditional and contemporary desks.

Though the majority of desks are usually single- or double-pedestal types, some fall into neither category. These are writing desks, drop-lid desks, and secretaries (Illus. 8-3). These desks cannot be built with casework techniques and will not be dealt with here.

Illus. 8-1. A double-pedestal traditional desk. (Drawing courtesy of Ethan Allen, Inc.)

Illus. 8-2. A traditional single-pedestal desk and chest. (Drawing courtesy of Ethan Allen, Inc.)

GOV. WINTHROP

WRITING DESK

Illus. 8-3. Examples of other styles of desks. (Drawing courtesy of Ethan Allen, Inc.)

SECRETARY

DROPLID

Basic Sizes

Desks are commonly manufactured in three sizes. These sizes are definitely related to the way the desk is used, either in the home or office. They are described below:

Student Desk

This desk is designed to meet the needs of the high school or college student. It is usually somewhat smaller than other desks and is often combined with a small chest of drawers, as shown in Illus. 8-2. Storage of file folders is not a prime requisite of the student desk, and this means that the width of the drawers can be narrowed considerably. The kneehole of any desk must be designed a minimum width of 22 inches. This is essential, because most chairs are 18 to 20 inches wide at the seat and must, of course, be able to slide into the kneehole space. If you want to build a smaller desk, subtract the width from the drawers or make a desk with only one pedestal.

A standard student desk is usually 40 to 48 inches long, 23 to 24 inches deep, and 30 inches high.

Library Desk

This desk is one that is found most often in the den, the home office, or the library of a home. It is intermediate in size, usually has two pedestals, and contains a drawer or drawers for the storage of standard file folders (Illus. 8-4). Library desks are usually 50 to 56 inches wide, 24 to 26 inches deep, and the standard 30 inches high.

Office Desk

These desks are quite large, befitting the importance of the executive office. They contain file drawers, a lock on the center drawer (and often on the other drawers as well), and may have pullout writing boards above the pedestals (Illus. 8-5). A typical office desk will be

Illus. 8-4. A traditional library desk. (Drawing courtesy of Ethan Allen, Inc.)

Illus. 8-5. The office, or executive, desk. (Drawing courtesy of Ethan Allen, Inc.)

60 to 78 inches wide, 30 to 36 inches deep, and the usual 30 inches high.

Location of Desk

Another consideration for the desk builder is whether or not the desk is to be completely finished. If the desk will be placed against a wall where the rear of the desk will not be seen, then only the front and two sides of the desk should be of finished construction. However, if the desk will be placed where the rear of the desk may be seen—in the center of a room or office, for example—then the desk should be finished on all four sides. A considerable savings in both material and labor is realized finishing the desk on only three sides, but, needless to say, most desks are completed on all four.

Base Options Another factor to consider is the type of base the desk will have. If a traditional desk is being built, the options for base construction are the same as those for traditional chests of drawers. (See Chapter 6.) The contemporary desk does not have as many types of bases as a traditional one, but it can have turned and tapered legs, a simple platform base, or a tapered pedestal base.

Drawer Requirements for Storing File Folders

If the desk requires a drawer or drawers for the storage of file folders, you will have to carefully plan so that the inside measurements of these drawers will handle a standard $11\frac{3}{4} \times 9\frac{1}{2}$-inch file folder. If the drawer will store legal-size file folders, it must be even wider. If hanging files are being considered, those required measurements must be calculated. The required outside width of the drawer must then be calculated from the *inside* width, and the face-frame opening calculated from the outside width. For example, a drawer with an inside width of 12 inches and built with $\frac{1}{2}$-inch sides will require a face frame designed with a width opening of $13\frac{3}{16}$ inches. Remember that $\frac{3}{16}$ inch should be allowed for the correct "play" for thumbtack glides and for proper drawer clearance. If the drawer must be built $9\frac{3}{4}$ inches deep on the inside, the drawer sides should be $10\frac{5}{16}$ inches high. (Add the $\frac{1}{4}$-inch plywood bottom and the $\frac{5}{16}$-inch bottom inset to the inside required depth to arrive at the $10\frac{5}{16}$-inch drawer side.) The face-frame opening must therefore be designed $10\frac{7}{16}$ inches high, to ensure a completed drawer with the needed inside measurements and the extra $\frac{1}{8}$ inch for thumbtacks and "play." Therefore, a desk drawer large enough to accommodate standard file folders will require a face-frame opening $13\frac{3}{16}$ inches wide $\times$ $10\frac{7}{16}$ inches high.

For narrower desks that require file folder storage, build narrow drawers but store the file folders parallel to the drawer sides rather than parallel to the front (Illus. 8-6).

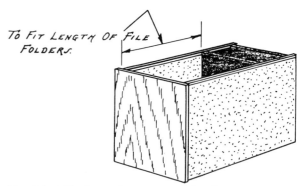

Illus. 8-6. A file drawer for a narrow pedestal.

Kneehole Drawer This drawer also needs some careful attention because if it is made too deep it could interfere with the knee space available for the person sitting at the desk. The standard height of a chair seat is 18 inches. Add *at least* 5 inches to this for a person's "thigh room," for a total of 23 inches. The standard height of the desk is 30 inches. However, from this measurement subtract $\frac{3}{4}$ inch (or more) for the desk top and $2\frac{3}{4}$ inches for the top and the first drawer rails, for a total of $3\frac{1}{2}$ inches. This leaves $3\frac{1}{2}$ inches for the face-frame height of the kneehole drawer. In fact, a desk designer might want to make this 3 inches, for the height of the face-frame opening. The top drawers of the two side rows of drawers will, of course, be the same height as the kneehole drawer.

A nice touch for the kneehole drawer is to build a pencil tray for the inside of the drawer (Illus. 8-7).

BUILDING A TRADITIONAL DESK

The traditional desk project selected for presentation in this chapter is a mid-size library desk (Illus. 8-8). This desk will fit nicely into

Illus. 8-7. A shop-built pencil tray for the kneehole drawer.

a home office, den, or even a student's bedroom. It has two narrow drawers for file folder storage, and a total of seven drawers. It has been designed so that the four side panels and the back and top panels can all be obtained from one 4 × 8-foot piece of ¼-inch plywood. Because of this efficient use of material, this is a fairly inexpensive piece of furniture to build.

DESK CONSTRUCTION

An examination of Illus. 8-9 reveals that a desk is simply two basic boxes joined together by a face frame. When the top and the base construction are stripped away, the two basic boxes can easily be distinguished. The desk can be built in much the same way as the chest of drawers presented in Chapter Six.

BUILDING THE FACE FRAME

As with all casework projects, first build the face frame, because all the width and height measurements are calculated from this assem-

bly. Study Illus. 8-10 to determine the building techniques. Note that the desk's face frame is similar to the face frame for a chest of drawers. Rabbet the stiles to accept ¼-inch side panels, screw the joints together, and bundle the rails together and notch them to fit around the four stiles. All of these are techniques presented in Chapter Six and will not be repeated in this chapter.

Bill of Materials

These following pieces are required to complete the face frame:

End stiles: Two pieces ¾ × 1½ × 24 inches

Kneehole stiles: Two pieces ¾ × 1½ × 22 inches

Top rail: One piece ¾ × 2 × 44½ inches

First drawer rail: One piece ¾ × 1¾ × 46 inches

Second drawer rails: Two pieces ¾ × 1¾ × 11¼ inches

Facing strips: Two pieces ¾ × ¾ × 9¾ inches

Illus. 8-8. This double-pedestal traditional desk is the first desk project. (Photo courtesy of Mr. and Mrs. Datlof Weseloh, Hutchinson, MN.)

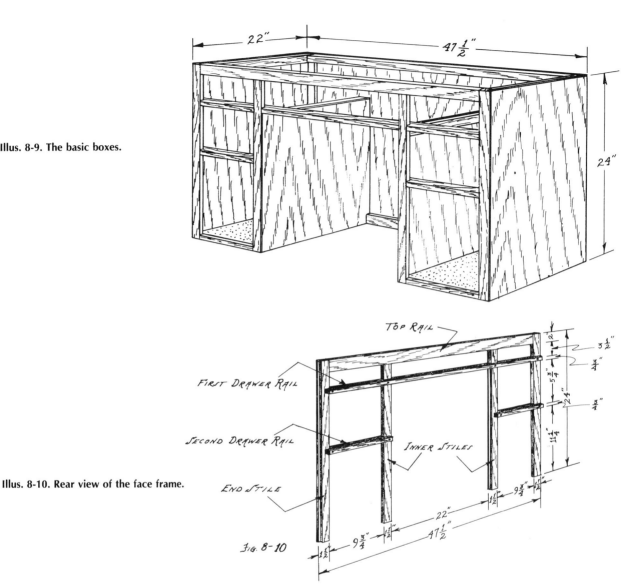

Illus. 8-9. The basic boxes.

TOP RAIL

FIRST DRAWER RAIL

SECOND DRAWER RAIL

INNER STILES

END STILE

FIG. 8-10

Illus. 8-10. Rear view of the face frame.

Cut these pieces to the net dimensions as listed above from the cabinet wood selected. Be absolutely certain that end cuts on all of the pieces are square so the butt joints, when screwed together, will be square.

Machining the Face-Frame Pieces

Rabbeting the Stiles All of the pieces will require some machining. Start with the rabbets needed on the four stiles, as shown in Illus. 8-11. Refer to Chapter Six for the machining techniques.

Notching the Rails The three drawer rails must be bundled together as shown in Illus. 8-12. Make the notches on the table saw with the saw blade exactly as high as the thickness of the face-frame material. The two interior notches are 1½ inches wide, and the end notches are ¾ inch long. Remember, the top rail must be exactly as long as the first drawer rail between the two outside notches (Illus. 8-13).

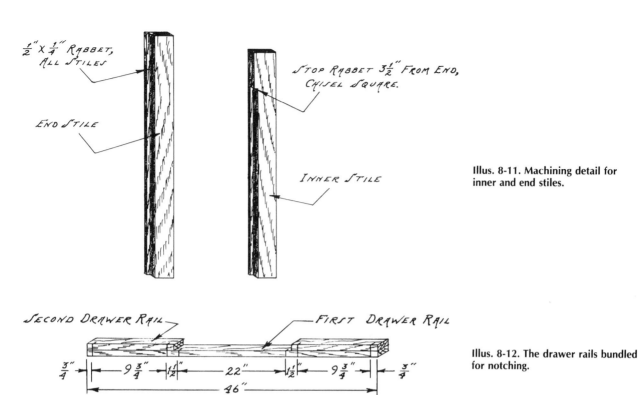

Illus. 8-11. Machining detail for inner and end stiles.

$\frac{1}{2}$" X $\frac{1}{4}$" RABBET, ALL STILES

END STILE

STOP RABBET 3$\frac{1}{2}$" FROM END, CHISEL SQUARE.

INNER STILE

SECOND DRAWER RAIL

FIRST DRAWER RAIL

$\frac{3}{4}$"   9$\frac{3}{4}$"   1$\frac{1}{2}$"   22"   1$\frac{1}{2}$"   9$\frac{3}{4}$" $\frac{3}{4}$"

46"

Illus. 8-12. The drawer rails bundled for notching.

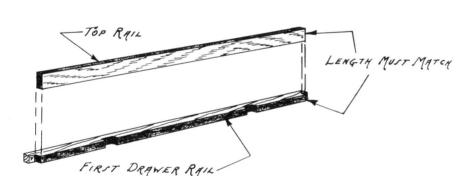

TOP RAIL

LENGTH MUST MATCH

FIRST DRAWER RAIL

Illus. 8-13. The top rail must match the length of the first drawer rail between notches.

Assembling the Face Frame

Step One   Join the two end stiles to the top rail with screw joints using the same techniques as described in Chapter 6. Make sure that the rabbets in these stiles face in the correct direction. Check the squareness of this first assembly.

Step Two   Glue and screw the first drawer rail in position to the rear of the stiles using 1¼-inch, #8 flathead screws. Use a gauge stick 3 or 3½ inches long (depending upon the desired depth of the kneehole drawer) to locate the position of the rail on the stiles.

Step Three   Fasten the two short stiles to the top rail. Hold these pieces in position with a C-clamp and a block of wood, as shown in Illus. 8-14. Glue and fasten them in place with one 2½-inch, #8 flathead wood screw that is counterbored ½ inch deep. Fasten the first drawer rail to the short stiles with glue and 1¼-inch, #8 flathead screws, again using the gauge stick to locate the exact position of the rail.

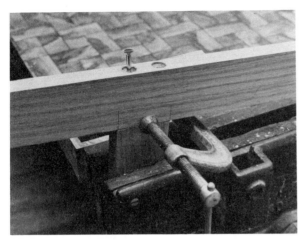

Illus. 8-14. Use a vise and C-clamp to hold the short stiles while they are fastened to the top rail.

21-inch length is 1 inch less than the overall depth (front to back) of the desk.

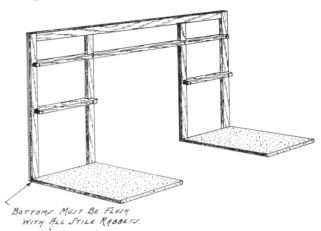

Bottoms Must Be Flush With All Stile Rabbets.

Illus. 8-15. The bottoms are as wide as the pedestal face-frame rabbets.

Step Four Fasten the two short rails to the stiles using glue and the same size screws. Position these stiles below the first drawer rail using a gauge stick 5¾ inches long. This will provide for a 10½-inch opening for the file drawers after the ¾-inch bottom is installed later. This completes the face-frame assembly.

Note: The location dimensions for the drawer rails shown in Illus. 8-10 are correct if ¾-inch lumber is used as specified in the bill of materials. If ¹³/₁₆-inch hardwood is used, some vertical dimension adjustments will have to be made to the drawer rail locations.

FABRICATING THE BOTTOMS

Make the bottoms for the two basic boxes from either ¾-inch particle board or plywood. Do not attempt to save on material costs by using thinner material, because this can affect the strength of the desk.

Bottom Sizes These two bottoms should measure about 12¼ inches wide by 21 inches long. Check the width by measuring the distance between the rabbets on the stiles. The bottom should be exactly as wide as the distance between these rabbets (Illus. 8-15). The

FABRICATING THE BACK

For clarity, when instructions are given for the front of the desk, they refer to the side of the desk with the drawer fronts. When instructions are given for the desk back, they refer to the plywood panel on the opposite side.

The first decision that will have to be made regarding the back panel is the type of corner joint that will be made. This joint can be mitred, filled with a matching hardwood strip, or a veneered joint may be used. A veneered corner joint will be used in this presentation, but the builder may prefer to use one of the other means of fastening the corners together.

ROUGH-CUTTING THE PANELS FROM A PLYWOOD SHEET

At this time, mark and saw the various desk panels from the ¼ inch × 4 foot × 8-foot plywood panel. Illus. 8-16 shows the size of each panel and the cutting sequence used so that all of the pieces may be obtained from the one piece of plywood. Note that the panel for the desk back and the piece for the outside end panels are the first two cuts made on the table saw. Each of these pieces will measure 24 inches, with the grain running in the 24-inch direction. One of these 48 × 24-inch panels will be cut into two pieces and will be used for the outside end panels. The remaining 4 × 4-foot piece is ripped down the middle into two 24 × 48-inch pieces. One of these is set aside for the top panel and the other will be cut into two pieces to be used for the inside kneehole panels.

PREPARING THE DESK BACK

Use the first 48 × 24-inch piece cut from the plywood panel for the desk back. Several pine reinforcing pieces will be needed for this back panel. The overall width of the finished desk will be 47½ inches, so the back panel will have to be about 47⁹⁄₁₆ inches long. Prepare the veneer joint very carefully, as described in Chapter Six. It would be wise to review the information on the veneer joint before proceeding. Make the first cut along both 24-inch edges, leaving only slightly more than the thickness of the veneer. Make the second saw cuts so that the distance remaining between the saw cuts exactly equals the distance between the outside rabbets of the face frame. After the veneer cuts are completed, handle the panel with care so that the thin veneers remaining on each end of the panel are not damaged.

Next, prepare four ¾ × 1½ × 23¼-inch pine reinforcing strips. These strips are cut ¾ inch shorter than the height of the back panel to allow for the particle-board bottoms. Glue and clamp two of these pine pieces to the inside of the back panel flush with the inside edge of the veneer rabbet. Be sure to allow ¾ inch for the thickness of the bottom at the lower edge (Illus. 8-17). Cushion the C-clamps with scrap plywood so that the back panel will not be marred by clamp marks.

Next, prepare a top reinforcing piece that is ¾ inch × 2 inches and about 46 inches

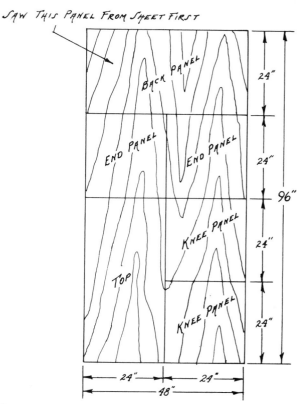

Illus. 8-16. Cutting plan for the required ¼-inch plywood panels.

long. Cut this piece to fit between the two end reinforcing pieces, and glue and clamp it to the top edge of the plywood back. Remember, this desk will be finished on all four sides; do *not* use any nails to attach the reinforcers.

The two inside kneehole reinforcing strips must be located very accurately. Measure the distance from rabbet to rabbet on the face frame across the pedestals. Transfer this distance to the back panel to locate the inner reinforcing strips. Draw vertical lines from these marks with the framing square. Now, glue these strips in position, using concrete blocks for weights. The outside edges of the reinforcers should line up exactly with the edges of the particle-board bottoms (Illus. 8-17).

ASSEMBLING THE FACE FRAME, BOTTOMS, AND BACK PANEL

Although all of the desk side panels still have

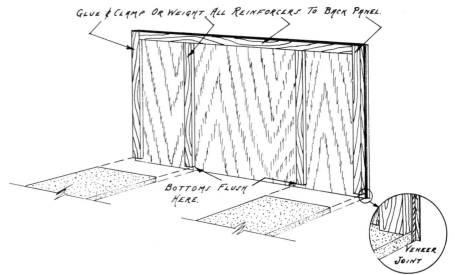

GLUE & CLAMP OR WEIGHT ALL REINFORCERS TO BACK PANEL.

BOTTOMS FLUSH HERE.

VENEER JOINT

Illus. 8-17. Reinforcers must be added to the back panel to match the width of the bottoms.

to be cut to size and installed, to be able to obtain accurate measurements for these panels it is necessary to assemble the face frame, bottoms, and the desk back.

Attaching the Bottoms to the Face Frame

Prepare two 22-inch-long supporting pieces of scrap plywood. They can be ¼-inch plywood pieces that are 4 to 6 inches wide. Tack-nail these pieces firmly to the top rail of the face frame. These two pieces will support the face frame even with the bottoms, as shown in Illus. 8-18. Line up the bottom panels flush with the rabbets in the stiles, and then glue and nail the stiles to the bottoms using two 4d finish nails in each stile. To prevent splitting the end of the stiles, use a 4d

nail in the electric drill and drill pilot holes for the nails about ⅜ inch from the end on all four stiles. Set the nails and fill the resulting holes with matching plastic wood.

Installing the Back Panel

Step One   Stand the face frame/bottom assembly vertically so that it is resting on the bottom panels. Place the back panel in position and tack-nail the supporting plywood strips to the top edge of the back (Illus. 8-19).

Step Two   Gently and carefully tip the assembly over so that it rests with the face frame on the floor. Line up the bottom edge of the back panel flush with the particle-board bot-

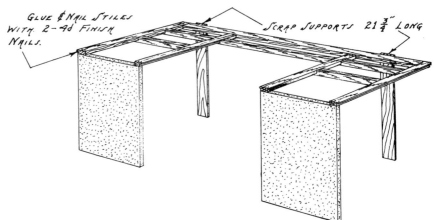

GLUE & NAIL STILES WITH 2-4d FINISH NAILS.

SCRAP SUPPORTS 21¾" LONG

Illus. 8-18. Temporary supports hold the face frame at the correct height.

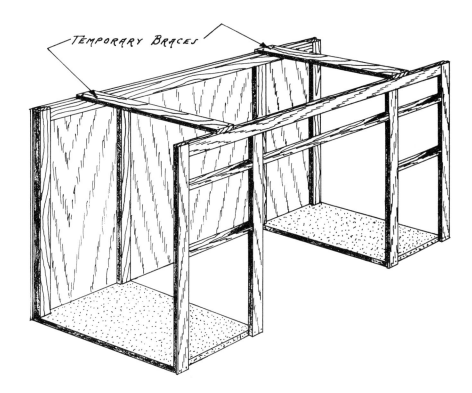

toms, making certain that all edges of the reinforcing strips and the rabbets at the veneer joints are correctly aligned. Finally, glue and nail the lower edge of the back to the bottoms using 1-inch brads. Set these brads and fill the holes with matching plastic wood.

FABRICATING AND INSTALLING THE FOUR SIDE PANELS

With the above assembly completed, it is now possible to make accurate measurements for the cutting of the end panels and kneehole panels.

Machining and Installing the Two End Panels

Measure the distance from the face-frame rabbet to the veneer joint rabbet. It should be about $21^{11}/_{16}$ inches. Use two of the $24 \times 24 \times \frac{1}{4}$-inch panels for the desk sides. Make

sure that the grain of these panels runs vertically.

To machine the two end panels, first joint a 5-degree angle on the edge that will fit into the face-frame rabbet. Then saw the panel to the correct width, allowing an extra $\frac{1}{32}$ to $\frac{1}{16}$ inch for jointing the rear edge. Joint the rear edge of the side panel until it fits exactly into the rabbet.

Next, glue and nail the panel in position. Start by nailing $\frac{3}{4}$-inch brads along the face-frame rabbet. Next, glue the veneer over the rear edge of the side panel and hold the veneer tightly in place by applying strips of masking tape across the veneer. Nail the side panel to the back reinforcing strip at this same time with $\frac{3}{4}$-inch brads. Finally, nail along the edge of the desk bottom using 1-inch brads. Pull everything into square with the side panel as you continue with the installation (Illus. 8-20). Set all the nails and brads and fill the holes with matching plastic wood.

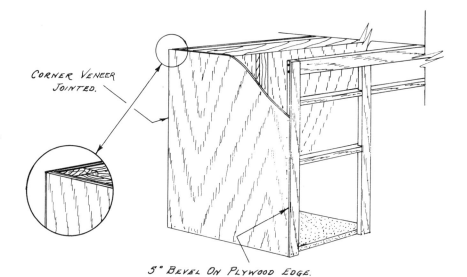

CORNER VENEER JOINTED.

Illus. 8-20. Install the end panels with veneered corner joints.

5° BEVEL ON PLYWOOD EDGE.

Machining and Installing the Kneehole Panels

Measure the exact distance from the face-frame rabbet to the desk back, where the side panels will be installed in the kneehole of the desk. Cut the two kneehole panels from one of the two remaining 2 × 4-foot pieces of ¼-inch plywood. (The last piece will be used for the desk top.) Joint the front edge at a 5-degree angle so it will fit into the face-frame rabbet, and then rip the panel to the correct width, allowing about ¹⁄₃₂ inch for the final jointing so that the panel fits snugly. Glue and

nail these panels in place, again using ¾- and 1-inch brads. Set these nails and fill the holes (Illus. 8-21).

MAKING AND INSTALLING THE PANEL REINFORCING PIECES

Glue and clamp a pine reinforcing piece to the top of each of the four side panels (Illus. 8-22). These pieces will be ¾ × 2 inches × the measured length. Again, use cushioning pieces under the C-clamps, so the panels are not marred by the clamps.

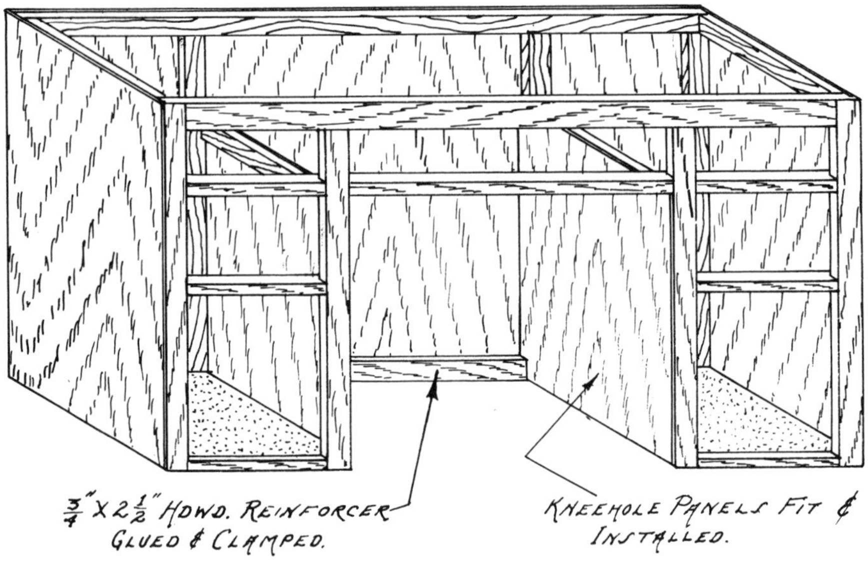

Illus. 8-21. Install the kneehole panels next.

¾" X 2½" HDWD. REINFORCER GLUED & CLAMPED.

KNEEHOLE PANELS FIT & INSTALLED.

MAKING AND INSTALLING THE CROSS-BRACES

Three pieces that measure $\frac{3}{4} \times 2 \times$ approximately $20\frac{3}{4}$ inches must be fabricated and installed at the top of the desk. These pieces not only brace the entire structure, but also act as upper runners for the drawers so that they do not tip when pulled from the desk. Also prepare six small blocks of pine that measure $\frac{3}{4} \times 2 \times 4$ inches. These blocks will be used as mounting blocks for these braces.

Glue and clamp three mounting blocks to the rear of the face frame, installing each block so that the upper runners, when installed, will be about in the center of each of the top drawer openings. Glue and clamp the remaining three blocks to the pine reinforcing strip across the top of the desk back. Use the framing square to install these directly across from the front blocks. After the glue has set, install the upper runners by gluing and screwing them to the mounting blocks with $1\frac{1}{2}$-inch, #8 flathead wood screws (Illus. 8-22). Hold the runners in position with a bar clamp while installing them.

COMPLETING THE BASIC BOXES

To complete the basic boxes, apply the $\frac{3}{4} \times \frac{3}{4}$-inch facing strips to the front edges of the bottom with glue and 4d finish nails. Also, you can install four rub-glued blocks in the four major corners to give them additional strength.

Use plastic wood to fill all nail holes, any small flaws in the face-frame joints, and any small openings along the seams where the plywood fits into the face-frame rabbets. After the plastic wood has thoroughly dried, use a hook scraper and sander to work the excess plastic wood away. Belt-sand the face frame, and then sand it with the finish sander. Remove the masking-tape pieces from the veneer joints and plane and sand the veneer down, to create an attractive corner. A well-sharpened block plane set for a very light cut works nicely for this job. Using the finish sander and

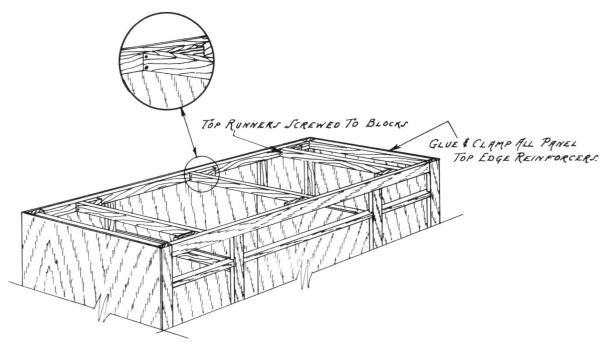

Illus. 8-22. The installation of the cross-braces and the end-panel reinforcers.

120-grit paper, give the entire desk a final sanding, paying particular attention to the plastic-wood-filled areas to be sure that all residue has been removed from around the holes and seams.

CONSTRUCTING THE BASE FOR THE DESK

Chapter Six contains the information needed to determine which type of base to use on the desk. The traditional desk has "coved-and-rolled" legs, a solid base that is coved and rolled, or a pattern-sawed straight base. Each of these features is described in Chapter Six, as are the building techniques for each. For purposes of these instructions, the cabriole, or "rolled-and-coved," legs that were built for the chest of drawers will also be used for the desk, with some adaptations.

Fabricating and Installing the Bottom Moulding

A bottom moulding must be installed around the bottoms on all four sides of the two basic boxes. The following material is required for this moulding:

Four pieces ¾ × 2 × approximately 24 inches

Four pieces ¾ × 2 × approximately 14 inches

The length dimensions are approximate, because the pieces must be long enough to allow for the mitred ends on each piece. When rough-cutting these pieces to length, take this into consideration.

Shaping the Edges Before cutting the pieces to their approximate lengths, shape the edges of the longer pieces with the router, the spindle shaper, or the moulding head in the table saw. The preferred pattern is cut with the Delta cutter 09-136, which has a bead-and-cove profile. This pattern is also available for the Delta moulding head for use on the table saw. If only a router is available, use a Roman ogee cutter. This will produce a nice-looking edge (Illus. 8-23).

Mitring the Pieces After the eight pieces have been cut to the rough lengths required, install them. The upper edge of the bottom moulding should extend beyond the basic box about ⅛ inch (Illus. 8-24).

Start by mitring one end of one of the longer pieces. Be sure to use a well-sharpened saw in the mitre box, an accurately set mitre

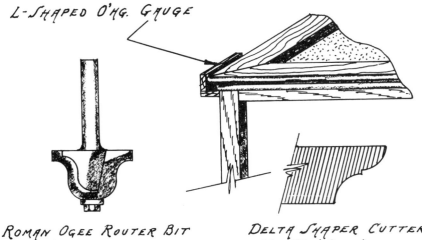

Illus. 8-23. Detail for fabricating and positioning bottom moulding.

L-SHAPED O'HG. GAUGE

ROMAN OGEE ROUTER BIT FOR ALTERNATIVE EDGE.

DELTA SHAPER CUTTER 09-136 (STEEL)

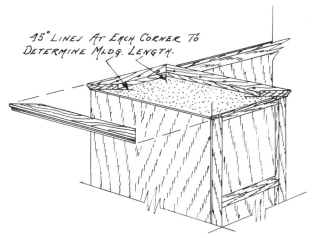

45° LINES AT EACH CORNER TO DETERMINE MLDG. LENGTH.

Illus. 8-24. Installing the four sides of the bottom moulding.

gauge for the table saw, or, best of all, a mitring jig as described in Chapter Six. Using a combination square, draw a 45-degree line exactly through each corner of the bottom. Make a small L-shaped jig from scrap plywood that will determine the amount of overhang (about ⅝ inch) the pieces will have (Illus. 8-23). Place the bottom moulding piece in position, line up the mitred end with the 45-degree pencil line, use the jig to determine the amount of overhang, and tack-nail the first piece to the bottom near both ends.

Next, determine the length of the piece that is near the 45-degree pencil mark at the unmitred end (Illus. 8-24). Transfer this mark to the bottom piece, remove the piece from the bottom, and mitre this end in the opposite direction from the first end. Place the piece back on the bottom, using the same nail holes so that it is positioned exactly where it originally was.

Work around the bottom using the same technique. Do the following: mitre one end, place it in position by lining up the first mitres, use the overhang jig, mark the length by using the 45-degree lines, mitre the opposite end, and return the piece to its original position. Occasionally, you will have to adjust a

mitred joint slightly using the disc sander, but accurate cutting and location of the pieces will result in accurate mitre joints.

After all the pieces are mitred and fit together, glue and screw the bottom mouldings to the desk bottom using glue and 1¼-inch, #8 flathead screws. Place glue in each mitre joint. Then drill holes for one 4d finish nail in the side of each mitre joint and drive the nails in, for additional holding power.

COMPLETING THE DESK

Refer to Chapter Six for information on final completion techniques.

Fabricating and Installing the Desk Base
After selecting the type of base desired for the traditional desk, proceed to make and install the legs as described in Chapter Six. Eight sets of cabriole legs will be needed for this desk, if that is the style selected.

Building the Drawers
The drawers for this desk are lipped drawers. Chapter Seven gives complete instructions for building and installing these drawers and other types of drawer. Remember, it is important to install the drawers in the desk prior to building and installing the top, because access is needed into the interior of the desk.

Fabricating and Installing the Desk Top
The only difference between the desk top and the chest top is that the desk top is finished on all four sides. Machine four panel retaining pieces and then install them by mitring the four corner joints very carefully. Install top-panel support pieces flush with the rabbet in the panel retainers, and then machine and install the ¼-inch plywood top. Install a ¾ × ¾-inch cove moulding beneath the top to create the bead-and-cove effect.

Most of the major building tasks are now completed. All that remains is to fill any imperfections with matching plastic wood, sand the entire project with the finish sander using 220-grit paper, and then proceed to stain and finish the desk following a finishing technique similar to that outlined in Chapter Six.

The final task is to select nice-looking, period-styled drawer pulls and install them on the fronts of the desk drawers.

BUILDING A CONTEMPORARY DESK

The contemporary desk shown in Illus. 8-25 is somewhat easier to build than the traditional desk, but the basic techniques are very similar. There are no cabriole legs or other complicated base structures to contend with, and the top of the contemporary desk is much simpler to build than the inset panelled top of the traditional desk. Many hobbyists prefer to cover the desk top with plastic laminate to secure a top that is fine-looking and durable. The overall size of this desk will be almost identical to the traditional chest presented earlier in this chapter.

BUILDING THE FACE FRAME

Illus. 8-16 depicts the face frame to be used

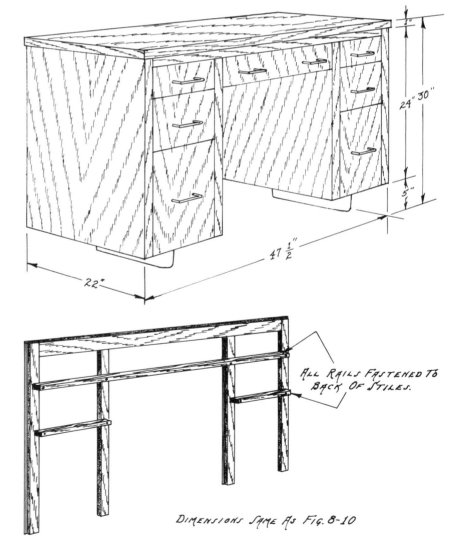

Illus. 8-25. A contemporary desk project.

Illus. 8-26. Rear view of contemporary desk face frame.

ALL RAILS FASTENED TO BACK OF STILES.

DIMENSIONS SAME AS FIG. 8-10

for this desk. Because the desk will have flush drawers, screw and glue the first and second drawer rails to the rear of the stiles rather than notching them flush with the stiles, as was done for the traditional desk. Join the top rail to the two end stiles with screw joints. Also join the two shorter stiles at the kneehole positions with screw joints. Machine $\frac{1}{4} \times \frac{1}{2}$-inch rabbets into the edges of each of the stiles to accept the $\frac{1}{4}$-inch plywood end and the kneehole panels.

Bill of Materials

The four stiles and the top rail should all be made from the cabinet wood selected. The drawer rails, however, may be made from less expensive wood because they will not be seen. The following pieces are needed for the face frame:

End stiles: Two pieces $\frac{3}{4} \times 1\frac{1}{2} \times 24$ inches
Inner stiles: Two pieces $\frac{3}{4} \times 1\frac{1}{2} \times 22$ inches
Top rail: One piece $\frac{3}{4} \times 2 \times 44\frac{1}{2}$ inches
First drawer rail: One piece $\frac{3}{4} \times 1\frac{3}{4} \times 46$ inches
Second drawer rail: Two pieces $\frac{3}{4} \times 1\frac{3}{4} \times 11\frac{1}{4}$ inches

FABRICATING THE BASIC BOXES

After assembling the face frame, use the same techniques as for the traditional desk and proceed to complete the basic boxes of the desk as follows:

1. Cut the bottoms to size and attach these to the face frame.
2. Prepare the back panel by cutting the veneer for veneer joints on each end and gluing the reinforcing strips in place. Attach the back to the subassembly of the face frame and the bottoms.
3. Machine the $\frac{1}{4}$-inch plywood end panels and the kneehole panels to size and install them.

4. Make and install all top-panel reinforcers as well as the three cross-braces that act as top runners for the drawers.

MAKING THE BASE STRUCTURE

Refer to the section in Chapter Six on building the base structure for a contemporary chest, and decide which of the base or leg options will be used for the desk. The techniques and the designs will be similar, only the height of the base will change. The base or legs for the contemporary desk should be $5\frac{1}{4}$ inches high.

FABRICATING AND INSTALLING THE DRAWERS

The drawers for this contemporary desk will be flush drawers that have matching, vertical-grained drawer fronts. Chapter Seven contains all of the required information on building and installing this type of drawer.

Building the Top

Again, refer to Chapter Six and the material on contemporary chest tops to determine what type of top and edging to use on this desk. If a plastic-laminate top is to be used, refer to Chapter Fifteen for techniques for fabricating a furniture top to be covered with laminate.

COMPLETING THE DESK

The finishing procedure for a contemporary desk is the same as for the traditional desk. Sand, fill any defects, and proceed with a good finishing procedure. Finally, select a contemporary-styled drawer pull for installation on all of the drawers.

BUILDING A TRADITIONAL SINGLE-PEDESTAL DESK

A single-pedestal desk that contains just one

row of drawers is another desk that can double as a small dresser. The advantage of this desk is that its drawers can be made somewhat wider than the drawers in a double-pedestal desk. The overall size of this desk is about the same as the other desks presented in this chapter, so it will fit nicely in a student's room. If desired, you can design the drawers to accept file folders or they may be smaller to accommodate other storage.

You do need a turning lathe to fabricate the two end legs on this traditional desk. Also, dowel joints are used to assemble the leg structure to the desk proper. One option for assembling the legs and their stretchers is to counterbore 3-inch screws, and hide their heads with matching wooden buttons. You can also fasten the leg assembly to the desk structure using the same technique. Just be certain that the buttons match the type of wood being used for the desk itself.

BUILDING THE FACE FRAME

Study Illus. 8-28 and 8-29 for the details of the face frame and its assembly. This face frame is constructed in exactly the same way as the face frames for the dressers and desks that have been presented earlier. Machine the rails and stiles to their correct sizes, and then bundle the rails together to do the notching. Cut ¼ × ½-inch rabbets on the stiles. The ¼-inch plywood end panels will later be fit into these rabbets.

Bill of Materials   These are the pieces required for building the face frame:

Left stile: One piece ¾ × 1½ × 24 inches
Right stile: One piece ¾ × 1½ × 22½ inches
Short right stile: One piece ¾ × 1½ × 5¼ inches
Top rail: One piece ¾ × 1½ × 42 inches.
First drawer: One piece ¾ × 1¾ × 43½ inches
Other rails: Three pieces ¾ × 1¾ × 21½ inches
   (If fewer drawers are being built into the desk, fewer rails will be needed.)
Bottom facing strips: One piece ¾ × ¾ × 20 inches

Machining the Face-Frame Pieces
Only the longer left and right stiles will re-

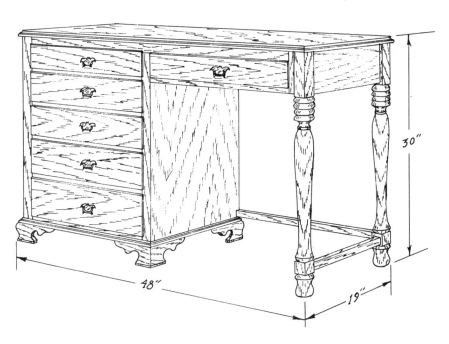

Illus. 8-27. A traditional single-pedestal chest and desk.

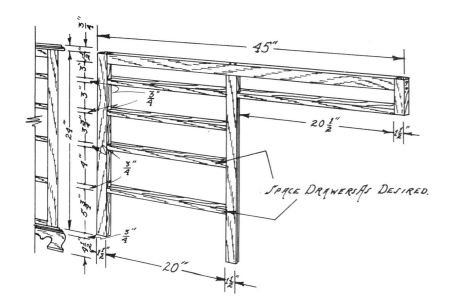

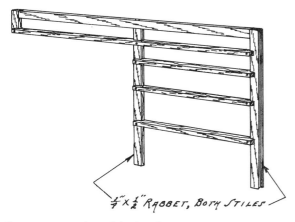

Illus. 8-29. Rear view of the face frame.

quire a ¼ × ½-inch rabbet. Do not rabbet the short stile on its right end, because it butts against the upper portion of the turned leg.

Bundle the rails together by nailing the shorter ones to the first drawer rail, and carefully and clearly mark the notches on the bundle. Notch the first drawer rail so that it fits behind both the left stile and the short right end stile. Notch the rails on the table saw and disassemble the bundle, taking care not to mar the edges that will be visible on the finished desk.

Assembling the Face Frame   Join both

end stiles to the top rail using screw joints and 2½-inch, #8 flathead wood screws and glue. Next, glue and screw the first drawer rail to the rear of the stiles with 1½ inch, #8 flathead screws. Use the proper spacers to position all the rails. Fasten the 22½-inch kneehole stile to the top rail, again using 2½-inch screws and glue. Then install the remaining drawer rails, spacing them as desired. When calculating the drawer space, make allowance for the ¾-inch particle-board bottom.

BUILDING THE BACK

An odd-shaped piece of ¼-inch fir plywood (or other inexpensive ¼-inch material) will be needed for the back. Illus. 8-42 shows the back shape. The section of the back for the chest portion of the desk must be exactly as wide as the face-frame stile rabbets and 24 inches high. The narrow portion of the back that extends to the right must be 5¼ inches high and 22¼ inches long. The back will be approximately 44¾ inches long. Obtain the exact length by measuring the rear of the face frame.

Make reinforcing strips that are ¾ × 1½ inches. Glue and nail these strips to the ply-

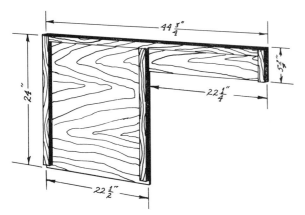

Illus. 8-30. Back panel for the chest and desk.

wood as shown in Illus. 8-30. Be sure to allow ¾ inch for the particle-board bottom.

BUILDING THE BOTTOM

Cut a piece of ¾-inch particle board or ply-wood for the desk bottom that measures approximately 23½ × 18 inches. Remember, the bottom must fit flush with the stile rabbets on the face frame and be 1 inch less than the depth of the desk.

ASSEMBLING THE COMPONENTS

Assemble the face frame, bottom, and back as shown in Illus. 8-31. Use 19-inch scrap support strips to hold the face frame in position when nailing the back to the bottom and when fastening the face frame to the bottom. Install the ¾ × ¾-inch bottom facing strip at this time.

The assembly techniques from here on are identical to those presented for earlier chests and desks. Machine and install the two ¼-inch plywood end panels, and then glue and clamp reinforcing strips across their top edges. Install ¾ × 1½-inch cross-braces from front to back that will also act as upper runners for the drawers.

BUILDING THE BASE

The base structure, consisting of two pairs of rolled-and-coved legs, two single legs, and the bottom moulding, is fabricated in the same manner as was described earlier in Chapter Six. Follow these building and installation instructions, changing only the dimensions if required.

BUILDING THE LEG ASSEMBLY

Set the cabinet structure aside for a while and fabricate the leg structure next. The legs should be turned first. Use either solid-lumber squares or glued-up blocks measuring 2 inches square. Turning instructions are given below:

Turning the Desk Legs Two pieces 2 × 2 × 29¼ inches will be needed for these turned legs. Follow the turning dimensions and details shown in Illus. 8-32 precisely. Lay out the square portions of the legs on the turning squares first, and then mount the leg blank

Illus. 8-31. Assembly of face frame, bottom, and back.

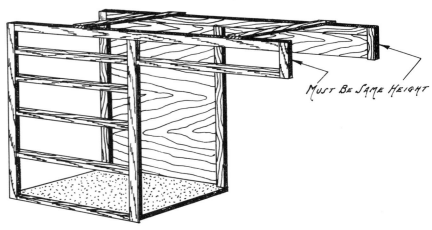

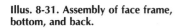

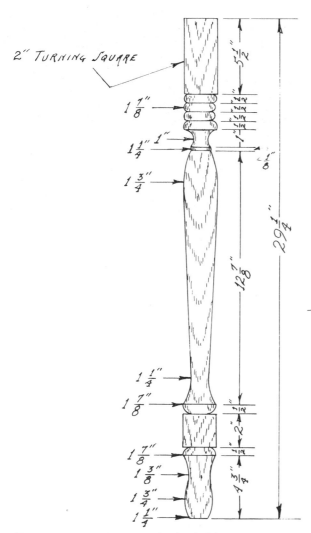

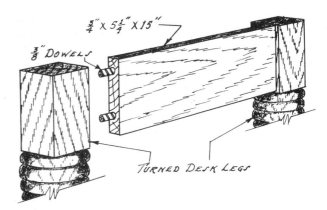

2" TURNING SQUARE

5½"

1 7/8"

1 1/4" 1"

1 3/4"

1/8"

29¼"

12 7/8"

1 1/4"

1 7/8"

2"

1 7/8"
1 3/8"
1 3/4"
1 1/4"

4 3/4"

Illus. 8-32. Turning dimensions for the desk legs.

¾" × 5¼" × 15"

⅜" DOWELS

TURNED DESK LEGS

Illus. 8-33. Detail of the top of the stretcher assembly. (Screws and wooden buttons can also be used for assembly.)

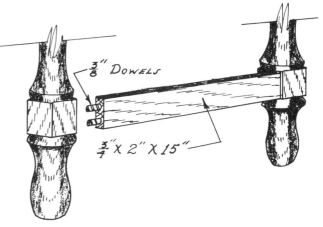

⅜" DOWELS

¾" × 2" × 15"

Illus. 8-34. Lower assembly detail of leg stretcher.

in the lathe. The corners of a square on a turning can sometimes be chipped where they meet with a rounded portion. To prevent this, saw just a short way into each corner with a fine-toothed saw (Illus. 8-33). Use the parting tool to carefully work next to the saw lines. Work the parting tool down until the largest diameter is arrived at and the parting tool is cutting completely around the blank. Rough out the leg blank between the square portions to this largest diameter, 1⅞ inches. Remember, these diameter dimensions can be varied slightly. The squared parts of the legs, however, must be located and followed carefully, because they must match the heights of the

cabinet portion of the desk.

Lay out the length dimensions on the rounded portions of the leg and proceed to turn the leg to the diameters and shapes indicated in Illus. 8-32. Sand the turning using increasingly finer grits of sandpaper, starting with 80-grit and finishing with 220-grit paper.

Now mount the second leg blank in the lathe and duplicate the first. A competent turner can do a respectable job of duplication if he uses his calipers carefully and has a good eye for shape and form.

Preparing the Stretchers

The top stretcher is a piece of ¾-inch lumber or plywood that measures 5½ × 15 inches

(Illus. 8-33). The lower stretcher between the legs (Illus. 8-34) measures ¾ × 2 × 15 inches, and the longer, lower back stretcher measures ¾ × 2 × 23 inches.

Making the Dowel Joints

Machine and sand these stretchers and drill two ⅜-inch holes into each end to receive the dowel pins. Lay out and center these holes precisely with a square and rule. Center-punch the holes to locate the drill point exactly.

If a dowelling jig is available, position it and drill the holes about ½ to ¾ inch deep. The centers for the matching holes on the legs must be located just as precisely. The stretchers are inset on the legs about ⅛ inch from the edge, so take this into consideration when making the layout. This means that the centers will be ½ inch from the edge of the leg, rather than ⅜ inch.

Again, position the dowelling jig on the legs and drill the companion holes with the ⅜-inch drill bit. The dowelling jig cannot be used to drill the holes in the cabinet for the long back stretcher, so locate and drill these holes by eye.

If a dowelling jig is not available, use metal dowel centers to transfer the centers from one piece to another. Simply drill the

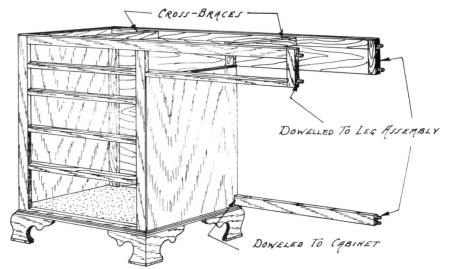

Illus. 8-35. Bottom moulding and legs installed on the basic box.

Illus. 8-36. Details of the top construction.

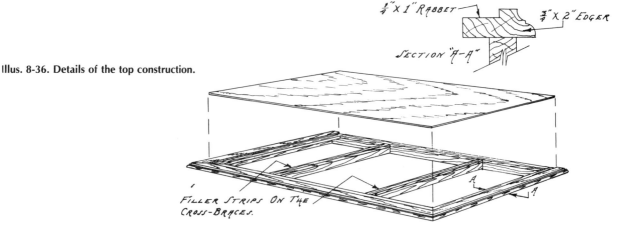

first two holes as accurately and as straight as possible, insert the metal centers, and press the pieces together, transferring the centers. Drill the companion holes, insert the dowel pins, and make a trial assembly. If metal centers are unavailable, drive small brads into the center marks of the holes.

Drilling the holes straight and true is extremely important when making dowel joints. Use a drill press if one is available. Prepare the dowel joints used to attach the legs to the main cabinet at this time.

You can purchase wooden dowels with spiral grooves that allow both air and excess glue to escape from the hole, or cut short dowel pegs from a 3/8-inch dowel rod that is available at any hardware store. If the dowels are cut from a dowel rod, they, too, should be scratched along their lengths several times to allow glue and air to escape.

ASSEMBLING THE LEG STRUCTURE

After the trial assembly is made and the joints all fit satisfactorily, square, glue, and clamp the two legs and their stretchers. Use bar clamps with cushioning material under the jaws so the pieces are not marred. Use epoxy glue. It has a slower setting time that works very well for this assembly and is exceedingly strong. Do not attempt to use the "five-minute" epoxy glue, because this glue does not have enough "open" time before the glue starts to set. Be certain to wipe off any excess glue with lacquer thinner, because it is extremely difficult to remove after it has set. Yellow carpenter's glue will work for this assembly as well.

Attaching the Leg Assembly to the Cabinet
Finally, apply glue and insert the dowel pegs into the holes at the ends of the face frame and the back, as well as those in the back leg for the bottom back stretcher. Then apply glue to the visible dowel pegs and the surface areas to be joined, fit all the assemblage together, and clamp it with long pipe clamps until the glue has set.

BUILDING AND INSTALLING THE DRAWERS

Before installing the top, build and install all of the drawers following the directions presented in Chapter Seven.

FABRICATING AND INSTALLING THE DESK TOP

The top for this single-pedestal desk is different from the framed-and-panelled tops used on previous desks and chests. This top will not have a cove moulding installed beneath it, and will have an overhang of only 1/2 inch. Shape the edge of the top pieces as shown in Illus. 8-36. Use two pieces for the top edging that are 3/4 × 2 × approximately 23 inches, and one piece that is 3/4 × 2 × approximately 50 inches. Run the moulding on the edges before machining the 1/4 × 1-inch rabbet on each piece. Prepare and install filler strips as required, to support the top panel.

Mitre and install the pieces as described previously in this chapter. Screw each piece to the top edges of the desk using 1-inch, #8 flathead wood screws. Place the screws into the rabbeted area so that their heads will be covered by the plywood top panel.

Prepare and install the 1/4-inch plywood top panel also as instructed in Chapter Seven.

Give the desk its final sanding and proceed with the finishing schedule selected. Finally, purchase enough traditional drawer pulls for the number of drawers built, and install these pulls on each drawer to complete this single-pedestal desk.

CHAPTER NINE

Bookcases, China Cabinets and Hutches

Cabinets, hutches, and bookcases with visible interiors can be built using the casework system, although it has to be adapted somewhat. Also, many of these projects have glass-paned doors with which the builder will have to contend. Chapter Eleven deals with cabinet and furniture doors of all types. This chapter contains instructions for building furniture with visible interiors.

VISIBLE-INTERIOR CABINETS

So far only furniture pieces have been presented that have been fit with drawers and/or doors that completely hide the interior of the furniture. This enables the builder to fabricate the sides, bottoms, and tops of ¼-inch plywood of the A-D grade and less expensive material such as particle board, fir, or Lauan plywood. The D side of the plywood, with its knots and blemishes, is not revealed in the finished project. However, in furniture and cabinets designed with open shelves and glass-paned doors, using the visible and blemished

D side of ¼-inch plywood is completely unacceptable.

One of the basic principles of the casework system is the use of a face frame assembled with screws that are hidden by ¼-inch side panels rabbeted into the face-frame stiles. However, ¼-inch hardwood plywood in grade A-2 is not stocked by local lumber dealers, and even wholesalers who supply cabinet shops rarely offer anything but oak and birch in the A-1 grade. One-quarter-inch plywood in the A-2 grade in walnut, cherry, mahogany, and most other species is either not made or not stocked. Because it is extremely difficult to purchase ¼-inch plywood in anything but the A-D grade, in many cases the ¼-inch plywood sides must be abandoned and ¾-inch plywood substituted. If a bookcase, for example, is going to be "built in"—that is, fastened to the wall with neither outside end visible— then ¼-inch A-D plywood can still be used. If, however, the bookcase will be freestanding and the outside ends will be visible, then ¼-inch plywood cannot be used, with the exception of birch or oak, if it is available.

USING ¾-INCH PLYWOOD

Having to use ¾-inch plywood for furniture sides will result in some fabrication problems and, of course, extra cost. The screwed face frame can still be used; this avoids the use of the mortise-and-tenon joint or the dowel joint. Rabbet the ¾-inch plywood edge to match the rabbet in the stile of the face frame (Illus. 9-1). This is not a difficult operation, and will cover the heads of the screws used in the screw joint. Though using ¾-inch plywood will cost more, some material and labor is saved. Reinforcing strips will not be required, as they were for the ¼-inch side and back panels. Also, the furniture back can be rabbeted into the sides (Illus. 9-2).

DESIGNING BOOKCASES

Bookcases can range from relatively simple pieces of furniture to complicated installations that fill an entire wall. They are often combined with other furniture and cabinets, and a bookcase in the hands of today's interior decorators will be put to use displaying all manner of bric-a-brac. Small wonder that homes of today possess several types of freestanding bookcases as well as built-in, library-type shelving to hold and display not only books, but everything from fine china pieces to other assorted collectibles.

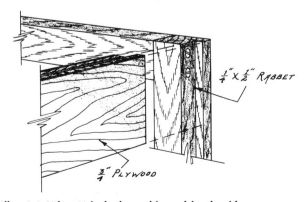

Illus. 9-1. When ¾-inch plywood is used for the sides, a companion rabbet is made to fit the face-frame rabbet.

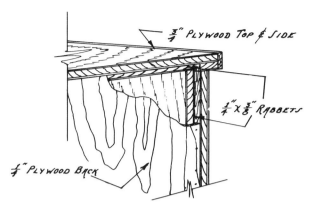

Illus. 9-2. Detail of plywood back installed in ¾-inch side panels.

DEPTH AND LENGTH OF SHELVING

It is recommended that you build bookshelves no less than 10 inches deep and no longer than 32 to 34 inches long. The 10-inch depth will accommodate even large reference books, and the 32- to 34-inch length will hold a reasonably heavy load of books with little danger of sagging. Nothing seems to be more unsightly than a bookcase with 4- or even 5-foot shelves that have sagged under the weight of a full shelf of books.

TYPES OF SHELVING

Should the shelves in a bookcase be permanently fixed or adjustable? Although this can be a matter of personal preference, the adjustable shelf would seem to be the most practical in light of the varied use made of bookshelves in today's homes. The wide variety of inexpensive hardware available for adjusting shelves would also contribute to the practicality of having moveable shelves. Adjustable shelf hardware is available in a metal or plastic shelf standard, or "track," that uses metal clips to support the shelves, as well as in many designs of "pin-style" shelf supports that fit into equally spaced holes in the cabinet sides.

DOES A BOOKCASE REQUIRE A BACK?

In the interests of strength and rigidity, add a back to the freestanding bookcase. A freestanding bookcase that does not have a back and holds a full load of books is always in danger of collapse. However, a built-in bookcase which has the walls for support often does not have a back installed. Instead, the decorator will paint or wallpaper the back wall to match the decor of the room.

DOES A BOOKCASE REQUIRE A FACE FRAME?

The inexpensive bookcases found in discount stores all lack face frames. However, the wall units manufactured by the leading furniture builders all seem to possess face frames. No doubt, the face frame adds a certain amount of strength and rigidity to the sides of the structure, but it also adds additional cost.

The face frame can be used to add decor to the bookcase when flute or beads are added to its stiles, the base is adorned with a "plinth," and the top is given traditional-styled mouldings. If a face frame is not used, the sides must be edge-banded (unless solid lumber is used). This is a time-consuming job for the amateur woodworker. Whether a face frame is built or not is determined by the machinery available, the skill level of the woodworker, and the use that is to be made of the finished product.

BUILDING THE FREESTANDING BOOKCASE

Illus. 9-3 and 9-4 show two basic freestanding bookcases. The width and height of a case is a matter of available space and personal preference, but the depth should be about 10 inches. Bookcases over 34 to 36 inches long are built in multiples of 30 to 36 inches. For example, a bookcase that is designed 60 inches long should have a divider in the middle so the shelves remain at the 30-inch length. A bookcase 48 inches long will have a divider placed in its middle, even though the shelves will now be less than 24 inches long. Sometimes it is possible to eliminate the middle divider by using extra shelf supports on the rear of the center face-frame stile and in the middle of the back panel. However, the principle remains the same insofar as the length of the shelf is concerned. They are either made 30 to 34 inches long or they must be supported at those intervals.

BUILDING A FACE-FRAMED BOOKCASE

Following are instructions for building the face-framed bookcase shown in Illus. 9-3. Although this bookcase is 60 inches long, it can be easily adapted to any desired length as long as the 30- to 34-inch intervals are observed. So can its height. The building directions remain the same, and the overall dimensions can easily be adapted to meet the requirements of the builder.

Bill of Materials   The directions that follow are for building the case from ¾-inch plywood or veneered particle board. If solid lumber is to be used, the shelves and top will not have to be edge-banded. If you use lumber, you will also probably have to glue up panels from narrower pieces to meet the 10-inch width requirement of most of the pieces. Blemish-free lumber in 10-inch widths is expensive and often difficult to find at the local lumberyard. For these reasons, the use of plywood is recommended.

As usual, start building this bookcase by making the face frame. Where a length measurement is given as approximate, cut that piece about ¼ to ½ inch longer than the di-

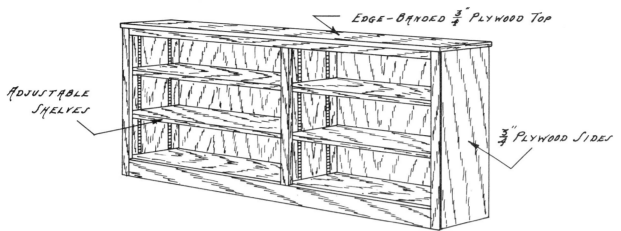

Illus. 9-3. A face-framed freestanding bookcase.

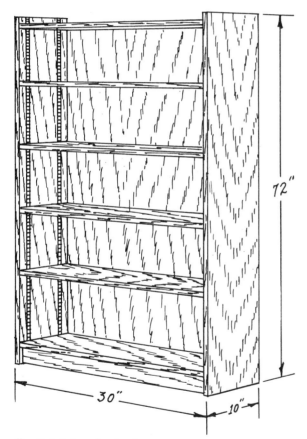

Illus. 9-4. A frameless bookcase.

mension listed. Take the actual measurement off the bookcase as assembly proceeds.

Face Frame (solid lumber)

End stiles: Two pieces ¾ × 2 × 29¼ inches

Center stile: One piece ¾ × 2 × approximately 23¼ inches

Top rail: One piece ¾ × 2 × 56 inches

Bottom rail: One piece ¾ × 3 × 56 inches

Ends, Divider, Bottom, and Top (¾-inch plywood)

Ends: Two pieces ¾ × 9¾ × 29¼ inches

Center divider: One piece ¾ × 8¾ × 23¼ inches

Bottom: One piece ¾ × 8¾ × approximately 59¼ inches

(Note: The bottom should be 59¼ inches long if rabbeted into the sides. If it will be butted to the ends, it should be 58½ inches long.)

Top: One piece ¾ × 10¼ × 60½ inches (The top will be edge-banded with ¼-inch strips on front and both ends, for an overall size of 10½ × 61 inches.)

Back

Two pieces ¼-inch plywood approximately 29¼ × 29⅝ inches (The back pieces will be spliced on the center divider. Measure the exact fit after assembly.)

Shelves

Four pieces ¾ × 8¾ × approximately 28⅞ inches (The length of the shelves is approximate and will depend upon whether a shelf support is used and, if it is, its type. A ¼-inch edge-banding will be applied to the shelves' front edges.)

Machining and Assembling the Face Frame

After the pieces listed above are machined to their correct sizes, rabbet the two end stiles. As shown in Illus. 9-5, the rabbets are ¼ × ½ inch. Assemble the face frame with screw joints, as described in Chapter 6. Fasten both the top rail and the bottom rail with glue and 2½-inch, #8 flathead wood screws. Make sure that the frame is square when completed. This is usually no problem if the ends of the rails have been sawed perfectly square and if the screws have been pulled up tightly.

Next, locate and mark the position for the center stile. Remember, this piece was cut to its approximate length, so now measure on the partially assembled face frame to obtain its exact length. Hold it in position by using C-clamps and blocks of scrap wood. Assemble the top joint by counterboring two ½-inch holes about ½ inch deep and driving two 2½-inch, #8 screws into the joint. Assemble the lower joint by counterboring two ½-inch holes

about 1½ inches deep and driving 3- or 3½-inch screws into the joint (Illus. 9-5).

Machining the Ends, Bottom, and Center Divider

Start by running out the two end pieces, which are the same width, and then ripping the bottom and the center divider, which are also the same width. Finally, rip the top to its correct width. Cut all pieces to their correct lengths on the table saw.

Note: When plywood is crosscut on the table saw, the veneer next to the cut edge often splinters. This can be prevented by scoring the veneer with a sharp knife next to where the saw cut will be made. Some craftspersons apply masking tape over the veneer and along the path of the saw blade, but scoring seems to work better. A sharp, smooth-cutting saw blade is essential for crosscutting plywood.

Several operations must be performed on the end pieces before the bookcase can be assembled. Be sure to plan for a right and left end.

1. A matching tongue must be machined on the front edge of the end panels

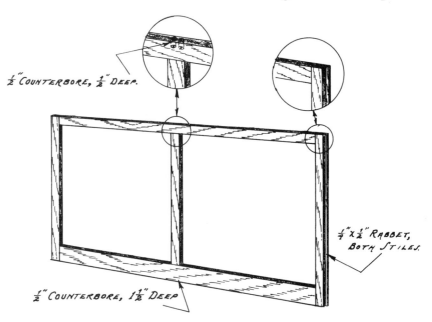

Illus. 9-5. Details of the face frame used on a face-framed bookcase.

½" COUNTERBORE, ½" DEEP.

¼" × ½" RABBET, BOTH STILES.

½" COUNTERBORE, 1½" DEEP

that will fit into the rabbets on the face-frame stiles. Do this by machining a ½ × ½-inch rabbet on the inside edge of the panel. Use scrap plywood to run test rabbets before actually running the rabbet on the end pieces. Joint a 5-degree bevel along the edge that fits into the face frame (Illus. 9-6).

2. Machine a ¼ × ⅜-inch rabbet along the rear edge of the end pieces to receive the ¼-inch plywood back.

3. Machine a ¾ × ⅜-inch dado to receive the bookcase bottom, as shown in Illus. 9-6. Remember, plan for a left and right end. The top edge of the dado must be exactly 3 inches from the bottom, to match the top edge of the bottom rail.

4. If shelf standard is going to be used, machine grooves into the side pieces and the center divider to receive this track. The shelf track may simply be nailed to the surface of the plywood if desired, but it looks much better if rabbeted. If pin shelf supports are to be used, drill the holes for these at this time. A drilling jig for making equally spaced holes is shown in Illus. 9-7.

Machining the Top Panel A rabbet must be machined along the rear edge of the top to receive the plywood back. This rabbet should be ¼ × ⅜ inch and should be machined at the same time the end panels are rabbeted for the back. This rabbet can be run along the full length of the back edge, because it will not be visible after the edge-banding is applied to the top.

Also edge-band the top panel, the front edge, and the two ends at this time. Following are instructions for effectively preparing and applying solid-wood edge-banding. Of course, a veneer edge-banding such as Plyedge or Edgemate may be used, but solid-wood edging is much more durable.

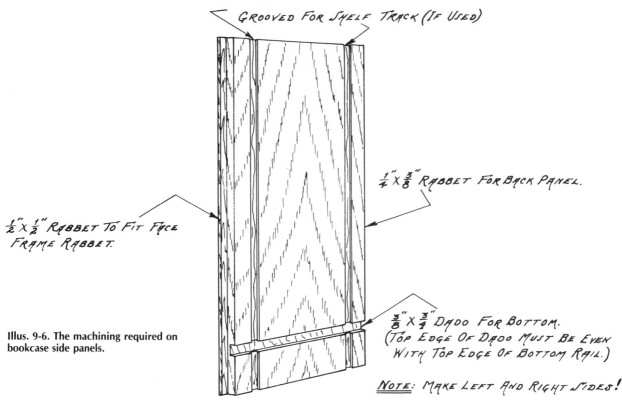

GROOVED FOR SHELF TRACK (IF USED)

½" X ¾" RABBET FOR BACK PANEL.

½" X ½" RABBET TO FIT FACE FRAME RABBET.

⅜" X ¾" DADO FOR BOTTOM. (TOP EDGE OF DADO MUST BE EVEN WITH TOP EDGE OF BOTTOM RAIL.)

NOTE: MAKE LEFT AND RIGHT SIDES!

Illus. 9-6. The machining required on bookcase side panels.

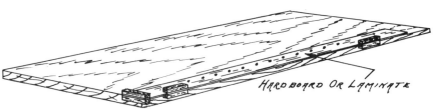

Illus. 9-7. A shop-made spacing jig for adjustable shelf pins.

HARDBOARD OR LAMINATE

FLIP JIG OVER TO DRILL OTHER EDGE

1. Joint the edge of the board from which the ¼-inch strip will be ripped. Rip this strip from the board, but do not joint the opposite side.

2. Apply the short pieces to the ends first by mitring one end and gluing and nailing the piece in place with ¾-inch brads that have predrilled holes to prevent splitting (Illus. 9-8). Place the smooth side against the plywood edge. Set the nails rather deep, fill the resulting holes with matching plastic wood, and let it dry thoroughly. Then smooth these rough edges on the jointer or, if the piece is too long for this, use a hand plane or even the belt sander. Fit and mitre the ends of the front strip and apply it in the same manner. Fill all holes and any opening in the joints and seams with matching plastic wood and then scrape, sand, and plane all edges flush and even.

Assembling the Bookcase
Sand the various pieces with the finish sander prior to assembly because it is often difficult to sand on the interior of the bookcase.

Start the assembly by gluing and nailing the sides to the face frame with 1-inch brads. Pull the tongue of the side pieces tightly against the rabbet in the face frame (Illus. 9-9). Next, measure the exact length of the bottom from dado to dado and cut the bottom panel to this length. Apply glue and slip the bottom into position. Nail the bottom in place by driving 6d finish nails through the sides into the ends of the bottom. Nail the face frame to the bottom with 4d finish nails. Measure the exact height of the center divider, cut it to length, and glue and nail it in position by nailing it through the bottom and nailing the face frame to it (Illus. 9-10).

Simply nail the top in place or screw it in position by using cleats and 1¼-inch, #8 flat-head wood screws from underneath (Illus. 9-11).

Finally, fit the back plywood panels in place and glue and nail them in position using 1-inch nails or brads. The grain of the back panels should run vertically. This will make it necessary to splice the two pieces on the center divider, as shown in Illus. 9-11.

Preparing the Shelves
Cut the shelves to their proper length, allowing some space for easy installation. Edge-band the front edge of all shelves using the techniques described previously. Then fill and sand them so they are ready for finishing.

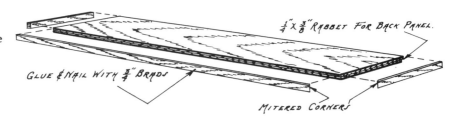

Illus. 9-8. Edge-banding the bookcase top.

¼"x⅜" RABBET FOR BACK PANEL.

GLUE & NAIL WITH ¾" BRADS

MITERED CORNERS

Illus. 9-9. Installation of bookcase bottom.

GLUE & NAIL IN RABBET WITH ¾" BRADS

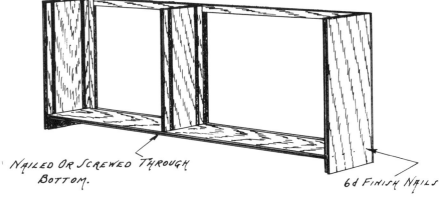

Illus. 9-10. Installation of bookcase divider.

NAILED OR SCREWED THROUGH BOTTOM.

6d FINISH NAILS

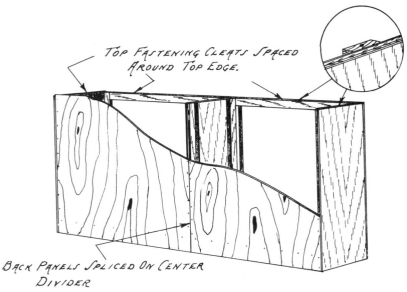

TOP FASTENING CLEATS SPACED AROUND TOP EDGE.

Illus. 9-11. Installation of back panels and cleats for fastening the top.

BACK PANELS SPLICED ON CENTER DIVIDER

Completing the Bookcase Carefully sand the entire structure, filling any flaws, nail holes, etc., to prepare the bookcase for finishing. Then proceed with your favorite finishing schedule. Finally, install the shelf track or shelf pins, and place the shelves in position.

BUILDING A FRAMELESS BOOKCASE

A simpler but serviceable bookcase can be built with no face frame. However, unless lumber is used, more edge-banding will have to be done to mask the raw edges of the plywood or particle board. Illus. 9-4 shows a typical frameless bookcase. The shelves in this type of bookcase should be adjustable, but can be permanently dadoed into the sides if desired.

Bill of Materials
The size of this bookcase can easily be adjusted to meet the individual's needs, but the bill of materials presented is for the bookcase shown in Illus. 9-4.

Sides (plywood or veneered particle board)
Two pieces ¾ × 9¾ × 71¾ inches
Top and Bottom (same material)
Top: One piece ¾ × 9¾ × 29¼ inches
Bottom: One piece ¾ × 9½ × 29¼ inches
Kicker or Bottom Filler (plywood or particle board)
One piece ¾ × 3 × 28½ inches

Shelves (plywood or particle board)
Four pieces ¾ × 9½ × approximately 28½ inches
Lumber
One 1 × 4 piece that's 8 feet long (Species to match plywood used.)

Machining the Bookcase Pieces
After the above required pieces are run out and jointed to the net dimensions listed, some machining will be needed before assembly.

Machining the Sides
Illus. 9-12 shows the machining that needs to be performed on the two side pieces. Dadoes will be needed for the top and bottom (and the shelves if they are to be permanently installed), and grooves or holes will be required for the adjustable shelf hardware of choice. The dadoes for the top and bottom must be chiselled flat and square near the end of the dado. If the dadoes are being made on the table saw, a "stop" dado must be made. A stop dado will stop short of the full width of the top and bottom pieces. Notch these two pieces to fit into the dadoes, and cover the end of the slot (Illus. 9-13). If the dadoes are made with the router, only the corners left rounded by the router cutter will have to be chiselled square.

The grooves for the shelf standard can also be made on the table saw with the dado set. If support pins are being used to support the shelves, use a drilling jig as shown in Illus. 9-7 to drill on these longer side pieces. Machine a ¼ × ⅜-inch rabbet along the back edges of the side pieces to receive the ¼-inch plywood back panel.

Edge-band the front and top edges of the sides with ¼ × ¾-inch lumber strips. This technique is described earlier in the chapter.

Machining the Top and Bottom Pieces
Machine a ¼ × ⅜-inch rabbet along the rear edge of the top member, to receive the back

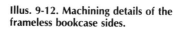
Illus. 9-12. Machining details of the frameless bookcase sides.

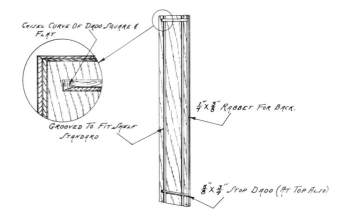

panel. This will not be necessary on the bottom because the panel is simply nailed to the back edge. Attach lumber strips to the edges of both pieces. Cut notches at the front corners of both pieces as shown in Illus. 9-13 so they will fit into and cover the dado.

Machining the Shelves Edge-band the four shelves (or more, if desired) and then cut them to their final lengths, so they can slip easily into position on the shelf supports. Sand all the pieces carefully with the finish sander prior to assembly. Use 220-grit paper for the final sanding.

Assembling the Bookcase Begin assembly by making a trial fit of the top and bottom in their respective dadoes. If they fit properly, either glue and nail or glue and clamp the two sides and the top and bottom together using bar clamps with cushions under the jaws to protect the veneer. If you are nailing the sides together, use 6d finish nails. Then set them and fill the holes with matching plastic wood. Check everything with the framing square, and nail temporary braces across

two of the corners to hold the bookcase in this position (Illus. 9-14).

Install the kicker piece by gluing and nailing it in position under the bottom and between the two sides. Install this piece about ½ inch to the rear of the front edges of the sides and bottom.

Check the exact dimensions of the back panel, saw it to size, and glue and nail it in place using 1-inch nails.

Completing the Bookcase

Look over the entire structure, filling any set nail holes, scraping away glue spots or blemishes, and give a final sanding to the bookcase. Remove any surplus glue or glue smudges. If stain is applied to areas with glue on them, it will not penetrate and these areas will appear as very unsightly light spots. Proceed with a good finishing schedule to complete the project.

BUILDING AN OPEN-SHELF BOOKCASE "UNIT"

Bookcases are often built in units 30 to 36 inches wide that are butted together to fill, or

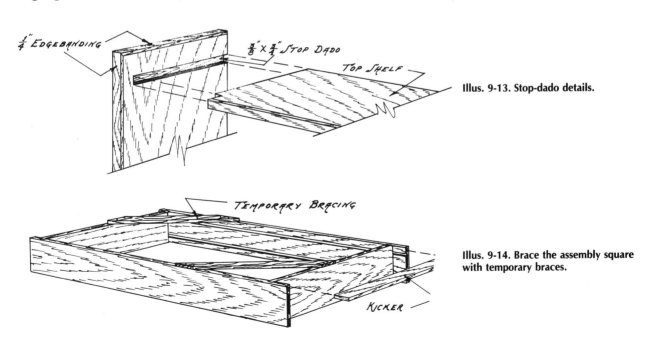

Illus. 9-13. Stop-dado details.

Illus. 9-14. Brace the assembly square with temporary braces.

nearly fill, a wall. Some of these units may be all shelving. Others may have doors mounted on the lower portion of the unit. Illus. 9-15 and 9-16 show the two designs that are used in combination with each other. For example, a wall-installed bookcase might have three units: two units with shelving only and one unit between them with lower doors (Illus. 9-17). This makes a very striking wall of cabinets, especially when built from a beautiful species of wood such as cherry, walnut, or oak.

Face-Frame Bill of Materials

The unit shown in Illus. 9-15 is not difficult to build. Begin construction with the fabrication of the face frame. These are the pieces needed for the face frame:

Stiles: Two pieces ¾ × 2 × 80 inches

Bottom rail: One piece ¾ × 4 × 30 inches
Top rail: One piece ¾ × 11 × 30 inches

Machining the Face Frame

As usual, the two stiles must be rabbeted to accept the ¾-inch plywood side panels. These rabbets measure ¼ × ½ inch.

Lay out the wide decorative top rail using the dimensions given in Illus. 9-18. Make the top rail layout on a large piece of cardboard, or similar material. Cut out this pattern carefully and use it to transfer the design to the wood. Using the sabre saw or band saw, cut the top rail to shape and sand the curved edge clean of saw marks before assembling the face frame.

Assembling the Face Frame

Assemble all the face-frame components using 2½-inch, #8 flathead wood screws and glue to hold the

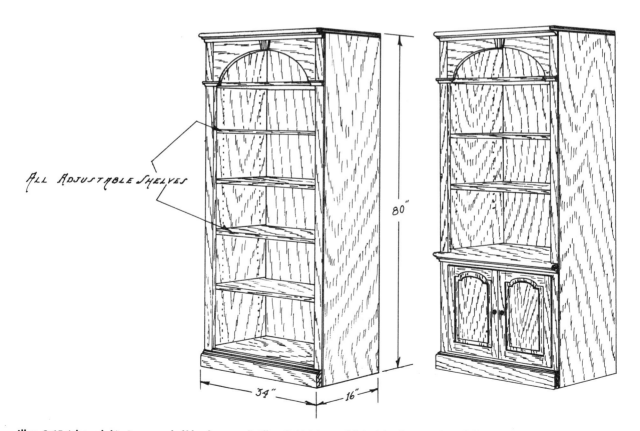

Illus. 9-15 (above left). An open-shelf bookcase unit. Illus. 9-16 (above right). A bookcase unit with lower doors.

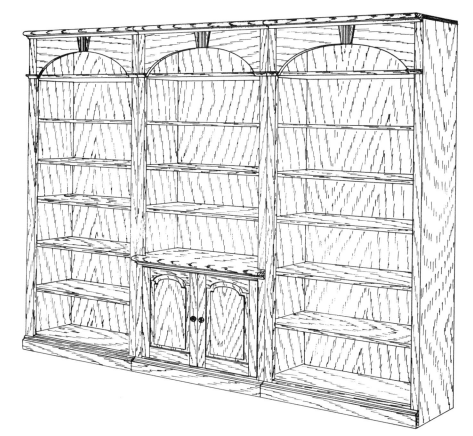

Illus. 9-17. Sectional bookcases can fill an entire wall.

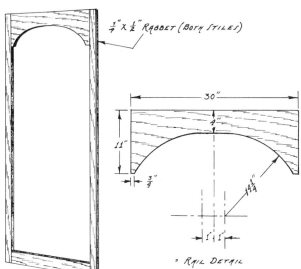

¼" × ½" RABBET (BOTH STILES)

30"

11"

4"

¾"

14½"

1½"

RAIL DETAIL

Illus. 9-18. Face-frame details for the open-shelf unit.

Machining the Top, Bottom, Sides, and Back

Use ¾-inch plywood, grade A2, with either veneer or particle core for the top, bottom, and sides. The back panel will require a piece of ¼-inch plywood, grade A-D.

Sides

Sides: Two pieces ¾ × 15¾ × 80 inches

Top: One piece ¾ × 16 × 34 inches

Bottom: One piece ¾ × 15 × approximately 33¼ inches

The bookcase sides for the smaller bookcase shown in Illus. 9-6 will require the exact same machining as the side pieces. The following dadoes and rabbets are needed:

1. A rabbet ½ × ½ inch along the front edge to fit into the rabbet of the face-frame stiles. Joint a 5-degree bevel along the front edge, so that this edge fits tightly against the face-frame rabbet.

pieces in the wood vise, as described previously. Check the face frame to be certain the assembly is square.

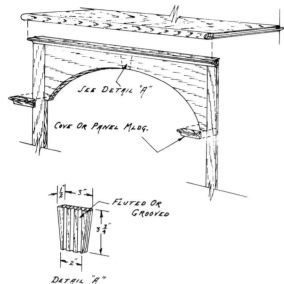

Illus. 9-19. Top and upper rail details for both units.

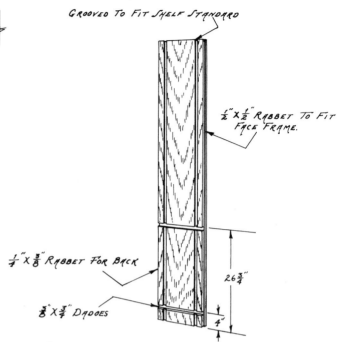

Illus. 9-21. Machining requirements for the sides of the lower door unit.

2. A $\frac{3}{8} \times \frac{3}{4}$-inch dado to accommodate the bottom panel. The top edge of this dado must be even with the top edge of the bottom rail of the face frame.
3. A $\frac{1}{4} \times \frac{3}{8}$-inch rabbet along the back edge to accommodate the $\frac{1}{4}$-inch plywood back panel
4. Two grooves into which the shelf standards will fit or, if shelf support pins are to be used, a series of holes drilled to accommodate the pins

The top panel must have a nosing glued to its front edge that measures $\frac{3}{4} \times 2\frac{1}{4} \times 34$ inches. Glue this piece in position and then shape it with the router after the glue has set. A simple $\frac{1}{2}$-round shape should be routed along this front edge. The top panel is the same 34-inch width as the bookcase proper. This means that the inner cores of the plywood top panel will be visible in the finished bookcase. Of course, if several units are butted together, only the end units will be visible. If this is objectionable, cut the top panel shorter and edge-band the exposed edge

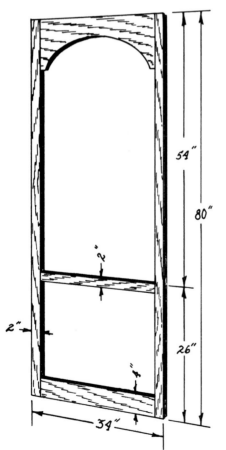

Illus. 9-20. Face-frame details for the bookcase with lower doors.

(or edges) to cover the unsightly inner core of the plywood.

Machine a ¼ × ⅜-inch rabbet along the back edge of the top panel to receive the bookcase back.

Other than machining the piece to exact size, no further work is needed on the bottom panel.

Machining the Decorative Pieces

These bookcase units have several decorative pieces. These pieces have to be machined and applied carefully to the face frame.

Cove Moulding About 4 feet of ¾ × ¾-inch cove moulding will be needed for installation under the front edge of the bookcase top and for the two short decorative pieces installed at the curved ends of the top rail (Illus. 9-19). Hopefully, this can be purchased from the local building supply dealer in the species required. If not, fabricate a satisfactory cove moulding using the router or the wood shaper, if one is available. You can use a small panel moulding in place of the cove for the decorative pieces at the ends of the top rail.

Bottom Decorative Facing Piece This piece is simply a ¾ × 3½ × 34-inch piece of lumber that has its top edge machined with a decorative shape. This may be a cove and bead shape or a Roman ogee shape, depending on which cutters are available for the router or shaper (Illus. 9-22). The shelf nosing, the cove moulding under the nosing, and the bottom decorative piece are all cut to length flush with the sides of the bookcase. This gives the entire assembly an unbroken look when the bookcases are butted together along the wall.

Small Finial This piece fits at the peak of the curve of the top rail. Cut it to an exact fit after positioning the cove moulding under the front edge of the top. The finial should measure about ½ × 3 × 3¾ inches, and is depicted in Detail A in Illus. 9-19. Do the grooving or fluting before tapering the sides, for ease in handling this small piece. It is also easier and safer to do this machining on a slightly longer piece. Cut this longer piece to its exact length and taper its sides after completing the fluting or grooving.

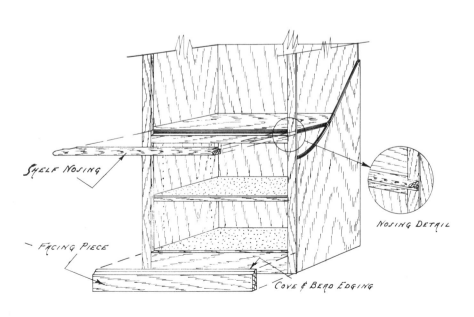

Illus. 9-22. Base and shelf detail for the lower door unit.

Assembling the Unit Bookcase Begin assembly by attaching the sides to the face frame using ¾- or 1-inch brads and glue. Cut the bottom panel to its exact length, so that it slides into its dadoes. Then glue and nail it in position. Next, nail the top in place. Finally, cut the ¼-inch plywood back panel to size, and glue and nail it in place in its rabbets along the rear edge of the sides and top.

Fill all set nail holes and any minor openings in the joints with matching plastic wood. Carefully belt-sand the face frame, and scrape and sand all excess plastic wood from the filled spots. Then sand with 150-grit sandpaper in the finish sander, and do final sanding with 220-grit paper. Apply the decorative pieces to the face frame by gluing and clamping them in place. Fasten the bottom decorative pieces to the bottom rail of the face frame by gluing and driving screws through the rear of the bottom rail.

Fabricating the Shelves Determine the number of shelves desired and rip these from ¾-inch plywood or veneered particle board. These pieces should measure ¾ × 14¾ × approximately 32½ inches. Apply ¼-inch lumber edge-banding to the front edge of each shelf, and sand the edge-banding free of machining marks and plastic wood. The ¼-inch edging brings the width of the shelves to the required 15 inches. Test-fit the shelves in the bookcase and joint or saw them to a loose fit as they rest upon the adjustable shelf supports.

BUILDING A BOOKCASE UNIT WITH LOWER DOORS

The unit pictured in Illus. 9-16 is built almost identical to the open-shelf unit. The only differences are the addition of a crossrail to the face frame, the permanent shelf that serves as a top to the lower section with doors, and the particle board that is used for the bottom and shelf in the lower section.

Building the Face Frame Illus. 9-20 shows the face-frame dimensions and the location of the top rail of the lower section. Although this rail is measured 26 inches from the bottom, it certainly may be adjusted slightly, according to the builder's desires. Other than the addition of this rail, proceed to fabricate the face frame exactly as was done for the open-shelf unit.

Fabricating and Machining the Sides The overall size of the side panels is the same as described for the open-shelf unit. The machining, too, is identical, with the exception of the additional dado needed for the top of the lower section. The top edge of this dado must be exactly ¾ inch *above* the top edge of the crossrail (Illus. 9-21). This allows room for a lumber nosing that will be applied to the front edge of the top panel for the lower section (Illus. 9-22).

Making the Top, Bottom, and Doored-Section Top The top of this bookcase is identical in size and machining requirements to the top of the open-shelf unit. However, the bottom, although identical in size to the bottom of the open-shelf unit, is made of particle board. The top of the doored section is exactly the same size as the bottom, but is made from the same material as the side panels.

Fabricating the Shelf Nosing This piece must be made from lumber, and will measure ¾ × 2¼ × 34 inches. Round the front edge to a half-round shape using the router or shaper. Carefully notch this nosing piece to fit between the stiles of the face frame and against the top of the lower section. The horn ends of the nosing should be flush with the sides of the bookcase, as shown in the detail drawing in Illus. 9-22. Glue the nosing in place using bar clamps. Do this after installing the top of the lower section, but *before* nailing the back panel in place.

Decorative Pieces　All of the decorative pieces are identical to the pieces used on the open-shelf unit and should be installed in the same manner.

Assembling the Unit　After machining all the major components to size, proceed to assemble the bookcase using these steps:

1. Attach the two side panels to the face frame.
2. Determine the exact length of the bottom and permanent shelves, slip these shelves into their respective dadoes, and nail and glue them in place.
3. Nail the top in place.
4. Cut the permanent shelf nosing to fit in place, and glue and clamp it to the shelf using bar clamps.
5. Cut the back panel to size, and glue and nail it in position.

Fill all set nail holes and any flaws in the joints with matching plastic wood. Belt-sand the face frame, and then finish-sand it. Scrape and sand all excess plastic wood from the nail holes and finish-sand the entire structure. Fabricate the decorative pieces and attach these pieces to the face frame, using the same techniques as were performed on the open-shelf unit. Finally, make all of the shelves, including the particle-board shelf for the lower section. Edge-band all shelves, sand them with the finish sander, and cut them to a loose fit on the shelf supports.

Making the Doors for the Lower Section　Refer to the following chapter, Chapter Ten, which contains complete direc-

tions for the building and installation of nearly all types of furniture and cabinet doors.

CHINA CABINETS AND HUTCHES

Another rather ambitious project for the home woodworker is the building of a china cabinet or hutch. The china cabinet and hutch are treated as one project because a hutch is simply a china cabinet that has no glass-paned doors. These units are built in a variety of styles, but the traditional or period-styled pieces seem to be the most popular. Here design principles will be presented for china cabinets, and full directions and plans will be given for building both types of units.

DESIGNING A CHINA CABINET OR HUTCH

A china cabinet or hutch can be built as one complete cabinet or, more commonly, in two separate pieces with the top piece resting on or fastened to the bottom cabinet. Several traditional china cabinet tops and bottoms are shown in Illus. 9-23. Upper and lower units for a hutch are shown in Illus. 9-24. The units on commercially manufactured china cabinets vary considerably in size. Some are built as long as 75 inches. The length of the project is of less importance to the craftsperson than are the other dimensions, because the builder will usually construct the unit to fit an available space in the home.

Typically, the base units (or buffets as they are called) are built 30 to 33 inches high and 19 to 20½ inches deep. Again, the height will vary, and some base units will be designed as high as 34½ inches. Be aware that the height of the base unit is closely related to the overall height of the combined upper and lower units, which should probably fall somewhere between 72 and 80 inches. The height of the usual interior door of a home is 80 inches, so a hutch is rarely built higher than this.

The upper units of both the china cabinet and the hutch will be 43 to 47 inches high. Thus, the designer and builder will simply have to decide on the overall height of the project by determining the desired height of the lower unit and matching an upper unit with it to secure the combined total height. The upper unit should be designed to be 12 to 13½ inches deep. Sometimes a foot is designed at the base of the upper unit on some china cabinets and hutches. This foot will of-

ten be 15 inches deep. However, the main portion or enclosed part of the unit will be 12 to 13½ inches deep. Study Illus. 9-23 and 9-24 carefully to become familiar with the variations in design and sizes.

EARLY AMERICAN OR COUNTRY-STYLE CHINA CABINET

The china cabinet pictured in Illus. 9-25 is a small but nicely proportioned piece that was designed and built to fit a particular small space in the author's summer home. It is a painted unit because it had to conform to the decor of the summer place and because the author salvaged a great amount of veneered

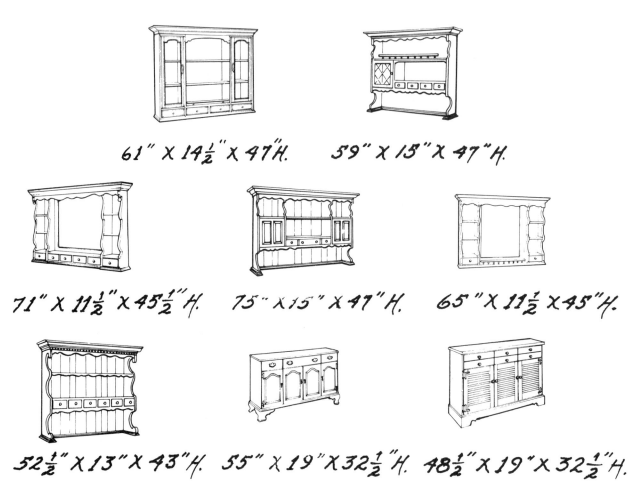

Illus. 9-23. Upper and lower units that can be found on hutches. (Drawing courtesy of Ethan Allen, Inc.)

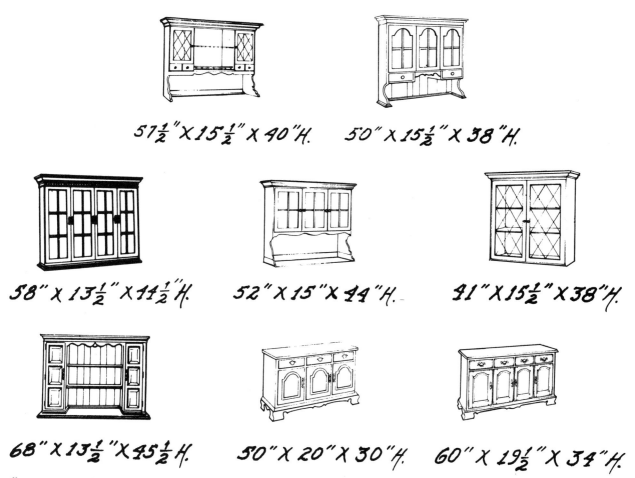

$57\frac{1}{2}'' \times 15\frac{1}{2}'' \times 40''H.$ $50'' \times 15\frac{1}{2}'' \times 38''H.$

$58'' \times 13\frac{1}{2}'' \times 44\frac{1}{2}''H.$ $52'' \times 15'' \times 44''H.$ $41'' \times 15\frac{1}{2}'' \times 38''H.$

$68'' \times 13\frac{1}{2}'' \times 45\frac{1}{2}''H.$ $50'' \times 20'' \times 30''H.$ $60'' \times 19\frac{1}{2}'' \times 34''H.$

Illus. 9-24. Examples of upper and lower units on china cabinets. (Drawing Courtesy of Ethan Allen, Inc.)

particle board from a local bank remodelling project! One long drawer (rather than two smaller drawers) was designed for this cabinet because a place was needed to store table linens near the eating area. It was built in two pieces. The upper section was fastened to the lower unit by screws through the back panel, which extends down ¾ inch behind the top of the lower section. (Fastening the two pieces is really not necessary, because the upper cabinets on most commercial cabinets simply rest upon the lower unit.)

Building the Lower Unit

The base unit of a china cabinet or hutch is almost identical in construction to a chest of drawers. This is typical casework cabinetry, and is covered in Chapter Six in great detail. If building a china cabinet is your first attempt at casework construction, study all of the pertinent information in Chapter Six very carefully because it will not be repeated in this chapter.

Illus. 9-25 presents the overall dimensions of the combined units and the sizes of the individual upper and lower units.

Face Frame for the Basic Box Illus.
9-26 gives the dimensions of the basic box. After the dimensions for the height of the legs, the bottom moulding, and the top are subtracted, the basic box measures 27½ inches

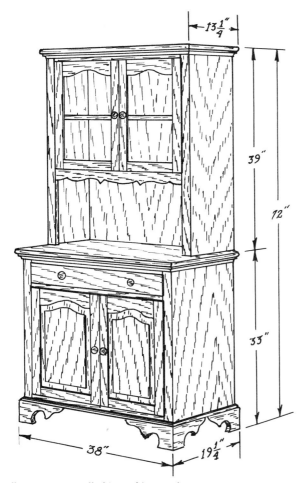

Illus. 9-25. A small china cabinet project.

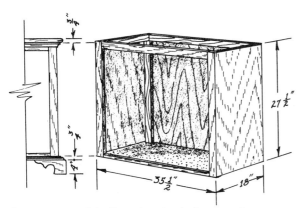

Illus. 9-26. Basic-box dimensions for the lower section.

high by 35½ inches long by 18 inches deep. As is usual in the casework system, the construction begins with the face frame, as shown

in Illus. 9-27. The craftsperson will have to decide if one drawer or two will be built into the cabinet. These are the pieces required for the face frame:

Stiles: Two pieces ¾ × 1¾ × 27½ inches
Top rail: One piece ¾ × 2 × 32 inches
First drawer rail: One piece ¾ × 1¾ × 33½ inches
Drawer divider stile (if desired): One piece ¾ × 2 × 4½ inches
Bottom facing strip: One piece ¾ × ¾ × 32 inches

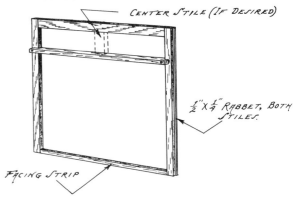

Illus. 9-27. Face-frame detail for the base.

Face Frame for the Upper Unit To save time and machine setups, build the face frame for the upper unit at the same time as the face frame for the basic box. Illus. 9-28 shows this face frame. The following pieces are required:

Stiles: Two pieces ¾ × 1¾ × 38¼ inches
Top rail: One piece ¾ × 2 × 32 inches
Decorative lower crossrail: One piece ¾ × 2½ × 32 inches

Run out the required pieces for both face frames from the type of wood desired. Lay out and cut the decorative pattern on the lower crossrail. Sand the edges and then run ¼ × ½-inch rabbets along the outer edges of the four stiles of both of the face frames. Assemble both face frames using screw joints as learned in Chapter Six.

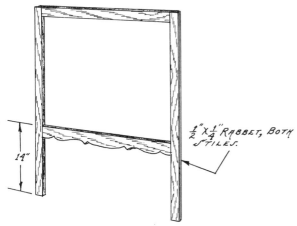
Illus. 9-28. Face-frame detail for the upper unit.

Back, Bottom, and Side Panels for the Basic Box
Fabricate the bottom from ⅝- or ¾-inch particle board or plywood. It should measure 17¾ × 34½ inches. Always check the exact length for the bottom by measuring from the bottom of the rabbets on the face frame.

The back should be made of ¼-inch material. Plywood, hardboard, or even particle or flake board may be used. Apply 2-inch reinforcing strips along the sides and the top. Remember to cut the side strips ¾ inch (or ⅝ inch, if that is the thickness used) shorter than the side panel to allow for the thickness of the bottom panel.

Glue and nail the back-panel assembly to the bottom, and then fasten the face frame to the bottom, supporting it with scrap strips, as was done with the chest of drawers in Chapter Six.

The side panels are made from ¼-inch plywood, and measure 17¾ × 27½ inches. Again, double-check these measurements by measuring the basic box assembly. Joint a 5-degree bevel along the front edge of the side panels, and then glue and nail them in place with ¾-inch brads and 4d finish nails. Square the basic box by pulling everything to the shape of the side panels. Set the nails and then fill all nail holes with matching plastic wood.

Scrape and sand the plastic wood after it thoroughly dries.

The bottom facing strip should be glued and nailed to the exposed raw edge of the bottom. Set the nails, and then fill the holes and any minor flaws in the joints. Then sand the entire face frame with a belt sander, followed by the finish sander.

Glue and clamp the side-panel top reinforcers in place, and then make and install two cross-braces that will also act as top drawer runners.

Bottom Leg Assembly
The type of leg to be used on this china cabinet is a matter of personal preference. One of the styles shown in Illus. 6-7 can be used. Rolled-and-coved legs look very nice. Legs can also be made uncoved, which is an easier process and makes for a simpler country look. The cabinet shown in Illus. 9-25 has these straight legs that seem to go well with this design. Review the information provided in Chapter Six on making these legs.

Fabricate the bottom moulding and attach it to the front and two sides of the bottom of the basic box using glue and 1¼-inch, #8 flathead wood screws, with the corners of the moulding mitred nicely. Then attach the leg assemblies to the bottom moulding and install all reinforcing for the legs and along the rear between the legs.

Drawers for the Lower Unit
Following the directions given in Chapter Seven, make and install the drawer (or drawers) and their runners.

Top for the Lower Unit
Make the top from reinforced ¼-inch plywood as was done for the chest of drawers, or from ¾-inch plywood, to which a half-round nosing is applied along the front and two sides. If you will fasten the upper and lower sections together, ma-

chine a ¼-inch rabbet along the rear of the top to accommodate the ¼-inch back of the upper unit. This back is extended from the upper unit to fit into this rabbet, and is fastened to the rear of the lower unit with screws. This will prevent any possibility of the upper unit tipping. This detail is shown in Illus. 9-33. Sand the top carefully, and then apply a ¾ × ¾-inch cove moulding below the top along the front and two sides.

Shelf for the Lower Unit

One shelf should suffice for the lower unit, although more can certainly be used if desired. These may be adjustable or permanent shelves. If adjustable shelves are desired and ¼-inch plywood has been used for the side panels, install the shelf track to the back side of the face frame and to the back-panel reinforcing strips. If permanent shelves are to be used, install cleats to the inside of the side panels. Glue and nail the cleats in place by nailing through the side panels.

Making the Doors for the Lower Unit

The doors for both the upper and lower units should be made at the same time. The techniques for fabricating cabinet doors are described in Chapter Eleven.

Building the Upper Unit

The face frame for the upper unit has already been fabricated, and the remainder of the construction calls for some techniques that are not casework-related. The side panels in the casework system are usually made from ¼-inch plywood. However, in the case of an interior-visible cabinet such as this china cabinet, ¾-inch plywood must be used. The fabrication techniques for building a unit with a screwed face frame and ¾-inch plywood side panels are presented in this section.

Making the Three Panels for the Upper Unit

Three panels of ¾-inch plywood must be made for the upper unit. Two of these panels will be for the sides and the other will be for the bottom. The two side panels should measure ¾ × 11¾ × 38¼ inches. The bottom panel should measure ¾ × 11½ × approximately 34¾ inches.

The length of the bottom piece is approximate because the exact length should be measured after the side panels are attached to the face frame. Note also that the bottom panel is ¼ inch narrower than the sides. This allows space for the back panel.

Machining the Side Panels

The two side pieces will need several machining operations. Remember, a left and right side will have to be made! The first operation will be to machine rabbets along their front edges that will fit into the corresponding rabbets of the face frame. Illus. 9-29 shows this in detail. After making the rabbets, joint a 5-degree bevel along this edge to secure a nice tight fit in the face-frame rabbet.

Machine a ¼ × ¼-inch rabbet along the rear of the side panels to receive the ¼-inch plywood back panel. Finally, run a dado in the side panels to receive the ¾-inch bottom piece. Locate this dado so that it will be exactly even with the top edge of the decorative crosspiece on the face frame.

Some thought should be given at this time as to the type of shelves desired in the upper unit. If permanent shelves are wanted, cut additional dadoes in the side panels to accommodate these shelves. However, if adjustable shelves are desired, select the type of shelf tracks or pins. Some adjustable shelf track is applied to the surface, and another type of shelf track is set into a groove. Groove and/or drill the holes for the pins in the side panels at this time.

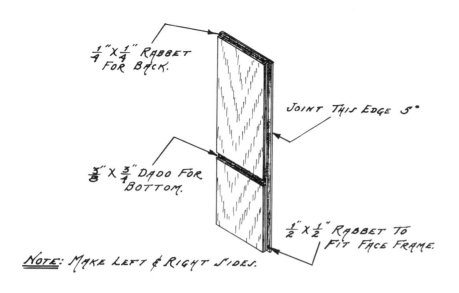

$\frac{1}{4}" \times \frac{1}{4}"$ RABBET FOR BACK.

$\frac{3}{8}" \times \frac{3}{4}"$ DADO FOR BOTTOM.

JOINT THIS EDGE 5°

$\frac{1}{2}" \times \frac{1}{2}"$ RABBET TO FIT FACE FRAME.

NOTE: MAKE LEFT & RIGHT SIDES.

Illus. 9-29. The side panel machining detail for the upper unit.

If the shelves are to be of the permanent variety, machine them to size at this time. They will have to be edge-banded along the front edge with ¼- or ½-inch wood strips. One or two pieces are needed for the shelves. The pieces should be ¾ × 10⅞ × 34¾ inches. They should be as long as the bottom panel and should be machined at the same time.

Assembling the Upper Unit

The best assembly technique is to first attach the side panels to the face frame. Glue and nail them to the face frame using ¾- or 1-inch brads. Stand the face frame and one side panel erect to accomplish this operation. Pull (or use a bar clamp) the side panel tightly into the face-frame rabbet while nailing (Illus. 9-30).

After attaching both sides, measure for the exact length of the bottom panel and cut it to its required length. Slip the bottom into the dadoes and glue and nail it in position through the sides with 4d or 6d finish nails. Install permanent shelves at this time as well. You can also clamp the entire assembly together with bar clamps, thus avoiding the use of nails.

Belt-sand the face frame at this time, and then finish-sand it. Set the brads used to fasten the sides to the face frame. Then fill the

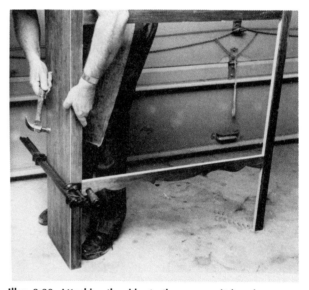

Illus. 9-30. Attaching the sides to the upper-unit face frame.

holes, and scrape and sand the filler after it is thoroughly dry.

Top for the Upper Unit

The top for the upper unit should overhang the cabinet portion by 1¼ inch on the front and both ends. It should be flush with the rear edge of the side panels. The top should be made from a piece of ¾-inch plywood that has a half-round nosing applied to its three exposed edges (Illus. 9-31). It is also possible to use ¼-inch plywood for the top. This panel will have to be

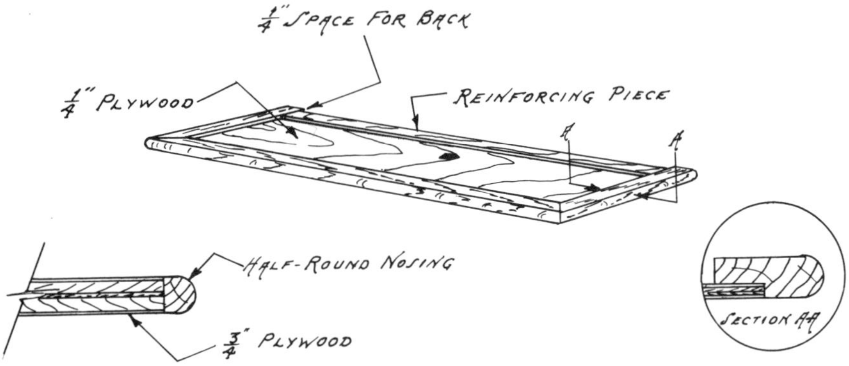

Illus. 9-31. Detail of the top for the
upper unit.

reinforced with lumber pieces that are rabbeted to receive the ¼-inch plywood. This is
very similar to building a top for a chest of
drawers, except that the assembly is fastened
to the cabinet top with the plywood facing
down, as shown in Illus. 9-31. No matter
which type of top is used, cut a rabbet in the
rear edge of the top to receive the ¼-inch
plywood back panel. This can be done with
the router or the spindle shaper, if one is available.

After fastening the top in place, install a
¾ × ¾-inch cove moulding below the top
along the front and two sides.

Fabricating and Installing the Back Panel

Measure the space for the cabinet
back. The grain on the back panel should run
vertically. (If the unit is to be painted, use

¼-inch hardboard for the back. This saves a
great deal of money.)

The back can be fabricated and installed
in one of two ways. If the units will not be
fastened together, a ¾ × 2 × 34-inch reinforcing piece must be glued and nailed to the
back panel between the sides (Illus. 9-32).

If the units are to be fastened together,
then the reinforcing piece is not required but
the back panel should be cut ¾ inch longer
than the sides. Then fasten the units together
by driving screws through the back panel into
the rear edge of the top of the lower unit (Illus. 9-33).

Making Adjustable Shelves

Techniques for the attachment of permanent
shelves have been described previously. Only
one or possibly two shelves can be used in

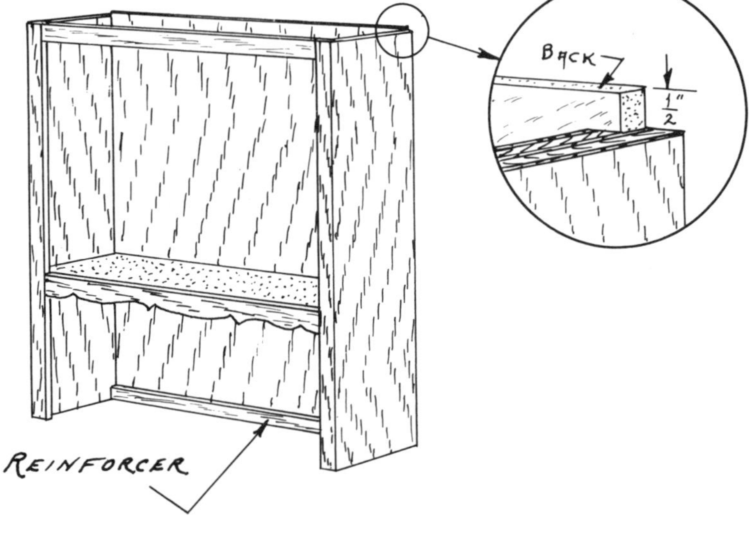

Illus. 9-32. Detail of the back-panel
installation.

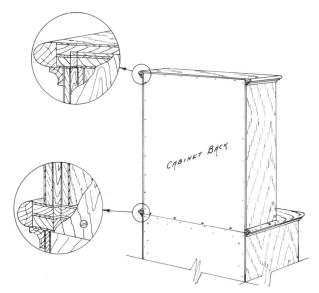

Illus. 9-33. Extend the back panel to fasten the two units together.

this upper unit. They should measure $3/4 \times 10^{7}/8 \times 33^{7}/8$ inches. The $10^{7}/8$-inch width should include the edge-banding along the front edge. The exact length will depend upon the type of shelf standard or pins used.

Making the Doors Building the two sets of doors for the cabinet is the last procedure. Chapter Eleven contains all of the information needed to fabricate the glass-paned doors for the upper unit and the panelled doors for the lower cabinet.

Applying the Finishing Touches Look over the entire project and make sure that all nail holes, seams, and joints are filled with wood filler. Sand the entire cabinet with 220-grit sandpaper on the finishing sander, and then proceed with a preferred finishing schedule.

HUTCH CABINET

The only difference between a china cabinet and a hutch cabinet is that the hutch usually has no doors on the upper unit. Some furniture designers will not follow this rule at all times and will place small side doors with glass panes on the upper units of their hutches. However, by far the vast majority of hutch cabinets will have just open shelves in the upper units. In this section, only the upper units will be described, because there really is no difference between the lower units on china and hutch cabinets.

Designing a hutch cabinet is simply a matter of determining the overall dimensions desired, deciding upon the style of doors and base structure, and positioning the drawers (if any) in the face-frame layout.

As was discovered earlier in this chapter, building a base unit is a straightforward casework job of cabinet building. It should be built with very few problems.

Several different hutch upper units are shown in Illus. 9-23. The one selected for instructional purposes in this section is similar to those illustrated.

Building an Upper Unit

Illus. 9-34 shows the upper unit selected for instructional purposes. It is a rather simple, open-shelf unit. Certainly other designs may be selected that meet with the builder's desires, but this unit is built with techniques that are basic to most open-shelf hutch tops. The lower shelf is decorated with a plate rail that is made of equally spaced gallery spindles. These may usually be purchased in a selection of hardwoods from woodworker's supply houses, and are quite inexpensive.

Designing and Fabricating the Sides

First, decide whether to make the side pieces for this upper unit from 3/4-inch plywood or lumber. Although plywood panels are, no doubt, easier to use, the unsightly raw edges of the plywood must be edge-banded. This limits the design to be used on the sides to rather gentle curves that will lend themselves to veneer edge-banding. If lumber is used, the

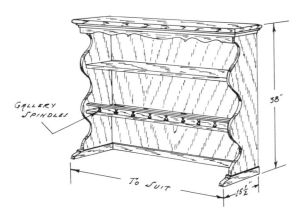

Illus. 9-34. A hutch open-shelf upper unit.

panels will probably have to be glued up from narrower boards. Although this entails much scraping, planing, and sanding, any design can be used on the sides, no matter how intricate. Again, this decision is up to the woodworker.

Make the side panels first. Two pieces are needed. They should measure $\frac{3}{4} \times 12 \times 35\frac{1}{4}$ inches. (The $35\frac{1}{4}$-inch length is calculated by subtracting the $\frac{3}{4}$-inch top plus 2 inches for the foot from the total height of 38 inches.) Lay out the spacing of the two shelves and mark where the stop dadoes will be machined on the sides. Remember to make a left and right side! Machine the stop dadoes prior to cutting out the curved pattern with a band saw (Illus. 9-35). Plan the dadoes carefully by marking on the saw table or rip fence exactly where the dado is to be stopped. Test-cut a scrap piece before cutting the side pieces. The rip fence can be used as a length stop, so that

the opposite dadoes will be the same distance from the ends. After the dadoes are run, use a sharp wood chisel to square their ends and remove the curved portion left by the dado blades.

The router can also be used for this operation. Use a $\frac{3}{4}$-inch straight cutter with an edge guide for the base of the router. A narrower straight cutter can be used, but that would necessitate moving the guide piece for a second cut. The edge guide must be located exactly and squarely so that the cutter cuts the dado where planned.

There are two advantages to using the router for this operation. First, the cutter can be observed while the machining is going on and can be stopped precisely where desired. Second, no work with the chisel is required to remove the curved bottom of the dado left by a dado head.

Run the $\frac{1}{4} \times \frac{3}{8}$-inch rabbets along the rear of each side piece for the $\frac{1}{4}$-inch back panel. Then, using a band saw, jigsaw, or sabre saw, cut the pattern for each side panel. Sand and file the edges of the curves smooth, and then apply edge-banding if the side panels are made of plywood. Sand the side panels with the finish sander, using 120-grit sandpaper.

Making and Attaching the Foot Pieces

Fabricate the two foot pieces for the sides next. These should measure $1\frac{1}{8} \times 2 \times 15$ inches. Although $1\frac{1}{8}$-inch material is pre-

Illus. 9-35. Detail of the blind dado at the end of the shelf.

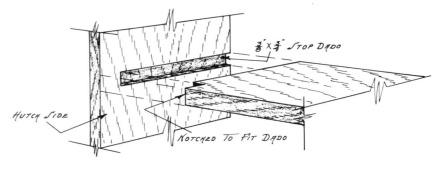

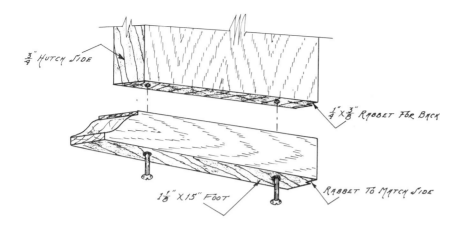

ferred for the feet, stock 1 inch thick will do quite well. Band-saw the selected pattern on the front end, sand the curves and the other surfaces, and then drill the holes used to attach the feet to the bottom edge of the sides (Illus. 9-36). Drill the holes ³⁄₁₆ inch in diameter and countersink them. Attach the feet to the side panels with 3-inch flathead wood screws. Another technique is to counterbore ½-inch holes about 1 inch deep and attach the feet with 2½-inch screws.

Making the Shelves

Two pieces of ¾-inch plywood or lumber will be needed for the shelves. They should measure ¾ × 11 × ¾ inches less than the overall length.

If plywood is used, edge-band the front edges and then cut the notches at each end to fit the stop dadoes machined in the sides.

Making and Installing the Gallery Rail

Make the top rail first (Illus. 9-37). Using the router, machine a nice-looking beading along the edges of a ¾-inch piece of lumber that's 2 or 3 inches wide. (This piece may be left with square edges, if preferred, and only the corners eased slightly.) After machining the beading, rip ½ inch off the board using the table saw. Then smooth the sawn edge on the jointer, taking a light cut. It is much easier to use the router on the edges of a wider board than to try to machine a narrow

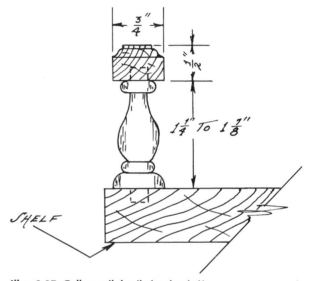

Illus. 9-37. Gallery rail details for the shelf.

strip of wood. Cut this top rail to an approximate length at this time, because it will be cut to its exact length after the sides are attached to the shelves.

Next, make the layout for the required matching holes for the spindles along the top rail and the shelf. Center and drill these holes very exactly using the drill press, if available, and a depth gauge to control the exact depth needed. After a trial assembly, glue the spindles in their proper holes in the top rail only. Lay this assembly aside until the sides and shelves are put together.

Assembling the Upper Unit

Make a trial assembly of the two sides and the two

shelves to see that everything fits together correctly. If all is satisfactory, proceed with the assembly. Either attach the sides to the shelves with nails or screws, or glue and clamp the entire unit together. If screws are being used, the heads can be concealed with wood buttons or plugs of a matching variety. Using plugs or buttons requires counterboring with the proper-size drill bit to accommodate the button. Check the assembly with the framing square and tack a couple of angle braces across the back edges to hold the hutch in this square position while assembling it.

Install the gallery rail next. Check and cut the top rail to the exact length needed. This will require that you saw off some of each end of the rail, so the matching holes for the spindles are properly aligned. Drive a 1- or 1¼-inch brad through the side panel into the end of the rail to secure it in place. First, however, drill a hole for this brad into the end of the rail using a ¹⁄₁₆-inch drill bit in the electric drill, to prevent splitting the narrow rail.

Making the Decorative Crossrail

Lay out the pattern for the upper rail on a piece of lumber that measures ¾ × 2½ inches × the length required. Either fit the top rail between the sides or attach it to the front upper edge of the sides. Cut the pattern and sand the edges smooth, removing all traces of saw marks. Fasten the top rail in position using either nails or button-capped screws.

Making the Top
The directions previously given in this chapter for making the top for a china cabinet apply equally to the top for a hutch. The top can be made from either ¾-inch plywood with an applied half-round lumber nosing or from ¼-inch plywood with rabbeted lumber edges. Plan the size of the top so that it overhangs the body of the hutch 1¼ inch on the front and both sides. Also remember to machine a ¼ × ³⁄₈-inch rabbet along the rear edge of the top that will accept the ¼-inch back panel. When you have completed and finish-sanded the top, nail it in position and then apply ¾ × ¾-inch cove moulding along the front and two sides.

Attaching the Back Panel
Measure the required size for the ¼-inch back panel and sand it with the finish sander, using 120-grit sandpaper, before installing it. Glue and nail it in position using any small box nail.

The lower edge of the back panel will need a reinforcing piece that measures ¾ × 2 or 2½ inches × the required length. This piece can be left square, or a routed pattern can be machined along the upper inside edge. Glue and clamp this piece in place using scrap-wood cushions under the C-clamp jaws so that the board does not get marred.

Finishing Touches
Look the project over for any flaws. Cover these flaws and any nail holes with matching plastic wood. Scrape and sand the plastic wood clean after it has dried thoroughly and then sand the entire unit with 220-grit paper to prepare for finishing. Check Chapter Sixteen for information on wood finishing and a good finishing schedule.

CHAPTER TEN

Gun Cabinets

For the outdoor sportsman who has a nice collection of firearms, a beautiful hardwood gun cabinet will make a nice addition to the den or recreation room (Illus. 10-1). This type of cabinet has a visible interior and is almost always equipped with glass-paned doors so as to display the contents. These doors should be equipped with locks to keep children or other individuals from gaining easy access to the contents of the cabinet. Often, the interior is provided with a light to enhance the display of guns. This project lends itself quite well to the casework method, and several examples of gun cabinets are included in this chapter.

DESIGNING A TRADITIONAL GUN CABINET

Most gun cabinets are designed and built in two sections. The upper section is used for the storage of guns, and the smaller, lower section is equipped with either drawers or doors and is used for storing ammunition, cleaning equipment, or other gun-related paraphernalia. Gun cabinets are determined in size by the

Illus. 10-1. A traditional-styled gun cabinet (Photo courtesy of Mr. and Mrs. Ivan Larson, Hutchinson, Mn.)

197

number of guns the cabinet is meant to store, hence the designations, 6 gun, 8 gun, 12 gun, etc. The guns can be stored either horizontally or vertically in the cabinet, although horizontal storage will result in a very long cabinet that is often up to 6 feet in length. Usually the guns are stored vertically. An average-size cabinet can store 6 or 8 guns. The interior of the storage area must have felt-lined barrel rests, and the bottom of the cabinet is felt-lined, with routed stock rests. Designing and building a gun cabinet is very similar to building a china cabinet. The cabinet is built in two sections. However, its base section is lower and its upper section higher than those sections on the usual china cabinet.

DETERMINING THE REQUIRED SIZE

It is quite simple to design the height and depth of a gun cabinet, but its length must be determined by the number of guns to be stored. For the custom cabinet or furniture builder, size is a matter of personal preference. However, some standard guidelines might assist you in arriving at a pleasing design.

DETERMINING THE LENGTH

Display cabinets for the storage of guns are seldom built for fewer than six shotguns and rifles. Storing less than that number would result in a very narrow cabinet that would not be worth building. Some suggested lengths for vertical storage for 6, 8, 10, and 12 guns are as follows: 6 guns, 24 inches; 8 guns, 30 inches; 10 guns, 34 inches; and 12 guns, 36 inches.

These lengths are for the interior requirements of the cabinet. To calculate the overall lengths needed, add the thickness of the end panels to these dimensions.

DESIGNING THE LOWER SECTION

The lower section is a separate cabinet that is built about 18 to 20 inches high by 12 to 14 inches deep. The base structure may be any of the various traditional styles shown in Chapter Six. The rolled-and-coved legs, for example, are usually made 4 inches high. Other features of the traditional bases are the same as for the china cabinet and chests already described in previous chapters.

DESIGNING THE UPPER SECTION

The upper cabinet that contains the actual storage facilities for the firearms must be designed with some care. The overall size of the upper section should be about 10 to 12 inches deep and 52 to 55 inches high. It should be exactly as wide as the lower unit. The barrel rests and stock rests must be designed to accommodate the number of guns the cabinet is to store. This is described in the section on building an upper unit.

BUILDING A TRADITIONAL GUN CABINET

The gun cabinet depicted in Illus. 10-2 is a 8-gun cabinet that will hold both rifles and shotguns. It should be built of a beautiful cabinet hardwood because it is sure to become the focal point of a den or recreation room. Below are instructions for building this cabinet:

BUILDING THE LOWER UNIT

The basic box of the lower unit is shown in Illus 10-3. It is 33½ inches long, 14½ inches high, and 14 inches deep. This, again, is typical casework construction, and the face frame should be built first. Build the face frames for both the upper and lower units at the same time. This will save considerable time making

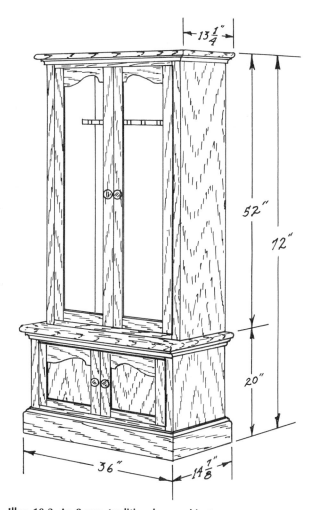

Illus. 10-2. An 8-gun, traditional gun cabinet.

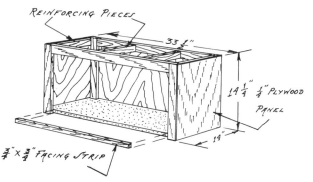

Illus. 10-3. Basic-box detail for lower section.

machine setups. The basic box for the upper unit will measure $33\frac{1}{2} \times 71\frac{1}{4} \times 12$ inches.

Building the Face Frames

The bill of materials for both face frames is as follow:

Lower Unit
Stiles: Two pieces $\frac{3}{4} \times 1\frac{3}{4} \times 14\frac{1}{4}$ inches
Top rail: One piece $\frac{3}{4} \times 2 \times 30$ inches
Facing strip: One piece $\frac{3}{4} \times \frac{3}{4} \times 30$ inches
Upper Unit
Stiles: Two pieces $\frac{3}{4} \times 1\frac{3}{4} \times 51\frac{1}{4}$ inches
Top rail: One piece $\frac{3}{4} \times 2 \times 30$ inches
Facing strip: One piece $\frac{3}{4} \times \frac{3}{4} \times 30$ inches

Machining the Stiles Machine the standard rabbets on all four stiles, as shown in Illus. 10-4. They should be $\frac{1}{4} \times \frac{1}{2}$ inch.

Assembling the Face Frames Using the techniques learned in Chapter Six, assemble the face frames with screw joints.

Making the Bottom, Back, and Side Panels

Bottom Make the bottom from a piece of $\frac{3}{4}$- or $\frac{5}{8}$-inch particle board that measures approximately 13×33 inches. Check the exact required length of the bottom by measuring from rabbet to rabbet on the back of the face frame.

Back From $\frac{1}{4}$-inch plywood or hardboard, cut the back panel exactly as long as the bottom and as high as the face frame ($14\frac{1}{4}$ inches). Nail $\frac{3}{4} \times 2$-inch lumber strips along the sides and along the top edge, allowing $\frac{3}{4}$-inch spaces at the lower end of the side strips to have space for the bottom panel (Illus. 10-5).

Side Panels Make the side panels from $\frac{1}{4}$-inch hardwood plywood that measures approximately $13\frac{3}{4} \times 14\frac{1}{4}$ inches. Check the assembled face frame, bottom, and back for the exact size. The grain of the side pieces should be vertical. Joint a 5-degree bevel along the front edge of these panels so that they will fit tightly in the face-frame rabbet.

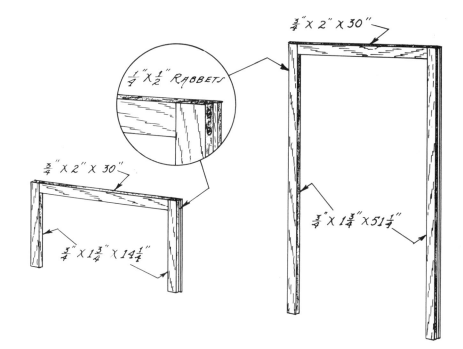

Illus. 10-4. Face-frame detail for the upper and lower sections.

$\frac{3}{4}" \times 2" \times 30"$

$\frac{1}{4}" \times \frac{1}{2}"$ RABBETS

$\frac{3}{4}" \times 2" \times 30"$

$\frac{3}{4}" \times 1\frac{3}{4}" \times 51\frac{1}{2}"$

$\frac{3}{4}" \times 1\frac{3}{4}" \times 14\frac{1}{4}"$

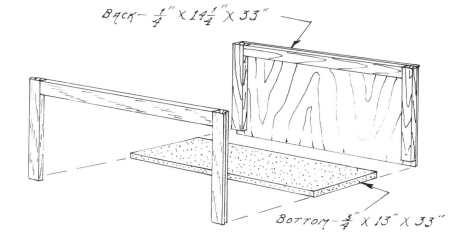

Illus. 10-5. Assembly detail for the lower section.

BACK— $\frac{1}{4}" \times 14\frac{1}{4}" \times 33"$

BOTTOM— $\frac{3}{4}" \times 13" \times 33"$

Assembling the Basic Box

First, attach the back panel to the rear edge of the bottom using glue and small box nails. Glue and nail the face frame to the bottom, using support strips to hold it in position. Use 4d finish nails for this. Drill holes for the nails before nailing them in by using a 4d nail in the electric drill; this will prevent the nails from splitting the stiles. Finally, check the size and fit of the side panels and glue and nail the panels in place using ¾- and 1-inch brads. Apply the facing strip to the exposed raw edge of the particle-board bottom using 4d finish nails and glue. Set the nails and fill all the nail holes and any joint imperfections with matching plastic wood. Allow the plastic wood to thoroughly dry; then scrape and sand the filled areas.

Using the belt sander, sand the face frame carefully. Follow this by sanding the entire structure with the finishing sander and 120-grit sandpaper.

200

Installing the Reinforcing Pieces

Glue and clamp reinforcers at the top of the side panels. Install two more reinforcing pieces between the face frame and the back panel (Illus. 10-3). Nail these pieces in position or attach blocks to the rear of the face frame and screw the reinforcers to the blocks.

Building the Base Structure

Select the style of cabinet base or legs desired. The legs or pedestal base, if used, should be 4 inches high. The gun cabinet shown in Illus. 10-2 has rolled-and-coved legs, and the cabinet shown in Illus. 10-2 has a pedestal base. These are just two examples of typical base structures that can be built. Refer to the information and building techniques presented ın Chapter Six for complete details on building base structures. No matter which base design is selected, a $\frac{3}{4} \times 2\frac{1}{2}$-inch bottom moulding will have to be made and installed on the bottom of the basic box along the front and two sides (Illus. 10-6). Then fasten the leg structures to the bottom moulding using $\frac{3}{4} \times \frac{3}{4}$-inch mounting pieces as shown in Illus. 10-6. Install a reinforcing piece between the back legs to further strengthen the base assembly.

Making the Top for the Basic Box

Because the top of the basic box will be covered by the upper section of the gun cabinet, no actual top need be made. Instead, a pseudo-top can be made from $\frac{3}{4} \times 3$-inch lumber pieces that are mitred at the corners (Illus. 10-7). Either rout an edging on the outside edges of these pieces or simply round them with a $\frac{3}{8}$-inch rounding-over bit in the router. Make a $\frac{1}{4} \times 1\frac{1}{2}$-inch cut on the rear of each side piece. These cuts will allow the back panel of the upper unit to fit flush with the rear of the lower unit (Illus. 10-7). Attach these pieces to the top of the basic box with $1\frac{1}{2}$-inch flathead wood screws and then install $\frac{3}{4} \times \frac{3}{4}$-inch cove moulding under the top edges. Install a filler strip along the back edge that is recessed $\frac{1}{4}$ inch. This will accommodate the $\frac{1}{4}$-inch plywood back panel of the upper unit when the two sections are fastened together (Illus. 10-7). When the time comes, you will fasten the upper cabinet to the lower unit by driving screws through these top pieces into the bottom of the upper unit.

BUILDING THE UPPER UNIT

The upper case is a typical "visible-interior" cabinet, and building this unit presents no new challenges that have not been covered in Chapter Nine on china cabinets and hutches. The only problem that will be encountered will be the layout for the barrel and stock rests. This is covered in this section.

Building the Face Frame   The dimensions for the three face-frame pieces are detailed in Illus. 10-4. Both face frames should be made at the same time. The machining on both face frames is identical, so machine setup time can easily be saved.

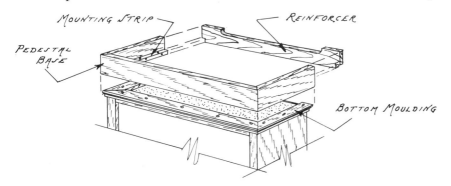

Illus. 10-6. Detail of a pedestal base for the lower unit.

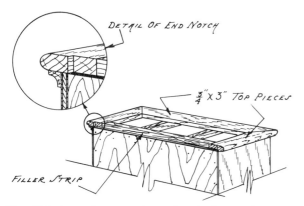

Illus. 10-7. A pseudo-top can be used on the lower unit.

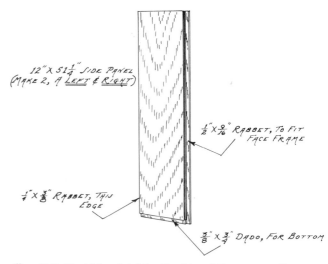

Illus. 10-8. Machining detail for the sides of the upper section.

Making the Back and Side Panels

The sides will have to be made from ¾-inch hardwood plywood or veneered particle board because all will be visible through the glass doors. The back will be made of ¼-inch plywood.

Side Panels Two pieces of ¾-inch hardwood plywood or veneered particle board will be required for the sides. These should be of the A2 grade and should measure 11¾ × 51¼ inches. Note that the overhang of the top has been subtracted from the 13¼-inch overall dimension to arrive at a basic box depth of 12 inches. Also, ¾ inch, the thickness of the top, has been subtracted from the 52-inch overall height of the top unit, to obtain the 51¼-inch length of the side panels.

Machine a ¼ × ⁹⁄₁₆-inch rabbet along the front edge of the side panels. These rabbets must fit into the rabbets along the edges of the face frame, so be sure to check these carefully for a nice fit. Machine a ¼ × ⅜-inch rabbet along the back edges to accommodate the ¼-inch plywood back panel. Machine a ⅜ × ¾-inch dado along the bottom edge of each side piece to accommodate the bottom panel (Illus. 10-8). Joint a 5-degree bevel along the lip of the rabbet on the front edge to secure a nice fit in the face-frame rabbet. Sand the side panels with the finish sander using 120-grit sandpaper.

Back Panel The back panel will measure 33 × 52¼ inches. Check the exact width of this panel by measuring from rabbet to rabbet on the rear of the face frame. The height of the back panel is 1 inch longer than the face frame and the side panels. This allows ½ inch to fit into rabbets along the rear edge of the tops of both the upper and lower units, so the two sections can be fastened together.

Making the Bottom

The bottom of the upper section should be made from ¾-inch hardwood plywood or veneered particle board and should measure 11 × 32¾ inches. Remember, ⅜ inch on each end of the bottom panel will fit into the dadoes on the sides.

Stock Rest Layout

The next step is to lay out the stock rests on the bottom panel. The stock rests can either be laid out at a slant or perpendicular to the back. This is a matter of personal preference, but slanted stock rests highlight the beauty of the guns more than the straight layout does.

Locating the stock rests takes some

thought and calculation. How far from the back wall of the cabinet should the stock rests be located? The builder must calculate the "drop" of the gun stock to the gun barrel to determine this distance. Place the gun barrel against a wall and measure the drop distance at the end of the gun stock (Illus. 10-9 and 10-10). Hopefully, all guns in the collection will possess the same drop, but in reality they will probably vary somewhat. Determine an average drop distance by measuring several guns and use this distance to locate the stock rests.

Illus. 10-10. Interior view showing stock and barrel rests for both shotguns and rifles.

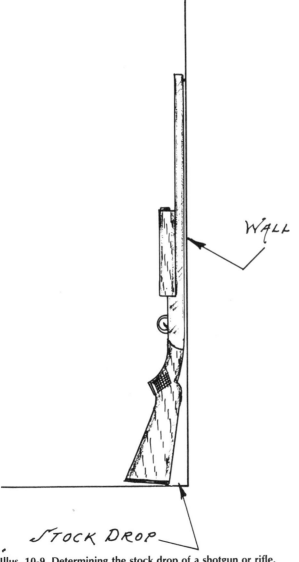

Illus. 10-9. Determining the stock drop of a shotgun or rifle.

One other factor must be taken into consideration before the actual layout can be made. The piece that contains the barrel rests will keep the guns about ¾ to 1 inch away from the cabinet back. Design the piece for the barrel slots so that there is ¾ inch of material remaining at the rear of the slot. Then add this ¾ inch to the calculated drop distance (Illus. 10-11). If the average drop distance is, for example, 1¾ inches and ¾ inch is added for the barrel rests, the stock rests will be located 2½ inches from the rear of the cabinet. Draw a line along the bottom panel 2½ inches from and parallel to the rear edge of the bottom piece. In Illus. 10-12, this is designated by line A.

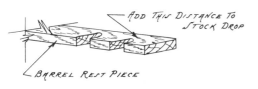

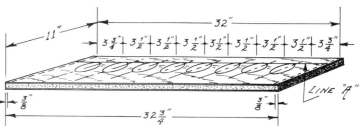

Illus. 10-11 (above). Add the thickness of the barrel rest to the stock drop. Illus. 10-12 (right). Lay out the stock rests on the bottom panel.

Next, design a cardboard pattern for the stock rests that is shaped somewhat similar to the shape of a gun butt and is a bit larger all around than the largest gun butt. Draw a centerline through the pattern so that it can be easily lined up with the locating centerlines that will be drawn on the cabinet bottom.

Space the stock rests evenly on the bottom piece. Remember, the bottom panel of an eight-gun cabinet must be divided into nine equal spaces. The bottom of a ten-gun cabinet will be divided into eleven spaces, etc. After you subtract ¾ inch from the bottom length (the amount that fits into the dadoes on the sides), the actual usable length of the bottom will be 32 inches. Dividing 32 inches by 9 results in slightly over 3½ inches. If the centerlines for the stock rests are located 3½ inches apart and there are seven spaces between stock rests, the following calculation will result: $7 \times 3\frac{1}{2}$ inches $= 24\frac{1}{2}$ inches. Now, subtracting 24½ inches from the overall length of 32 inches leaves 7½ inches. This amount can be divided to obtain end spaces of 3¾ inches each. Illus. 10-12 shows this layout, which provides about 1¼ inches between stock rests.

Routing the Stock Rests

This is an easy task for the router if the following three accessories are available: template guides for the router; a shop-made plywood routing template; and a mortising bit for the router. Template guides are inexpensive and can usually be purchased as an accessory to the router from the place of business where the router was purchased.

These guides simply screw onto the bottom of the router and act as a metal sleeve surrounding the cutting bit (Illus. 10-13). The metal sleeve rubs against the template and follows the pattern, but does not allow the router bit to touch and cut into the template. The guides are usually purchased in sets of three with the following diameters available: 5/16, 7/16, and 5/8 inch. For this routing operation, a ½-inch mortising bit works nicely with the 5/8-inch-diameter template guide.

Illus. 10-13. Template guide on the bottom of the router.

Fabricate a template from ⅜- or ½-inch plywood or similar material. Use the cardboard pattern prepared previously for the general layout as a starting point for the template. However, the template will have to be larger than this pattern to accommodate the routing guide. If a ½-inch bit is used with the 5/8-inch guide, the template will have to be 1/16 inch larger all around to rout a stock rest the size of the original pattern. Use a jigsaw or sabre saw to remove the center portion of the template

CENTER LINE OF TEMPLATE ALIGNED WITH CENTER LINES ON BOTTOM & LINE #

and sand the inside edges of the template smooth and even. Be certain that the template has a centerline so that it can be aligned with the centerlines already drawn on the bottom panel. Tack-nail the template to the bottom panel, lining it up exactly in the correct position (10–14). With the router cutter set about ¼ inch deep, carefully follow the edge of the template first and then remove the center material. Good routing technique calls for making two passes each ¼ inch deep, for a total depth of ½ inch. Move the template to the next stock rest position and duplicate the procedure until all rests have been routed.

Sand the bottom panel with the finish sander using 120-grit paper.

Assembling the Upper Unit

Attach the sides to the face frame using glue and ¾-inch brads. Pull the rabbets together as tightly as possible; use a bar clamp, if necessary. This operation is shown in Illus. 9-34. After the sides are attached, check the bottom panel to ensure that it fits in the dadoes. Glue and nail the bottom in place using 4d finish nails through the sides.

Check the fit of the ¼-inch plywood back panel in the rabbets machined along the back edges of the sides. Glue and nail the panel in place, remembering that the back will extend ½ inch at the bottom and the top. Pull everything into square while installing the back.

Next, install the barrel rest piece (or two pieces, if one has been prepared for rifles). Locate this piece so that the guns rest in their slots about 4 or 5 inches from the end of the gun barrels.

Set all nails and fill the holes with matching plastic wood. Also add plastic wood to all joints and seams that may need filling. After the filler has been allowed to dry thoroughly, scrape and sand it clean.

Making the Upper Unit Top

The same type of top may be fabricated for the gun cabinet as was made for the china cabinet in Chapter Nine. Machine a rabbet into the rear edge of the top to receive the ¼-inch back panel. Nail the top in position, allowing 1¼-inch overhang along the front and both sides. Install ¾ × ¾-inch cove moulding under the top to give the cabinet a bead-and-cove look.

Assembling the Upper and Lower Units

Attach the upper unit to the lower unit by driving 1¼-inch screws through the top pieces of the lower cabinet into the bottom of the upper unit. Also glue and nail the plywood back panel to the lower unit along the rear edge of the lower cabinet. A small decorative moulding can be used to cover the joint between the upper and lower cabinets (Illus. 10-15).

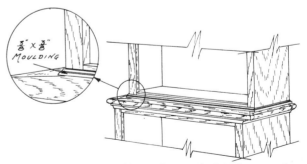

⅜″ × ⅜″ MOULDING

Illus. 10-15. A small moulding will cover the joint between the upper and lower units.

Final Touches

Fill any remaining nail holes with matching plastic wood, sand the entire structure with 220-grit sandpaper in the finishing sander, and proceed with a favorite finishing schedule. After the finishing procedure is completed, line the stock and the barrel rests with green felt. The instructions and procedures for building the glass-paned doors are addressed in Chapter Eleven.

BUILDING A HORIZONTAL-STORAGE GUN CABINET

The craftsperson who owns a large collection of shotguns and rifles may want to build a cabinet with the guns displayed horizontally rather than in the traditional vertical fashion. This type of cabinet can be rather large and thus will take much more wall space, but probably better displays the guns. The gun cabinet shown in Illus. 10-16 measures 58 inches long × 15 inches deep × 72 inches high. It is built in two sections, and will hold about 12 guns.

BUILDING THE LOWER SECTION

Illus. 10-17 gives the dimensions for the bottom section of this gun cabinet. As usual, isolate the basic box by disregarding the top, the base structure, and the bottom moulding. This results in a basic box that measures 55½ × 13¾ × 14½ inches.

Building the Face Frames Build the face frames for both the upper and lower sections at the same time to save machine setup time (Illus. 10-18). The lower section of this cabinet has two drawers in the middle and two doors on either end. Of course, this can be changed to suit the builder, but if this design is acceptable, the following is the bill of materials for the lower-section face frame:

End stiles: Two pieces ¾ × 1¾ × 14½ inches
Short stiles: Two pieces ¾ × 1¾ × 12½ inches

Top rail: One piece ¾ × 2 × 52 inches
Drawer rail: One piece ¾ × 1¾ × 25½ inches
Facing strips: One piece ¾ × ¾ × approximately 50 inches, to be cut into three facing strips

The bill of materials for the face frame for the upper section is as follows:

Stiles: Two pieces ¾ × 1¾ × 51¼ inches
Top rail: One piece ¾ × 2 × 52 inches
Facing strip: One piece ¾ × ¾ × 52 inches

Machine ¼ × ½-inch rabbets along one edge of each of the stiles to receive the rabbet that will be machined on the side panels. Assemble the face frames with screw joints, fastening the stiles to each end of the top rail. Locate the position of the short stiles and counterbore ½-inch holes in the top rail about 1 inch deep, as shown in Illus. 9-5 in the previous chapter. Fasten the short stiles in place with 2½-inch, #8 flathead wood screws. Cut

Illus. 10-16. A cabinet for the horizontal storage of guns.

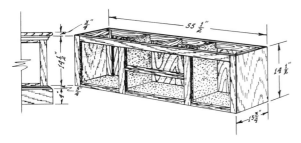

Illus. 10-17. The basic box for the cabinet.

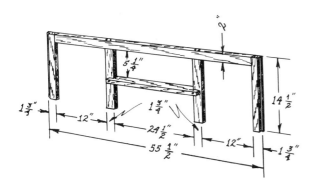

Illus. 10-18. Face-frame detail of the lower unit.

a ¾ × ¾-inch notch into each end of the drawer rail. Lay the notches out carefully so that the drawer rail will fit snugly between the short stiles.

Making the Back, Bottom, Dividers, and Sides

Other than their sizes, the bottom, back, and sides for this gun cabinet are built exactly the same as those for the china cabinets and the traditional gun cabinet.

Bottom Use a piece of ¾- or ⅝-inch particle board or inexpensive plywood for the bottom. The bottom will measure 55 × 12¾ inches. Check its exact length by measuring from rabbet to rabbet on the rear of the face frame.

Back Use a piece of ¼-inch plywood or hardboard for the back. This piece must measure 55 × 14½ inches. Remember, the exact length must match the length of the bottom.

Use ¾ × 2-inch pine (or other inexpensive lumber) strips to reinforce the top edge and the ends of the plywood back. Be certain to allow ¾ inch for the bottom when applying the end reinforcing strips, as is shown in Illus. 10-5.

Sides Make the side panels from ¼-inch hardwood plywood that matches the face-frame material. The dimensions given in Illus. 10-17 are for side panels made with ¼-inch plywood end panels.

Dividers Two dividers must be placed in the bottom cabinet to separate the storage sections from the drawer section. These may be made from either ½-inch particle board or plywood. Illus. 10-19 shows one of the dividers in position. Cut a ¾ × 2-inch notch into it to fit the reinforcing strip along the upper edge of the cabinet back. Fasten the dividers in place by nailing small box nails through the bottom and back, and two 4d finish nails through the face frame.

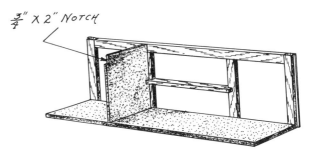

Illus. 10-19. Divider positioned in the lower cabinet.

Base and Top for the Lower Section

Make the base structure and the top for the lower section exactly as the base and top for the traditional gun cabinet. Refer to Illus. 10-6 and 10-7 for details on this construction.

Drawers and Drawer Runners

Make the two drawers by following the building directions presented in Chapter Seven. Note that the opening for the top drawer is 5¼ inches, and that for the bottom drawer is 6½ inches. The cabinet will be more appealing visually if the lower drawer is built slightly deeper than the upper drawer. Follow the directions in Chapter Seven for making the drawer runners and installing the drawers in the cabinet.

BUILDING THE UPPER SECTION

The upper section, although larger, is built using the identical methods previously described for the china cabinet and the traditional gun cabinet. Start by fabricating the face frame, whose dimensions were given previously. Machine the side panels from ¾-inch plywood and make the back panel from ¼-inch hardwood plywood. Because the cabinet is 52 inches wide, the back panel will have to be spliced. Use a reinforcer to back up the splice. Use the same techniques for assembly and for making the top.

The directions for building the glass-paned doors are given in Chapter Eleven.

Making the Gun Hangers

Wooden hangers will have to be made to hold the guns in the upper section. Two different patterns will be needed: one for the gun barrels and the other for the gun stocks. These patterns are given in Illus. 10-20. Make the rests from matching hardwood, cut them to shape with a band saw, and rout all but the back edges with a small-radius round-over cutter. A nice touch is to line the barrel and stock-rest portions of the hangers with green felt.

Install the rests in the upper cabinet by driving screws driven through the ¼-inch back panel into the rear of the hanger. Install the hangers so that the gun barrels are perfectly horizontal or level in the cabinet. To accomplish this, install the stock rests so that they are somewhat lower than the barrel rests. Install the stock rests just behind the trigger guard. Each gun may have a slightly different drop, so some trial and error may be necessary to obtain a nice-looking arrangement of the guns in the cabinet.

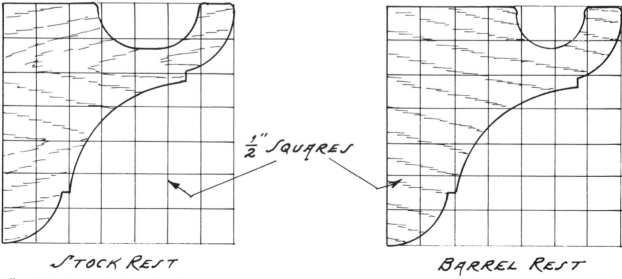

STOCK REST

½" SQUARES

BARREL REST

Illus. 10-20. Patterns for the stock and barrel rests.

Designing and Building Furniture Doors

Certainly one of the distinguishing features of furniture is its doors. Along with the top and the legs, the doors contribute a great deal to the motif of the furniture piece. After all, it is these three features that determine the style of the furniture. Become thoroughly acquainted with the various door styles described below and the methods of building them. Apply them to your projects, to give them a professional look.

TYPES OF DOOR

Most traditional furniture manufactured today has some type of panelled or glass-paned door. In its simplest form, such a door is a wooden frame into which a plywood panel or a pane of glass has been inserted. In its more intricate form, a solid-wood panel, with its edges shaped, is inserted into the wooden frame whose members have been cut and shaped into any of a number of patterns. These are termed raised panelled doors.

Contemporary furniture, on the other hand, has ¾-inch plywood doors with little, if any, embellishment or adornment on the surface of the plywood. It can also use plate-glass sliding or swinging doors, which give a modern motif to the furniture piece. All of these types of furniture doors, as well as several others, are described in this chapter. The workshop equipment owned and the level of skill the craftsperson possesses are really the only limits to designing and building beautiful doors for furniture projects.

FURNITURE DOORS IN RELATION TO THE FACE FRAME

Besides the style of the door, another distinguishing feature of furniture doors is the fit of the door against or into the face frame or the basic box. Three types of door characterized by the way they fit into the face frame are the ⅜-inch lipped door, the flush door, and the overlaid door. The style of door can usually be fabricated for any of these three mountings. For example, a panelled door can be made with a ⅜-inch lip, installed flush with the face frame, or hung in the overlaid position.

⅜-Inch Lipped Door   This type of door has a ⅜-inch rabbet machined around all four of its edges. A ⅜-inch inset hinge is used to mount or "hang" the door on the face frame (Illus. 11-1). In the past, lipped doors have been the doors most frequently attached to furniture and cabinets. However, in the last few years new hinges have been designed and manufactured that have made the lipped door much less popular. Perhaps it was the savings in labor costs in not having to machine the rabbets that persuaded furniture builders to abandon the lipped door.

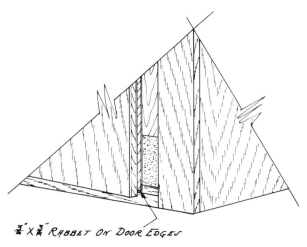

⅜″ × ⅜″ RABBET ON DOOR EDGES

Illus. 11-1. The lipped door overlaps the face frame.

The lipped door is still one of the more popular doors for the amateur woodworker, for three reasons. First, because the lip covers the crack between the door and frame, it conceals any minor problems of squareness in the face frame. Second, if the lipped door is made properly, it is easy to hang because no fitting is necessary. Third, a lipped door requires no sophisticated machinery to make and thus lends itself nicely to the woodworker with minimum equipment.

Flush Door   This type of furniture door is seldom seen anymore on popular furniture. This door fits *into* the face frame, and the surface of the door is flush with the surface of the face frame (Illus. 11-2). Ordinarily, the flush door is ¾ inch thick and is mounted with butt hinges (although surface hinges may be used) that must be mortised into both the door edge and the face frame. This is a time-consuming operation that calls for a certain level of skill. Also, the door must fit exactly all around its edges, so it does not rub or bind in its opening. This, too, takes time and skill. If the margin or gap between the door and the face frame is too large, a very poor-looking piece of furniture is the result. All in all, flush doors are just not used much today because they require many more hours of labor and demand a higher degree of skill.

Illus. 11-2. Flush doors are installed even with the face frame.

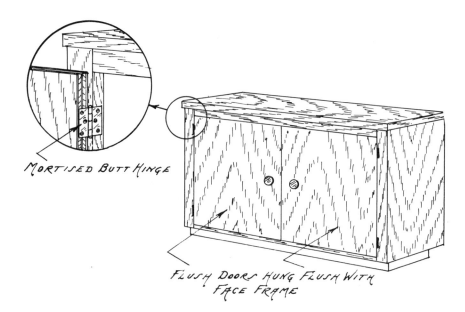

MORTISED BUTT HINGE

FLUSH DOORS HUNG FLUSH WITH FACE FRAME

Overlaid Door   This is the type of door that is found on most popular furniture today. It is usually a ¾-inch-thick door that is mounted *in front of* the face frame, and thus requires no machining for a lip or laborious fitting (Illus. 11-3). The overlaid door can be used on almost all types of furniture. Also, it is easy to determine the size of the overlaid door required.

A fairly recent innovation among furniture and cabinet builders is the "frameless" look that came to this country from Europe. This style makes use of the overlaid door extensively, but it requires the use of a special two-piece "clip" hinge that was developed especially for this type of door (Illus. 11-4).

MAKING THE LIPPED DOOR

Most doors, with the exception of the overlaid door, can be made with a ⅜-inch lip. For example, a lipped door can be made of ¾-inch plywood or veneered particle board, or a ⅜-inch rabbet can be machined on the edges of panelled doors of various styles.

One reason for the popularity of the ¾-inch plywood lipped door is its versatility. It can be left plain with just the ⅜-inch rabbet, or have its surfaces embellished with grooves, mouldings, or overlays.

DETERMINING THE DOOR'S OVERALL SIZE

There is an easy-to-remember rule for cutting lip doors to their correct overall size in relation to the face-frame opening. This rule applies to either a single door or a pair of doors. It is as follows: Measure the face-frame opening exactly. Add ½ inch to the width of the opening. Also add ½ inch to the height of the opening.

This will provide for the thickness of the ⅜-inch inset hinge, the proper allowance of "play" between the doors, plus the necessary space allowance so the door or doors do not touch the face frame after mounting (Illus. 11-5).

The rule applies equally well when you are cutting a pair of doors to fit an opening. Measure the opening, add ½ inch to its height and width, and saw the plywood panel to this size first. Next, rip the panel down the middle to make the pair of doors. This saw cut (plus a very light jointer cut) will provide the necessary space for the other pair of hinges and

Illus. 11-3 (above left). Overlay doors are installed completely in front of the face frame. Illus. 11-4 (above right). The two-piece clip hinge. (Photo courtesy of Julius Blum, Inc.)

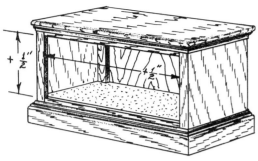

NOTE: MEASURING RULE APPLIES TO BOTH SINGLE OR DOUBLE DOORS

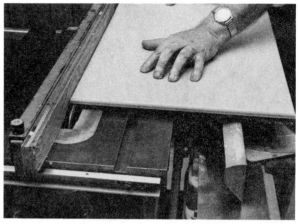

Illus. 11-6. The table saw and dado head can be used to lip doors.

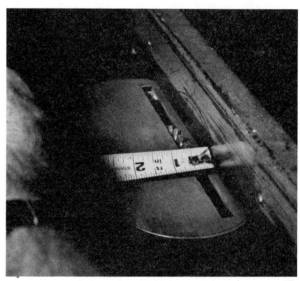

Illus. 11-7. To cut a door lip, set the saw blade ⅜ inch high and measure ⅜ inch to the left of the blade.

for the allowance needed in the middle so the doors do not touch. Using this method for a pair of doors will also ensure that the grain of the doors can be matched. Mark the doors with unobtrusive pencil marks so that the matching grains can be remembered.

MACHINING THE LIPPED DOOR

Remember, one of the advantages of using plywood lipped doors is that sophisticated machinery is not required. After the doors have been cut to their correct sizes, machine the rabbet according to the equipment available in the workshop.

Using a Table Saw

If the table saw is the only machine available, use the dado head (or other grooving device) to make the ⅜ × ⅜-inch rabbet. Lacking even that accessory, you can make the rabbet using just the saw blade. If using the dado head, use an auxiliary wooden fence attachment to ensure that the cutters machine just ⅜ inch wide (Illus. 11-6). Set the dado head ⅜ inch high and make tests cuts until the rabbet is the correct size.

If you use only the table-saw blade, you will have to make two passes over the saw to make the rabbets. Set the saw blade exactly ⅜ inch high and ⅜ inch from the saw fence to the *left side* of the blade (Illus. 11-7). To obtain an accurate cut, measure from the fence to a saw tooth that is set to the left. Make test cuts

in scrap wood to be certain that the rabbet measures exactly ⅜ × ⅜ inch. First run the door over the blade with the panel resting on the saw table (Illus. 11-8) and then make the second pass with the panel in a vertical position and against the saw fence (Illus. 11-9). Sand the rabbets smooth using a sanding block and 80-grit sandpaper.

Using a Router

Using the router, if available, is preferred because it is a faster operation and no sanding of the rabbets is required. A ⅜-inch rabbeting bit is needed for this operation. So, too, is a small rounding-over cut-

Illus. 11-8. Make the first cut for the lip with the door in a horizontal position.

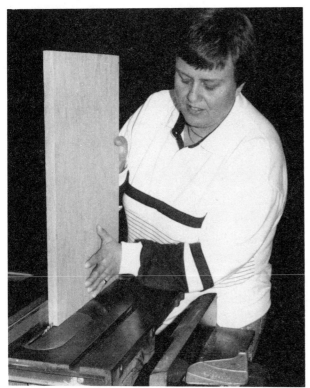

Illus. 11-9. Make the second cut with the door in a vertical position.

ter for decorating the lip. If the lip to be machined will be rounded somewhat, do this first (Illus. 11-10). Otherwise, no material remains for the guide pin of the cutter to run against.

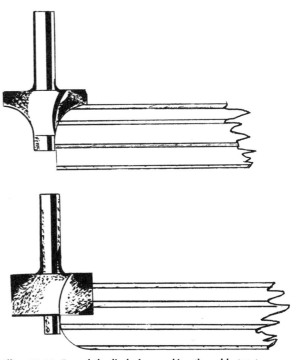

Illus. 11-10. Round the lip before making the rabbet cut.

After rounding the lip with a router, machine the ⅜ × ⅜-inch rabbets on the three or four door edges as required. Remember, do not rabbet the meeting edges of a pair of doors. The easiest way to prevent the door panel from shifting around while routing it is to lay the door on a rubber router pad. These pads can be inexpensively purchased from various woodworking supply houses.

Using a Spindle Shaper

For the woodworker who has a spindle shaper, a straight knife on this machine does a fast and neat job of cutting rabbets. Knives are even available that will machine the rabbet and round the lip all in one pass (Illus. 11-11). For the average home builder, however, either the table saw or the router will have to do the job.

Illus. 11-11. A cutter for the spindle shaper will machine the lip and the rabbet in one pass.

ROUNDING THE DOOR LIP

It is up to the builder to determine the amount of rounding, if any, to machine on the lip of the furniture doors. Many craftpersons prefer to machine a full quarter-round on the lip of their plywood furniture door edges, others run less of a curve, and still others allow the lip to remain square with the sharp corner slightly eased by sanding. When determining how much to round the door lip, remember that the more curve that is routed or shaped on the lip, the more inner core will be exposed. With veneered particle board this is not too objectionable because the edge can be sanded smooth and, when finished, looks presentable. This is not the case with the exposed edge

grain of plywood, because there are often voids in the layers of the plywood that require filling. Even after the edges are sanded, stained, and varnished, the alternate layers of the inner plies are often quite noticeable.

DECORATING THE DOOR

Several types of adornment are often seen on ¾-inch plywood lipped doors that add a certain decor to the door. Some of these adornments are described below:

Pattern Routing Jig   A routing jig is available on the market that provides several patterns for routing a stylized groove on the surface of the door and on the drawer fronts (Illus. 11-12). These jigs are available from some mail-order houses, woodworking tool suppliers, and building material centers (Illus. 11-13). Of course, a routing template made from ⅜- or ½-inch plywood can be readily made by the craftsperson to do this job if only a couple of doors or drawers of the same size are to be routed. The advantage of the commercial template is that it can be easily adjusted to accommodate doors of various sizes.

Illus. 11-12. Cabinet and furniture doors can be decorated with routed fluting.

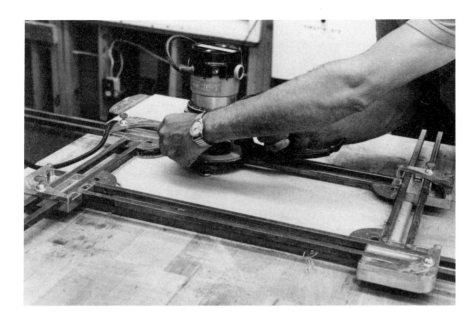

Moulding

Moulding is often applied to a plywood door or drawer front to give it a traditional or provincial style. This moulding is available from cabinet supply houses and specialty woodworker's stores in both straight lengths and curved sections already mitred at the correct angle. Apply the moulding to the surface of the door or drawer front in the pattern desired with glue and small brads (Illus. 11-14).

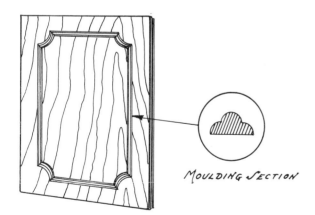

Illus. 11-14. Applied decorative moulding will embellish a door.

Wood Overlays

A plywood door can also be adorned with various types of routed overlays that provide the motif for the style de-sired (Illus. 11-15). These overlays usually are made from lumber. Their patterns are sawed out with a band saw or jigsaw and their edges are then routed with a cutter with an attractive shape. Then they are glued to the surface of the door after the components are given their final sanding.

INSTALLING THE LIPPED DOOR

The lipped door is fairly easy to install. Below are instructions for installing a lipped door:

Selecting and Fastening the Hinges

Any catalogue from a good woodworker's supply house lists a wide variety of hinges for many different thicknesses and styles of furniture doors. It is simply up to the furniture builder to select the type that best fits the door or doors built for the project. The ⅜-inch inset hinge is the one most often selected for hanging the ⅜-inch lipped door. These are available in any number of styles and finishes, including polished brass, antique brass, satin brass, and hammered copper. Most discount stores and building centers carry large displays of furniture and cabinet hardware. Self-closing (or spring-action) hinges are available

215

Illus. 11-15. Applied wood overlays are often used on furniture doors.

that require no catches to keep the door closed. Usually only two hinges are required per door, but for a large or heavy door three or even four hinges are often used.

Position the hinges on the door by measuring an equal distance at the top and bottom of the door with a combination square (Illus. 11-16). If more than two hinges are used, locate the others by measuring carefully. Drill pilot holes for the screws using a $\frac{7}{32}$-inch drill bit. It sometimes helps to use a nail set or other punch to determine the exact center where the hole is to be drilled. A bit of beeswax on the screw threads will help to drive the screws into hardwood. An electric screwdriver can be used to efficiently drive in the many screws the hinges require (Illus. 11-17).

Illus. 11-17. The electric screwdriver can be used to quickly attach hinges.

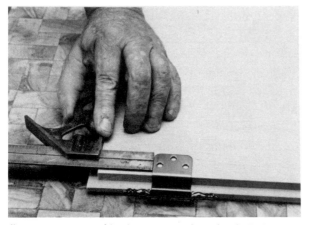

Illus. 11-16. The combination square makes a handy jig for installing hinges.

Hanging a Single Door If it is convenient to do so, lay the piece of furniture on its back to facilitate the hanging of the door. Position the door in its opening and shift it

216

around to feel that the door is not touching the face frame at any of its four edges. Make sure that the bottom edge of the door is parallel to the lower edge of the cabinet. If everything is aligned, simply drill the holes for the hinge screws in the face frame and drive the screws home. Swing the door open to determine that nothing touches or binds against the face frame.

If the furniture piece must remain in an upright position, rip a strip of wood about 3/32 to 1/8 inch thick and about 3/4 inch wide. Cut this strip to a length that is slightly shorter than the width of the door opening. Place the lipped door in position in the face-frame opening. This allows the rabbet on the door to rest on the strip of wood (Illus. 11-18). This will give the door the proper amount of vertical play and will keep it parallel with the lower edge of the furniture piece.

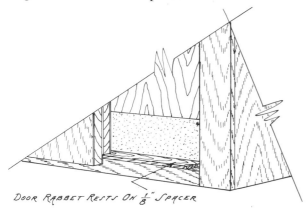

DOOR RABBET RESTS ON 1/8" SPACER

Illus. 11-18. A 1/8-inch shim under the door lip provides the correct spacing when you are hanging a lipped door.

Shift the door from left to right to determine that it is not touching the face frame on the sides. If self-closing or spring-loaded hinges are being used, push the door firmly against the face frame in order to spread the hinges to their proper position. Drill the holes for the hinges and attach the door to the face frame. Swing the door open, remove the spacing strip, and check to see that the door swings free and clear all around.

Hanging a Pair of Doors

Again, if it is convenient, lay the project on its back to install the doors. Prepare two spacers of 1/16-inch material (scrap plastic laminate works well for this) and hang the spacers by a finish nail between the doors to provide for the proper amount of middle play (Illus. 11-19). Shift the doors around in the opening to feel that they are not touching the face frame; keep the bottom edges parallel with the lower edge of the furniture piece when doing this. Again, if self-closing hinges are being used, push the doors tightly against the face frame to position the hinges correctly. When everything is aligned, drill the screw holes and fasten the doors in place.

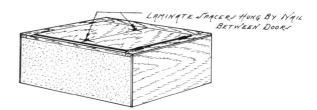

LAMINATE SPACERS HUNG BY NAIL BETWEEN DOORS

Illus. 11-19. Laminate spacers provide the proper play between a pair of doors.

If the furniture piece must remain in an upright position, again use a 3/32- or 1/8-inch wooden spacer strip that's cut a bit shorter than the door opening to properly position the doors. Place both doors in the opening, resting the rabbets on the spacer strip. Place a 1/16-inch laminate spacer between the doors at the bottom and hang another spacer between the doors at the top. Shift the doors from left to right to determine that they are not touching the face frame on the sides. Then push the doors tightly against the face frame (if self-closing hinges are being used) and drill the holes for the hinge screws. Sometimes it seems that extra assistance is needed to hang a pair of doors in the vertical position, because one of the doors will fall forward as the other door is being held and the holes drilled. To prevent this from happening, carefully remove one of the doors from the opening after they have been correctly located, and hang just one door first. Then return the other door to its position, insert the middle spacers, and hang the second door.

Selecting and Installing Door Catches

If a more positive closing is desired for the doors beyond that provided by the self-closing hinges, the furniture builder may prefer installing door catches. A door catch such as a friction catch can be used to pull a slightly warped door into place.

Catches are available in a wide variety of types ranging from friction to magnetic (Illus. 11-20). Magnetic touch catches are now sold that firmly hold the door shut, yet allow it to swing open when it is slightly pushed. These are sold for either a single door or a pair of doors. Elbow catches are often used when a pair of doors is to be equipped with a lock. The left-hand door is secured by elbow catches, and the lock is installed in the right-hand door. The locking mechanism swings behind the left-hand door, providing a secure lock for the two doors. Simple roller spring or magnetic catches are sold at discount stores and building supply dealers. Woodworker's

supply catalogues carry the more sophisticated types of catches.

Installing Friction and Magnetic Catches

Catches are usually mounted at the top of the door to lessen the chances of any interference. To install almost any type of door catch on a piece of furniture made with a face frame, you have to glue a ¾ × ¾ × 4-inch piece of wood to the inside of the top rail (Illus. 11-21). This block can be of pine or of wood that matches the face frame. This piece is needed in order to obtain enough mounting surface for the catch.

To install catches on a pair of doors, always fasten the bayonet or the magnetic plate portion of the catch to the door first. Next, put the body of the catch on the bayonet or magnetic plate, close the door—leaving the other door open—and reach inside to mark the location of the catch whose mounting holes are slotted for adjustment. Drill pilot holes for screws in approximately the middle of the slotted space, fasten the body of the catch loosely in place, and then, before tightening the screws, adjust it so that the door closes properly.

For a single door, mount the body of the catch first about ⅜ inch from the front edge of the face frame by drilling the screw holes ap-

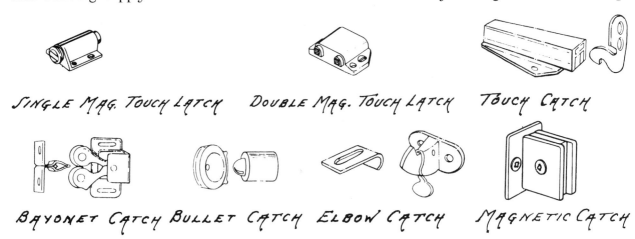

SINGLE MAG. TOUCH LATCH   DOUBLE MAG. TOUCH LATCH   TOUCH CATCH

BAYONET CATCH   BULLET CATCH   ELBOW CATCH   MAGNETIC CATCH

Illus. 11-20. Many types of door catches are available.

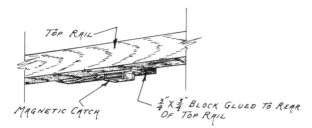

Illus. 11-21. A mounting block is often needed for the catch.

proximately in the middle of the slotted area. Attach the plate or bayonet to the door so that it is correctly aligned with the body of the catch. A little practice will make the installation of catches an easy task.

BUILDING PLAIN PANELLED DOORS

As described before, the panelled door is really a wooden frame with a plywood panel insert. The design and construction of panel doors will depend to a great extent upon the machines the craftsperson has available. If you do not have a spindle shaper or a heavy-duty router that will take ½-inch-shank cutters, you will have to make panel doors that are plain. However, nice-looking panel doors can be made with just the table saw and a small router.

DESIGNING AND BUILDING THE FRAME

A well-designed simple, rectangular panel door with a ¼-inch plywood insert will have stiles and top rails that are the same width and a bottom rail that is somewhat wider. If the panel door is also to be a lipped door, the stiles and top rail will have to be approximately 2 inches wide. This dimension is arrived at by adding the ⅜-inch lip, 1³⁄₁₆ inches for the inside leaf of the offset hinge, and ⅜ to ½ inch for the groove for the plywood panel. This totals just a bit over 2 inches. Although

the ¼-inch groove does not directly affect the width of the door stile, door rails and stiles 1¾ to 2 inches long will look nice. If a ⅜-inch rabbet for a piece of glass will be machined on the inside edge of the stile, then the 2-inch width is an absolute minimum. If the stiles are 2 inches wide, the bottom rail should be 2½ to 3 inches wide (Illus. 11-22).

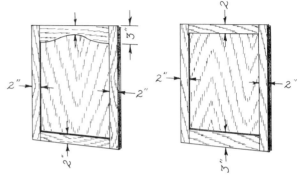

Illus. 11-22. Standard dimensions for panelled door frames.

For a panel door with a curve designed into the top rail, the top rail will have to be made considerably wider. The narrowest width of the curved portion of the rail should be designed so it is about the same width as the stiles. The ends of the curved rail should be 3 to 3½ inches wide (Illus. 11-22). The bottom rail on doors with a curved top rail should be the same width as the stiles. Although these dimensions do not have to be exact, if they are generally followed the result will be a well-proportioned and pleasing door (Illus. 11-23).

DETERMINING THE OVERALL SIZE OF THE DOOR

If the door is to be a lipped door, use the sizing formula presented earlier in this chapter. Add ½ inch to both the length and width of the face-frame opening to arrive at the overall size of the door. If the opening is to have a pair of doors, add ⁹⁄₁₆ inch (rather than ½ inch) to the face-frame width. This will result

Illus. 11-23. Two excellent examples of panelled doors.

in doors that might be a bit too wide for the opening. These doors, however, can easily be made to their exact sizes, after the lips are machined, by running the meeting rails over the jointer. Remember, doors that are too large can easily be trimmed, but those that are too small are useless.

DETERMINING THE LENGTH OF THE RAILS AND STILES

Calculating the length of the stiles is not a problem, because they will be just ½ inch longer than the height of the face-frame opening. The rails must be calculated very carefully. Calculate the net length of the rail by subtracting the width of both stiles from the finished width, and then adding the stub tenon on each end. For example, if the finished width (including the lips) of a single door is to be 14½ inches, 4 inches must be subtracted for the two stiles, leaving 10½ inches. The groove for the plywood panel should be machined about ⅜ inch deep, so the stub tenons will each be that length. Therefore, ¾ inch will be added to the 10½ inches to arrive at an overall length of 11¼ inches (Illus. 11-24).

Following is an example of a bill of materials that can be used for a panel door when the face-frame opening measures 14 × 20 inches:

Stiles: Two pieces ¾ × 2 × 20½ inches
Top rail: One piece ¾ × 2 × 11¼ inches
Bottom rail: One piece ¾ × 3 × 11¼ inches
Plywood panel: One piece ¼ × 11³⁄₁₆ × 16³⁄₁₆ inches (One-sixteenth inch is allowed for "play" from each dimension.)

The size of the plywood panel can be verified after a trial assembly of the door frame is made. Be sure to select absolutely straight stock for the rails and stiles. Pieces with even a slight warp or twist can result in a panel door that fits very poorly.

MACHINING THE STILES AND RAILS

As long as the style of the door calls for no curves, all of the machining can be done on the table saw. Even the curve on the door lips can be made by using the moulding head in the table saw if no router is available.

GROOVES FOR THE PLYWOOD PANEL

After the rails and stiles have been made, machine the grooves for the plywood panel. Make the groove cuts with the dado head (or other grooving device) set to cut ¼-inch wide. Check the exact thickness of the plywood to be used for the panel. Usually hardwood plywood is a bit thinner than ¼-inch, so no shims are necessary for the dado head. Remember, ¼-inch material will not slide into a ¼-inch groove—some play is necessary! Test-fit the

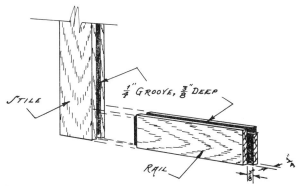

Illus. 11-24. Details for fabricating stub tenons.

plywood by cutting the groove on a piece of scrap.

Set the saw fence so that the groove is machined in the middle of the edges of the rails and stiles. Cut the grooves ⅜ inch deep. The groove can extend the full length of all the pieces. This is the simplest type of frame construction for panel doors, and the stub tenons glued into the grooves make a perfectly satisfactory joint.

STUB TENONS ON THE RAILS

Machining the stub tenons requires the same setup and technique as was described in Chapter 5. Using the dado head and the saw fence as a length jig, cut the stub tenons on the ends of the rails to exactly fit into the grooves run in the stiles.

PLYWOOD PANEL

Make a trial assembly of the door frame and then measure for the exact size of the ¼-inch plywood panel. Allow about 1/16 inch for play when cutting the panel to size. The grain of the panel should run the vertical dimension of the door. Sand the panel with the finish sander before assembly.

ASSEMBLING THE DOOR

Using bar clamps, glue and clamp the door together, checking the assembly for square-

ness. Cushion the clamp jaws with plywood scraps to prevent the door edges from being marred. The panel is not glued in the grooves, but is allowed to "float" in the grooves and expand and contract independent of the frame.

SANDING

Sand the frame of the panel door with the belt sander, and then with the finish sander. Use the same sanding techniques as were used to sand the face frames.

EDGE-SHAPING THE DOOR

If the door is to be lipped, cut the ⅜ × ⅜-inch rabbet using the dado head in the table saw. If the router is going to be used, use the methods described earlier in this chapter. Be certain that the overall dimensions of the door are correct before doing the final edge-shaping and lipping. Finally, sand the routed lip with the finish sander using 120-grit paper and then 220-grit paper.

BUILDING THE PLAIN PANELLED DOOR WITH A CURVED DESIGN

After the desired pattern has been designed for the top rail (and often the bottom rail as well), the procedure for building this door is very similar to that already described for the rectangular door. The only change will be in the techniques used to mill the curved portions of the door frame.

Machining the Stiles and Rails

Cut all pieces to their proper dimensions and cut the grooves in the bottom rail and the stiles. Some craftspersons machine the stub tenons on the rails before cutting the curves that are required. It makes very little difference, however, if the curves are cut before or after the tenons are machined, because the mitre gauge can simply be reversed in the table saw so that the straight edge of the rail can be held firmly. Cut the curves with a band saw, jigsaw, or sabre saw, sand the piece nicely, and then groove it with the router. A cutter for the router is available that will cut a ¼-inch slot about ½ inch deep (Illus. 11-25). This is a bit deeper than required, but will cause no problems. You can cut the grooves by holding the pieces on a rubber routing pad or by mounting the router in the routing table. The latter method makes this procedure somewhat easier because the cutter is fixed and the wood is moved into the cutter.

ROUTER 3-WING SLOTTING CUTTER

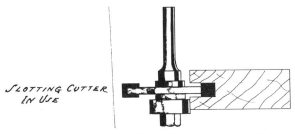

SLOTTING CUTTER IN USE

Illus. 11-25. A slot cutter can be used in the router to cut the grooves in the stiles and rails.

Although this book is written for the person who has a limited amount of woodworking equipment, the craftsperson should be aware that the most satisfactory machine to use for machining curves on the edges of rails and stiles is the spindle shaper. Methods for using this machine are described in the section on raised panel doors.

Preparing the ¼-Inch Plywood Panel
After completing the rails and stiles and making a trial assembly, cut the ¼-inch panel to fit the top rail. Cut the panel to its exact width first, but do not cut it to length as yet. Using the top rail as a pattern, transfer the curve to the upper end of the panel. Saw the curve to shape and then determine the length of the panel. This is accomplished by assembling the two stiles and the top rail and inserting the panel in its grooves.

Next, with the bottom rail in place *on top of* the stiles but even with the lower ends of the stiles, mark the length of the plywood panel, remembering to allow for the ⅜ inch that must go into the groove. Cut the panel to its correct length and then sand the panel prior to the final assembly of the door.

Assembling and Sanding the Door
These final operations are identical to those already described for the rectangular panelled door.

ADDING AN OVERLAY PANEL
You can give the plain-panelled door a more ornate look by overlaying another panel on top of the ¼-inch inserted panel. This gives the door a simulated raised panel look that is surprisingly effective. The china cabinet shown in Illus. 9-25 has doors with overlay panels in its lower cupboard. Illus. 11-26 shows another panelled door with an overlay panel. The overlays on this door look very much like raised panels.

Preparing the Overlay Panel
The overlay panel is glued to the lower panel after the door has been assembled. The overlay can be made of ¼-, ⅜-, or even ½-inch plywood, if it is available. Because ¼-inch plywood is more readily available, it is most often used. Allow a margin of about 1½ inches completely around the frame of the door. Then cut the overlay panel with the same curve as the inner panel. Routing a small cove around the outer

Illus. 11-26. A panelled door with a ¼-inch overlay panel.

edge of the overlay adds a nice touch. Be aware, however, that with ¼-inch material, very little material remains for the depth bead of the router cutter to run against. To accomplish this routing without gouging the panel, cut another panel of inexpensive plywood exactly the same size and shape as the overlay panel. Fasten the two panels together with tiny brads or double-sided tape. Now the guide of the router cutter has something against which it can run.

Installing the Overlay Panel   Mark the exact location of the overlay panel and glue it in place using weights such as concrete blocks. Support the underside of the inserted panel with a scrap piece of ¼-inch plywood, so that it cannot sag from the weights. Double-check to see that the overlay panel does not shift position when the weights are applied.

BUILDING AND INSTALLING FLUSH DOORS

Although flush doors are not used nearly as often as they were years ago, occasionally a craftsperson will want to duplicate an Early American piece that has these doors. The flush door was most often a rectangular panelled door or a panelled door with a curved top rail. Because the flush door (whether it is panelled or a solid door of plywood) must be made to fit inside the face-frame opening, this fit must be skillfully accomplished so that the margin between the door and frame is the same on all sides. If the face frame is slightly out of square, the door must be planed or jointed to fit the opening. No wonder most furniture builders build lipped and overlaid doors.

BUILDING THE DOOR

Because there are no rabbets and lips to account for, the dimensions of the rails and stiles are easy to calculate. Cut the stiles about ⅛ inch shorter than the height of the opening, and calculate the length of the rails by subtracting the width of the stiles plus ⅛ inch more. The ⅛ inch in each case provides for a ¹⁄₁₆-inch margin at the top, bottom, and two sides of the door. Some woodworkers build their flush doors a bit oversize, so that they will have enough wood to plane or joint when fitting the door. The procedure for building this door is exactly the same as for the lipped panelled door.

SELECTING HINGES FOR THE DOOR

Butt hinges for hanging flush doors are available at most hardware stores. These hinges can be used to hang the flush door, but they should be mortised into the edge of the door and the face frame for their best appearance. This is shown in Illus. 11-2. Most woodworker's supply catalogues carry a number of different designs and types of hinges for flush doors. Amerock, one of the nation's leading manufacturers of cabinet and furniture hardware, makes hinges for flush doors in a wide variety of styles and finishes. These hinges are usually designed to be mounted on the surface of the door and the surface of the face frame.

HANGING THE DOOR

The most difficult aspect of hanging a flush door is fitting it into the opening so that the margins around the perimeter of the door are equal. What is the proper width of this margin? One old-time woodworker believed that a margin that's the thickness of a 4d finish nail at the top, bottom, and doorknob edge is about right. If mortised butt hinges are used, the margin on the hinge side would naturally be less.

If surface hinges are being used, first attach the hinges to the door. Then place the door in the opening and use 4d finish nails along the bottom and the sides to wedge the door in place while fastening the hinges to the face frame. If a pair of doors is being installed, use plastic laminate spacers between the doors for proper spacing. Remember, these doors will swell and shrink somewhat with the changing seasons, so allow enough play so that the doors do not bind when the humidity is high.

BUILDING AND INSTALLING OVERLAID DOORS

Overlaid doors are probably the most popular type of door used by furniture manufacturers. There are two reasons for this popularity: the door is easy to install and can be used in an unlimited variety of designs. Illus. 11-15 shows an attractive overlaid door. The one drawback of the overlaid door is that it is not as dustproof as either the lipped or the flush door.

HINGES

Before attempting to make overlaid doors, it is necessary to become familiar with the hinges available for hanging these doors, because the hinge will in most cases affect the size of the door.

Basically, there are just two types of hinges that are used with overlaid doors. These are the variable-overlay hinge and the ½-inch-overlay hinge (Illus. 11-27).

Variable-Overlay Hinge   This hinge is so named not because the hinge itself is variable, but because it can be used with doors of almost infinite size. The hinge, as shown in Illus. 11-27, is mounted under the surface of the door and onto the surface of the face frame. When this hinge is used, the door can be made to overlay the opening by almost any amount the builder desires.

Illus. 11-27. The two types of hinges used on overlay doors.

The ½-Inch-Overlay Hinge   Note that this hinge is mounted on the face-frame edge and that the overlay is limited to ½ inch on the hinge side. Because the hinge is set back ½ inch, most builders will construct the door with this same amount of overlay on the other three edges. Both types of hinges are available in the self-closing variety.

BUILDING THE DOOR

After determining the size of the door, decide what style of door is desired. Overlaid doors can have plain or raised panels, plain ¾-inch plywood, or plywood with decorative cutouts glued to its surface. If ¾-inch plywood is used for the doors, edge-band the edges to hide the inner plies. Study furniture catalogues to determine what style of doors lend themselves to overlaid construction.

INSTALLING THE DOOR

Doors equipped with ½-inch overlay hinges are very easy to install because the hinge itself determines the horizontal position of the door on the face frame. To determine the vertical position, simply look over the door to see that it covers the face-frame opening an equal amount at the top and bottom.

Doors equipped with variable-overlay hinges must be located so there is an equal amount of margin at the top and bottom and the sides of the door. This can be accomplished by measurement and marking where the door should be positioned. If a pair of doors is being installed, always make certain that the doors form a straight line along their bottom edges, and that the top corners of the meeting edges are exactly even. Nothing is more disappointing than to see doors that are hung slightly out of plumb or door corners that do not meet the way they should.

BUILDING FURNITURE DOORS WITH GLASS PANES

China and gun cabinets are just two of many furniture pieces that have doors with glass panes inset within their frames. In fact, the glass-paned door is very similar to the plain-panelled door except that the door must be built so that the glass can be replaced if it breaks. This necessitates that some changes in building technique be made. Because the glass pane must rest in a rabbet machined along the inside edge of the door frame, some special construction problems are also encountered.

Traditionally, most glass-paned doors are built using a spindle shaper for the intricate patterns that are machined along the inside edges of the framework and for the tightly fitted coped joints where the rails and stiles meet (Illus. 11-28). However, this section of the chapter deals with much simpler methods that will still result in nice-looking doors.

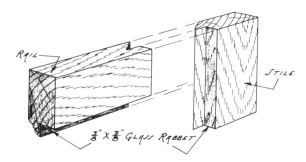

Illus. 11-28. Glass-paned doors usually have coped joints.

PLYWOOD GLASS-PANED LIPPED DOOR

Although some woodworking "purists" may shudder a bit at this method of making glass-paned doors, for the beginner or craftsperson with a minimum number of woodworking tools this is a unique and easy method that results in a nice-looking door. For lack of a better name, it will be called the "plywood method."

In the plywood method, a lipped door of ¾-inch plywood is made and then its inner part is sawed out, leaving a framework that will be rabbeted to hold the glass (Illus. 11-29 and 11-30). This method has several advantages over more traditional methods of fabricating framed doors. They are as follow: (1) the stiles and rails do not have to be machined; (2) the parts do not have to be assembled or glued; (3) the danger of the door twisting or warping is greatly reduced because veneered particle board is very stable; (4) more ornate doors such as those with curved rails can be easily duplicated; and (5) the glass does not have to be cut to a curved pattern, but can be placed in the door with square corners. The

Illus. 11-29. Example of plywood glass-paned china cabinet doors.

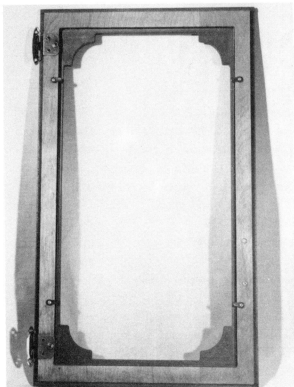

Illus. 11-30. Inside view of the plywood glass-paned door.

one main disadvantage is that the grain of the door will run all in the same direction; that is whereas the grain of the rails is usually horizontal on traditional doors, the grain on the rail area will run vertically. The other possible disadvantage is that the inner core of the ply-

wood is exposed, as is true on all plywood doors. If the edges of the plywood are sanded very smooth, they can be finished very nicely and will not be unsightly.

Making the Layout   Follow the directions presented earlier in this chapter for making ³⁄₄-inch plywood lipped doors for either a single door or a pair of doors. Machine the rabbets on the outside edge to make the lip of the door before proceeding to work on the inside of the door.

Draw the layout of the simulated rails and stiles on the rear surface of the plywood, allowing a minimum of 2 inches for their width. The lines drawn should represent the *inner edge* of the glass rabbet. The top and bottom "rails" can be curved in any of a number of patterns, if desired. The bottom "rail" can also be made wider than 2 inches, if desired. Illus. 11-31 shows some possible variations of curved patterns in the traditional mode.

Machining the Inner Portion of the Plywood   The method of machining the inner portion of the plywood door will depend upon whether the door is a simple rectangular door or one with a curved top and/or bottom.

LEFT & RIGHT REQ'D.

Illus. 11-31. Panel door frames come in many designs.

The Rectangular Door After making the layout on the rear of the door, drill a pilot hole for the sabre-saw blade and then proceed to saw on the lines as marked to remove the inner "cutaway" portion of the door. Sand all four of these inside edges smooth and even. Using a router equipped with a ⅜-inch rabbet cutter, run a ⅜ × ⅜-inch rabbet around the four inside edges of the door. Square the four corners with a chisel (Illus. 11-32).

The Curved-Top Door The techniques presented in the preceding section work equally well for a curved-top door if the glass is to be cut to fit the patterned rabbet. Using a square piece of glass in a curved-top door requires a different approach. Lay out the pattern lines used to remove the inner cutaway, drawing the curved top and bottom lines as desired. Cut the inner portion free with a sabre saw and remove this portion from the door. Rout a ⅜ × ⅜-inch rabbet along all edges. Using a router that is set to cut ⅜ inch deep and is equipped with a ⅜-inch straight cutter, rout a groove along the top edge of the door and along the two sides above the curved portion of the door (Illus. 11-33). This groove must match the rabbet for the glass that is already machined along the inner edges of the door. To accomplish this, use the width guide that some routers have as an accessory that can be set for the exact distance from the edge the groove is to be routed. Woodworkers often design their own width guides by making jigs that can be fastened to the base of their router, which will maintain the specific distance that the groove is to be machined from the edge of a board. Illus. 11-34 shows a simple Plexiglas™ router guide that can be easily made to fit almost any router. Remove the regular base of the router when this Plexiglas base guide is to be used.

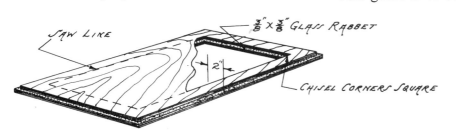

SAW LINE

⅜" × ⅜" GLASS RABBET

2"

CHISEL CORNERS SQUARE

Illus. 11-32. Detail for routing a rectangular, plywood glass-paned door.

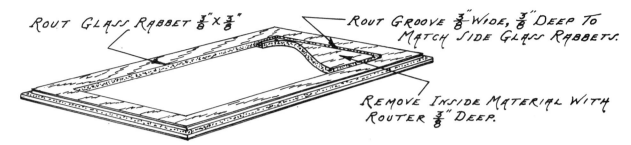

Illus. 11-33. Technique for routing a curved-top, glass-paned plywood door.

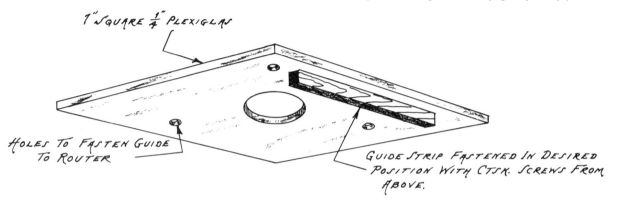

NOTE: REMOVE REGULAR BASE FROM ROUTER

Illus. 11-34. A shop-built, Plexiglas router width guide.

After cutting the groove, simply rout away the material above the curved line. It may help to place the inner cutaway piece of plywood back into position to help support the base of the router while doing this operation. Again, chisel the two upper corners square. The door is now ready to receive the glass.

Overlaid and Flush Plywood Glass-Paned Doors

The procedure for making flush and overlaid glass-paned doors is not very different from the methods used for the lipped doors. First fabricate the plywood doors to their correct overall sizes using the methods described earlier in the chapter. Of course, you will have to edge-band an overlay plywood door to cover the unsightly inner core or plies of the panel. Then lay out the pattern desired on the rear of the plywood panel, and saw the inner cutaway

portion free with the sabre saw. Next, cut the rabbet for the glass with the router and, if a square pane of glass is to be used, rout away the upper portion of the door for the glass as described in the preceding section.

TRADITIONAL METHODS OF MAKING GLASS-PANED DOORS

There are several methods of fabricating glass-paned doors that require more machinery and skill. Making door frames with lumber rails and stiles is first described. Then methods for shaping the edges of the rails and stiles and making coped joints are presented.

Door Frames with Square Edges If the interior edges of the door frames are left square and a $3/8 \times 3/8$-inch glass rabbet is machined along the same edges, some special joinery problems are encountered. The rails can only be joined to the stiles with a mortise-and-tenon or dowel joint. Illus. 11-35 shows how this joint is usually made. The glass bead must be sawed and chiselled away so that the rail fits flush against the stile. A dowel joint is fairly easy to make and will provide satisfactory strength for the door. Chapter five contained instructions for making dowel joints. Review it before attempting to make one for the first time. One method of decorating the glass bead is to rout a small cove around the inside edge (Illus. 11-36).

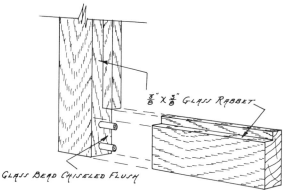

Illus. 11-35. Lumber door frames require dowel or mortise-and-tenon joints.

Door Frames with Moulded Glass
Bead Most commercially made glass-paned doors have the glass bead edged with a moulding, as shown in Illus. 11-28. This is usually done with a spindle shaper and matching cutters that will produce the moulded edge on the stiles and the matching "female" cut on the end of the rails. Because the shaper is an expensive machine and the matching cutters can cost hundreds of dollars, these techniques will not be described. However, there are on the market router cutters that do a fairly good job of producing moulded edges and coped joints for glass-paned doors and raised-panelled doors (Illus. 11-37). These cutters are available in either ¼-inch or ½-inch shanks and should be used with the router mounted in a router table (Illus. 11-38). It is a good technique to make several shallow cuts using these

cutters rather than one heavy cut, especially in hardwoods. Although these cutters are made for panelled doors, it is a simple matter to cut away the material to make the rabbet for the pane of glass (Illus. 11-39).

Another technique sometimes used is to mitre the corners where the rails and stiles meet. However, the mitre joint is not strong, and if the rails and stiles are of different widths, it cannot be used.

Glass-Retaining Methods
There are several methods for retaining the pane of glass in a door frame. In the last few years, new devices have been marketed that

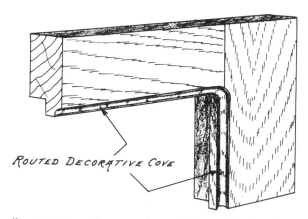

Illus. 11-36. A small cove can be routed around the door frame, for decoration.

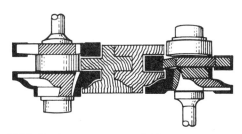

Illus. 11-37. Router cutters are available to make coped door joints. (Drawing courtesy of MLCS Ltd.)

229

Illus. 11-38. The mounted router is excellent for machining coped joints.

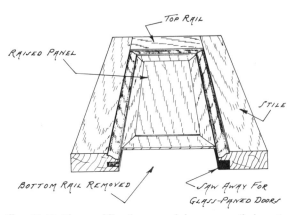

Illus. 11-39. The moulding for a panel door can easily be cut away for a glass-paned door.

retain the glass with very little effort upon the part of the builder. These devices are available from woodworker's supply catalogues. In this section of the chapter both traditional and modern methods of retaining glass are described.

Wood Bead This is the oldest method of retaining a glass pane in a door frame, but it works well on only rectangular doors. Cut a simple wood beading to its correct size (approximately ¼ × ¼ inch, depending upon

the thickness of the glass used). The beading is often machined with a slight rounding, to give it a nicer appearance. Mitre it at the corners and fasten it in place with small, thin brads. Drill holes for these brads before nailing them in place, to prevent splitting the narrow pieces (Illus. 11-40).

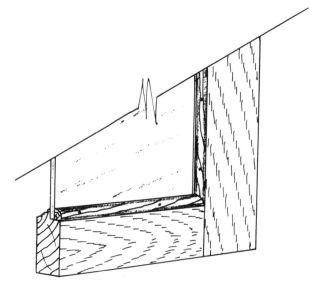

Illus. 11-40. A wood bead is a common means of retaining glass in a door frame.

Retaining Buttons

These buttons are available in different sizes and shapes (Illus. 11-41). No machining or recessing is required on the plastic offset button because the button has a lip that holds the glass firmly in place. The disc retaining button must be recessed into the frame so that it is flush with the glass surface. It has a flat spot on its edge which, when rotated, allows for easy installation and removal of the glass.

Screw Retainer

This device holds the glass firmly in place and also adjusts to any thickness of glass (Illus. 11-41). The screw has a plastic tip, to prevent the glass from cracking when pressure is applied.

PLASTIC OFFSET   DISC

SCREW-TYPE

Illus. 11-41. Three newer types of glass retainers.

Plastic Retaining Strips

Plastic stripping is sold in two styles. One style is designed to slip into a groove cut into the door frame. The other is stapled or tacked in position (Illus. 11-42). Both work well on straight frames or frames with gentle curves. The strips are usually available in walnut and a fruitwood color. Since the advent of retainer screws and buttons, plastic strips are not used as often.

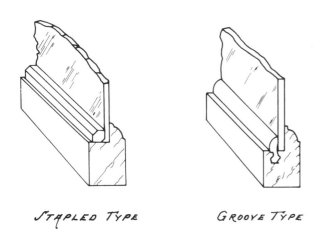

STAPLED TYPE   GROOVE TYPE

Illus. 11-42. Plastic strips are used to retain glass.

Glazier Points

Although these are ordinarily used to retain glass in a window sash and are then covered with putty, they can also be used in a furniture door. They are rather unsightly compared to the other devices already described. However, glazier points would be an inexpensive and quick means of installing glass in the frame of a door that will not be opened often.

BUILDING RAISED-PANELLED DOORS

Probably nothing can surpass the beauty of a traditional piece of furniture with solid raised-panelled doors. Raised-panelled doors have become increasingly popular over the last two decades, and many craftspersons would like to be able to duplicate them in their home shops. However, these doors are usually made with heavy-duty spindle shapers and large, expensive shaper cutters. These methods will not be described here. There are, however, ways of producing an attractive raised panel with either a table saw or router. These methods are explored in this section of the chapter.

A raised-panelled door has exactly the same door frame as a plain-panelled door. The edges of the stiles and rails can be square or moulded, but making the panel requires additional expertise and skill. The door itself can be lipped, overlaid, or even flush, because the raised panel fits nicely with either style.

Illus. 11-43 shows raised panels. The panel itself is made from glued-up, solid lumber that is 5/8 inch thick. With the proper machinery, any of a number of shapes can be milled along the edges of this panel to give it the raised effect (Illus. 11-44). The home woodworker, however, will be restricted to making panels with less elaborate designs with the router or the table saw.

After deciding upon the type of door—lipped, flush, or overlaid—calculate the overall size of the door or doors and run out the rails and stiles as required. If moulded edges

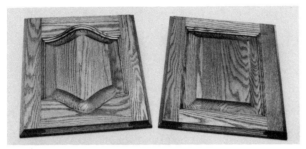

Illus. 11-43. Two examples of high-styled raised-panelled doors.

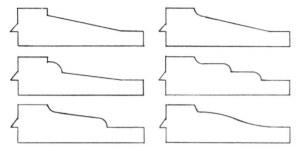

Illus. 11-44. The panels can be given a number of shapes.

and coped joints are being used, take into account the distance the moulded edge of the stile penetrates the "female" cut in the rail when calculating the length of the rail.

USING A TABLE SAW

If the door frame that will contain the raised panel is rectangular, a satisfactory raised panel can be made by using just the table saw, although some laborious sanding will be required to make it look presentable. If the edges of the rails and stiles are to remain square, the procedure for machining these is exactly as described in the section on plain-panelled doors.

The bevelled edges of the raised panel are usually 1½ inches wide, excluding the portion that fits into the door-frame groove. Set the saw blade at an angle of about 12 degrees. Because the blades on almost all tilting arbor saws tilt to the right, move the saw fence to the left of the blade for this operation (Illus. 11-45). Raise the blade 1⅝ inches high and set the fence so that a tongue slightly less than ¼ inch will be cut along the outside edge of the panel. This portion of the panel must fit into the groove machined into the rails and stiles. Set the fence just far enough from the

Illus. 11-45. Table saw setup for machining a raised panel.

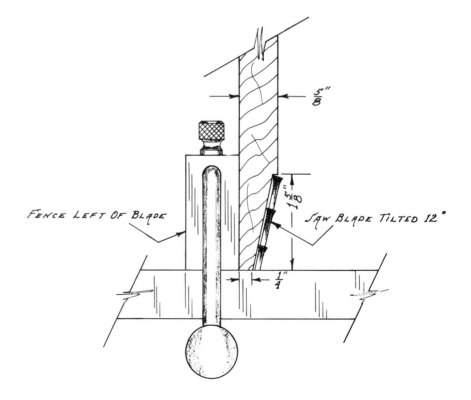

FENCE LEFT OF BLADE

$\frac{5}{8}''$

$1\frac{5}{8}''$

SAW BLADE TILTED 12°

$\frac{1}{4}''$

saw blade so that a ⅛-inch rabbet is cut along the inner edge of the bevelled portion. You will probably have to readjust the fence and make test cuts on scrap wood before the bevel is perfect.

If the raised panels are quite large, attach an auxiliary wooden fence to the regular saw fence; this will help steady the pieces as they are being machined. Cut the bevel along all four edges of the panel, and then sand the bevels smooth and clean of all traces of saw marks. Start with 60-grit sandpaper and use finer grades as the sanding proceeds. Usually some of the sanding can be done with the finish sander, which will remove the sanding marks on the bevels that were cut across the grain of the wood. Check the fit of the panel in the grooves on the door frame. If the grooves are too tight, plane them to a nice fit using a hand plane. Assemble the door by gluing and clamping it with bar clamps. Cushion the clamps so as not to mar the stiles. Remember, do not glue the raised panel in the groove, but allow it to "float" so that it can expand and contract as the humidity dictates.

USING A ROUTER

The router cutters shown in Illus. 11-37 are used to make raised-panelled doors and glass-paned doors. With these cutters, the edges of the rails and stiles can be moulded and the coped joints made. Curved rails can be machined with these cutters, so Gothic panelled doors can be built.

One other router cutter is required to create raised panels. This cutter is shown in Illus. 11-46. Although this cutter will cut bevels only about 1 inch wide, an attractive raised panel can be fabricated. The full set of router cutters with either ¼- or ½-inch shanks needed to make raised-panelled doors costs under $100. These cutters are sold by MLCS Ltd., P.O. Box 4053DA, Rydal, PA 19046.

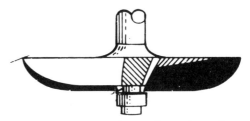
Illus. 11-46. A router cutter that can be used to make a raised panel. (Drawing courtesy of MLCS Ltd.)

BUILDING PIVOT OR POCKET DOORS

A fairly new concept in furniture doors is the pivot or pocket door, as it is termed by some manufacturers (Illus. 11-47). This is the type of door often found in entertainment centers, because the doors open and then push back into the cabinet, allowing an unobstructed view and access to the television, VCR, stereo, etc. Several manufacturers now make the hardware for installing pivot doors. Although this hardware is similar in principle, it is applied and installed differently.

One advantage of the pocket door is that almost any style of door can be used with the available hardware: a plain ¾-inch plywood

Illus. 11-47. The pocket door is a common feature on entertainment centers. (Photo courtesy of Julius Blum, Inc.)

door, a plain- or raised-panelled door, or a door with overlaid cutouts glued to the surface. Although the style can vary, the type of door cannot, as only a flush door can be used. The edges of the door should be left basically square, although a routed edge would be permissible and would not interfere with the installation of this type of door.

SELECTING THE HARDWARE

This is not a hardware item that is stocked by the average building supply dealer or hardware store (Illus. 11-48). Wholesale cabinet hardware suppliers in larger cities usually list this item in their catalogues. So, too, do the leading woodworker's supply houses. The cost for a complete set of hardware depends upon the length of the metal slide travellers, which are directly related to the depth of the piece of furniture being built. The metal slides are available in lengths that will accommodate doors from 14 to 24 inches wide. A set refers to the hardware required for just one door, so it is necessary to purchase two sets for a pair of doors that front an entertainment center. It is important to note that the depth of the cabinet must be as much as 3½ inches greater than the width of the door to fully recess the door. This will vary from manufacturer to manufacturer, so it is a good idea to secure the hardware while the project is in the planning stage.

The hardware can be installed so that the door slides either vertically or horizontally (Illus. 11-49).

POCKET DOOR REQUIREMENTS

Gap Dimensions   As with all flush doors, there must be a gap between the door and the furniture case. This gap should be ¹⁄₁₆ to ³⁄₃₂ inch on the top, bottom, and sides of the doors. If a pair of doors is to be installed, the doors should meet nicely at the middle, just short of actually touching.

Thickness Restrictions   The thickness of the door can vary from ⅝ to 1¼ inches, although this will depend upon the hardware.

The knob or pull used on the door may

Illus. 11-48. The hardware set needed to install pocket doors. (Photo courtesy of Julius Blum, Inc.)

234

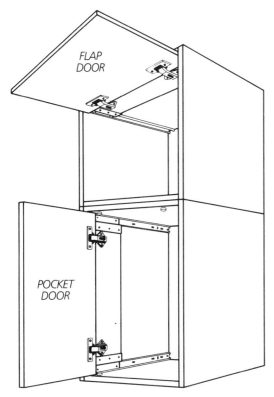

Illus. 11-49. Pocket doors can be used in two positions. (Drawing courtesy of Alfit America Inc.)

cause some problems. Check the side-gap allowance of the hardware to be certain there is enough room for the track, the door thickness, and the knob. If there is not enough room for the knob, the door will not be able to fully recess into the cabinet. If this is the case, a flush or recessed finger pull might have to be used.

Door Size Restrictions This must be carefully checked, also, for some hardware restricts the door height to be between $19^{11}/_{16}$ and $39^{3}/_{8}$ inches. Other hardware does not restrict the height because the metal travellers are not connected by anything but the door itself. Of course, if larger doors are used, extra hardware sets would also have to be used to bear the load.

Furniture Construction Requirements Pivot-door hardware is

primarily made to be installed on frameless cabinetry. If the pivot-door hardware is to be used on a face-framed cabinet, place wood blocks under the track so that it is flush with the door edge of the face frame. This, too, is important to know while the project is being planned.

INSTALLING THE HARDWARE AND THE PIVOT DOORS

The instructions that come with each set of hardware are very specific and should be followed to the letter (Illus. 11-50). Simple installation jigs for obtaining parallel tracks can easily be made from scraps of wood. The hardware sets come complete with European two-piece clip hinges that have to be installed precisely to function properly. These hinges are described below. Read this section before attempting to install these hinges in a door.

EUROPEAN CLIP HINGES

Many changes have taken place in the cabinet and furniture industry in the last 20 to 30 years, much of which has occurred in Europe. After World War II, because of the resulting serious shortage of skilled labor Europeans designed simple, straight-line cabinets and furniture that did not have the usual face frame. This furniture and these cabinets could be mass-produced and required few skilled artisans because the machinery, once set up, could be run by unskilled people. Discarding the face frame also meant discarding the $3/_8$-inch inset hinge, because there simply was not enough room to hang adjoining doors on a $3/_4$-inch cabinet division. The Europeans quickly designed a completely concealed, compound-action hinge that allows adjoining doors to be opened without hitting the neighboring door. This is accomplished by moving the door out and away from the cabinet while

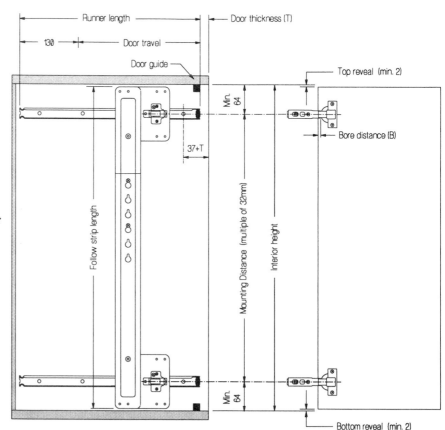

Illus. 11-50. Mounting instructions for pocket doors. (Drawing courtesy of Julius Blum, Inc.)

Illus. 11-51. One style of concealed European hinge is used on frameless furniture. (Photo courtesy of Julius Blum, Inc.)

the door is being opened (Illus. 11-51). In this way, doors could be hung side by side and almost completely cover the basic box.

APPLICATIONS AND FEATURES

These hinges have three advantages. First, they can be used in almost any door application. They are made for a wide range of opening angles—100, 110, 125, and 170 degrees—and can be used on almost any type of door. There are also concealed hinges that can be used on face frames (Illus. 11-52).

Second, these hinges possess a "slide-on" action that allows the two parts of the hinge to be mounted separately. The door, with its portion of the hinge installed, is then slid into that part of the hinge mounted on the inside of the furniture piece. Third, the self-closing hinge (and thus the door) is adjustable in any of three directions after the door is hung.

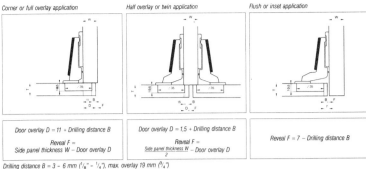

Corner or full overlay application

Half overlay or twin application

Flush or inset application

Door overlay D = 11 + Drilling distance B

Reveal F =
Side panel thickness W − Door overlay D

Door overlay D = 1,5 + Drilling distance B

Reveal F =
Side panel thickness W − Door overlay D
2

Reveal F = 7 − Drilling distance B

Drilling distance B = 3 - 6 mm ($^1/_8$" - $^1/_4$"), max. overlay 19 mm ($^3/_4$")

Illus. 11-52 (left). Another style of European hinge is used for face-frame furniture. (Photo courtesy of Julius Blum, Inc.) Illus. 11-53 (above). Three different mounting applications for the European hinge. (Photo courtesy of Julius Blum, Inc.)

DOORS THAT CAN BE USED WITH EURO-HINGES

Illus. 11-53 pictures the three basic mounting variations: full overlay, half overlay, and inset or flush. The full overlay and the inset or flush applications are self-explanatory. The half-overlay hinge is used where a pair of doors must be hung on a center divider.

Typically, these hinges are most often associated with a contemporary, plastic-laminate-covered door, but can be used on almost any style of door. The only design restriction is that the door stiles be made wide enough to accept the circular door portion of the hinge—about 1¾ to 2 inches.

DOOR-SIZE AND HINGE-NUMBER REQUIREMENTS

The width of the door is quite important when these hinges are to be used. The height is not that important. Study Illus. 11-53 carefully. Note that the "reveal" (or amount the door is made smaller than the exterior of the basic box) and B (the distance from the edge of the door that the hinge hole is drilled) are very important. This is not as forbidding as it seems. Distance B is usually ¹⁄₁₆ to ³⁄₃₂ inch, and, if the door is a bit too wide, simply run it over the jointer until it works properly! Re-

member, it's easy to remove and reattach the door with these hinges.

The number of hinges to use per door depends upon the size and weight of the door.

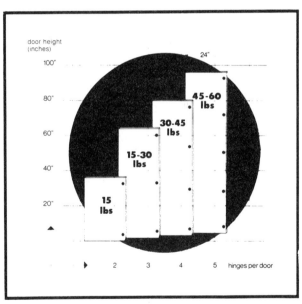

Illus. 11-54. Hinge requirements for different-size doors. (Drawing courtesy of Julius Blum, Inc.)

Illus. 11-54 shows the hinge requirements for doors of various heights and weights.

INSTALLING THE HINGES

As Illus. 11-55 reveals, the two parts of the hinge are mounted separately. Both locations

237

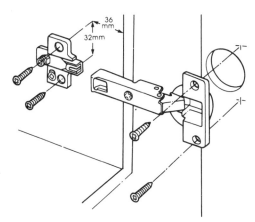

Illus. 11-55. The European hinge is mounted in two parts.

are very important. Install the door portion of the hinge by drilling a 1⅜-inch hole usually ½ inch deep and ⅟₁₆ to ³⁄₃₂ inch from the edge of the door (Illus. 11-56). This requires the special Forstner bit shown in Illus. 11-57. Use this bit in a drill press, to obtain a straight and true drilling. Mount the door portion of the hinge, making sure that the arm is square with the door edge.

Next, position the door exactly as desired in relation to the basic box and transfer the hinge centerlines to the inside of the furniture piece. The holes for the mounting strip of the hinge are located exactly 1⁷⁄₁₆ inches (37 mm) from the front edge. Here a simple drilling jig comes in handy, especially if a number of

hinges are to be installed (Illus. 11-58). This jig can easily be made in the shop. If a flush door is being hung, add the thickness of the door to the 1⁷⁄₁₆-inch set back dimension. This will ensure that the plate is located properly to bring the face of the door flush with the furniture piece.

Finally, snap the door into place and give it a trial swing or two. Perhaps a few adjustments will be needed but the advantage of these hinges is that they are adjustable in three directions. After you have worked with these hinges a few times, they will become easy to handle and install. Just be certain to purchase the correct hinge for the application desired, and always follow the directions included with the brand of hinge purchased.

GLASS DOORS FOR FURNITURE

Contemporary furniture often has frameless plate-glass doors. These doors will either be sliding glass doors or hinged glass doors. Special hardware and some building modifications are required to install these doors.

PLATE-GLASS SLIDING DOORS

China cabinets and other interior-visible fur-

Illus. 11-56. Drilling detail for mounting the concealed hinge.

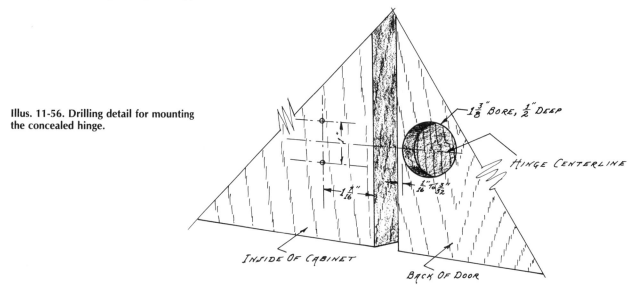

238

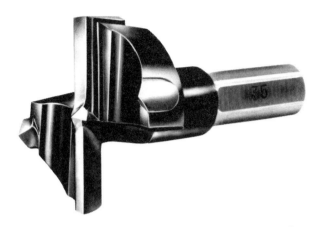

Illus. 11-57. A 35-mm Forstner drill bit is needed to mount the concealed hinge. (Drawing courtesy of Stanley Hardware, Division of the Stanley Works)

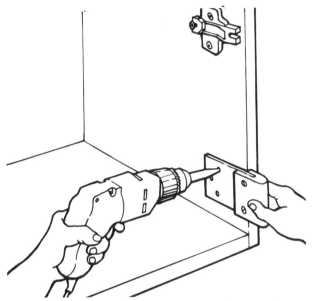

Illus. 11-58. A simple jig can be used to locate the mounting plate holes.

niture designed in the modern motif often are equipped with plate-glass sliding doors. These doors display the contents of the cabinet clearly and, with the proper hardware, slide very easily.

Designing the Cabinet No major building modifications are required to accommodate plate-glass sliding doors in a china or gun cabinet. Of course, the cabinet will be of the visible-interior type that has been described in the previous chapters. About the only modi-

fication necessary is to widen the stiles so that the doors do not slide behind the stiles. The upper rail may also have to be widened to accommodate the upper track. This is a simple matter of gluing and clamping a ¾-inch piece to the inside of the stiles and rail to widen these pieces to 1½ inches.

Pay careful attention to the weight of plate-glass sliding doors. Their weight could cause the bottom of an unsupported cabinet to sag after a while. Keep the span or width of the cabinet opening to a minimum, to prevent this. A china cabinet does not have this problem if the upper unit rests on and is supported by the lower unit. Fortunately, this is the way most of these furniture pieces are designed.

Ordering Plate-Glass Sliding Doors

When most of the furniture piece is completed, order the plate-glass sliding doors from a glass specialty house. All the dealer requires is the exact size of the opening—width first, then the height. The dealer will then order the doors from a supplier or make them up in his own shop if it is so equipped. If finger slots are desired, these, too, must be ordered, because there is usually an extra charge for grinding finger slots. The doors are delivered complete with the track. The builder simply installs the doors in the completed piece.

Track and Hardware

Cabinet supply houses and woodworker's specialty catalogues usually carry plate-glass sliding tracks and special locks for glass doors. For an inexpensive sliding door installation, use a simple wood, plastic, or aluminum track (Illus. 11-59). This same type of track is also used for ¼-inch plywood sliding doors. Better-quality plate-glass sliding doors have a ball-bearing track assembly that allows the doors to slide with minimum effort (Illus. 11-60).

Installing the Track and Doors   Screw

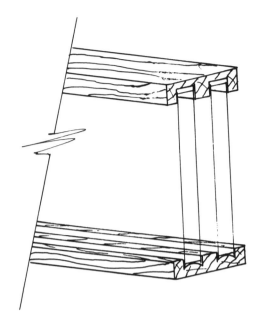

Illus. 11-59. Wood, metal, or plastic track is available for use with sliding glass doors.

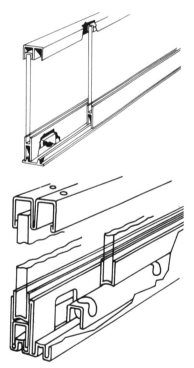

Illus. 11-60. A more sophisticated ball-bearing track is often used for plate-glass sliding doors.

the track to the top rail and the bottom of the cabinet. The cabinet must be exactly square for the doors to meet the stiles properly when

closed. There is practically no adjustment possible other than shimming the lower track slightly to make glass doors fit.

NO-BORE HINGES

These hinges are fairly new in the furniture hardware field, and make working with glass doors very easy. There are sets of hinges for several different types of door applications as well as door pulls and strike plates for magnetic catches. The hinges are held to the glass with pressure screws that will hold ¼-inch plate glass securely in place with no glass drilling required. This hardware is available in brass and chrome.

Pivot Hinges for New Furniture Pieces
This pivot-door installation requires drilling holes for two metal bushings at the top and bottom of the cabinet opening. Pins on the hinges ride in these bushings, and provide the swinging mechanism. These hinges are used on inset or flush glass doors only (Illus. 11-61).

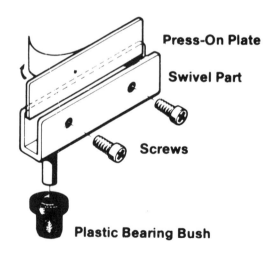

Illus. 11-61. A type of no-drill hinge used to install glass doors in new furniture.

Pivot Hinges for Existing Furniture
Use these hinges if you want to modernize and upgrade an older piece of furniture with

glass doors. The hinge comes with a mounting bracket that is screwed to the inside of the cabinet and is used for flush or inset glass doors (Illus. 11-62).

Pivot Hinges for Overlay Glass Doors
This is a rather unique hinge in that it allows a $7/16$-inch overlay on all edges of a glass door, rather than requiring that the door be inset or flush with the cabinet edges.

Catches for Glass Doors
The most used and probably the most convenient type of catch for the pivot glass door is the magnetic touch latch—either double or single, as needed. A no-bore metal strike plate is fastened to the door with a self-adhesive foam rubber pad. This strike plate will hold the door securely closed against the magnetic touch latch, and a simple push against the door gently opens the door. These magnetic touch catches are shown in Illus. 11-20.

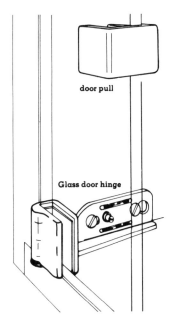

door pull

Glass door hinge

Illus. 11-62. No-drill hinge used to install glass doors in old work.

CHAPTER TWELVE

Headboards and Bedside Tables

Bed headboards and bedside tables or nightstands can also be built very handily in the home woodworking shop with the casework method. The home craftsperson may decide to build a headboard and night tables that match one of the chests of drawers featured in Chapter Six. Again, a word of caution: Do not attempt to build the projects contained in this chapter until the lessons and woodworking techniques presented in Chapter Six have been mastered.

DESIGNING HEADBOARDS

There are two types of headboard generally used in today's bedrooms: the decorative headboard and the bookcase headboard. In this chapter only the bookcase headboard will be addressed. Sliding doors are the common feature of this type of headboard. Other factors play a part in determining the design. These include the style (contemporary or traditional), the number of compartments built into the headboard, the motif used on the sliding doors, and, of course, the species of wood and other materials used in its construction.

DETERMINING THE SIZE OF THE HEADBOARD

The dimensions of headboards vary considerably and are directly related to the size and type of bed that will be used with the headboard. Probably most beds used with bookcase headboards are supported by a metal frame that is equipped with casters and is adjustable to the size of the box spring and mattress. At the head of the frame are metal plates with screw holes, so, if desired, the metal frame may be permanently fastened to the headboard. Permanent legs are screwed or bolted directly to the underside of some box springs. There are also bedsteads that are complete with side rails that fasten to the head and tail boards.

Standard Box Springs and Mattresses

There are four types of box springs and mattresses in general use. The sizes of these box springs have a direct bearing on the dimensions of the bookcase headboard. These box springs come in twin, double, queen, and king sizes. The designer needs to know the width and length dimensions of each to properly design a matching headboard. They are as follows:

Twin: 39 inches wide × 75 or 80 inches long
Double: 54 inches wide × 75 or 80 inches long
Queen: 60 inches wide × 80 inches long
King: 76 inches wide × 80 inches long

On occasion two twin beds will be used side-by-side to look like one complete king-size bed covered by one large bedspread. When this is done, the combined width of the two beds is 78 inches. Illus. 12-1 shows a headboard built for this arrangement. The castered metal frame is really a necessity to allow the two twin beds to be easily rolled apart for bed-making purposes.

Bookcase headboards are usually built the same width as the mattress, or just an inch or two wider. The depth of the headboard will vary from 9 to 12 inches, with 9 inches the most-used depth. Most commercially built bookcase headboards are made 40 inches high. Check the combined height of the legs (or metal frame) and the box spring and mattress that is to be used to determine if 40 inches is the proper height. It is a simple matter to make dimension and design adjustments while planning rather than to have to rework a project after it is underway.

A KING-SIZE HEADBOARD

The headboard shown in Illus. 12-1 and 12-2

Illus. 12-1. A headboard with sliding doors and side cabinets for two twin beds made up as a king-size bed.

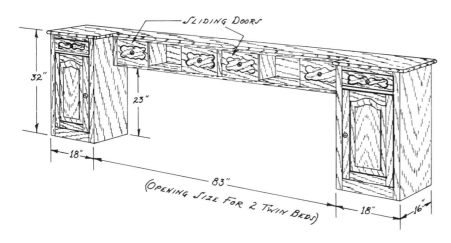

Illus. 12-2. Overall dimensions of the king-size headboard.

is unique in that it is not only a bookcase equipped with sliding doors, but it also has bedside cabinets to make one very functional piece of bedroom furniture. Because the headboard is 119 inches long, it must be built in three separate pieces to facilitate moving it into the bedroom and through narrow hallways. The three sections are joined by screws, and the entire unit is attached with a one-piece top. It takes just a few minutes to disassemble the headboard when it has to be moved to a different location. The scrolled design on the sliding doors and the drawer fronts and the panelled cabinet doors with their curved top rails give the headboard a traditional look. You can adapt this type of headboard to meet personal requirements.

ADAPTING THE MEASUREMENTS

Illus. 12-2 gives the overall measurements of the headboard. The area between the side cabinets is 83 inches. This area accommodates two side-by-side twin beds plus an additional two inches on each side, so you can roll the beds in and out between the cabinets without scratching them. If you are changing the width to make use of a narrower box spring and mattress, be sure to allow this same margin for the bed to fit between the side cabinets. For a double bed, allow 58 inches as the length of the bookcase section, for a queen size 64 inches, etc. Check the height of the box spring, mattress, and legs to determine if the height to the bottom of the bookcase section is correct. It is a simple matter to adjust the height of the side cabinets so the bed assembly just slips under the middle section of the headboard. Note in Illus. 12-1 that when the bed is made up and the pillows are in place, the sliding doors are partially covered by the pillows. Some builders may prefer making the entire structure slightly higher to expose the sliding doors completely.

BUILDING THE SIDE CABINETS

Build the two side cabinets using the casework methods as presented in various chapters throughout this text. Make sure that you are thoroughly familiar with these methods before attempting this project, because all of those techniques will not be repeated in this chapter.

FABRICATING THE FACE FRAMES, BACKS, AND BOTTOMS

Begin by making two face frames as shown in Illus. 12-3. The bill of material for both face frames is as follows:

Stiles: Four pieces ¾ × 1½ × 31¾ inches
Top rails: Two pieces ¾ × 2 × 14 inches

Bottom rails: Two pieces ¾ × 3 × 15 inches
Drawer rails: Two pieces ¾ × 1¾ × 16½ inches

On the top rails, machine special grooves the width of the table-saw blade. Locate these grooves ⅜ inches from the upper edge of the top rail. They will be used for the metal top fasteners that hold the top in place. Illus. 12-5 shows this groove in detail. Next, run ¼ × ½-inch rabbets along one edge of each stile and then assemble the face frames using screw joints. Locate the drawer rail 4 inches from the top rail and notch it so it fits between the stiles. Then glue and screw it in place.

Backs

Use two pieces of ¼-inch hardboard or plywood that measure 17½ inches wide × 31¼ inches high for the backs. As usual, check the exact dimensions by measuring on the basic face frame. Glue and nail ¾ × 2-inch pine reinforcers to the sides and the tops of these panels, as shown in Illus. 12-4. Note in Illus. 12-5 that the groove for the tabletop fasteners is run in the top reinforcing piece, as was done on the top rail of the face frames. Nail the reinforcers to the plywood by nailing from the

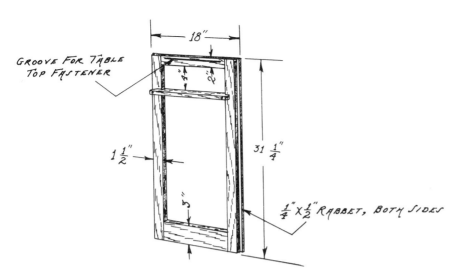

back side of the plywood panels into the pine pieces.

Bottoms   Use ⅝- or ¾-inch particle board or plywood for the bottoms. The bottoms should measure 17½ inches wide × 15 inches deep. Cut notches at the back corners to fit around the pine reinforcers nailed to the back panels. Again, check the face frames and backs for the exact width.

Assembly   Nail the backs to the bottoms. The upper surface of the bottoms must be exactly even with the top edge of the lower rail of the face frames, which are 3 inches high. Then fasten the face frames to the bottoms using two support strips to hold the face frames in place. Glue and nail the face frames to the bottoms using 4d finish nails (Illus. 12-4).

FABRICATING THE SIDE PANELS

Cut four pieces of matching ¼-inch hardwood plywood that measure 15¾ × 31¼ inches. Double-check their exact sizes by measuring the partially assembled cabinets. Joint a 5-degree bevel along the edges of the panels that will fit into the rabbets on the face frames. Glue and nail the panels in place using ¾-inch

brads along the rabbets and 4d finish nails along the other edges. Be certain to pull the cabinets into alignment with the side panels to ensure that the cabinets are square.

Illus. 12-4. Assembly technique for the side cabinets.

MAKING AND INSTALLING THE REINFORCING PIECES

The pine reinforcing pieces that are glued and clamped to the top edges of the side panels must be grooved to accommodate the tabletop fasteners as shown in Illus. 12-5. These reinforcers should measure ¾ × 2 inches × the appropriate length to fit. Make and install the ¾- × 2-inch upper drawer runner at this time.

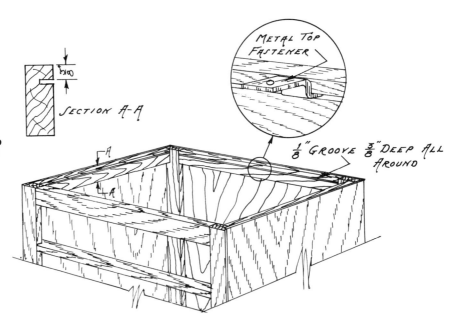

SECTION A-A

METAL TOP FASTENER

⅛" GROOVE ⅜" DEEP ALL AROUND

Illus. 12-5. Reinforcer details and top attachment method. Note: the upper drawer runner is omitted for clarity.

MAKING THE DRAWERS

The drawers for the side cabinets are standard lipped drawers made according to the directions in Chapter Seven. Only the building of the drawer front itself requires some instruction. The directions that follow apply to making a scroll-sawed, overlay drawer front, as shown in Illus. 12-1. Make the fronts from three pieces of ¼-inch hardwood plywood that are cut to the overall drawer-front size by following the formula in Chapter Seven. Glue two of the pieces together to form a piece ½ inch thick. Draw the pattern for the scrollwork on the third piece, cut it out with the jigsaw, and cove the inner edge with a small cove bit in the router (Illus. 12-6). Finally, glue the third piece to the previously glued ½-inch piece to bring the total thickness of the drawer front to ¾ inch. Then machine the rabbets for the four edges of the drawers according to the directions in Chapter Seven.

COMPLETING THE SIDE CABINETS

Sand the face frames with a belt sander and then sand both the face frames and the side panels with the finish sander. Next, make the drawer runners and install the drawers in the cabinets. After choosing the design desired for the doors, make the type of doors selected and sand them ready for finishing. Prepare one (or two, if desired) shelves for the side cabinets and install the shelf tracks for adjustable shelving.

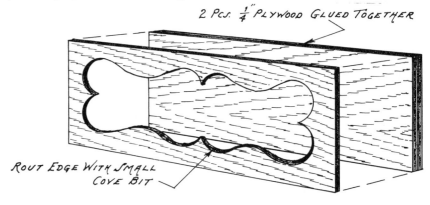

2 PCS. ¼" PLYWOOD GLUED TOGETHER

ROUT EDGE WITH SMALL COVE BIT

Illus. 12-6. Method of fabricating the scrolled drawer front.

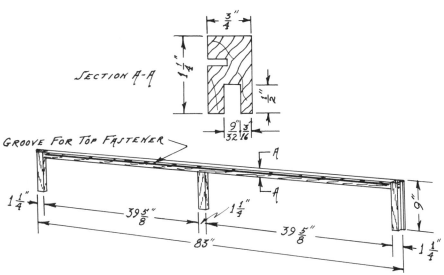

Illus. 12-7. Face-frame details for the center section.

BUILDING THE CENTER SECTION

The center section is an interior-visible cabinet with some sections open and other sections covered with sliding doors. All the doors slide in a single grooved track.

Making the Face Frame

The members of the face frame are narrowed considerably for this long but thin section of cabinetry. The bill of materials for the face frame is as follows:

End stiles: Two pieces $\frac{3}{4} \times 1\frac{1}{4} \times 9$ inches
Short stile: One piece $\frac{3}{4} \times 1\frac{1}{4} \times 7\frac{3}{4}$ inches
Top rail: One piece $\frac{3}{4} \times 1\frac{1}{4} \times 80\frac{1}{2}$ inches
Facing strips: Two pieces $\frac{3}{4} \times \frac{3}{4} \times$ approximately $39\frac{5}{8}$ inches

There is considerable machining required on the face-frame pieces. Machine a $\frac{1}{4}$- × $\frac{1}{2}$-inch rabbet along one edge of each of the end stiles. Run two grooves in the top rail, as detailed in Illus. 12-7. Make the groove along the lower edge $\frac{1}{2}$ inch deep and slightly wider than $\frac{1}{4}$ inch. It is in this groove that the upper edge of the sliding door will ride. Widen the groove by placing one or two shims between the blades of the dado head. Make another groove just the width of the saw blade along the inside of the top rail for the metal top

fasteners that are shown in Illus. 12-5.

Assemble the face frame using $1\frac{1}{2}$- or 2-inch flathead wood screws for the screw joints. Be careful not to place a screw where it will end up in the groove made for the sliding doors.

Making the Ends and the Dividers

Make the two end pieces from either $\frac{3}{4}$-inch lumber or $\frac{3}{4}$-inch veneered particle board or plywood. Edge-band the interior dividers, if they are made from plywood or particle core, to hide the interior core. To make the end pieces, you will need two pieces $\frac{3}{4}$ inch thick × $9\frac{1}{2}$ inches wide × 9 inches high. To make the dividers, you will need five pieces $\frac{3}{4}$ inch thick × $8\frac{3}{4}$ inches wide × $8\frac{1}{4}$ inches high. As detailed in Illus. 12-8, you will have to cut rabbets and dadoes in the end pieces. Also, joint a 5-degree bevel along the $\frac{1}{4}$-inch edge that will fit into the rabbet of the stile. Make a notch cut at the upper back corner of the dividers to fit around the back panel reinforcer, as shown in Illus. 12-8.

Making the Bottom
Make the bottom from $\frac{3}{4}$-inch lumber, veneered particle core, or plywood. The bottom should measure $\frac{3}{4} \times 8\frac{3}{4} \times 82\frac{1}{2}$ inches. Double-check the exact

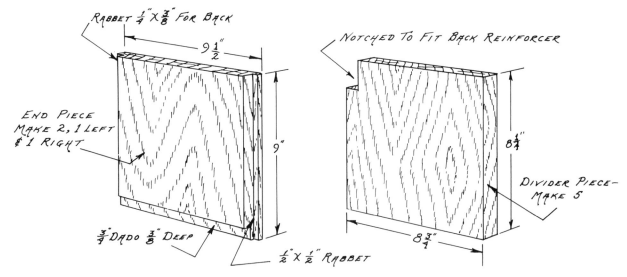

RABBET 1/4" X 3/8" FOR BACK

9 1/2"

END PIECE
MAKE 2, 1 LEFT
& 1 RIGHT

9"

3/4" DADO 3/8" DEEP

1/2" X 1/2" RABBET

NOTCHED TO FIT BACK REINFORCER

8 1/4"

DIVIDER PIECE—
MAKE 5

8 3/4"

Illus. 12-8. End panels and dividers for the center section.

length of the bottom after fastening the side pieces to the stiles of the face frame.

Starting the Assembly Sand the bottom and the end pieces before beginning to assemble the piece. Check the fit of the end pieces in the stile rabbets and make any adjustments necessary to ensure a tight fit. Glue and nail the ends into the rabbets on the stiles using 3/4-inch brads. Next, check the exact length the bottom needs to be and slip the bottom into the dadoes. Glue and nail the bottom in place using 4d finish nails.

Locate the position of all five dividers and fasten them in place by nailing through the bottom and the top rail using 4d finish nails. Measure and lay out the six spaces formed by the dividers so that they are all equal (Illus. 12-9).

Making the Back and the Back Reinforcer Make the back from 1/4-inch matching-hardwood plywood. Check the exact size needed by measuring on the partially assembled piece. The reinforcing strip is 3/4 × 1 1/4 × 82 1/4 inches. Cut a groove the width of the saw blade on the full length of this piece to

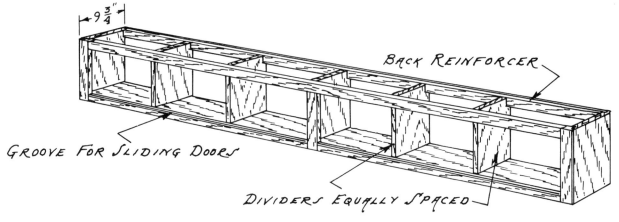

9 3/4"

BACK REINFORCER

GROOVE FOR SLIDING DOORS

DIVIDERS EQUALLY SPACED

Illus. 12-9. Assembly of the center section.

fit into the top fasteners (Illus. 12-10). Glue and nail the reinforcer in place in the notches of the dividers, checking each divider for squareness. Nail through the end pieces into the ends of the reinforcer. Glue and nail the ¼-inch plywood back in place using 1-inch nails.

Making the Facing Strips

Two pieces ¾ × ¾ × about 39⅝ inches are needed for the facing strips along the front edge of the bottom piece. Machine a groove in these strips to match the groove made in the top rail; this groove should be only ¼ inch deep. The lower edge of the sliding doors will run in this groove. Glue and nail the strips in place, taking care that no nails go through the grooved space (Illus. 12-10).

Making the Sliding Doors

The sliding doors are made of two thicknesses of ¼-inch plywood that are glued together. Make the pattern for the first, or outside, layer and cut it out with a scroll saw. This pattern should match the pattern used on the drawer fronts. As you will note from Illus. 12-11, only the rear piece of ¼-inch plywood slides in the grooves provided in the top rail and the bottom facing strip. In order to install the sliding door, you must raise this back piece into the

upper groove and then drop it into the lower groove. That is why the upper groove was machined ½ inch deep and the lower groove only ¼ inch deep.

Measure and cut the rear piece carefully. Make sure that it can be installed into the grooves before gluing the scrolled piece in position. Make the scrolled piece almost ¾ inch less in height than the rear piece so that the sliding doors can be installed. To accomplish this, locate the scrolled piece approximately 5⁄16 inch above the lower edge of the back piece and slightly more than ½ inch below the top edge.

ASSEMBLING THE THREE UNITS

Some assistance may be needed in assembling the three units. The best method of assembly is to have a helper lift and hold the center piece in place while you apply C-clamps to hold the sections firmly together. Then fasten the two end units to the center assembly by driving 1½-inch, #8 flathead wood screws through the upper reinforcers of the end cabinets into the ends of the sliding-door cabinet. Drive two more screws through the ¼-inch plywood sides of the end cabinets into the ends of the sliding-door unit. Use ¾-inch, #8 flathead wood screws. A total of four screws

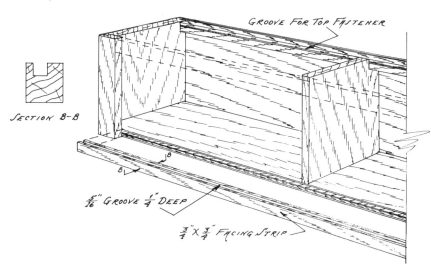

SECTION B-B

GROOVE FOR TOP FASTENER

5⁄16" GROOVE ¼" DEEP

¾" × ¾" FACING STRIP

Illus. 12-10. Detail of the sliding-door groove in the facing strip.

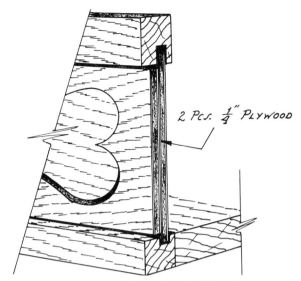

2 PCS. $\frac{1}{4}''$ PLYWOOD

Illus. 12-11. Fabricating technique for the sliding doors.

should be used to hold each end cabinet to the sliding door section.

MAKING THE TOP

If you are building the headboard for two twin beds as planned for in this chapter, the top, because of its length, will probably have to be made from hardwood lumber that will be edge-glued to form the required widths. If you have adapted the headboard for a smaller-size bed and the top is less than 96 inches long, you can use ¾-inch plywood for the top. If using ¾-inch plywood, you must apply a hardwood edging to all exposed edges. Before applying the edging, machine it with the desired moulding and mitre the corners exactly while installing the edging.

If a lumber top is being made, rout the edges with the desired cutter after cutting the top to its exact size. Plan for a ¾-inch overhang on all edges except the rear (Illus. 12-12). The two interior corners of the top may require some diligent carving to blend the routed edges together. Sand the lumber top with the belt sander and then the finish sander, using 220-grit sandpaper for the final sanding. Sand the plywood top only with the finish sander.

INSTALLING THE TOP

Remember, the three sections of the headboard were grooved near their upper edges to accept metal tabletop fasteners. These fasteners are available from most woodworker's supply catalogues such as the Woodworker's Store, Rogers, MN 55374; they cost only a few cents each. Use 14 to 16 fasteners. If obtaining or using these fasteners is a problem, you can hold the top in place with strategically located wooden cleats and screws.

The easiest means of installing the top is to turn it upside down on cushioned sawhorses or on a blanket on the shop floor. Place the assembled sections upside down on the top and locate the cabinets with the proper overhang all around. Slip the metal fasteners into the grooves and attach them to the underside of the top with ⅝- or ¾-inch roundhead screws.

ADDING A FINISH

If the headboard must be taken apart so it can be moved into the bedroom, do this prior to finishing. Proceed with a favorite finishing

Illus. 12-12. Details of the headboard top.

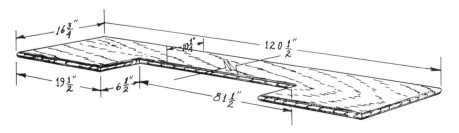

schedule after giving all sections a final cleanup sanding. When the finishing has been completed, reattach the doors, install all knobs and pulls, move the headboard into the bedroom, and reassemble the units.

BOOKCASE HEADBOARD

The bookcase headboard is one of the more common pieces of bedroom furniture and is relatively easy to build. The easiest material to use is lumber, because the headboard is made only 8 to 10 inches deep and lumber can be purchased in these widths. Although ¾-inch plywood or veneered particle board can be used, this entails a lot of laborious edge-banding that can just as well be avoided.

Bookcase headboards may be of the open-shelf variety or they may be equipped with sliding doors and partitions. Both types will be presented in this section.

DESIGNING THE HEADBOARD

The first dimension that must be determined is the desired width of the headboard. This is determined by the type of box spring and mattress to be used—twin, double, queen, or king. These widths are presented on page 243. The headboard should be made just an inch or two wider than the mattress size.

The headboard is usually 40 to 40½ inches high. It varies in depth from 8 to 10 inches. The width can be obtained from a 10-inch hardwood board. Illus. 12-13 shows a typical open-shelf bookcase headboard and its overall dimensions. A decorative top rail added to a headboard with no sliding doors or partitions will help embellish the design.

BUILDING THE OPEN-SHELF BOOKCASE HEADBOARD

After the width of the headboard has been

calculated, determine the other dimensions. These dimensions are presented in Illus. 12-13.

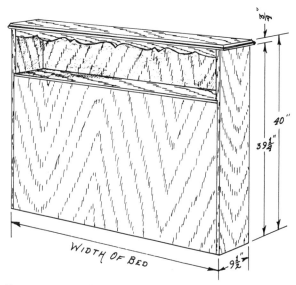

Illus. 12-13. Overall dimensions of the bookcase headboard.

Building and Machining the Side Pieces and the Shelf

The two side pieces are the most exacting in the headboard and must be planned carefully. Each side piece should be ¾ × 9½ × 39¼ inches. The piece for the shelf should measure ¾ × 9¼ inches × ¾ inch less than the total length of the headboard.

Run these pieces out to their finished dimensions. Then machine on the side pieces a ¾-inch dado ⅜ inch deep and 12 inches from the upper end. Note: A left and right side must be made! Using a router or spindle shaper, run a rabbet ⅜ inch wide and ¼ inch deep along the front edge of each side piece (Illus. 12-14). This must be a "stop" rabbet that is machined from the lower end up to the ¾-inch dado. Run the same stop rabbet along the rear edges of the side pieces from the upper end down to the ¾-inch dado. The front edge of the shelf will receive this same rabbet.

Make a ¾ × 4-inch reinforcing piece that fits between the two sides. This piece will

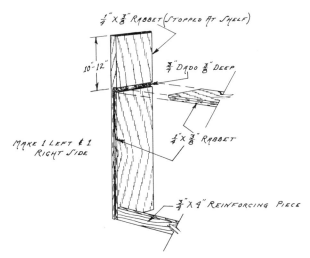

Illus. 12-14. The machining needed on the headboard sides.

strengthen and reinforce the ¼-inch plywood front panel of the headboard and may be made from either inexpensive lumber or a scrap strip of ¾-inch plywood.

Assembling the Sides and the Shelf

Fit the shelf into the dado and glue and nail it in place. Next, nail the reinforcer between the two sides. Then square the assembly and hold it in that position with temporary angle braces.

Preparing and Installing the Front ¼-Inch Panel

The front panel should have its grain running vertically, if possible. If the headboard is 48 inches wide or less, this is not a problem. However, if it is over 48 inches wide, either splice the plywood or the grain on the panel will have to run horizontally.

Splicing the Plywood Panel Prepare a ¾-inch backup board that's about 2 to 3 inches wide. Cut this board so that it is 4 inches short of the panel on its lower edge to allow room for the reinforcing piece, and about ½ inch short on the upper end for the rabbet in the shelf (Illus. 12-15). Joint 5-degree bevels along the meeting edges of the panels and check to see that a tight fit is obtained along

the length of the seam. Also check to see that the two panels have a matching grain pattern, if possible. Glue and clamp one edge of the plywood panel to the splicing piece and, after the glue has set, glue and nail the other panel in place with brads. Set all the brads and fill the holes and any seam gaps with matching plastic wood. After this has dried, scrape and sand the filler clean.

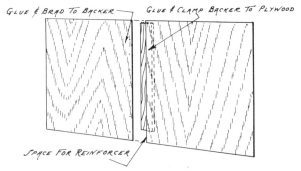

Illus. 12-15. The method used to splice ¼-inch plywood.

Next, install the front ¼-inch plywood panel so that it fits nicely into the rabbets along the shelf front and the sides. First, joint a 5-degree bevel along the top edge of the panel and saw the panel to its correct height. Then joint a 5-degree bevel along one edge of the panel and see how the panel fits into the rabbets along the top and this one side. Do any necessary hand-planing or jointing to make sure these two edges fit into the rabbets correctly. Finally, saw the panel to its proper length, allowing about ⅟32 to ⅟16 inch for joint-ing this remaining edge. Joint this final edge at 5 degrees and see how it fits into the rabbet. Continue jointing with very shallow cuts until the panel just drops into the rabbet. Glue and brad the panel in place using ¾-inch brads. Set the nails and fill the holes and any seam gaps with plastic wood. Sand and scrape the filler clean after it has dried.

Making and Installing the Top and the Decorative Rail

The top should measure ¾ × 10¼ × 1½

inches longer than the headboard structure. These dimensions allow for a ¾-inch overhang along the front and both ends. Machine a selected edging along the front and the ends. This may be a simple half-rounding, bead and cove, or other selected moulding. Machine a ¼ × ⅜-inch rabbet on the back edge that starts and stops just short of the ends of the top. This rabbet should not be exposed at the ends of the finished top.

The decorative rail must fit exactly between the sides. This top rail should measure ¾ × 2½ inches and should be of the appropriate length. Lay out the desired pattern and saw it to shape using a band saw or a sabre saw. File and sand the patterned edges smooth, cleaning off all of the saw marks. Sand the surface of the rail at this time as well. Install the rail in place between the sides using nails or counterbored and plugged screws.

Either simply nail the top in place or screw it in place. Counterbore the screw heads and cover them with matching wooden plugs. Then fit the ¼-inch plywood back into the rabbets and install it with short nails and glue.

Fastening a Bedframe to the Headboard

If the metal bedframe is to be permanently bolted to the headboard, glue wood reinforcing pieces to the inside of the front panel. This will strengthen the ¼-inch panel so it will not be marred by the bolts (Illus. 12-16).

BOOKCASE HEADBOARD WITH SLIDING DOORS

The bookcase headboard can easily be equipped with partitions and sliding doors. The basic structure remains the same as just described. Only the shelf section needs altering.

MAKING THE GROOVES FOR THE SLIDING DOORS

Cut grooves in the bookcase section to provide spaces for the upper and lower runners of the sliding doors. You can easily cut the lower groove if you use a dado head set slightly wider than ¼ inch. Either make the upper groove in the underside of the top or make a special top rail. It is somewhat easier to make, groove, and install a special top rail than it is to groove the underside of the top.

Make a top rail ¾ × 1¼ inches × the required length between the sides. Then run a ⁵⁄₃₂-inch groove that is ½ inch deep along its entire length (Illus. 12-17). Fasten this rail in place using the same method as was used for installing the decorative rail in the previous headboard. Cut the groove in the shelf only ¼ inch deep and locate it so it matches the groove in the top rail and so that only about ⅛ inch remains between the back of the sliding doors and the partitions. To machine a groove on the underside of the top, use a ¼-inch

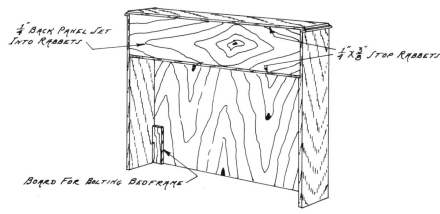

Illus. 12-16. Reinforcers are needed if the bed frame is to be bolted to the headboard.

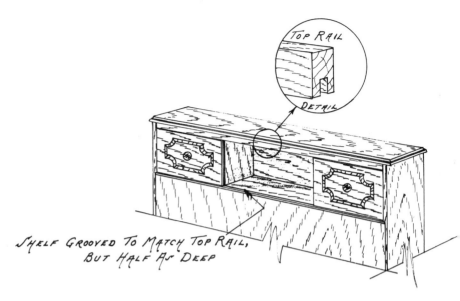

TOP RAIL

DETAIL

Illus. 12-17. Groove details for the sliding doors.

SHELF GROOVED TO MATCH TOP RAIL, BUT HALF AS DEEP

straight cutter bit in a router and make a "blind," or stop, groove that is located to match the groove in the shelf. A blind groove is one that is started and stopped far enough from the ends so that it cannot be seen. Using a strip of wood for a straightedge, clamp this piece to the underside of the top at exactly the right distance from the front edge of the shelf so the router cutter will machine the groove where planned.

MAKING THE PARTITIONS FOR THE BOOKCASE SECTION

Make the partitions to fit behind the top rail. They only have to be 8½ inches wide. Position the partitions so the center space of the bookshelf area is slightly larger than the two side spaces. Install each partition by nailing from the underside of the shelf and through the ¼-inch plywood back.

MAKING THE SLIDING DOORS

The length of the sliding doors must correspond to the location of the partitions and should be long enough to cover the edge of the partition. If scrolled and laminated doors are desired, follow the same directions as were presented in the previous section of this chap-

ter. Always use a ¼-inch plywood panel for the basic sliding door regardless of the treatment to the front of the panel. Illus. 12-17 shows an overlaid raised panel that is glued to the basic sliding panel. Any number of designs, overlays, or even applied moulding can be used to decorate the front of the sliding doors.

BEDSIDE TABLES

Some craftspersons may want to add bedside tables to their bedrooms. If the techniques of the casework system have been mastered, the builder will discover that bedside tables present no new woodworking challenges.

DESIGNING A BEDSIDE TABLE

Bedside tables are small pieces of furniture designed to be placed on either side of the bed. These furniture pieces are seldom wider than 24 inches and usually no higher than 26 inches. They have a standard depth of 16 inches. They may be fitted with drawers and doors or they may have just one drawer across the top and the portion below the drawer may be left completely open. Bedside tables may be adapted to almost any style of furniture, either contemporary or traditional. Illus.

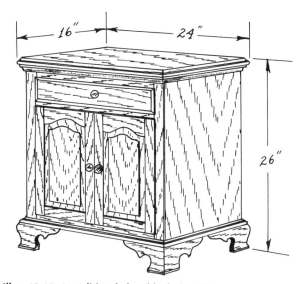

Illus. 12-18. A traditional closed bedside table.

12-18 shows a traditional closed bedside table. Instead of building doors on the lower portion, it would be a simple matter to equip this furniture piece with all drawers. Illus. 12-21 shows an open bedside table with one shelf in the open portion. Some open bedside tables do not have any shelf in the lower space. If you plan to build a traditional bedside table, there are several ways to treat the legs. Any of the leg treatments presented earlier for chests of drawers and desks may also be used on bedside tables.

A TRADITIONAL CLOSED BEDSIDE TABLE

Both open and closed bedside tables lend themselves nicely to casework construction. The sides and top of the closed unit can be made of ¼-inch plywood, but the open type will probably require ¾-inch plywood or veneered particle board unless thinner material can be located that is good on both sides. Complete step-by-step instructions will not be repeated in this section as they are exactly the same as presented for many of the earlier projects. Just a few of the general techniques will be reviewed.

BUILDING THE FACE FRAME

Illus. 12-19 shows the basic box with its essential dimensions. As usual, first fabricate the face frame. On a small unit such as this, it is good design practice to narrow the stiles. In this case, the stiles have been narrowed to 1½ inches. The top rail should remain at about 2 inches because a cove moulding is placed under the top overhang. The bill of materials for the face frame is as follows:

Stiles: Two pieces ¾ × 1½ × 20½ inches
Top rail: One piece ¾ × 2 × 19½ inches
Drawer rail: One piece ¾ × 1¾ × 21 inches
Facing strip: One piece ¾ × ¾ × 19½ inches

If you are eliminating the doors to add more drawers, of course, more drawer rails will be required.

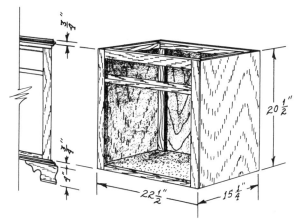

Illus. 12-19. The basic box of the closed bedside table.

COMPLETING THE CLOSED BEDSIDE TABLE

Assemble the face frame with screw joints (Illus. 12-20) and then fabricate the bottom, back, side panels, and all reinforcing pieces, including the upper drawer runner. If any problems are encountered, review the techniques as presented in Chapter Six. Drawer building is described in Chapter Seven, and doors in Chapter Eleven.

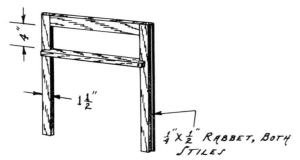

Illus. 12-20. Face-frame details for the closed bedside table.

OPEN BEDSIDE TABLE

Because this is an interior-visible cabinet, plywood or veneered particle board that is good on both sides must be used. The techniques for using thicker material for the side panels in connection with the casework method are presented in Chapter Nine. Review those operations if necessary. Illus. 12-21 shows a bedside table of the open variety that may be built of either edge-banded ¾-inch plywood or veneered particle board or of glued-up panels of solid lumber.

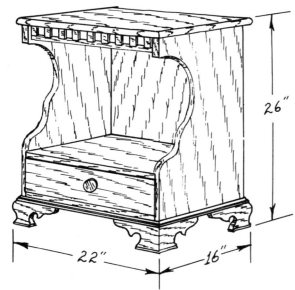

Illus. 12-21. A traditional open bedside table.

BUILDING THE BASIC BOX

This open bedside table does not have a face frame because of the curves that are cut in the

side panels. This means that if plywood is used for these panels, they must be edge-banded. Be sure to plan for gentle curves in the side panels so the thin edge-banding can be applied without breaking.

Side Panels   The side panels measure 15¼ × 21½ inches. Run the dadoes before cutting the curves, and plan for a lower drawer that is 4 to 5 inches deep. Machine a rabbet along the back edge to accommodate the ¼-inch back panel.

Shelf and Bottom   These two members will measure 19¾ × 15 inches. They are ¼ inch less in depth than the sides because of the ¼-inch plywood back panel.

Decorative Top Rail   The decorative rail is actually two pieces (Illus. 12-22). The back piece measures ¾ × 2 × 20½ inches. The overlay is a piece that measures ⅝ × 1½ × 20½ inches. Cut the evenly spaced dadoes on the table saw using the dado head. Machine a simple ogee moulding along the lower edge using the router, and then glue the two pieces together. Fasten the top rail in position by either nailing through the sides or screwing the piece in place and covering the heads with plugs or buttons.

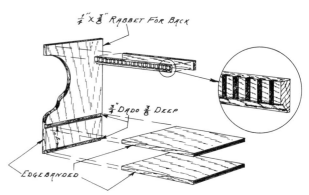

Illus. 12-22. Machining and assembly detail of the open bedside table.

Top and Back The top overhangs the front and two sides by ¾ inch. Make the top from plywood and apply a half-round nosing to it. Another alternative would be to make the top from ¼-inch plywood and lumber as was done for the chests in Chapter Six. No cove moulding is used under the top.

Cut the back panel to size and glue and nail it in the rabbets along the rear of the side panels and to the back edge of the shelf and the bottom.

COMPLETING THE OPEN BEDSIDE TABLE

After the basic box has been built, build the drawer to fit the opening. Then fabricate the base structure using the type of leg desired. The height dimensions for the base are exactly the same as given for the closed bedside table in Illus. 12-19.

Sand the entire structure with the finish sander and finish it with a favorite finishing schedule.

CHAPTER THIRTEEN

Entertainment Centers and Armoires

It might come as a surprise to some woodworkers to find armoires included in the same chapter with entertainment centers. Armoires, however, are much more than freestanding clothes closets, which was their historic origin. They are certainly used for wardrobes, but they are also used as entertainment centers, bars, and as shelf storage for a wide range of items.

In this chapter, the emphasis is on the design and construction of the entertainment center and the adaptation of the armoire to this use. Several interior designs are also presented for the use of the armoire as a wardrobe and closet.

DESIGNING AN ENTERTAINMENT CENTER

An entertainment center is designed to accommodate the entertainment equipment being stored: television set, VCR, compact disc player, etc. It takes a considerable expenditure of labor and financial investment in material and hardware to build an entertainment center. In this chapter, general plans are presented for armoires and entertainment centers, but it is up to you to adapt the interior features of these pieces to fit the electronic equipment to be placed within them.

FEATURES AND DIMENSIONS

There are two general types of entertainment centers. The first is the type most often seen in the furniture section of large discount stores. These are inexpensive and manufactured of very thin laminate-covered particle board. Some are equipped with swinging glass and plywood doors, and others have no front closures whatsoever. The second type can be found in any first-class retail furniture establishment. These fine pieces of furniture contain a pullout rotating television shelf, pullout turntable slide, pocket doors, and built-in storage for records and videotapes. Some are equipped with interior electrical outlets to accommodate the many electronic devices that are housed within the unit.

Though the first type of entertainment center is functional, it is poorly designed and constructed. These types are not deep enough to accommodate 23- to 27-inch television sets.

Therefore, the rear of the television set must stick out behind the unit, rather than be enclosed as it would be in a customized unit. Needless to say, the projects presented in this chapter will be of the second type.

DESIGN RECOMMENDATIONS

The entertainment center should be built 22½ to 24 inches deep so that it will accept larger television sets. Nearly all of the shelves should be adjustable. Adjustable shelves can accommodate the varying heights of tape recorders, VCRs, CD players, etc. Pocket doors are recommended for the television enclosure section because they disappear within the cabinet and offer no obstruction to television viewing. Be aware, however, that pocket doors make use of considerable interior space, and extra construction features are necessary to use adjustable shelves in a pocket-door unit.

A pullout rotating television shelf is very desirable in a cabinet-type enclosure to allow viewing from various angles in the room. Adequate ventilation must be provided, as well, because electronic equipment requires circulation to prevent damage from overheating. Provision should be made to accommodate all the connecting wires, cables, and cords that connect the units. This is generally achieved by creating openings in the back panel of the entertainment center. Finally, customized drawers or sections of the center should be built to store videotapes, CDs, recording tapes, and records. Again, the equipment you own will determine the features to be built into the center.

When designing an entertainment center, it is best to house the television set and the VCR on one side of the unit and the sound and recording items on the adjacent side. Often these centers are made in separate units much like those found in bookcase walls, with each unit approximately 36 inches wide.

DIMENSION RECOMMENDATIONS FOR AUDIO AND TELEVISION UNITS

A storage unit that will accommodate a 25- to 27-inch television set and pocket doors will have to be a minimum of 33 inches wide. The hardware for the pocket doors and the doors themselves will usually occupy a minimum of 2 to 3 inches on each side of the cabinet's interior. Determine the specifications for the pocket-door hardware prior to designing the unit, to ensure that the correct width is planned. The height of the television unit will depend upon the placement of the VCR and whether or not a pull-out rotating TV shelf is to be used. If all of these items are to be placed into a single unit, about 36 inches of height will be needed. The entertainment centers, as previously stated, should be 22½ to 24 inches deep.

The audio portion of the center that will house the sound and recording compartments should be about 24 inches wide and equipped with adjustable shelves. Tape storage drawers or doored cabinet areas are usually designed below the audio and television portions of the center and should be about 20 to 24 inches high. The overall height of the combined units is 55 to 60 inches.

BUILDING A CONTEMPORARY ENTERTAINMENT CENTER

With the general design and dimension guidelines in mind, the first project will be a contemporary entertainment center (Illus. 13-1). This center features a space for the television set that is equipped with pocket doors, a glass-paned door on the audio portion of the center, and a good-size drawer below for the storage of tapes, etc. This unit is designed with a toe

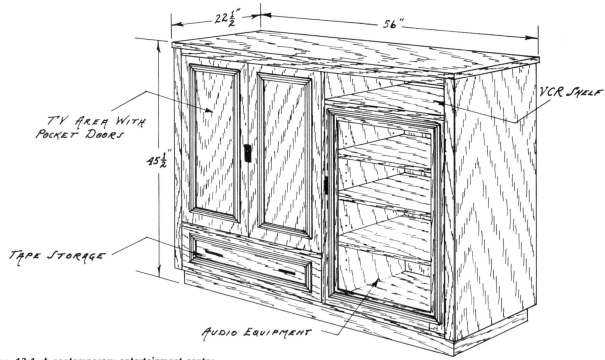

Illus. 13-1. A contemporary entertainment center.

space and has only a partial face frame, which will present some new and interesting woodworking challenges. Because all of the interior of this entertainment center will be visible, it should be constructed of one type of plywood and lumber.

BUILDING THE BASIC BOX

When the entertainment center is stripped of its toe-space platform, its doors, and its drawer, a basic box appears that has a face frame along the two sides and the top (Illus. 13-2). The interior partitions are made from ¾-inch material that will require edge-banding. The dimensions as given apply to the entertainment center shown in Illus. 13-1. If you make changes to adapt the center to the equipment you own, remember to make the necessary dimension changes.

Making the Face Frame
This face frame is a very basic one that should require no explanatory illustration. The bill of materials is as follows:

Stiles: Two pieces ¾ × 1½ × 41¾ inches
Top rail: One piece ¾ × 2 × 52 inches
Bottom facing piece: One piece ¾ × ¾ × approximately 52 inches
Center facing piece: One piece ¾ × ¾ × approximately 40 inches
VCR facing piece: One piece ¾ × ¾ × approximately 23 inches
Television facing piece: One piece ¾ × ¾ × approximately 29 inches
Note: All facing piece lengths are approximate because they are cut to fit after the basic box is assembled.

Machine the usual ¼ × ½-inch rabbets along one side of each stile and assemble the face frame with screws.

Making the Toe-Space Assembly
Illus. 13-2 gives the toe-space dimensions and assembly details. Note that only the front and two end pieces need to be of hardwood to match that being used for the cabinet. All of the other pieces may be of inexpensive lumber

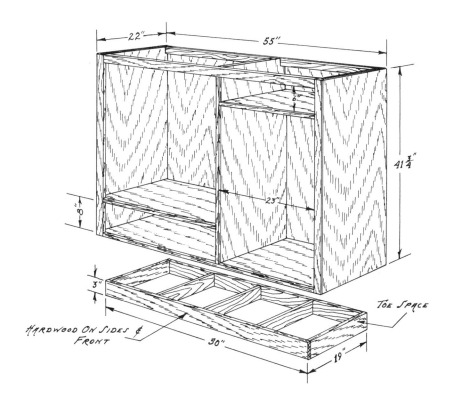

Illus. 13-2. The basic box and the toe-space assembly.

or scrap plywood. The toe space is designed for a 3-inch overhang along the front and both sides, but it will be even with the rear edge of the bottom panel. After the exact length of the bottom panel has been determined, simply nail the bottom to the toe-space assembly.

Making and Assembling the Box

Run out all the panels as indicated in Illus. 13-3. Mark the locations and machine the dadoes, which measure ¾ × ⅜ inch. Make the dadoes either with a dado head in the table saw or a straightedge and a router. Machine ½ × ½-inch rabbets along the front edge of each side panel and ¼ × ⅜-inch rabbets along the rear edge of these same panels. Joint a 5-degree bevel along the lip of the front rabbets so they fit tightly into the stile rabbet. Cut a notch in the upper rear corner of the partition piece that will fit around the back-panel reinforcer.

Decide which type of adjustable shelf system will be used. Then either drill the holes for peg shelves, or machine grooves for metal shelf standards, if these are to be installed.

Making the Two Shelves
The shelf that will hold the VCR should measure ¾ × 24½ × 20¼ inches. The shelf that will hold the TV should measure ¾ × 29¾ × 20¼ inches.

Begin assembly by gluing the lip along the front edge of the side panels into the rabbets on the stiles using ¾-inch brads. After the sides are attached, measure to determine the exact length of the bottom. After cutting the bottom to length, nail it to the toe-space assembly. Then slip the bottom, with the toe space attached, into the rabbets along the bottom edge of the sides. Glue and nail the bottom in place using 4d finish nails. Square the sides and bottom and nail temporary braces in place to hold the assembly square.

Make a back-panel reinforcer of inexpensive lumber that measures ¾ × 2 inches × the length as measured between the side panels. Nail the reinforcer in place by nailing

261

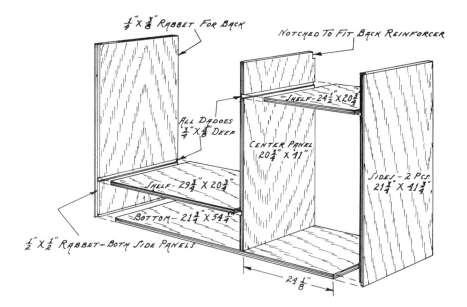

Illus. 13-3. Size and machining detail for all panels.

through the sides into the ends of the reinforcing pieces. Position the center division panel and nail through the bottom into the lower edge of this panel. Square it vertically and fasten it in place by nailing through the back-panel reinforcer.

Slip the two shelves into their respective dadoes from the rear and glue and nail them in place using 4d finish nails. Measure the required size needed for the back panel, machine it to size, and glue and nail it in position.

Fit, glue, and nail all facing strips in place. Then set all the nails and fill the resulting holes with matching plastic wood. Also use matching plastic wood on any flaws in the seams and joints of the face frame. Belt-sand the entire face frame, and complete the sanding with the finish sander.

MAKING THE TOP, DOORS, AND DRAWER

Top The top may be made from ¾-inch plywood or veneered particle board to which a solid-wood square edging is applied. The edging should measure ½ × 1 or 1¼ inch to give the top some appearance of thickness. The top may also be fabricated from ¼-inch plywood

and reinforced with ¾ × 2-inch strips of inexpensive lumber as was instructed in Chapter Six in the section on contemporary chests. Edge this top with ½ × 1-inch wood also.

Doors Instructions for building glass-paned doors are given in Chapter Eleven. If you are applying a fluted moulding to the rails and stiles of the glass-paned door, widen the members of the door slightly. The door shown in Illus. 13-4 is a flush door rather than a lipped door.

Make pocket or pivot doors with a ¹⁄₁₆- to ⅛-inch margin along the top, bottom, and sides. Shim the pivot-door hardware on the left side so it is exactly flush with the inner edge of the face frame. Install the doors according to the directions furnished with the hardware. Concealed European hinges are often used to attach the doors to the slides. If this is the case, a 1⅜-inch Forstner drill bit will have to be purchased in order to install these hinges in the doors.

Drawer The drawer is a standard flush drawer built according to the directions given in Chapter Seven. If the drawer is to be used to store videotapes, be certain to check the

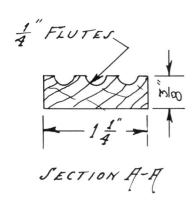

$\frac{1}{4}''$ FLUTES

$\frac{3}{8}''$

$1\frac{1}{4}''$

SECTION A-A

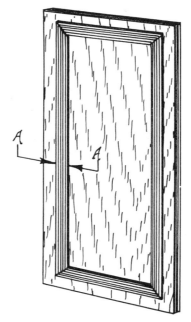

Illus. 13-4. Details of the applied door and drawer moulding.

dimension of the tapes and adjust the depth of the drawer accordingly. You may want to design and install slotted partitions that hold tapes to better organize the storage of tapes.

INSTALLING A TELEVISION EXTENSION PULLOUT

Almost all entertainment centers have television sections with extending, swivel pullouts (Illus. 13-5 and 13-6). The hardware for these pullouts can be purchased from any good mail-order woodworker's supply house. Make sure that you firmly and securely fasten the slides to the bottom shelf of the television section because they must carry the full weight of the TV set (Illus. 13-7). The pullout hardware is rated by the pounds the hardware is designed to carry, and priced accordingly. The swivel plate is not large enough to hold the television set, so attach a plywood piece to the plate that is large enough for the set to rest upon. Often a finger grip is machined on the underside of this piece or a front piece is attached that hides the slide and also provides a means of gripping and pulling the television set out of the cabinet. Most types of pullout hardware allow the TV set to be extended only about 7 inches. There is a real danger that if the set is extended much beyond this distance, the entire cabinet might topple forward due to the weight of the TV set.

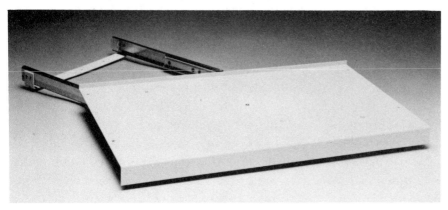

Illus. 13-5. The pullout television swivel. (Photo courtesy of Alfit America, Richmond, VA.)

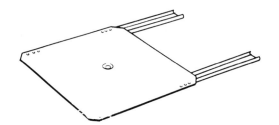
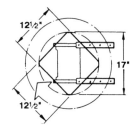

Illus. 13-6. Swivel details of the
television pullout.

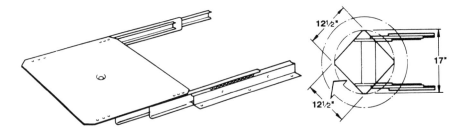

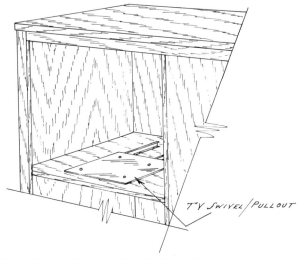

TV SWIVEL/PULLOUT

Illus. 13-7. Installation of the television pullout.

COMPLETING THE ENTERTAINMENT CENTER

Give the entire structure its final sanding with
220-grit paper and proceed with a favorite finishing schedule. Install all the hardware and
hang the doors. The entertainment center can
be moved into the den or recreation room.

BUILDING A TRADITIONAL ENTERTAINMENT CENTER

For the person who owns just a television set
and a VCR, the entertainment center shown
in Illus. 13-8 will make a nice furniture unit.
The base of this center may be designed and
built with any of the legs or bases described in
Chapter Six and need not have the coved and
curved legs as illustrated.

BUILDING THE BASIC BOX

Illus. 13-8 shows the basic box, which is the
entertainment center with the base structure,
top, and doors all removed. The legs and the
bottom moulding are 4¾ inches high, and the
top is ¾ inch thick. This adds up to a total of
5½ inches, which is added to the 45½-inch
height of the basic box for a total height of 51
inches. Note that the two tops are designed to
overhang the basic box by 1¼ inches along
the front and two sides.

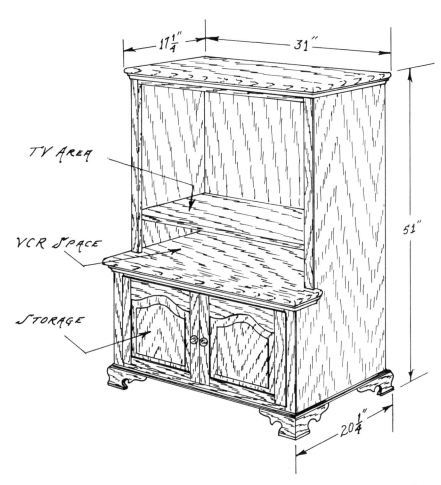

Illus. 13-8. A traditional entertainment center.

BUILDING THE FACE FRAMES

As usual, build the face frames first. These are not illustrated because both face frames are standard casework face frames that have been illustrated many times throughout this book. The bill of materials for the face frames is as follows:

Upper Face Frame

Stiles: Two pieces ¾ × 1½ × 28¾ inches
Top rail: One piece ¾ × 2 × 25½ inches
Facing strip: One piece ¾ × ¾ × approximately 25½ inches

Lower face frame

Stiles: Two pieces ¾ × 1½ × 16 inches
Top rail: One piece ¾ × 2 × 25½ inches

Facing strip: One piece ¾ × ¾ × approximately 25½ inches

Run out these pieces to the exact measurements given and machine ¼ × ½-inch rabbets along one edge of each stile. Assemble the face frames using the typical casework screw joint technique.

MAKING THE SIDE PANELS

The dimensions for the side panels are given in Illus. 13-10. Use two pieces of ¾-inch plywood or veneered particle board that measure 18¾ × 45½ inches. Run the two pieces out first and then lay out the lines on each side panel for the dadoes. It is easier to machine the dadoes before sawing the 3-inch setback. Machine the dadoes using the dado head in the table saw or a router and a straightedge.

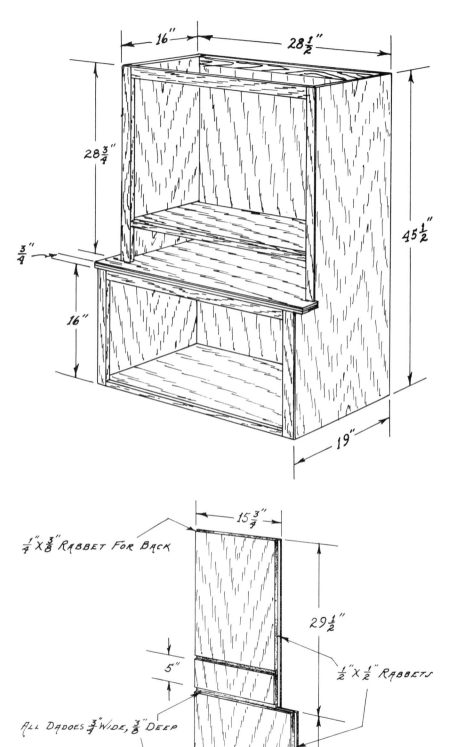

Illus. 13-9. The dimensioned basic box for the traditional unit.

16"

28½"

28¾"

45½"

¾"

16"

19"

Illus. 13-10. Size and machining detail of the side panels.

15¾"

¼" X ⅜" RABBET FOR BACK

29½"

5"

½" X ½" RABBETS

ALL DADOES ¾" WIDE, ⅜" DEEP

16"

18¾"

NOTE: MAKE RIGHT & LEFT SIDES!

266

Next, lay out the 3-inch setback on each panel and saw the panel out on the table saw. Remember, a right and left side must be made! Saw the right-side panel first, using the table-saw fence set with 15¾ inches between the blade and the fence. (The right side is to your right as you face the cabinet.) A slight undercutting will occur when the blade arrives at the stop mark, but this creates no problem because the saw mark will be on the inside of the cabinet. Use a sabre saw, handsaw, or table saw to saw the 3-inch distance and free the inset piece.

The left-side panel will have to be handled differently. With the fence still set at 15¾ inches, drop the panel carefully onto the saw blade well away from the 3-inch inset mark. With a firm grip on the panel, pull the panel so the saw blade is cutting *rearwards*. Saw very slowly rearwards just up to the inset mark. This is not a dangerous operation—just cut slowly and make sure that the blade you are using is sharp. After this has been accomplished, complete the saw cut by pushing the panel through the saw to the end of the panel.

Machine the ¼ × ⅜-inch rabbets for the back panel using either a router or a dado head in a table saw.

Finally, machine the ½ × ½-inch rabbets along the front edges of the sides to create the ¼-inch lips that will fit into the face-frame rabbets. You can easily cut the rabbets on the lower or wider portion of the side panels using a dado head on the table saw and an auxiliary wooden fence that you fasten to the metal fence. Make up the dado head with enough blades to cut ⅝ inch wide. Set the dado head and fence so the rabbet is machined slightly wider than ½ inch. Raise the dado head so that the resulting lip is slightly thinner than ¼ inch and cut the lower rabbets on both side panels.

To cut these same rabbets on the upper portion of the sides, you will have to set the table saw up carefully. Remove the auxiliary fence and set the metal fence at about 15¾ inches from the *left* side of the dado head to the fence. Do not change the height of the dado head. Run the right-side panel into the dado head, just barely touching the wood for a test cut. Make whatever fence adjustments are needed so the resulting rabbet is exactly the same as that machined on the lower portion of the panel.

When all machine adjustments are satisfactory, run the dado head along the edge; continue slightly past the 3-inch setback spot. This results in an undercutting but, again, it will not be seen because it will be on the inside of the cabinet. For the left side, again drop the panel onto the dado head just slightly beyond the 3-inch inset and then run the panel through.

If the slight undercutting seems objectionable, cut all of the rabbets using a router and a straightedge. This, however, will probably require a lot of test-cutting and straightedge setting.

MAKING THE SHELF, BOTTOM, AND LOWER SECTION TOP

Illus. 13-11 contains the dimensions for the TV shelf and the bottom. The bottom may be

Illus. 13-11. Assembly of the basic box.

made from particle board. Machine these two pieces to the required sizes.

The top for the lower section is shown in Illus. 13-12. The overall size of this piece is 29½ inches wide × 18½ inches deep. Cut the insets on each side to the dimensions shown, making certain that the width of the rear portion exactly matches the 27¾-inch width of the bottom and the TV shelf. Apply ¾-inch-wide half-round nosing to the exposed edges of this top before installing the piece. Make sure that the mitre joints at the corners are neat and then sand the nosing flush with the top veneer. Apply nosing to the short 3½-inch side projections as shown in Illus. 13-13. Apply the very short nosing pieces at the rear of the projections after installing the top.

ASSEMBLING THE BASIC BOX

Glue and nail the bottom and TV shelf in place using 4d finish nails. Slip the lower top into its dadoes and fasten it in place by nailing through the sides. Square the structure with the framing square and support it with scrapwood angled braces.

Belt- and finish-sand both face frames before installing them. Place the lower face frame in place and install it using ¾-inch brads and glue. Do the same with the upper face frame. Make certain that the lower ends of the stiles rest firmly against the top of the lower section. Prepare the back panel and glue and nail it in place. Make a ¾ × 2-inch back reinforcer and install it at the top of the back panel. Nail through the sides into the ends of the reinforcer, but glue and clamp the piece to

the back panel. Glue and nail the facing strips to the front edges of the TV shelf and the bottom. Then set all nails and brads, and fill the holes and any flaws along the face-frame seams with matching plastic wood.

BUILDING THE BASE STRUCTURE

Select the type of leg or base structure desired from the examples illustrated in Chapter Six. Prepare the bottom moulding and install it along the front and two sides of the bottom of the cabinet. After preparing the base structure, install the legs or base by fastening the units in position on the bottom moulding. Make and install a reinforcer between the legs at the rear and install other reinforcers as required to strengthen the entire structure. These techniques were all presented in Chapter Six.

Completing the Top, Doors, and Lower Shelf

Either make the top from ¾-inch material or fabricate a ¼-inch plywood panelled top with a hardwood edge. The top should overhang the basic box by 1¼ inches on the front and sides. Prepare enough ¾-inch cove moulding to install under the top and the lower shelf.

Make the doors in the style desired fol-

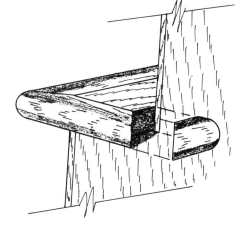

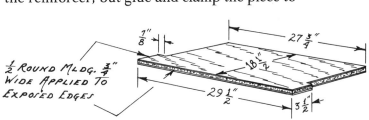

Illus. 13-12 (above left). Detail of the top of the lower section. Illus. 13-13 (above right). Nosing detail of the lower section top.

lowing the directions as presented in Chapter Eleven.

The lower section of the entertainment center should have at least one adjustable shelf. Prepare this shelf from particle board and band the front edge with a ¼-inch strip of matching hardwood.

Final Touches

After the cabinet has been given its final sanding and the staining and finishing are completed, select and install all hardware. If a television swivel pullout is desired, install the slide in the television section with a properly sized plywood platform that will hold the television set. Cut or drill holes in the ¼-inch plywood back so the connecting cords and cables can be installed between the television set and the VCR.

ARMOIRE

The armoire was originally used as a free-standing clothes closet, but today it is adapted for other uses, one of which is as an entertainment center. It is a spacious piece of furniture that can hold many sound and video components and still be a beautiful addition to any living space.

DESIGNING THE ARMOIRE

Whether it is going to be used as an entertainment center or a closet, the armoire is usually 36 to 48 inches wide, 21 to 22 inches deep, and 74 to 80 inches high. When used as an entertainment center, the front of the armoire is often designed with two large doors above and two smaller doors below. The upper portion will house the television set, the VCR, and perhaps the turntable. The lower section will have storage facilities for the tape deck, radio, CD player, and other sound components, as well as room for storage of tapes and even records. It is not unusual to see an ar-

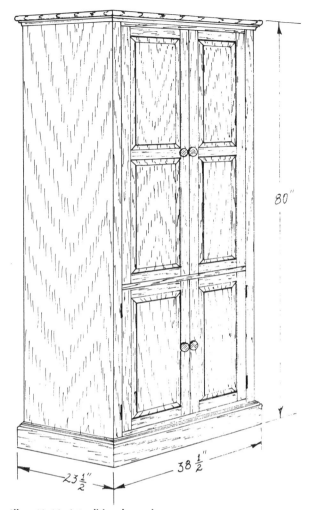

Illus. 13-14. A traditional armoire.

moire entertainment center built to be part of a total cabinet wall and matched with the bookcases and other wall units.

The doors on the television portion of the cabinet are very often pocket doors, but those on the lower section are most often installed with traditional hinges.

The armoire is usually built in the traditional or period style. No doubt, this is because the armoire is a replica of a very old piece of furniture and lends itself quite well to this style.

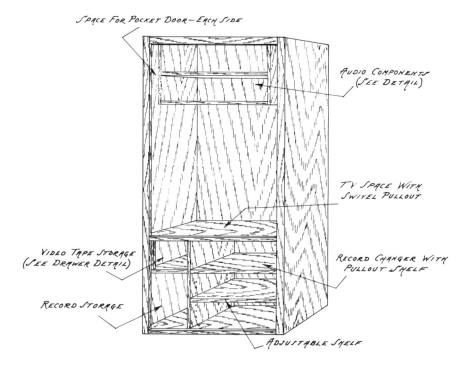

SPACE FOR POCKET DOOR — EACH SIDE

AUDIO COMPONENTS
(SEE DETAIL)

TV SPACE WITH
SWIVEL PULLOUT

VIDEO TAPE STORAGE
(SEE DRAWER DETAIL)

RECORD CHANGER WITH
PULLOUT SHELF

RECORD STORAGE

ADJUSTABLE SHELF

Illus. 13-15. The interior detail of the armoire entertainment center.

BUILDING THE ARMOIRE ENTERTAINMENT CENTER

Do not hesitate to undertake the building of an armoire. The woodworking challenges involved in this construction are no more difficult than many of the projects in this book—only the project itself is larger. If you have mastered the techniques for the handling and machining of large pieces of plywood, and if the shop has the suggested jigs and fixtures for ease in handling these larger pieces, you should have no difficulty in completing this excellent storage facility for audio and video components. Illus. 13-14 shows an armoire entertainment center. Although the doors as shown are raised-panelled doors, you can change them to a style you prefer. The interior of the armoire is shown in Illus. 13-15. This, too, may be changed to more efficiently house the audio and video units you own.

Building the Basic Box

Face Frame Although not illustrated, the face frame is standard casework. The bill of materials is as follows:

Stiles: Two pieces ¾ × 1½ × 74 inches
Top rail: One piece ¾ × 2 × 32 inches
Facing strips: Two pieces ¾ × ¾ × 32 inches

Cut ¼ × ½-inch rabbets along one edge of each stile and assemble the face frame with screw joints.

Box The parts to the basic box are given in Illus. 13-16, less the upper shelf insert and the adjustable shelf in the bottom section. The dimensions for these pieces are all listed in the dimension chart. These dimensions include the front edging that must be applied to pieces C, D, and E and to the adjustable shelf when that is made. (Note: You may want to wait to run out some of these pieces until the measurements can be verified on the cabinet after it has been partially assembled.) All of the lower interior shelves that will be behind closed doors most of the time may be made from particle board if you want to save the

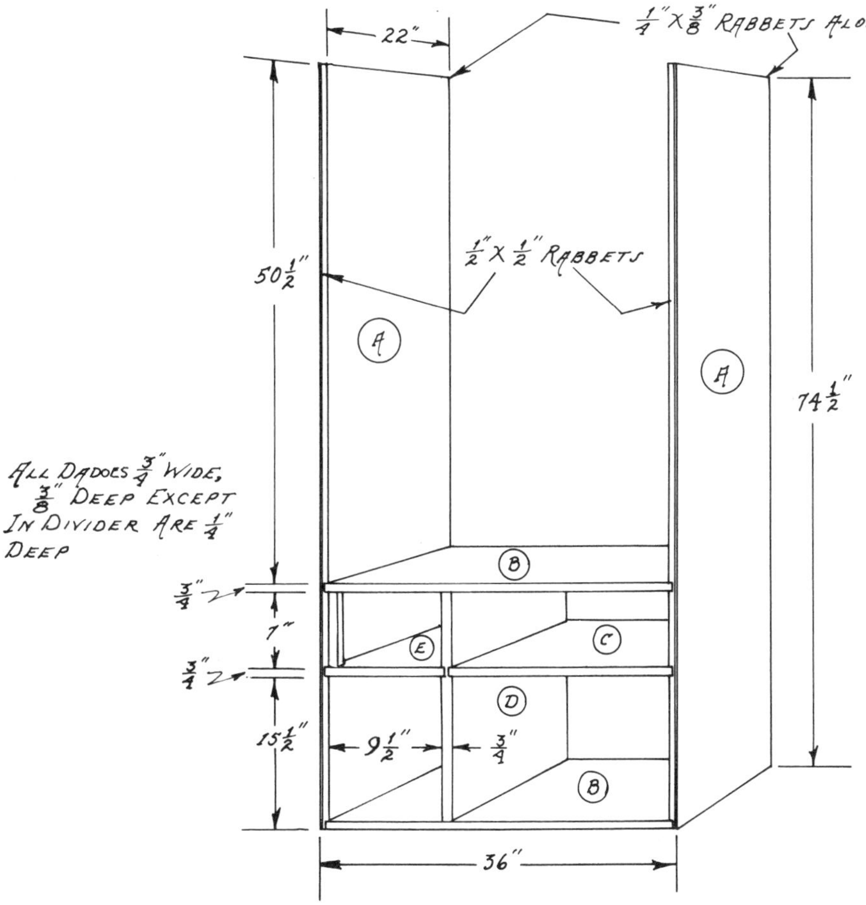

A	SIDES	22" X 74 1/2"
B	SHELF & BOTT.	35 1/4" X 21 1/4"
C	SHELF	24 7/8" X 21 1/4"
D	DIVIDER	21 1/4" X 22 1/2"
E	SHELF	10 7/8" X 21 1/4"
F	FILLER	3/4" X 1 X 7"
	DIMENSIONS INCLUDE EDGE BANDING	

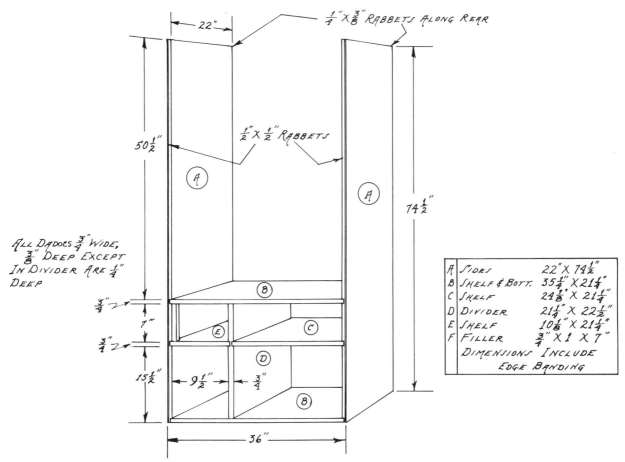

Illus. 13-16. Panel sizes and machining detail.

expense of using hardwood plywood in this section. Do not apply the edging to pieces C and E until they have been installed. The divider (D) should have one continuous piece of edging. These same three pieces are 3/4 inch less in depth than the shelf and bottom (B) because the shelf and bottom will have a 3/4-inch facing strip applied. This will allow room for the doors that will be installed on the lower section of the armoire.

Machine the two side pieces (A) with the same rabbets and dadoes as were used on the sides for the two previous projects—only the dimensions and locations are different. Again, remember to make a left and right side!

The filler strip is needed if a tape storage drawer is to be installed as shown in Illus. 13-15. The filler piece allows the drawer to be pulled from the armoire and not hit the face frame.

Begin assembly by gluing and nailing parts B into their respective dadoes in the side panels. Square and add braces to the structure. Next, install the face frame by gluing and nailing the lips of the front rabbets on the side panels into the rabbets of the face frame. Position and install D (the divider). Then slip C and E into place and nail and glue where applicable. Apply the facing strips to B and two thin edgings to parts C and E. Simply glue and clamp the filler strip in place against the side panel.

Next, machine the back panel to size and install it. Rather than use a reinforcer across the top of the panel, allow the back to project upwards 1/2 inch so it can be nailed and glued

into a rabbet on the rear of the armoire top.

Fill all holes, open seams, and any joint flaws with matching plastic wood. After it has thoroughly dried, scrape and sand the filler flush with the veneer. Belt- and finish-sand the face frame and finish-sand the side panels as well. Proceed with the base structure and the top as designed. The top should probably be made of ¾-inch material because it will have to help carry the weight of the upper shelf structure that will be installed above the television area. Machine a ¼ × ⅜-inch blind rabbet along the rear edge of the top. Apply half-round nosing to the front and two sides of the top and install ¾-inch cove moulding under the top overhang after nailing it in place.

Building and Installing the Armoire's Interior Fittings

Videotape Drawer A simple flush drawer can easily be built to house videotapes as shown in Illus. 13-17. The drawer should be at least 7½ inches on the inside, because standard T-120 tapes measure 7⅜ inches long. If ½-inch drawer sides are to be used, the width of the drawer front will have to be 9½ inches. Either make the inside drawer slightly smaller

so the drawer will slide into the 9½-inch opening provided in the cabinet or narrow the filler piece slightly. Spacers between the tapes can be made from ¼ × ¼-inch wood strips as shown. You can add more tape drawers by changing the design slightly to allow for a vertical row of drawers along the left side. Use a ⁵⁄₁₆ × ¾-inch center drawer runner to guide the drawer into the opening.

Upper-Interior Shelf Structure This unit, shown in Illus. 13-18, must be built narrower than the armoire opening to accommodate the pocket, or recessing, doors. Provide about 1½ to 2 inches on each side for the door thickness and its hardware, depending upon the brand of hardware used. You can alter the dimensions of this interior unit as desired, depending upon the size of the television set to be installed in the armoire. Install the unit in the armoire by driving screws through the back and top into the rear and top edges of the unit.

Sliding Shelves for Audio Units For those shelves that should be equipped with pullout slides, such as the shelf upon which a record changer is mounted, select the proper slide from those illustrated in a woodworker's sup-

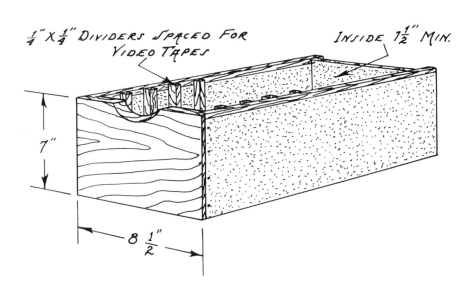

Illus. 13-17. Detail of the VCR tape storage drawer.

¼" X ¼" DIVIDERS SPACED FOR VIDEO TAPES

INSIDE 7½" MIN.

7"

8½"

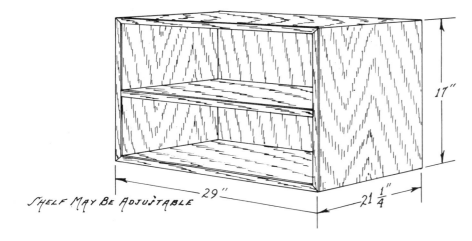

SHELF MAY BE ADJUSTABLE — 29" — 21 1/4" — 17"

Illus. 13-18. The detail of the upper shelf storage section.

ply catalogue. Slides are available with and without ball bearings. They also come with various degrees of extension. Some will allow the complete shelf to be pulled from the cabinet, and others only allow a part of the shelf to be pulled out. Check the load rating of the slide to be certain it is designed to carry the weight of the unit that is going to be installed on the shelf. Of course, the load rating, the presence of ball bearings, and the amount of shelf extension will all determine the cost of these slides.

Armoire's Doors

If pocket doors are going to be used, and it is highly recommended that they should be, follow the directions for this type of door presented in Chapter Eleven. Make the doors in the style desired and install them according to the directions included with the brand of hardware purchased.

The doors on the lower section of an armoire are usually hinged doors. These doors are also described in Chapter Eleven.

Finishing Touches

Give a final cleanup sanding to the entire project and proceed with a staining and finishing schedule that will bring out the beauty of the species of wood chosen for this fine piece of furniture.

TRADITIONAL CLOSET ARMOIRE

The closet armoire is usually somewhat wider than the armoire designed to hold audio and TV components. The entertainment center adaptation of the armoire was 36 to 40 inches wide, but the closet armoire will be 40 to 48 inches wide. The height and depth dimensions remain about the same. There are no new techniques involved in building the closet armoire, so this section will deal mainly with design rather than with construction details.

DESIGNING THE CLOSET ARMOIRE

As mentioned, the armoire designed to hold clothes is 4 to 12 inches wider than the entertainment center armoire. However, the height remains approximately 80 inches, and the depth about 22 inches. Illus. 13-19 shows a typical closet armoire. It is not unusual to see these units designed with two wide drawers below, instead of just one as shown. Decreasing the size of the upper doors is always an advantage because large doors always are in danger of warping or twisting. Often, too, the frames for larger doors are made from 5/4 lumber which, when surfaced, finishes out at 1 1/16 inches thick. If you are using thicker lumber

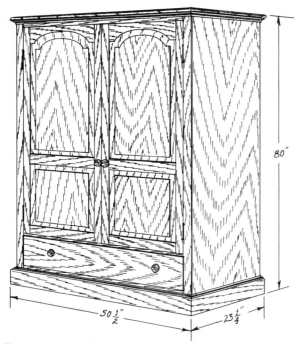

Illus. 13-19. A traditional-styled closet armoire.

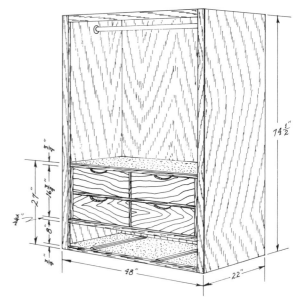

Illus. 13-20. Interior fittings of the closet armoire.

for the door frames, the face frames of the armoire will have to be made from the same material. Make the larger doors flush and mount them with loose-pin, mortised hinges much like those used on ordinary house doors.

INTERIOR FITTINGS

Often a clothes armoire is outfitted with flush, pullout drawers on the inside of the cabinet (Illus. 13-20). The number of pullouts can be changed, of course, as desired. Install a closet pole near the top of the interior. Many variations are possible for the interiors. Sometimes the pullouts are omitted and two closet poles are installed—one as shown in Illus. 13-20 and another about at the middle level of the cabinet. Adjustable side shelves may be installed on one side or the other as another variation, but doing this narrows the hanging area of the armoire. The possibilities are almost endless as to the storage and hanging

fittings within the armoire, so you can design the interiors as imaginatively as desired.

BUILDING THE CLOTHES ARMOIRE

The procedure for building this closet armoire is exactly the same as for the entertainment center. Suggested dimensions for the basic box and interior fittings are contained in Illus. 13-20, but they, and the overall design of the cabinet, can be easily adapted to suit your available space and needs. Start with the face frame. Then fabricate the side panels and do the required machining of rabbets and dadoes. Make the shelves and the bottom and assemble the unit, bringing it into square by installing the ¼-inch back panel. Make the interior fittings next, and then the lipped drawer and doors. Fabricate the top and the base structure to complete the construction, and then add a finish.

CHAPTER FOURTEEN

Designing and Building Corner Cupboards

Another piece of furniture that can add beauty to a home and supply excellent storage space is the corner cupboard. Corner cupboards make use of space that ordinarily is not used. No other furniture piece fills this exact need. Like the armoire, the corner cupboard originated in colonial times, but even modern homes will often have a corner cupboard in the dining room which holds fine china and silver pieces.

The corner cupboard is really two cupboards in one. The upper part most often is a china cabinet that is equipped with glass-paned doors (or just open shelves with no doors), and the lower section is a storage area with plywood or panelled doors. Illus. 14-1 suggests some typical front designs for corner cupboards.

DESIGNING THE CORNER CUPBOARD

The designer of a corner cupboard must pay particular attention to the relationship between the front width of the unit and the distance along the walls the cupboard will occupy in the corner. As the front width increases, so does the distance along each wall. For example, a corner unit that measures 25½ inches across the front will occupy about 18 inches along each wall in the corner. However, a cupboard that measures 34 inches across its front will use 24 inches of corner wall space.

There is another relationship that is equally as important, and that is the width of the front to the depth of the cupboard. A 25½-inch corner unit will have less than 12 inches of shelf depth, but a 34-inch front will have shelves approximately 14 to 15 inches deep at their middle, deepest points. Consider, too, that the usable space of a corner cupboard is quite limited due to the angled shelves that narrow drastically at each end.

Ideally, the corner cupboard should be 32 to 36 inches wide and around 80 to 84 inches high. Often, the cupboard is built to match the height of standard interior 6-foot 8-inch doors plus about 2 inches of casing, for a total height of slightly over 82 inches.

To obtain a genuine picture of the interior size of a proposed corner cupboard, make a full-size plan layout of the unit on a piece of

275

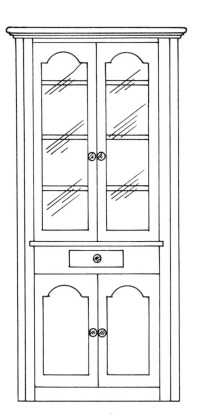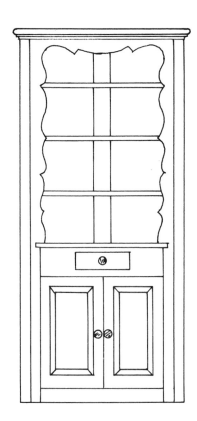

Illus. 14-1. Corner cupboards can be designed with doors or have open shelves.

plywood. From this plan, the exact size and shape of the shelves can be determined as well as the measurements of the face frame members (Illus. 14-2). From this plan, make a full-size shelf pattern that will be used to lay out the exact size and shape of the individual shelves.

Some corner cupboards have a small drawer built into the midsection that provides a nice design break between the upper and lower sections. This will have to be a fairly narrow drawer because the slant of the sides determines the length of the drawer sides.

Notice that most corner cupboards have pairs of stiles that meet at an angle of 22½ degrees, and thus they meet the walls at right angles. If this is not done, the edges of the stiles must be cut at 45 degrees to fit against the wall. This not only is not as attractive, but it is much more difficult to fit the back panels into that type of face frame. The stiles can vary considerably in width, but regardless, the

method for assembling the face frame is the same.

BUILDING THE CORNER CUPBOARD

Some interesting joinery problems are encountered when building a corner cupboard, although very few new techniques are used that have not been used on previous projects. Perhaps the single most exacting chore is to make the shelf template precisely and then run out the shelves so each shelf is an exact duplicate. The corner cupboard shown in Illus. 14-3 and Illus. 14-4 has been selected for building and for instructional purposes.

BUILDING THE FACE FRAME

As usual, the face frame should be built first. Unlike most other furniture projects, a corner cupboard has a triangular rather than a rectangular basic box. The ¾-inch top and the

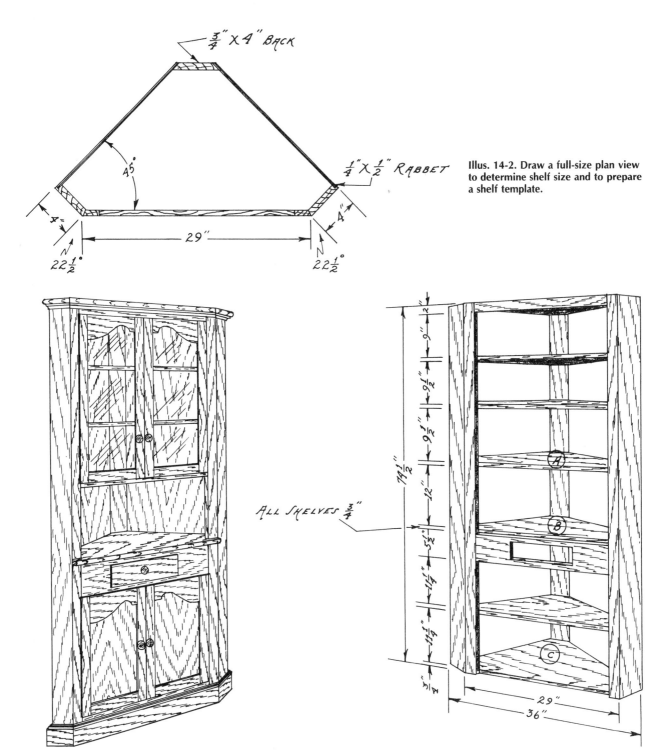

Illus. 14-2. Draw a full-size plan view to determine shelf size and to prepare a shelf template.

$\frac{3}{4}$" X 4" BACK

$\frac{1}{4}$" X $\frac{1}{2}$" RABBET

45°

4"

29"

4"

N

$22\frac{1}{2}$°

N

$22\frac{1}{2}$°

ALL SHELVES $\frac{3}{4}$"

$74\frac{1}{2}$"

2"

9"

$9\frac{1}{2}$"

$9\frac{1}{2}$"

12"

$5\frac{1}{2}$"

$11\frac{1}{4}$"

$11\frac{1}{4}$"

$\frac{3}{4}$"

A

B

C

29"

36"

Illus. 14-3 (above left). A traditional corner cupboard. Illus. 14-4 (above right). The triangular basic box.

4¾-inch base structure are subtracted from the total height of 80 inches, so the face-frame stiles should be 74½ inches long. The exact horizontal dimensions of all rails must be taken from the full-size plan drawing. Note that the corner cupboard has four stiles—two interior and two exterior—whose edges are jointed to make a 22½-degree angle (Illus.

277

14-5). The bill of materials for the face frame is as follows:

Interior stiles: Two pieces ¾ × 2 × 74½ inches

Exterior stiles: Two pieces ¾ × 4 × 74½ inches

Top rail: One piece ¾ × 2 × approximately 25 inches

Drawer rail: One piece ¾ × 5½ × approximately 25 inches

Facing strips: Two pieces ¾ × ¾ × approximately 25 inches

Nosing: One piece ¾ × 1¾ × approximately 25 inches

(Check all rail lengths on the full-size drawing!)

Although not part of the face frame, a ¾ × 4 × 79¼-inch piece of lumber or plywood back "spine" is required.

Machining Face-Frame Members

Prepare the four stiles and saw and joint the 22½-degree edge on each. Machine a ¼ × ½-inch rabbet along the outside edge of each exterior stile. This rabbet will accept the back panel when installed. Cut out the layout for the drawer in the drawer rail with a sabre saw. Drill a ⅜-inch hole in one corner of the layout as a starting point for the saw blade. Assemble the face frame with screw joints and then attach the exterior stile to the interior stile using 4d finish nails and glue. Nail through the exterior stile into the interior stile by using a nail in the drill and drilling parallel to the face of the frame. This will prevent any splitting and will also guide the nails straight into the interior stile.

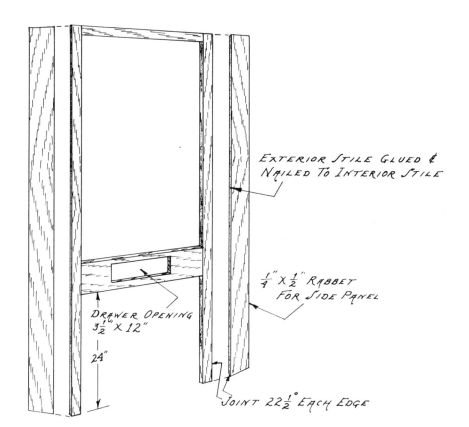

Illus. 14-5. Detail of the face-frame assembly.

EXTERIOR STILE GLUED & NAILED TO INTERIOR STILE

¼" × ½" RABBET FOR SIDE PANEL

DRAWER OPENING 3½" × 12"

24"

JOINT 22½° EACH EDGE

Preparing The Spine

The rear board or spine is 4 inches wide and has its edges ripped at 45 degrees. The spine is 4¾ inches longer than the basic box because it acts as a rear leg that supports the cupboard after the base structure is installed (Illus. 14-6). Mark all locations for the top, bottom, and all permanent shelves clearly on the spine. If the shelves in the upper and lower sections of the cupboard are to be adjustable, they need not be marked on the spine. However, most often the shelves in a corner cupboard are permanent shelves.

Make these same shelf location marks on the back side of the face frame so the shelves will be located exactly even with both the spine and the face frame.

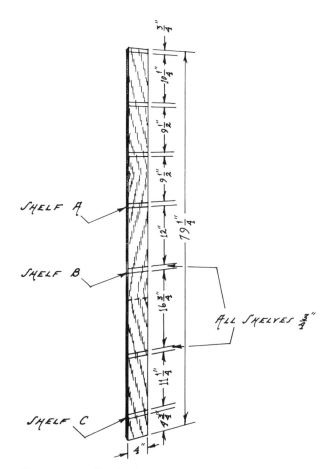

Illus. 14-6. Detail of the shelf layout on the spine board.

MAKING THE SHELVES

Using the shelf template prepared from the plan drawing, determine the depth of the shelves. All exposed shelves should be made of hardwood plywood, and those in the lower interior of the cupboard can be made of particle board. Make five shelves of ¾-inch hardwood plywood or veneered particle board and two of plain ¾-inch particle board. Rip a strip or strips of plywood from a 4 × 8-foot sheet that is ¹⁄₁₆ inch wider than the required depth of the shelves. (The extra ¹⁄₁₆ inch is for jointing the front edge.)

Using the shelf template, lay out the cutting pattern for the shelves (Illus. 14-7). A radial arm saw works the best for cutting the shelves at 45 degrees. If you do not have a radial arm saw, try a band saw. An alternative is to prepare a 45-degree cutting jig for the table saw similar to the 90-degree jig described in Chapter Five. After all the shelves are sawed to their basic shapes, mark and saw the short return at each end of the shelves. The shelves should be as identical in shape as possible, and they should fit nicely against the inside of the face frame.

If all shelves are permanent shelves, edge-band them after assembling the cupboard. If some of the shelves are to be adjustable, they can be edge-banded prior to installation. Be sure to make a dimension allowance for the edge-banding on the adjustable shelves so they still fit in the cupboard.

A nice touch for the shelves of china cabinets, hutches, and corner cabinets is to machine a plate groove near the rear edge of the shelves. This groove allows plates to stand against the cabinet back without slipping down. Machine this groove with the router using a grooving bit ¼ inch wide and run the groove about 2 inches from the rear edge of the shelves.

Illus. 14-7. Cutting pattern for the shelves.

ASSEMBLING THE CORNER CUPBOARD

Begin assembly by nailing each permanent shelf to the spine board in its exact location as marked previously. Line the shelves up squarely with the spine as you nail and glue them (Illus. 14-8).

Gently turn the assembly over so that the spine is resting on the floor. Temporarily nail a couple of brace pieces in place to prevent the assembly from tipping (Illus. 14-9). Place the assembled face frame in place on top of the shelves and glue and nail the face frame to each shelf using 4d or 6d finish nails. (Note that shelf B, which is the top of the lower section, is located ¾ inch above the drawer

rail. A nosing piece will be installed on the front of this shelf, as shown in Illus. 14-10).

Install the two facing strips on the cupboard bottom (shelf C) and the shelf that is the bottom of the upper section (shelf A). Install the edge-banding on the front edge of each of the other shelves and sand or scrape the edging flush with the upper surface of the shelves.

INSTALLING THE BACK PANELS

Determine the dimensions of the back panels and cut these to size. The backs fit into the rabbets that were machined along the edge of the exterior stiles. Glue and nail the backs in place by nailing them to each permanent shelf,

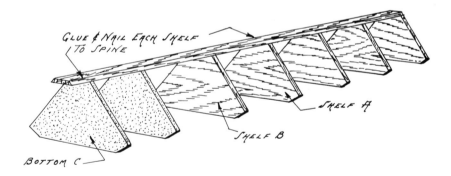

Illus. 14-8. Technique for attaching the shelves to the spine.

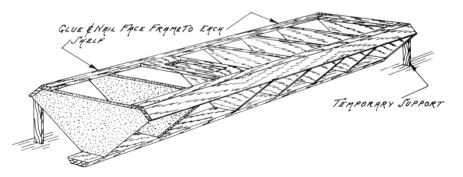

Illus. 14-9. Technique for attaching the face frame to the shelf assembly.

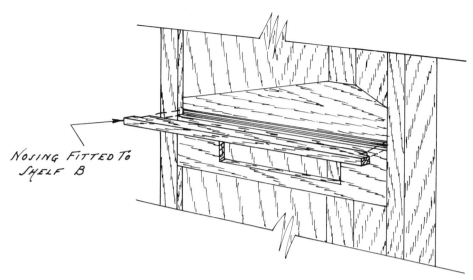

NOSING FITTED TO SHELF B

Illus. 14-10. Detail of the nosing applied to Shelf B.

the spine, and in the rabbets. Pull the entire structure into square when installing the backs.

FABRICATING AND INSTALLING THE BASE STRUCTURE

Prepare about 4 feet of ¾ × 2-inch patterned bottom moulding exactly the same as the moulding used on the chests in Chapter Six. Mitre the joints at 22½ degrees and fit and screw this moulding to the bottom of the cupboard. Next, prepare about 4 feet of ¾ × 4-inch baseboard. Machine a ⅜-inch rounding along the top edge of this piece. Mitre the joints at 22½ degrees and attach the base pieces to the bottom moulding. Prepare ¾ ×

¼-inch mounting strips to fasten the baseboard in position (Illus. 14-11). Install two bracing pieces at each end of the baseboards as shown in Illus. 14-12.

FABRICATING AND INSTALLING THE TOP MOULDING

Prepare about 4 feet of ¾ × 2½-inch top edging of lumber and rout or shape a half-round on one edge of the piece. This top moulding will overhang the edge of the cupboard by 1¼ inches. Mitre the joints at 22½ degrees and install the pieces by screwing them to the top shelf of the cupboard (Illus. 14-13). Install ¾ × ¾-inch cove moulding under the top pieces to complete the upper overhang.

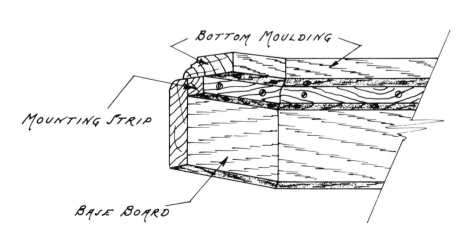

BOTTOM MOULDING

MOUNTING STRIP

BASE BOARD

Illus. 14-11. Rear view of the bottom moulding and base.

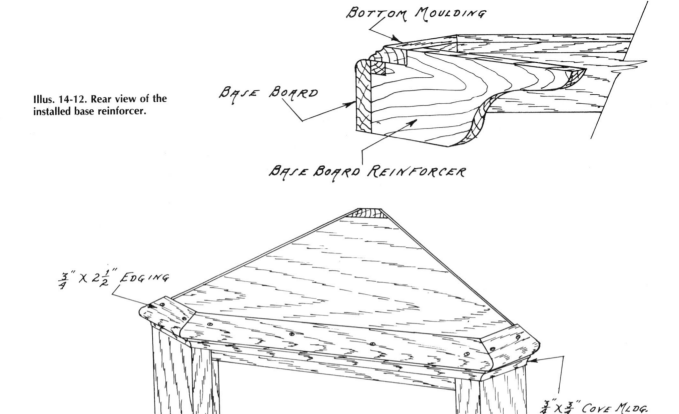

BOTTOM MOULDING

BASE BOARD

Illus. 14-12. Rear view of the installed base reinforcer.

BASE BOARD REINFORCER

¾" X 2½" EDGING

¾" X ¾" COVE MLDG.

Illus. 14-13. Top view of the installed top edging and cove moulding.

COMPLETING THE CORNER CUPBOARD

Fabricate and install the small drawer and then make the glass-paned doors for the upper section and the panel doors for the lower space. As on other projects, set all nails, fill any holes, and cover flaws and seams with matching plastic wood. Belt-sand the entire face frame and the doors, and then use the oscillating sander with 220-grit paper for the final sanding. Scrape and sand the plastic wood cleanly from the filled areas prior to the start of the finishing schedule.

After applying the selected finish, install all the cabinet hardware that is required. The corner cupboard is now ready to be placed in the home.

CHAPTER FIFTEEN

Plastic Laminate

Plastic laminates are used extensively on modern furniture, especially on tabletops. This is not surprising, because laminates are available in literally hundreds of patterns, colors, and beautiful wood grains. Plastic laminate is extremely durable and it can be worked with ordinary woodworking tools and machines. Sooner or later you will work with this material and should have some basic knowledge of handling and applying this modern covering.

Laminates appeared on the market shortly after World War II, having been developed as a hard, durable, inexpensive material for small machine gears. Soon they were marketed for the furniture and cabinet industries. At first the laminates were available only after they had been bonded to plywood; this could only be accomplished with special glues and high-pressure presses. Furniture builders fabricated tabletops from 4 × 8-foot (or larger) sheets of this pre-bonded product and finished the edges with metal mouldings of various shapes and sizes. This was short-lived, however, as contact cement was soon developed that allowed cabinet and furniture build-

ers to bond the laminates to the plywood backing and use the same material for edging the tabletop.

Today an almost unlimited variety of patterns are available under various trade names such as Formica, Wilson Art, Consoweld, and Nevarmar, to name just a few.

SIZE AND ORDERING INFORMATION

Laminate sheets are usually available in widths of 24, 30, 36, 48, and 60 inches, although this may vary somewhat from manufacturer to manufacturer. Most laminate sheets are furnished ½ to 1 inch oversize, which makes for economical cutting.

Laminate sheets are available in lengths (again, depending upon the manufacturer) of 60, 72, 84, 96, and 144 inches. Always carefully plan the use of the laminate so that the most economical use is made. This is an expensive product and you do not want to squander money on wasted material.

Laminate is available in three thicknesses. The standard thickness is ¹⁄₁₆ inch and is used for most tabletops, kitchen counters, and backsplash installations. Laminate that is ¹⁄₁₆ inch thick is also used for edging tabletops, especially if there are no particularly sharp bends to make.

Also available is a laminate that is ¹⁄₃₂ inch thick. This is used primarily for edging, where the edges have to be bent to a sharp radius. Also available is a ¹⁄₂₀-inch-thick laminate that is used for countertops that have curved front edges and backsplashes. However, fabricating those countertops requires sophisticated heating devices that the home woodworker would not have available.

Also available and in wide use by cabinet manufacturers is a pre-bonded laminate called melamine that has the laminate already bonded to particle board on either one surface or both. This product is widely used for making contemporary furniture and cabinets. It is available from cabinet builder supply houses and can probably be ordered by the local lumber dealer.

SOURCES FOR PLASTIC LAMINATE

Lumber dealers have sources available to them that can supply laminates in most colors, sizes, and patterns. Although they do not stock the laminates, they are very willing to order them for the customer and usually only a wait of a few days is needed for delivery. Discount home centers often carry a few standard patterns and sizes in stock, but these are very limited as to choice and size. However, they are often priced considerably less in discount home centers than other sources.

A visit to a local cabinet shop sometimes pays dividends because it often has leftovers that the home woodworker can use. They are eager to get rid of this excess and will usually price the laminate accordingly. The local cabinetmaker will have several suppliers and many, many different patterns and colors that are available. They often are willing to order a piece for a "do-it-yourselfer" if they will be sending in an order.

MACHINING PLASTIC LAMINATES

Because plastic laminate is a very hard, brittle material, ordinary woodworking tools dull rapidly when it is being cut and trimmed. Carbide tools are much more successful and stay sharper much longer. However, standard saw blades and router cutters can be used on a small installation if they are resharpened after use.

USING A TABLE SAW

Equipped with a fine-toothed carbide blade, the table saw is generally used to cut the sheets of laminate to the approximate size the job requires. Standard procedure calls for the tabletop pieces to be cut about ¼ inch oversize all around; then the excess is trimmed to exact size with the router or a laminate trimmer. Because the laminate is so thin, it will slip under the fence of many makes of table saws. A special auxiliary fence can easily be made from a strip of wood that is screwed to the fence and fits snugly against the saw table. If the saw fence is extended beyond the top of the table saw, an auxiliary fence that possesses a lip is fastened to the rip fence that will support the plastic while it is being ripped (Illus. 15-1).

The laminate is very brittle and the chips are thrown towards the operator when it is being ripped. It is good practice to wear safety glasses or goggles while cutting this material on the table saw.

Cutting a good-size piece of laminate on the table saw is really a two-person job. How-

Illus. 15-1. Use a lipped auxiliary fence when you are ripping laminate on the table saw.

ever, with the sawhorse supports and auxiliary roller supports presented in Chapter Five, one person can adequately handle this material. Another technique for cutting a large sheet of plastic into usable sizes is to lay the sheet on the shop floor, mark the cutting lines, and, with carefully positioned pieces of lumber under the laminate sheet, make the rough cuts with a portable circle saw. Be aware that a sheet of laminate can easily be broken and ruined by careless handling.

Although the jointer is not regularly used to cut laminate, there are times when it is indispensable. Occasionally, the laminate must be spliced to cover a tabletop. To ensure that the two pieces fit tightly, a jointer is required. Here again, a helper might be needed to handle the often awkward pieces while you are machining the edges on the jointer.

If several splices must be made, it might be worthwhile to make a splicing jig for the router. The jig holds both pieces firmly in place, and you can machine the two edges to be joined to an almost perfect match by running the router along both edges at the same time (Illus. 15-2).

Illus. 15-2. A shop-built jig is used with the router to make nice-fitting laminate joints.

USING A ROUTER

If there is any one machine that is indispensable for the home woodworker when working with plastic laminate, it is the router. Though special laminate trimmers are available on the market, the router does an excellent job of trimming laminate. The main difficulty encountered when using the router is that it cannot be used to trim the laminate close to a wall because the base of the router interferes. This is not a problem, however, for furniture builders because they have access to their projects from all four sides.

The least expensive means of routing and trimming plastic laminate is to use carbide trimming bits (Illus. 15-3). Only two cutters are needed to handle nearly all trimming operations. These are available from woodworking supply catalogues. The bevel trimming bit produces a 7½-degree bevel on the trimmed edge. The hole and flush-cut trimmer drills through the surface laminate into a precut opening in the underlayment and then trims the edge flush. Also available is a flush trimmer that will trim vertically with no bevel.

One very important precaution must be observed when using these carbide trimmer bits. When trimming laminate applied to the surface of a table, for example, make sure that you lubricate the laminate edging with Vaseline to prevent the trimmer from burning the laminate self-edging. If this is not done, the friction caused by the high-speed cutter would quickly burn the laminate.

SPECIAL HAND TOOLS

There are a few tools on the market that have been developed especially for use on plastic

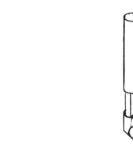

Illus. 15-3. Three types of carbide laminate trimmers for the router.

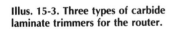
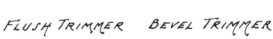

FLUSH TRIMMER   BEVEL TRIMMER   HOLE & FLUSH CUT TRIMMER

Illus. 15-4. Hand tools available for laminate fabrication.

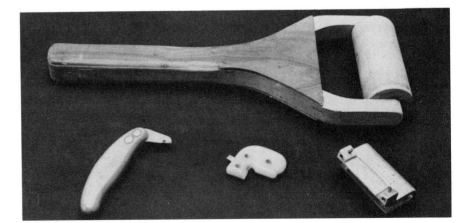

laminates (Illus. 15-4). These can be used in place of the router or in places where the router cannot be used. All are made of carbide and will do the job for which they were designed, although they are much slower than a router or a laminate trimmer.

Carbide Scribing Knife

This tool, similar to a linoleum knife but made with a carbide point, can be used to score and break plastic laminate (Illus. 15-5). Score the laminate on the surface by making several passes with the knife guided by a straightedge. Then break the laminate off at the scored line by bending or snapping the laminate *upwards* (Illus. 15-6). If pressure is applied downwards, the laminate will not break evenly along the scored line.

Hand Trimming Tool

This tool was designed to trim the laminate flush with the tabletop edging. It has two carbide points that score the laminate as the tool is held against the edge of the table or counter (Illus. 15-7). The tool will cut when moved in either direction. After scoring the laminate deeply, break the waste edge clean with the same upwards motion as was performed when using the scribing knife. Then file the rough edge to a smooth finish to complete the job.

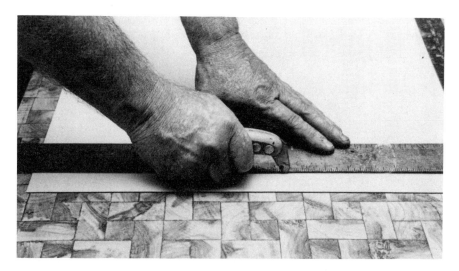

Illus. 15-5. The carbide scribe is used to score the laminate deeply.

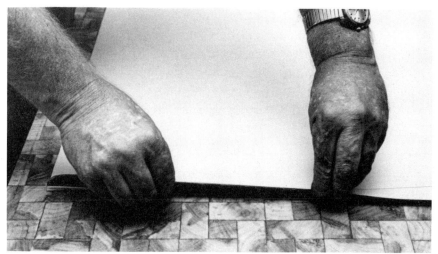

Illus. 15-6. After scoring, the laminate is broken with an upwards force.

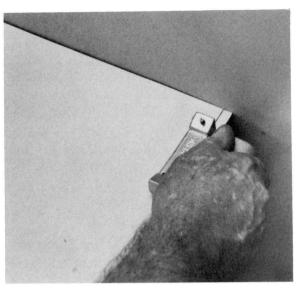

Illus. 15-7. The hand trimming tool can be used in places inaccessible to the router.

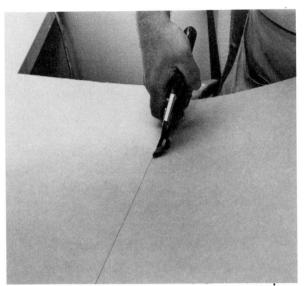

Illus. 15-9. The laminate snips do a nice job of cutting laminate.

Hand Bevelling Tool

This simple cutter contains a carbide knife that will produce a bevelled edge on the laminate. It saves a lot of hand filing and in certain situations is indispensable (Illus. 15-8).

Illus. 15-8. The hand bevelling tool is used to put a slightly bevelled edge on the laminate.

Laminate Snip

Built like small tin shears, this tool does an excellent job of cutting laminate quickly and cleanly (Illus. 15-9).

Laminate Roller

A roller is pressed over the laminate to create an excellent bond between the laminate and the particle board or plywood underlayment. Rollers are available from specialty woodworking catalogues. You can also easily make a roller if you have a lathe. The roller must be rugged enough to withstand the pressure exerted to bond the laminate and the underlayment firmly together. Illus. 15-20 shows a shop-made roller in use.

COMMON HAND TOOLS

Many of the common hand tools in your possession will at some time be used when you are covering a tabletop with plastic laminate. Squares, hacksaws, metal files, rubber mallets, hammers, straightedges, etc., will all be put to use at some stage of the fabrication.

CONTACT CEMENT

The development of special adhesives for use with laminates has made it practical and easy for the home woodworker to apply this material to furniture sides, shelf surfaces, and tops. These adhesives, called contact cement, are available at lumberyards, building supply dealers, and even the larger discount stores.

The surfaces coated with contact cement will adhere on contact. Apply the adhesive to both surfaces to be bonded, allow it to dry, and then press the surfaces together to make a firm bonding. Once brought into contact, the laminate cannot be adjusted, so extreme care must be taken to see that the laminate is in the correct position prior to making contact.

TYPES OF CONTACT CEMENT

There are several types of contact cement on the market. These are available from suppliers of plastic laminate in 1-gallon, 5-gallon, and drum sizes. Lumber dealers usually have the cement on hand in the 1-quart and 1-gallon sizes. These types are described below.

Industrial Contact Cement This grade is extremely volatile and is not available to the home-shop woodworker. It is ordinarily sprayed on the surfaces to be bonded or applied by automatic glue spreaders. It is used primarily by furniture and cabinet manufacturers who bond hundreds of square feet of plastic laminate.

Cabinet Shop-Grade Contact Cement Although this is also a volatile product, it is not nearly as fast-drying as the industrial grade. This is the type that is sold by building supply dealers. Always make sure there is adequate ventilation when using contact cement, for there is a danger of explosion if the fumes are allowed to accumulate. Also breathing the fumes for any length of time poses a health problem.

Water-Based Contact Cement
Gradually, the environmental protection agencies throughout the United States are outlawing the use of the volatile contact cements and lacquers. A water-based product that neither pollutes the atmosphere nor poses a danger to the user is becoming increasingly more popular. The one disadvantage this product has is its slow drying time when compared to the volatile types. On a hot day with low humidity, water-based contact cement dries quite rapidly, but on days when the temperature is low or the humidity is high the drying time slows down considerably. This is not a major problem for the occasional fabricator doing a small job, but when a great deal of laminating must be done, it can be very aggravating.

APPLYING CONTACT CEMENT

The occasional user of contact cement will apply it with either a brush or an inexpensive, throwaway paint roller. For coating narrow surfaces such as the edging around a tabletop, use a bristle brush. A nylon brush is not satisfactory for applying contact cement because the brush fibres will deteriorate because of the solvents in the cement. Special solvents are available for contact cement, although lacquer thinner is very suitable for cleanup.

Apply a coat of contact cement to the back of the laminate and also to the particle board or other backing material being used. A heavy, even coat is required. On porous material or end grain, more than one coat may be needed. Allow the adhesive to dry until no stickiness is noticeable. A recommended test for dryness is to touch the cement with a piece of brown wrapping paper. If the paper does not adhere to the contact cement, the surfaces are ready for joining. Open time for the coated surfaces is approximately an hour, but recoating might be required if the surfaces are left unassembled for much longer.

JOINING THE CEMENTED PLASTIC LAMINATE AND BACKING

As described previously, the material to be bonded must be carefully positioned, because after contact is made between the laminate and the backing no adjustment is possible.

One way to bond the material is to prepare strips of ¼-inch plywood about 1½ inches wide × 36 inches long to use to support the laminate above the underlayment (Illus. 15-10). Carefully clean and sand the strips so that chips or sawdust cannot accidently get between the surfaces to be bonded. Lay these strips about 12 to 14 inches apart on the length of the underlayment and then lay the laminate on top of the strips. Then adjust the laminate to its proper position and simply pull the strips out from under the laminate one by one, allowing the surfaces to come into contact. Then use a roller over the surface of the plastic to ensure good contact between the surfaces. If you do not have a roller, use a block of wood and a hammer or rubber mallet.

On small installations, strips of wood are not needed. Simply locate the laminate on one edge of the top and gradually lower it to the surface, maintaining the correct margin all around the tabletop.

REMOVING PLASTIC LAMINATE FROM BACKING

If a roller has not been used on the laminate,

it is sometimes possible to carefully separate the laminate by slowly pulling it up and away from the backing. This might take some of the backing material with it, however. If the backing surface is not too damaged, the surfaces can be recoated and reassembled.

You can also use a squirt-type oil can filled with lacquer thinner to help loosen and remove plastic from the backing. Pry a corner of the laminate loose and squirt the thinner underneath. By carefully pulling and squirting the solvent while separating the plastic, you can often successfully delaminate the two surfaces. However, if the bonded surfaces have been allowed to set for a day or longer, separation is nearly impossible without destroying the laminate.

APPLYING LAMINATE TO A CABINET OR TABLETOP

Following is a step-by-step method for fabricating a cabinet or tabletop and installing the plastic laminate on the surfaces. No sophisticated machines or tools are required to make an attractive top, but having a router available will save a lot of time and labor.

Illus. 15-10. Use strips of plywood to support the laminate above the cemented surface.

MAKING THE PARTICLE-BOARD TOP AND EDGING

The most successful underlayment material is high-density (45-pound) particle board. It has a smooth surface that does not absorb the contact cement or possess a wood grain that could possibly show through the laminate after it has been bonded. This sometimes happens to laminate after it is applied to plywood with a prominent grain.

Three-quarter-inch material is usually used for the top underlayment but, if properly supported underneath, ⅝- or even ½-inch material can be used. The edging is usually made of ½-inch material.

INSTALLING THE TOP

The basic top piece of underlayment (less the edging strips) should be made about 1/16 inch longer and wider than the cabinet or table on which it is to be installed. Joint the edges smooth and then screw or nail the particle board in place (Illus. 15-11).

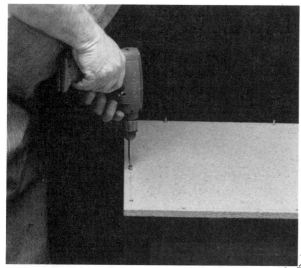

Illus. 15-11. Screw or nail in place the particle board used for the sub-top.

PREPARING AND INSTALLING THE EDGE STRIPS

Rip 1½-inch strips from ½-inch particle board

or plywood and glue and nail these strips to the edges of the top (Illus. 15-12). Although there is no specific rule as to the width of these strips, 1½-inch-wide strips make a nice-looking edge. However, you can make the strips any width desired.

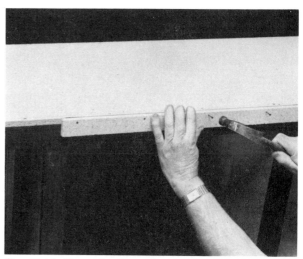

Illus. 15-12. Glue and nail the edges in place.

Some designers prefer to add a wood edging to the plastic-laminate top. This type of edging can be made in the shop and can have a variety of moulded edges (Illus. 15-13). If this type of edge is desired, install it after gluing the top laminate in place.

After the edging is in place, belt-sand the upper edge flush with the top (Illus. 15-14).

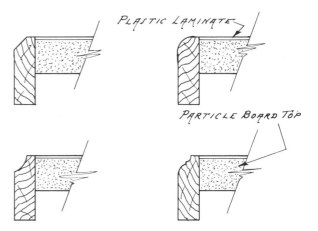

Illus. 15-13. A solid-wood edging is often used in place of laminate edging.

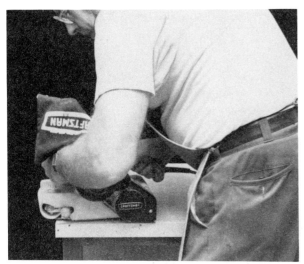

Illus. 15-14. Sand the edging flush with the particle-board surface.

INSTALLING PLASTIC LAMINATE SELF-EDGING

Rip strips of laminate about 1/16-inch wider than the underlayment edging. This is usually done on the table saw with the aid of a helper using the techniques described earlier in this chapter. Clamp featherboards to the saw fence to hold the laminate while you are sawing.

Apply the short ends of the top first. Cut the laminate strips about 1/2 inch longer than is needed, apply contact cement to both the laminate and edge of the top, and allow the adhesive to dry (Illus. 15-15). Use at least two coats of contact cement. Install the laminate strips, allowing the top edge to extend slightly above the surface of the particle board (Illus. 15-16). After the strips are in place, tap the laminate with a rubber mallet or the flat face of a claw hammer, being extremely careful not to mar the plastic (Illus. 15-17). Trim the extra length at the corners with a router or hacksaw and then file the laminate flush with the corner.

Apply the longer strips in the same manner. Trim the corners flush with a router and then file them smooth, rounding them slightly to remove their sharpness.

Next, remove that portion of the self-edging that extends above the surface of the underlayment. This can be done with a belt sander or the router (Illus. 15-18). If using the sander, make sure that you do not round the surface while sanding. If you do, the laminate, when installed, will not bend. Finish up with a flat file to be absolutely certain the edging is flush with the top surface.

APPLYING PLASTIC LAMINATE TO THE TOP UNDERLAYMENT

Cut the laminate so there is a 1/4- to 1/2-inch margin all around it. If a splice is required, joint the meeting edges, then test-fit and hand-

Illus. 15-15. Apply contact cement to the particle-board edging and the back of the laminate edging. Two coats may be needed.

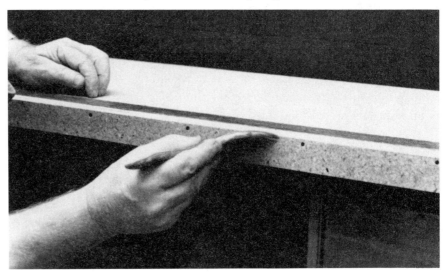

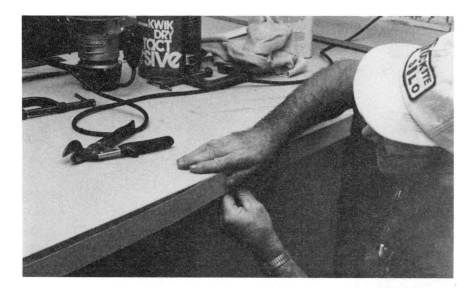

Illus. 15-16. Carefully position the laminate self-edging with the top edge so that it is slightly higher than the particle-board surface.

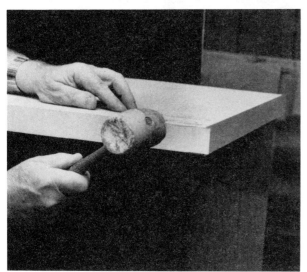

Illus. 15-17. Tap the self-edging with a rubber mallet to make good contact.

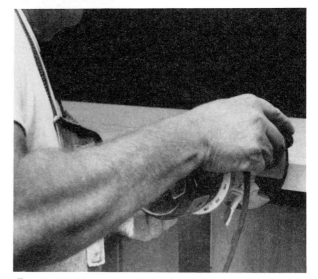

Illus. 15-18. Use a router to trim the self-edging flush with the particle-board surface.

file them, if necessary, to secure a tight-fitting seam. If several splices must be made, consideration might be given to making a splicing jig as shown earlier in Illus. 15-2.

As shown in Illus. 15-19, apply contact cement to both surfaces with a brush or roller, allow it to dry, and, using the supporting wood strips as shown in Illus. 15-10, position the laminate so there is an overhang all around. Remove the wood strips, allowing the laminate to make contact with the underlayment. Use a roller over the entire surface, to

ensure good contact between the laminate and underlayment (Illus. 15-20).

TRIMMING EXCESS PLASTIC LAMINATE

If a carbide trimming bit is used in the router, apply Vaseline to the self-edging to prevent the cutter from burning the plastic. Proceed to trim the entire perimeter of the top (Illus. 15-21). After trimming the top with a router, use a metal file to remove all of the sharp edges and corners (Illus. 15-22). You can remove

293

Illus. 15-19. Apply contact cement to the particle board and the back of the laminate.

Illus. 15-20. Use a shop-built roller to bond the laminate with the underlayment.

Illus. 15-21. Trim the laminate even with the self-edging. Note: Be sure to apply Vaseline™ to the self-edging to prevent it from being burned from friction.

Illus. 15-22. Smooth all sharp edges and corners with a file.

any excess contact cement quickly by dipping a cloth in lacquer thinner and rubbing it vigorously. Rubbing the cement with a dry cloth

works almost as well.

Special Note: If the top being laminated is L-shaped with an interior corner, round the laminate at the interior corner slightly. Do not file this corner to make it sharp. Stress causes the laminate in a sharp corner to crack, but this can be prevented if you leave the rounding that forms after using the trimmer cutter (Illus. 15-23).

DO NOT FILE SQUARE AT CORNER

Illus. 15-23. Do not file laminate inside corners so that they are sharp and square.

CHAPTER SIXTEEN

Adding a Finish

Some craftpersons believe that the most important step in building a piece of furniture is the final finishing. Knowledgeable and skillful application of stain and a protective clear finish to a project can enhance the beauty of the wood and its grain, but a careless finishing job can spoil what might have been an impressive piece of woodwork.

Wood requires a protective finish for two reasons: to protect it from the elements, and to bring out the natural beauty of the species being finished. This natural beauty can sometimes be enhanced by the application of a coloring agent known as stain. Sometimes just a transparent coating applied to the wood is enough to beautify and protect it.

Wood finishing can require years of study to master. But it is also possible that with a fundamental knowledge of the various finishing products on the market today and their proper use, an amateur can develop the skills to do fine finishing on home-built projects. This chapter presents information and application techniques on the four most commonly used finishing materials: shellac, lacquer, varnish, and the newer water-based finishes. It also describes the proper methods of preparing wood for finishing and how to rub the finish to its final lustre.

WOOD SPECIES

Some basic knowledge about the various woods used in cabinetmaking is required in order to do even an adequate finishing job. Each species has its own color, type and coarseness of grain, and ability to absorb and hold the finishing material. It would be foolish, for example, to paint walnut or mahogany, or to varnish basswood or poplar. Therefore, various species of woods are classified as to their finishing treatment, and the craftsperson should become acquainted with these classifications.

OPEN-GRAINED vs. CLOSED-GRAINED WOOD

All cabinet woods are classified as open grain or closed grain. Open-grain woods include walnut, mahogany, oak, butternut, and chestnut. Closed-grain woods include red gum, birch, cherry, maple, poplar, pine, fir, and basswood.

Open-grain woods are more difficult to finish because the grain is coarse and deeply pits the surface of the wood. Even though an oak board, for example, has several coats of varnish or paint, pinholes will still be revealed throughout the surface, indicating that the finish has not filled the porousness of the grain. If enough coats are applied, eventually these pinholes will be filled, but only after a large amount of finishing material is wasted.

PREPARING THE PROJECT FOR FINISHING

Many amateurs believe that finishing the wood will hide blemishes, flaws, poor joints, and poor workmanship. Exactly the opposite is true. Nothing is more important in the finishing process than preparing the project to receive the stain and final coating.

FINAL SANDING AND CLEANUP

Do the final sanding of the project with the finish sander and 180- or 220-grit sandpaper. As the final cleanup progresses, pay very close attention to discovering and repairing or removing even minute blemishes, dents, glue spots, sander scratches, remains of plastic wood, and other flaws. Following is information on how to remove and repair particular flaws.

Glue Spots

These are often hard to detect because the glue dries transparent, but the instant the stain or finish is applied, the glue residue appears as a white spot. Some finishers wipe the wood with mineral spirits at this stage to reveal glue spots. When detected, they can easily be removed with a sharp hook scraper followed by a light sanding. If you discover glue spots while applying stain, use the same technique and then reapply the stain. If glue remains that has seeped out of a joint, use a well-sharpened chisel to scrape and cut away the glue. When assembling a project with glue, it is a good idea to always wipe the joint and surrounding area with a damp cloth to remove any glue residue to save much work later.

Dents   The quickest and easiest means of removing a dent is to steam it out. A small electric soldering iron and a damp cloth do a very effective job of removing unsightly dents. The moist heat swells the wood fibres and, after the wood has dried and then been sanded, the dent is usually gone. If the dent has broken the fibres of the wood, steaming will not work. In this case, fill the area with matching plastic wood or stick shellac.

Scratches   In many ways scratches are the most serious flaws to handle. Usually the fibres of the wood are broken, so steaming is not effective. Scraping and sanding will remove a scratch from solid lumber, but this cannot be done on plywood to any extent because of the possibility of breaking through the veneer. Try steaming first, and then scraping and sanding. If neither works, fill the scratch with plastic wood and then scrape and sand the spot clean. A professional refinisher will use colored stick shellac to do these repairs. The sticks come in a wide array of colors to match almost any stained or natural wood. The shellac stick is melted with a hot knife and then quickly placed into the flaw. This technique takes expertise, but once mastered even serious flaws can be repaired. Stick shellac repair kits are sold by woodworking supply companies such as the Woodworker's Store in Rogers, MN.

Sander Scratches   The belt sander will often leave scratches on a face frame because of the cross-grain sanding that is done. Most of these are removed by later sanding with the finish sander but, inevitably, a few scratches remain. These can easily be removed by a few quick strokes with the hook scraper.

Plastic Wood Residue

Throughout this book, it has been recommended that flaws in joints and seams be filled with matching plastic wood. Select a color that closely matches the unfinished color of the wood. If the project is to be finished with a natural finish, the filled flaws are practically invisible. If the project is to be stained, the plastic wood takes the stain of the surrounding wood.

Some finishers prefer to wait to fill flaws until after the stain and one coat of finish is applied. They then fill the flaws with colored putty. This usually shrinks after a few days and is quite noticeable. Although plastic wood will take stain, the plastic wood residue must be removed because it contains lacquer and thus seals the wood surrounding the flaw. The stain or finish will not penetrate this sealed area and it appears as a lighter smudge which is quite noticeable. Careful scraping and sanding the immediate area around the filled spot will successfully prevent this from happening.

PREPARING OPEN-GRAIN WOOD

Using Paste Wood Filler

The easiest and quickest means of preparing open-grain wood for finishing is to fill the pores of the wood with a product called paste wood filler. This product should not be confused with other wood fillers such as Plastic Wood or Famowood that are made for filling and repairing blemishes in wood and flaws in joints. Paste wood filler is purchased at quality paint stores and comes in a semi-solid state. The basic ingredients of paste wood filler are silica, which is suspended in oils, and a drier. It is silica that is forced into the grain to fill the open pores and then allowed to dry.

Thinning Paste Wood Filler

Of course, the filler must be thinned to a working consistency. Most directions state that the filler should be thinned until it feels and looks like heavy cream. It can be thinned with any inexpensive paint thinner, which basically is mineral spirits. If the project is to be stained with a penetrating oil stain, many finishers will mix the stain right with the paste wood filler. This will thin the filler to almost the correct consistency, with perhaps just slightly more thinning needed with mineral spirits. Note that only an oil stain can be mixed with the filler. Disaster will result if a spirit or water stain is used!

When the filler is dry, it has a greyish cast to it that does not blend with the natural color of the wood. The filler is colored slightly with stain that blends with the finished color of the wood. This matches the color of the filler with the final color of the wood.

Applying Paste Wood Filler

Brush the filler onto the surfaces of the project with an ordinary paintbrush of a proper size for the project, working both with and across the grain (Illus. 16-1). Do only a small section at a time. Do not leave a heavy coat of filler on the surface, because it will only be wasted when rubbed off. Allow the filler to dry until it begins to look dull; this is essential to success. If the filler is wiped while still quite wet, it will not remain in the pores of the wood. If it dries too long, it is extremely difficult to remove.

Prepare a wiping cloth of a coarse material such as burlap for the initial removal of the filler. Some finishers make a 4- to 5-inch ball out of a piece of an old T-shirt filled with cotton. Wipe the filler off by going across the grain—pressing and packing the filler into the grain as it is wiped. Wipe the filler as clean as possible. Then complete the wiping by going with the grain with a clean cloth; wipe gently

Illus. 16-1. Stain and paste wood filler can be mixed and applied in one operation.

so as not to remove the filler from the pores. It is important to remove all excess filler because it is very unsightly if allowed to remain on the surfaces.

The top of the table or cabinet and other large surfaces are easy to do. Filling and wiping the curved and moulded areas requires patience and attention to detail. To remove the filler from these spots, try working with the cloth wrapped around a small screwdriver blade. In any event, remove the filler as cleanly and as completely as possible. Again, it is important not to fill too much surface at a time, to prevent the filler from drying hard before it can be removed.

Allow the filler to dry at least 24 hours under good drying conditions and even longer if the humidity is high or the temperature of the room low. Do not rush the drying process, because subsequent finish coats can "lift" the filler if it is not thoroughly dried. Sand very lightly with 220-grit paper to prepare the surfaces for finishing.

On wood that possesses a very open grain such as Lauan or Philippine mahogany, it is sometimes necessary to do the filling pro-cedure twice to be certain the wood is ready for finishing.

STAINING TECHNIQUE

If the wood is an open-grain variety, mix the stain with the paste wood filler. For closed-grain woods, apply the stain as a separate step in the finishing process. There are several types of wood stains available. Each requires some knowledge and skill in its application. The most important rule to observe when applying stains is to "always read the directions on the label of the product being used." Another good rule to follow is to always test the stain on scrap wood before applying it to the project. This not only reveals what the final color will be but also indicates what application techniques are required.

TYPES OF WOOD STAIN

Penetrating Oil Stain   This type of stain is the one most recommended for use by home woodworkers because it is easy to use and readily available at paint retailers everywhere. It comes in a wide variety of colors, and is simply applied and wiped off. After a thorough stirring or shaking, oil stain is usually applied to furniture pieces with a brush, allowed to remain on the wood until the wood absorbs all it is able to, and then the surplus is wiped with clean cloths. Applying more coats will usually not darken the initial application because the wood can absorb just so much of the stain. An oil stain can be lightened by thinning with mineral spirits, but a darker shade of stain of a similar kind must be added to secure a darker color. Allow a minimum of 24 hours drying time under good conditions when applying an oil stain to a project.

End grain will stain darker than other surfaces. To prevent it, apply a very thin coat of shellac to this area prior to staining. This will prevent the end grain from absorbing more stain than the other portions and keep the color more uniform.

Cleanup Clean the brushes with mineral spirits, fuel oil, kerosene, or turpentine, which is expensive. Do not use gasoline. Besides being dangerous, gasoline will harden the upper portion of the brush.

Water Stains
Water stains are soluble colors that dissolve in water. They are somewhat less expensive than other stains, but are more difficult to apply. Water stains are widely used in industry because of their many advantages. Many finishers prepare their own water stains by purchasing the dry powdered colors. There are a few commercially prepared water stains on the market, however.

Water stains have one serious shortcoming: they raise the grain of the wood upon drying. This problem can be handled in two ways. You can lightly sponge the entire project with water, allow it to dry, and then resand it. Possibly a better technique is to apply the stain and allow it to thoroughly dry. Then apply the first coat of sealer or other finish, allow it to dry, and then lightly sand it with a fine-grit sandpaper. Do not sand after the stain has been applied and dried, because it is virtually impossible to not sand through the stain to the raw wood underneath.

It is necessary to work fast when applying water stain and to use a fairly large brush to avoid lap marks. If a commercial water stain is being used, apply the stain over a reasonable area and then wipe with a damp cloth to remove the surplus and make the color more uniform. Then apply the sealer or first finish coat. When it has dried, sand the raised grain smooth. Sponging the end grain just before staining will prevent that area from darkening.

Cleanup Use soap and water to clean brushes and receptacles.

Alcohol or Spirit Stains
Aniline stains can be purchased that are soluble either in alcohol or water. Spirit stains dry too fast for the average finisher, and thus are often avoided. They have a tendency to fade rather rapidly, are comparatively expensive, and are not used extensively in industry. Because they dry so fast, it is difficult to stain a large surface an even color and to avoid lap marks. However, for a small project and one that the finisher wants to complete quickly, a spirit stain might be just the thing to use.

Cleanup Clean brushes and containers with denatured alcohol.

APPLYING TRANSPARENT FINISHES

After the project has been prepared for its final finishing coats, select which type of finish to apply. Four types of finish are generally used by home woodworkers: shellac, varnish, lacquer, and water-based varnish. Step-by-step procedures for applying each type are given below.

SHELLAC FINISH

Shellac is a gum produced by an insect that lives in India. When dissolved in alcohol, it actually becomes a spirit varnish. Two varieties are usually available. Orange shellac has an orange-brown color that some finishers object to, so it is bleached to produce white shellac, which is practically colorless. Shellac may be purchased from most paint retailers in containers labelled 4-pound cut. This simply means that 4 lbs. of shellac gum have been dissolved in one gallon of alcohol. Shellac is often thinned for use as a wash coat over stains and for the first one or two coats of a shellac finish.

Many amateurs prefer finishing with shellac because it dries fast, is easy to apply, and builds up to a nice finish with three or four coats. It is easily rubbed out with steel wool to a smooth, satin finish. Then it is given a coat of paste wax and a final polishing. Because of its short drying time, dust and other particles do not get much of a chance to adhere to a shellac surface.

Finishing Schedule Wipe all dust and dirt from the project and try to work in a fairly dust-free environment. A tack rag is often used to remove settled dust. (A tack rag is a soft, lintless cloth that has been dampened slightly with thin shellac or varnish and allowed to dry until it becomes sticky before being used.) There are five steps involved in applying shellac. They are described below:

Step One Using 4-pound cut shellac, pour enough into a glass or porcelain container. When applying each individual coat, thin these coats as follows: For the wash coat, add one part shellac to seven parts alcohol. For

the first coat, add one part alcohol and one part shellac. For the second coat, add two parts shellac and one part alcohol. (For additional coats, use the shellac as it comes from the can.)

Step Two Using a brush of suitable size, apply a fairly full coat of shellac, brushing with the direction of the grain only. Cover narrow strips the entire length, working as quickly and evenly as possible. Because shellac sets very quickly, work speedily or the shellac will begin to congeal on the laps. Do not go back and attempt to touch up spots that might be missed—the next coat will cover them. Remember, two thin coats are better than one heavy coat.

Except for the first thinned coats, allow at least two hours for drying time under good conditions. The first coats are usually dry in 15 to 30 minutes.

Step Three Rub down the project with either fine sandpaper (220-grit) or 00-grade steel wool. Steel wool works best because it does not clog up as sandpaper does.

Step Four Apply coats two and three, thinning each as directed above. The material is now heavier, sets more quickly, and is more likely to congeal on the laps. If the shellac is brushed too much, there is a danger of loosening the first coats. After drying, rub between coats with 00-grade steel wool.

Step Five After the final coat has dried at least overnight, rub the finish to its final lustre using finer grades of steel wool. Start by rubbing with 00 grade, then switch to 000 grade, and finally use 0000 grade. Rub strenuously, but be careful not to rub through the coats of shellac to the bare wood. This is easily done on curved work and at the edges. When the finish takes on a nice lustre, complete the process by applying a coat of good paste wax and buff it with a clean, dry cloth.

Cleanup   Clean shellac brushes and containers only with denatured alcohol.

Storage   Store shellac only in glass or porcelain jars. It will deteriorate rapidly if stored in an ordinary tin receptacle. The tin that the shellac is originally purchased in has a special treatment on the inside to prevent it from deteriorating.

POLYURETHANE VARNISH FINISH

The traditional oil varnish has all but disappeared from the shelves of paint retailers and has been replaced by polyurethane finishes. These finishes have become very popular with both amateur and professional finishers for a number of reasons.

They are extremely resistant to marring, abrasives, and stains, and are ideal for furniture and floor finishing. They are resistant to water, weather, and corrosion, and are therefore used widely in the marine industry. They dry rapidly, which results in less dust pickup and faster recoating. They retain their gloss and beauty longer than any other type of resinous finish. Finally, they are available in gloss, satin, and flat varieties. It is no wonder that with these attributes, polyurethane varnishes are so popular with wood finishers in both factory and home shops.

Sanding Sealer

Sanding sealers are high-solid varnish-like coatings that are applied to the bare wood as a first coat. They are less expensive than the varnishes. However, the main reason for using a sanding sealer is that it can be readily sanded without gumming up the sandpaper. When sanded with fine sandpaper, a fine, white, talcum-like powder is produced that is easily brushed or blown away. The resulting surface is very smooth, and succeeding coats of the final finish do not soak into the wood but remain on the surface as they should.

However, there is one important drawback to many sanding sealers. They cannot be used under polyurethane finishes. If you are interested in using a sanding sealer, be sure to check to see if it is formulated for use under polyurethane varnishes.

Finishing Schedule

(Note: Always read label directions prior to using any purchased finishing material.) It is recommended that satin polyurethane varnish be used for finishing furniture projects because it dries to a soft lustre with no rubbing required. This means that the sides and understructures of many woodworked pieces need only very little rubbing to secure the desired effect. Remember, you have to stir any product labelled satin, semi-gloss, or flat to distribute the solids and flattening agents in the mixture. This schedule, like the others presented, is based on the assumption that the project has been prepared for finishing, the grain filled (if it is of an open-grain variety) and stained or left natural, as desired.

Step One   Apply a coat of sanding sealer (if the sealer is compatible with polyurethane) and allow it to dry for three hours minimum. If sanding sealer is not used, thin the first coat of polyurethane slightly with mineral spirits. Sand lightly with 220-grit sandpaper.

Step Two   Apply a coat of polyurethane straight from the container. Brush on a full coat, but examine the surface to see that no spots are left uncovered. Do not continue to brush after the brush begins to drag. On vertical surfaces, check back often to see that no runs or sags have appeared. If some do appear, brush them out quickly before the finish sets up. Allow it to dry 24 hours. Although this finish will dry to the touch (and be dust-free) in three or four hours, it should be re-coated only after a 24-hour drying period. Sand lightly with 220-grit paper to remove any dust pips or other roughness.

Step Three Apply the final coat straight from the container and set the project aside to dry. Allow this final coat to dry and harden for several days before attempting to rub it out. Test the hardness of the finish by applying fingernail-pressure to it. When the finish cannot be dented by hard fingernail pressure, it is considered ready for the final rub.

Step Four Proceed to rub out the desired surfaces using the steel-wool method outlined in the shellac finishing schedule. If a higher sheen is desired, skip to the last section of this chapter, entitled "Rubbing a Finish to a High Lustre."

Cleanup Clean the brushes with mineral spirits, fuel oil, kerosene, or turpentine.

LACQUER FINISH

Lacquer has been the most popular industrial finish for many years. It is usually sprayed on rather than brushed, is very fast-drying, and is an extremely durable, water-resistant finish. Because of its very fast drying time, lacquer is difficult to apply with a brush. Manufacturers, however, have marketed brushing lacquers that are slow enough for the non-sprayer to handle. Probably the best known of the brushing lacquers is a product called Deft that is readily available at many paint retail stores. The finishing schedule described below is for brushing lacquer, because it is doubtful that many amateurs have air compressors in their woodshops.

It is very important to know that any lacquer product cannot be used over a non-lacquer finish like shellac, varnish, polyurethane, etc., because it will act as a paint remover and "lift" the undercoats. It is equally important to know that any lacquer product must be used with care because it is a volatile finish whose fumes can explode if allowed to build up in an unvented workspace. Prolonged breathing of these fumes can also cause serious disorientation. Because the ingredients in lacquer are also pollutants, the pollution control agencies of many states have begun to press for legislation to forbid the use of lacquer and lacquer-based products.

Brushing lacquers are still used by wood finishers who want to apply a fine finish to their product in as short a time as possible. Brushing lacquers are available in gloss, satin, and dull sheens.

Finishing Schedule The following steps are for a semi-gloss brushing lacquer:

Step One After making the project as dust-free as possible, apply a full, wet coat of brushing lacquer. Watch carefully for runs and sags on vertical surfaces and at corners. Because it will dry so rapidly (to the touch in 20 to 30 minutes), do not brush out much because the brush will soon start to drag and ridges will be left on the surface. The first coat will be ready to recoat in two hours. Sand it lightly with 220-grit sandpaper and clean the surfaces with a brush or tack cloth.

Step Two Apply additional coats at two-hour intervals. Sand lightly between all coats. Three coats are recommended for an alcohol- and water-resistant finish.

Step Three Allow the final coat to dry a minimum of 24 hours before rubbing to a desired lustre with steel wool as described previously.

Cleanup Only lacquer thinner can be used to clean brushes. It can be purchased at most paint and discount stores.

WATER-BASED FINISH

Water-based finishes are so new that many retail paint stores are just becoming aware of their presence. Professional finishers are well aware of their presence because these products are much safer than volatile finishes like lacquers. Water-based finishes have practically no odor, are fast-drying, dry clear with little if any yellowing, and can be cleaned up with soap and water! No wonder they are becoming popular.

The one serious disadvantage in using a water-based finish is that it will raise the grain of the wood. Another disadvantage is that water-based finishes at present are quite costly when compared to the more traditional finishes. Also, water-based finishes have a tendency to bubble when applied, although manufacturers are now adding debubbling agents to the finish.

Nearly all of the leading paint manufacturers are producing water-based finishes under the names Wood-Kote, Amity, Deft, and Hydrocote, to name a few. There is some confusion in the labelling of these products, because they are still referred to by their manufacturers as lacquers and polyurethanes. Reading the label seems to be the only sure way to secure the right product for the correct application. Some are formulated strictly for spraying, and others for brushing.

Finishing Schedule

Because raising the grain is a problem, it will be addressed first in this schedule.

Step One There are three ways to deal with raised grain. You can sponge the project with water, allow it to dry, and then sand the raised grain smooth. Or you can apply the first coat of finish, allow it to dry, and then sand the grain smooth again. The third choice is to apply a water-based sanding sealer to prevent the grain from being raised by the water-based finish, sand it smooth, and then proceed to apply the finish coats. Chances are that the firm selling the finish also will have the water-based sealer.

Tip: Use 3M Scotchbrite pads instead of steel wool for smoothing curved surfaces and intricate parts of a project. Do not use steel wool, because its minute particles sticking to the surfaces will rust.

If the project is to be stained with a penetrating oil stain, allow it to thoroughly dry before applying a water-based finish.

Step Two Strain the finish through a nylon stocking to remove any chunks of coagulated finish that have a tendency to gather inside the container.

Step Three Brush on the finish using a good-quality nylon brush. Do not overload the brush, and, if a sealer has not been used, make the first coat a thin one. The finish will have a milky coating when first applied, but it dries perfectly clear. Do not brush the finish a lot because of its quick setup time. In this respect, applying water-based finish is similar to applying shellac and brushing lacquer.

Step Four A drying time of one hour is usually needed between coats, although the finish will set up dust-free in about 15 minutes under good drying conditions. Sand it lightly with 220-grit sandpaper.

Step Five Apply second and third coats, sanding lightly between each coat. Water-based finishes build up rapidly because of their high solid content.

Step Six Use the fingernail test to determine

the hardness of the finish and if it is ready for the final rubbing. It may take several days for the finish to completely harden. Proceed to rub out the finish using the steel-wool method or according to the directions in the next section.

Application Tips   The finish can be rolled on large surfaces with a short-nap roller or applied with a painting pad. Very lightly drag a brush across the finish to eliminate air bubbles. Work quickly and don't try to rebrush, because of the fast set up time. This works on large objects such as doors, tabletops, and floors.

Cleanup   Use soap and water to clean the brushes.

RUBBING A FINISH TO A HIGH LUSTRE

So far only the steel wool rub-out method has been described. Although this results in a satisfactory lustre, another method will have to be used to produce a glass-like, high lustre on a furniture top. Although it is usually not practical to attempt to rub out an entire project, this is a decision that you will have to make. On a chest of drawers, for example, you may decide to rub out the finish on the top and drawer fronts using the method in this section, and the finish on the sides and the face frame with steel wool, followed by waxing. Apply three coats of the final finish and let them cure before attempting to obtain a gloss finish.

Each finisher will have a favorite method of rubbing out a final finish. The one described in this section is fairly fast, works well, and produces excellent results with a bit of practice.

Rubbing out a finish has its disadvantages. If the process is carried on too long, the finish can be rubbed right down to the bare wood. This usually happens when a finish is rubbed before it has properly cured or hardened. Arrises and corners can be rubbed through very quickly, and extra caution must be observed on those areas. However, when the method is used properly, the result will be a beautiful finish.

REQUIRED MATERIALS

Special materials are needed to rub out a finish to a beautiful lustre. Most of these are available at any good paint retailer or even at some hardware stores.

Wet-or-Dry Rubbing Paper   3M Company manufacturers a black, waterproof, silicone-carbide paper in various fine grits that is suitable for rubbing finishes. Purchase a sheet or two of the 400- and 600-grit paper. Water will be used as a lubricant for this rubbing method, hence the need for waterproof paper.

Rubbing Felt   This is a heavy felt pad about ½ inch thick that should measure about 2 × 4 inches. The pad should be large enough to fit the hand comfortably.

Pumice Stone   Although this comes in various grits, most often the box or can is simply labelled "pumice stone." Grit FF is used by many finishers, but any grade is suitable.

Rottenstone   This is simply a super-fine rubbing agent used to produce a high-gloss, mirror-like finish.

Rubbing Oil   This is *not* required, but some finishers do use it. However, water, used as a rubbing agent, is definitely cheaper and allows the abrasive to cut faster.

305

RUBBING PROCEDURE

After the finish has been properly cured and tested for hardness, the final rubbing can be done.

Step One   Cut a sheet of 400-grit rubbing paper into fourths. Soak the paper in a pan of water for a few minutes and then sprinkle water on the surface to be rubbed. Back the paper up with your hand and begin rubbing across the grain. This rubbing will generally level the surface by removing brush marks, dust pips, and any laps or sags. Next rub with the grain. Because more rubbing takes place in the middle of a panel, take extra strokes at both ends to compensate for this. Do not allow the rubbing paper to sag over the ends of the tabletop or it will soon rub through these edges.

Keep the rubbing paper clean by dipping it frequently in the water container and keep the surface wet. The water will soon turn a milky color, indicating that cutting action is taking place. Hook a corner of the rubbing paper between your thumb and forefinger to prevent the paper from slipping out of your grasp. The paper also seems to drag at this point. When the water begins to solidify into a film on the surface, it is time to wipe the surface dry and check your progress. Four-hundred-grit paper will cut rather rapidly, so do not continue this initial rubbing for too long.

Step Two   Switch to a quarter-sheet of 600-grit rubbing paper and continue rubbing out, using the same technique as in step one. The 600-grit paper will actually begin to polish the surface after the 400 paper evens or levels the surface. Continue to rub using your hand to back up the paper. To check your progress, wipe the surface free of water and allow it to dry. By checking against the light reflection, it is easy to see where more rubbing must be done. Where enough rubbing has taken place, a slight lustre should begin to appear and your hand should be reflected. When the entire surface appears to have been rubbed level and a slight lustre is evident, it is time to proceed to step three.

Step Three   Sprinkle water and pumice stone over the surface. If the pumice has been packed in a small can, punch a few holes in the cover so you can shake the pumice evenly on the surface. Dampen the felt rubbing pad and wring it dry. Start rubbing the pumice across the grain. Apply moderate pressure while rubbing. Raise the pad occasionally to keep the pumice under it and to keep the surface wet. Continue the rubbing action with the grain for a few minutes and then wipe the surface clean of the pumice/water slurry to determine its lustre. A definite low gloss should begin to be evident. After one or two more applications of pumice and water and continued rubbing, an even, medium lustre should be the result. The danger of rubbing through the finish is now quite high, so don't rub much longer. Most finishers will stop at this point and apply and buff a coating of paste wax to complete the finishing process.

Step Four   If a higher-gloss finish is desired, the final step is to continue using rottenstone as the rubbing agent. Rottenstone is a very fine abrasive agent and actually polishes more than it cuts. Continue to use water as a lubricant and sprinkle the rottenstone on the surface in the same manner as the pumice was applied. Rinse the felt pad of all pumice or use a separate pad for this final rub. Continue the rubbing until all the minute scratches left by the pumice have been removed. Finally, apply a coat of paste wax and buff the finish to a nice polish.

REPAIRING A RUBBED-THROUGH FINISH

Don't be disheartened if you have rubbed through the surface. This happens to all finishers. If bare spots appear where even the stain has been rubbed out, restain the areas and then apply new coats of finish. Allow the new coats to cure and then start the rubbing process all over.

If a few light spots appear on the edges or arrises, touch them up with stain. After the spots have dried, apply the paste wax and polish. There is no need to apply more finish to these small flaws.

Glossary

Actual Size   The size of lumber after being dried and planed.

Adhesive   A substance used to hold materials together by surface attachment. Includes glue, paste, cement, etc.

Air-Dried   Lumber that has been only dried in the open air for a period of time, as opposed to kiln-dried.

Aniline Dyes   Soluble colors made from coal-tar derivatives and used for staining wood.

Arbor   The assembly in a table saw that holds the saw blade and revolves and tilts.

Armoire   A freestanding closet structure originally used for the storage of clothes but today often used as an entertainment center.

Arris   The outside corner or edge formed by the meeting of two surfaces.

Basic Box   The box-like structure of a furniture piece that remains after the top, legs, doors, and drawers have all been removed.

Belt Sander   A portable or stationary mechanical sanding machine that uses an endless abrasive-coated belt.

Bleaching   Lightening the color of wood by applying a chemical solution.

Bleeding   The movement of stain or dye from the wood into surface coats. For example, mahogany stain under white enamel will bleed through and develop pink spots in the enamel.

Blemish   Any defect, scar, or mark that tends to detract from the appearance of a surface.

Blind Dado   A dado that does not completely travel across the board.

Board Foot   The standard unit of measure for lumber. A board foot measures 1 inch thick × 12 inches wide × 12 inches long.

Box Nail   A common nail with a head.

Brad   Small, almost headless, mild-steel nails that come in lengths from ¼ to 1½ inches and gauge sizes from 20 to 14.

Butt-Block Joint   A type of furniture face-frame joint that is strengthened and reinforced by gluing and nailing a wooden block to the back of the joint.

Cap Strips   Solid-wood strips applied to the top edge of plywood or particle-board drawer sides to cover the unsightly inner core material.

Carbide Tips A very hard material applied to the edges and tips of router cutters, saw blades, and shaper cutters that stays sharp much longer than tool steel.

Casework System A method of building furniture and cabinets that uses a screwed face frame and ¼-inch plywood for the sides, backs, and top.

Center Runner A type of drawer guide that is installed in the center of the drawer opening.

Chamfer An angled cut (usually 45 degrees) along the edge or edges of a piece of lumber or plywood.

Chipper Blades The inner cutter blades of a dado set.

Claw Hammer A type of hammer whose head has two curved, claw-like appendages that are used for driving and removing nails.

Closed Coat Abrasives on which the grits are applied very close together and completely cover the adhesive.

Contact Cement A latex- or butane-based adhesive that bonds on contact and requires no clamping. Widely used to apply plastic laminate to a core material.

Coped Joint A joint used on furniture and cabinet doors where the rails and stiles meet and the end of the rail is cut to fit the shaped edge of the stile.

Counterboring To enlarge a hole through part of its length by boring.

Countersink Tool used in the electric drill or drill press to provide a bevelled edge to the predrilled screw hole so the screw head may be driven flush with the wood surface.

Cove Moulding A type of wood trim that has its face milled with a concave pattern. It is used under beaded furniture tops to form the bead-and-cove top edging.

Cross Bands Layers of veneer that are glued together at 90 degrees to make plywood.

Crosscut To cut across the grain of wood. Also describes a saw blade designed to efficiently cut across the wood grain.

D (See penny.) A unit commonly used to designate nail sizes.

Dado A groove cut across the grain by using a dado head (or other type of dado cutter) on a table saw.

Dado Head A set, consisting of two outside saw blades plus several inside chipper blades, used to make dadoes and grooves in wood.

Dovetail Jig A metal template used with the router and a bevelled router bit to quickly and accurately machine dovetail joint members.

Dovetail Joint A special interlocking finger-type joint widely used in quality furniture to attach drawer sides to the drawer fronts.

Dowelling Jig A device for accurately centering and drilling the matching holes required to make a dowel joint.

Dowel Joint A furniture joint that is assembled with wooden pegs for reinforcement and strength.

Drawer Rail The cross-member in a face frame that supports a drawer directly above it.

Drier A catalyst added to paint and other finishing material to speed up the curing or drying time.

Edge-Banding Matching veneer or thin lumber strips applied to the edge of plywood or particle board to cover the inner core material.

Euro-Look A frameless style of furniture and cabinetry, also known as the 32-mm system, that was developed in Europe after World War II.

Face Frame The facing structure, usually made of hardwood, composed of horizontal and vertical pieces that form the openings for drawers and doors on a furniture piece.

Face Nail Driving nails through the visible surface of a piece of wood.

Facing Strips Lumber strips, ¾ × ¾ inch and usually of hardwood, that are glued to the edge of plywood or particle-board panels to cover the inner core material.

Featherboard A shop-made wooden hold-down cut from a ¾ × 2-inch piece of softwood with several saw cuts made to provide a spring action. Featherboards are clamped to the machine with C-clamps and adjusted to hold the work firmly while it is being machined.

Fibre Core A hardwood veneered panel that has its inner core composed of wood particles (shavings, chips, sawdust) bonded with a special adhesive.

Finish Nail Almost headless nails used in furniture building where the head of the nail is to be "set" below the surface of the wood. They vary in length from 1½ to 3 inches, and in gauge size from 5½ to 11½ inches.

Finish Sander (Orbital Sander) A high-speed, hand-held, mechanical sander that usually operates with an orbital action.

Flow The property of a finishing material to spread or level to an even film.

Freestanding A piece of furniture or cabinetry that is not fastened to the wall.

Gallery (See Plate Rail.)

Gloss The type of finish that dries to a shiny or highly lustrous surface.

Glue Blocks Small blocks of wood, usually triangular in shape, that are glued along the inside corner of a joint to add strength.

Green Lumber Lumber that has been through no drying process.

Groove The cut made in a piece of lumber by using the dado head in the table saw

and running the cut with the direction of the grain.

Hanger Strip The upper rear, interior board of a cabinet or furniture piece through which screws are driven to attach the piece to the wall.

Hold-Down A spring steel, adjustable, metal strip attached to a woodworking machine in pairs to hold the work firmly and safely while it is being machined.

Identification Index The stamp placed on plywood panels that informs the purchaser as to their grade, type, and use.

Inset Hinge A hinge for furniture and cabinet doors that is made to fit the ⅜-inch rabbet of lipped doors.

Jig A device that holds the work and/or guides the work while you are forming or assembling parts.

Joint A means of joining two pieces of wood together.

Kerf The path or cut made by a saw blade as it passes through a piece of wood.

Kiln-Dried Lumber dried in an oven-like chamber to reduce its moisture content to an acceptable level for the building of fine furniture.

Kneehole The open, center section between the pedestals of a desk where the knees of the desk user are placed.

Knife Marks The "ripples" or "planer waves" left on the surface of a board after it has been run through a planer or over a jointer.

Lacquer A highly volatile, nitrocellulose finishing material, usually applied by spraying, that dries quickly by evaporation and forms a protective film from its non-volatile components.

Mineral Spirits A petroleum solvent used as a substitute for turpentine.

Mitre Gauge A table-saw accessory that is used to support the wood as it is being cut across the grain either squarely or at an angle.

Mitre Joint   A joint used to fasten two pieces of wood together, usually at 45 degrees, that is used extensively on picture frames.

Moulding   Decorative or patterned wood strips used to decorate and trim furniture and cabinets.

Moulding Head   A table-saw accessory mounted on the saw arbor that is used to machine various-shaped edges on furniture tops, etc.

Mortise   The square hole machined in the stile to receive the tongue, or "tenon," machined on the end of the rail. Commonly used on face frames and window and door construction.

Naphtha   A volatile, inflammable liquid used as a solvent or thinner for paint and varnish.

Nominal   The stated size of lumber, which is somewhat larger than the actual size. Example: A 2 × 4 used in house construction is the nominal size; the actual size is 1½ × 3½ inches.

Offset Hinge   (See Inset Hinge.)

Open Coat   Coated abrasive on which the grit or abrasive grains are applied to 50 to 70 percent of the coated surface. Open-coat abrasives resist clogging and filling.

Overlay Drawer   A furniture or cabinet drawer whose front is built to be completely in front of the face frame.

Particle Board   A man-made composition panel made from chips, sawdust, shavings, etc., that is combined with adhesives. Widely used in the higher-density grades as a core material for plastic laminates and veneers.

Paste Wood Filler   A silica mixture used to fill the pores of open-grain wood.

Pedestal   The one or two side sections of a desk that hold the drawers.

Penny   The term used in reference to the size of nails. The symbol "d" refers to the penny size of nails.

Plain Panel Door   A framed furniture or cabinet door that has a ¼-inch plywood panel inset within its rails and stiles.

Plain Sliced   A method of making veneer where a section of a log is thrust down along a knife edge that sheers off the veneer in sheets. Slicing results in rather straight-grained veneers.

Plastic Laminate   A highly durable surfacing material used on furniture and cabinet tops.

Plate Groove   A shallow, routed groove machined near the back edge of a shelf to hold a plate securely in an upright position.

Plate Rail   A decorative railing made of small spindles and solid wood rails that is attached to the front of a shelf in a hutch cabinet.

Pocket Door   A furniture or cabinet door that swings open and then slides inside the cabinet on special hardware. It is widely used on entertainment centers.

Points Per Inch   The designation of the fineness or coarseness of a handsaw by measuring the number of tooth points in one inch of saw blade.

Polyurethane   A transparent finish that is tough, quick-drying, resistant to marring, water, and weather, and retains its gloss and beauty longer than other resinous finishes.

Pullout Shelf   A shelf that is built to be pulled out of the cabinet or furniture piece on slides or rollers to provide easy access to the furniture's contents.

Pumice   A powdered abrasive used to rub a finish to a desired gloss or lustre.

Quarter Round   A small moulding whose

shape in cross section is exactly one-fourth of a circle.

Rabbet An L-shaped or 90-degree shoulder cut along the edge of a board.

Rail The horizontal members of a face frame, furniture door frame, window sash, or house door.

Raised Panel The solid wood or plywood piece with bevelled, shaped edges that is inset within the framework of a furniture or cabinet door.

Raised-Panelled Door A style of cabinet or furniture door that has a solid wood or plywood panel inset within its rails and stiles.

Reduce To lower the viscosity of paint or other finishing material by the addition of solvent or thinner.

Resawing A sawing operation in which thinner boards are ripped from a wider, thicker piece of lumber.

Retainer Button A small button-like device used to keep glass in the rabbet of a furniture door.

Rip To saw in the direction of the grain of a piece of lumber.

Rotary Cut Method of cutting wood veneer where the entire log is centered on a huge lathe and turned against a broad knife. Rotary cutting results in a beautiful, wavy grain pattern.

Rottenstone A very fine abrasive powder used to bring a finish to a high gloss or lustre.

Scale The process of drawing large objects on paper by using a proportional value of the true size, such as using 1/4 inch to represent 1 foot.

Self-Edging Applying plastic laminate or veneer to the edge of a table or counter-top that is the same species, color, or pattern as that used on the top.

Set The amount of bend or slant given to alternate teeth of a saw blade to provide

a wider path or kerf than the thickness of the blade itself.

Shelf Track (Shelf Standard) A manufactured metal strip with regular perforations designed to accept metal "clips" or supports that allow furniture shelves to be adjusted to desired heights within the piece of furniture.

Shellac A transparent finishing material made by dissolving lac, a secretion from a bug native to India, in denatured alcohol to form orange shellac, which can be bleached to form white shellac.

Side Runner A type of drawer guide made to guide and support a drawer from the bottom, outside edges of the drawer.

Sinker A type of box nail, usually resin-coated, that has a slanted or bevelled undersurface on its head.

Solid-Lumber Core Plywood that has as its inner core pieces of solid lumber rather than cross-bands or layers of veneer.

Solids Material remaining in a finishing material after the solvents have evaporated.

Spline Joint A wood butt joint reinforced with a piece of 1/4-inch plywood set in a groove along the edges to be joined.

"Sticker Cutters" The shaper or router cutters that are used to run the desired pattern along the edges of door and window stiles and rails.

Stile The vertical members of a furniture or cabinet face frame, window sash, panelled house door, etc.

Stop Chamfer The woodworking operation of bevelling the edge of a board for only a portion of its length by stopping the bevel at a desired point.

Stop Dado (See Blind Dado.)

Stop Rabbet The L-shaped shoulder cut machined along the edge of a board that does not travel the full length of the board.

Table Insert The slotted metal piece that fits

in the recess in the saw tabletop around the saw blade. A wide-slotted insert is required when the dado head is to be used.

Tack Rag A piece of soft, lintless cloth soaked with varnish and allowed to partially dry until sticky that is used to remove dust and debris from a surface prior to finishing.

Template A pattern, guide, or model used to lay out work or check its accuracy.

Template Guide The sleeve-like device that is attached to the router base that surrounds the cutter and is used to follow the edges of a template.

Tenon The "tongue" that is cut on the end of the rail that is made to fit in the mortise, or squared hole, in the stile.

Three-Wing Cutter A patterned or straight-edged spindle shaper cutter that has three cutting edges set at 120 degrees around its center.

Thinners Volatile liquids used to regulate the consistency (thickness) of finishing materials.

Tilting Arbor The mechanism on a table saw that holds the saw blade and is used to tilt the blade up to 45 degrees.

Toe Space The 3- or 4-inch inset space built at the bottom of a cabinet or furniture piece so a person has foot room to stand comfortably close to the piece.

Vehicle The liquid part of paint or other finishing material.

Veneer A thin sheet of wood, either sliced, cut, or sawed. Veneer is referred to as a ply when assembled in a panel.

Veneer Core Plywood made with interior cross-bands or plies of less expensive wood.

Veneered Fibre Core (See Fibre Core.)

Water-Based Finish A recently developed transparent finishing material which has its solids dissolved or carried in water rather than in mineral spirits, alcohol, or other carriers.

Waterfall Design A contemporary chest or desk that has all of its edges rounded to a radius of about 1½ inches.

Water Stain Colored dyes that are soluble in water.

Metric Equivalents

INCHES TO MILLIMETRES AND CENTIMETRES

MM—millimetres   *CM—centimetres*

Inches	MM	CM	Inches	CM	Inches	CM
⅛	3	0.3	9	22.9	30	76.2
¼	6	0.6	10	25.4	31	78.7
⅜	10	1.0	11	27.9	32	81.3
½	13	1.3	12	30.5	33	83.8
⅝	16	1.6	13	33.0	34	86.4
¾	19	1.9	14	35.6	35	88.9
⅞	22	2.2	15	38.1	36	91.4
1	25	2.5	16	40.6	37	94.0
1¼	32	3.2	17	43.2	38	96.5
1½	38	3.8	18	45.7	39	99.1
1¾	44	4.4	19	48.3	40	101.6
2	51	5.1	20	50.8	41	104.1
2½	64	6.4	21	53.3	42	106.7
2	76	7.6	22	55.9	43	109.2
3½	89	8.9	23	58.4	44	111.8
4	102	10.2	24	61.0	45	114.3
4½	114	11.4	25	63.5	46	116.8
5	127	12.7	26	66.0	47	119.4
6	152	15.2	27	68.6	48	121.9
7	178	17.8	28	71.1	49	124.5
8	203	20.3	29	73.7	50	127.0

Index